A COOKBOOK OF BIG FLAVORS

BOLD

SUSANNA HOFFMAN AND VICTORIA WISE

WORKMAN PUBLISHING · NEW YORK

Library of Congress Cataloging-in-Publication Data

Hoffman, Susanna.

Bold : a cookbook of big flavors / by Susanna Hoffman and Victoria Wise.

pages cm

"Published simultaneously in Canada by Thomas Allen & Son Limited"--Title page verso.

ISBN 978-0-7611-3961-4 (alkaline paper) 1. Cooking, American. 2. Flavor. 3. Food portions.

I. Wise, Victoria. II. Title.

TX715.H72375 2013

641.5973—dc23   2013026709

Cover and book design by Lisa Hollander

Illustrations by Sudi McCollum

Workman books are available at special discounts when purchased in bulk for premiums and sales promotions as well as for fund-raising or educational use. Special editions or book excerpts can also be created to specification. For details, contact the Special Sales Director at the address below, or send an email to specialmarkets@workman.com.

Workman Publishing Company, Inc.

225 Varick Street

New York, NY 10014-4381

workman.com

WORKMAN is a registered trademark of Workman Publishing Co., Inc.

Printed in the United States of America

First printing December 2013

10 9 8 7 6 5 4 3 2 1

WE DEDICATE
THIS BOOK TO
EACH OTHER AND
OUR DECADES
OF COLLABORATING.

SPECIAL THANKS:

A BOOK CANNOT GET COOKED without the help of many.

As always, the people at Workman Publishing have been a dream team. We would like to thank Mary Goodbody for the first sharp-eyed read; Carol White, who oversaw the many details of copyediting and production; Julie Primavera for production; Selina Meere and Anwesha Basu, who handled the monumental publicity, Jessica Wiener for marketing, Barbara Peragine for typesetting, and the entire staff of the sales department for their efforts. Special thanks go in particular to Erin Klabunde, who facilitated all the book's back-and-forthing and Lisa Hollander for the stunning layout and design.

To our longtime caring editor, Suzanne Rafer, we honestly and truly cannot thank you enough. Our love and praise forever. Finally, in memoriam, we want to declare our heartfelt gratitude to Peter Workman for decades of encouragement and for whittling our original title down to one great word, not unlike his own character, BOLD.

For their ongoing encouragement and life support, abiding love and appreciation go to Rick Wise, Jenan Wise, Arayah and Paul Rude, Deborah and Jerry Budrick, Beverly Jenanyan, Gary Jenanyan, Kristine Potter, Jason Williams, Bob and Jean Goldberg, Barry and Barbara Deutsch, Dan and Deborah Kashinsky, Veronica Aiken, Martha Casselman, Gabriella Aratow, Jesse, Liza, and Kalea Aratow, Joe Cooley, Deborah and Levi Bendele, Levi and Isabelle Bendele, Rebekah and Harry Spetnagel, Mark Bendele, Marshall Whiting and Richard Arnold, Paula Moss and David Karabell, Anthony and Kerry Oliver-Smith, and to all our supportive and much loved community of friends in Telluride, New York, and California.

CONTENTS

AMERICAN COOKING

BOLD is a cookbook that celebrates the glorious cohesion of foods that make up American cuisine. Its cornucopia has been crafted from the stupendous ingredients, flavors, and dishes derived from all the people who have stepped upon its shores, east to west, northern tip to southern gulf, along with the inventive creations of the millions of the nation's residents. All of it has merged into a single fabulous, kaleidoscopic menu.

It is a bold cuisine. It steps away from traditions and strictures, it takes license for caprice with a fresh understanding of the old ways and uses them as leaven for the new. From its first days, America has been described as a melting pot. Used as a metaphor, the term first signified the hodgepodge of people who inhabit this nation. It referred to the great experiment where, for the first time in history and no matter what their origin, all people had to do was be born on the land or, once residents, pass a test to become fully vested citizens. But to the benefit of us all, the melting pot evolved into something much more than the people and a metaphor. It came to define the American plate.

Until recently, general opinion has held that the foods eaten in America, along with the cooking styles, remained disjointed according to differing ethnic groups. If there were any overarching opinion concerning American food, it was that the nation embraced the cooking of northern Europe as its culinary model. But from the get-go that was a myth. America's very melded, very mixed cuisine has, in fact, a long history. From the first days off the *Mayflower*, the Viking long boat, the Spanish galleon, the sustaining diet of the new arrivals incorporated the victuals already being hunted, fished, gathered, and grown by America's first settlers, the Native tribes, and many of the most widely eaten American foods did not exist in Europe.

What ensued has never happened before: An intermarriage took place, a crossing of ethnic and social boundaries forging with it a unique culinary fusion. At this point in American history, after four hundred years of pairing, few among the citizenry can boast a monochromatic heritage. Some dozen or more generations of mixed matrimony have produced offspring with a veritable potpourri of ethnic strains. Communities are populated by a splendiferous mishmash of cultural components. All partake of a multitude of differing foods in restaurants, friends' homes, and at their own tables.

American social organization has also involved a great deal of mobility. People of all backgrounds move about the country again and again until not only has the shared cuisine overarched ethnic diversity; it has collapsed much class distinction. Everyone's children eat pizza. The entire population eats pot stickers. Pretty much everybody partakes of the whole enchilada.

VIGOROUS NEW ADDITIONS TO THE BILL OF FARE

ON TOP OF ALL THAT, over the last three decades many other changes in the American diet have occurred. Trends appeared and spread, and from them people discovered yet more delectables and ways to cook. Beyond our time-honored dishes and the first exotic, often Chinese edibles, along came highly compelling California cuisine. The fanciful compositions of Pacific Rim cooking appeared, along with the toothsome tastes of northern Italian. Irresistible Japanese sushi changed the way we think of cooked and raw. Farmers' markets sprung up. Health concerns elicited the call for more vegetables and fish. The organic and locavore movements arose in response to foods shipped long distances or preserved for long shelf life to the detriment of both nutrition and flavor. The tide turned against pesticides and additives. In consequence, the populace evolved into not only worldly eaters but ones who are almost fanatic about fresh and wholesome food.

Together the culinary infusions and tantalizing trends swept over all, from coast to coast. While there remain cherished regional differences in American cuisine according to local food specialties and the customs of the original settlers, such variations prevail less and less. New England lobster feasts are held in the Great Basin states. People in Maine eat tacos. Minnesotans down Cajun blackened catfish, while folks in Louisiana eat New York cheesecake. Southeast Asians eat roast beef, falafel is relished by Italians on Philadelphia's South Side, and Jewish bagels have become the entire nation's quotidian breakfast. America is not only a wide-open world; it's *one world* when it comes to food.

Bold honors the great mélange. It is replete with recipes for the amazing, ever-changing round of dishes that make up American cooking today. It venerates traditional foods that Americans have long prepared—such as the thick-cut steak and the still-beloved mound of potatoes—but it also pays homage to the new styles and tastes the country's ethnic mix has added to the pot. It acclaims the heartland's bounty and extols the recent innovations, along with the fresh and healthy choices, that have come to be the dining preference over the last several decades as well. Call it a return, or call it a brand-new epiphany; both are accurate.

At the same time *Bold* celebrates a long-standing and revered American custom: the full plate. Many who arrived on America's soil were hungry. The new nation provided, often for the first time, a plenitude of food to eat, a dazzling opportunity to fill up and feel secure. Here privation was far from the door. Americans have long been rightly deemed the "People of Plenty," a people blessed with abundance. In consequence, the big, full meal became more than a gratification and more than a pleasure to most. It became a proudly displayed and ever-practiced custom. Indeed, it became a symbol. Despite the small plate fancy, trendy snack and tidbit meals, beyond the wave of dainties, mostly Americans want a big dinner. Now, though, we like that dinner bolder. We want our traditional copiousness, but we want it vivid, scrumptious, and varied.

Bold is also a storybook. It tells the tales of where the foods came from, of the people and what they brought, of the landscape and great cities, of personages who changed the American menu, and of American values. *Bold* recounts how the American menu evolved into what has become its national corpus of cookery.

OUR CULINARY COLLABORATION

BOLD **ALSO** **CELEBRATES** four decades of our, the authors', friendship. During that time we have operated two restaurants and worked on four previous cookbooks together. In both our restaurants and our writings, we have been part of and instrumental in America's culinary evolution.

A calico cat named Cato was the unwitting cause of our meeting. The year was 1971. Susanna was taking a breather from knocking down walls in the old house that was to become Berkeley's famed Chez Panisse restaurant, the font of California cuisine. She took a litter of kittens, the progeny of diffident Cato, to the sidewalk in the hope of donating the rascally brood to cat-loving passersby. A man strolled up and stopped to chat. Not interested in a kitten, he asked if Susanna would be interested in a friend who was a good cook? Definitely, answered Susanna, and a few hours later down the hill and up to the door came Victoria.

Our kinship was settled on first sight. We began talking as if we'd always been friends. Through the years those things have included shopping, eating, traveling, healing, feeding, nagging, lending, minding, sighing, sunning, and, above all, cooking.

Victoria became the first chef at Chez Panisse. She cooked dinners galore, going from just a few to 140 overnight. Susanna, after seeing the restaurant to its opening, returned to her anthropology professorship. From the lore and habits of wondrous isolated cultures by day, she came back to help in the restaurant kitchen. In the hectic years that followed, Victoria left Chez Panisse to open Pig-by-the-Tail Charcuterie, the first classic French delicatessen in the United States, which cinched the paparazzi tag "Berkeley's Gourmet Ghetto." Susanna started a family, two children in eighteen months, began to make ethnographic films, and turned her skills to writing her successful book, *The Classified Man,* all the while cooking up a storm. Susanna helped Victoria cook and cater and bestowed on the Pig

some of its most popular dishes. Victoria married, began supplying major stores and restaurants with her sublime edibles, and brought her delicatessen to national recognition. She wrote her first cookbook, *American Charcuterie,* in which she redefined the notion of delicatessen in America, and soon gave birth to her son.

OUR COOKBOOK CHRONICLE

IT WAS WHILE Victoria's son was a toddler that we began the first of our cookbooks together. We had already opened our own restaurant, the Good & Plenty Café, and named the book for it, *Good & Plenty: America's New Home Cooking.* We followed with three more cookbooks, *The Well-Filled Tortilla, The Well-Filled Microwave,* and after Susanna lost her home in the Oakland-Berkeley firestorm, her fire-born tome *The Olive and the Caper: Adventures in Greek Cooking,* with Victoria collaborating. Victoria has gone on to scribe ten food books of her own. Susanna revamped her academic interests to become a disaster anthropologist, writing books and articles, and lecturing on the subject worldwide.

Although we both grew up with largely conventional cooking, like most Americans we had on our platters a smattering of diverse legacies and comestibles. As individuals we encompass the sort of genetic hodgepodge that characterizes most Americans. We combine Armenian, Scotch, Irish, German, Dutch, French, Swedish, and Jewish. In *Bold,* we bring the elements of all our and the country's culinary legacies to our cooking as we delight in sharing our part in America's changing food consciousness.

The delight comes with a profound message. Americans today share not only rights, law, customs, and language; they also share food. In the world of everyday being, food is voice, food is identity; it is the bedrock of unity. America's incomparable, intermixed cuisine both empowers and endows us as a people. When we cook from its amazing variety, we partake of the mutual history and unparalleled uniqueness of the land we love.

BOLD STARTERS AND SNACKS

Meant to arouse the palate, for the first two centuries of American dining starters were not part of the meal. At the dinner hour most people were ready to tuck immediately into the main event. Over time our cuisine increasingly became a flavorful parade, and appetizers and snacks gave us a chance to sample exciting tastes and textures. Starting a meal with an interesting round of nibbles became our custom, and today appetizers are one of the most innovative aspects of American cuisine. We borrowed some; we innovated more. No matter what the cultural heritage, whether vegetable, cheese, meat, fowl, or fish, appetizers afford the cook creative leeway to cross boundaries, borrow, meld, and recombine ingredients from everywhere. The following pages showcase a bouquet of finger foods and small plates. Some are designed to spread informally across the coffee table or kitchen counter, while others are meant to serve at table to start the meal. If you enjoy grazing, a little of this and a little of that, without a main dish, you can make a whole meal out of a collection of these small treasures.

AVOCADO, RADISH, AND SUNFLOWER SEED DIP
WITH TORTILLA CHIPS

MAKES ABOUT 2 CUPS

INGREDIENTS:

4 flour tortillas, cut into 8 to 12 wedges, for serving

2 ripe but firm Hass avocados

2 medium-size red radishes, finely chopped

2 tablespoons roasted sunflower seeds, chopped

¼ cup finely chopped yellow or white onion

1½ tablespoons fresh lemon juice

⅛ teaspoon chopped fresh thyme

Small pinch of kosher or fine sea salt

½ cup radish or onion sprouts, for garnish

ALTHOUGH THEY TASTE LIKE A LUSCIOUS VEGETABLE, avocados are in fact a fruit. We like them sliced as a topping on hamburgers and fish, chunked in salads, and even smoothed in ice cream, but what has truly won American hearts is an avocado spread, such as this one. At first it held solely to Mexican-style guacamole, but the fulsome green taste and pudding-like texture of the fruit has engendered dozens of innovations. Here the green seeds of America's brilliant yellow sunflower add a pleasing crunch, and radishes, rather than chiles, supply the desired hot bite, while a touch of unexpected thyme adds intrigue. Luckily for us, each avocado tree produces about four hundred of the opulent fruit per year.

1. Preheat the oven to 400°F.

2. Set the tortilla wedges on a baking sheet without overlapping. Toast in the oven, turning once, until the wedges are slightly blistered and toasty on both sides, about 5 minutes per side.

Use right away or store in an airtight container up to overnight.

3. Halve and pit the avocados and scoop the pulp into a small bowl. Mash the pulp to break it up a bit, add the radishes, sunflower seeds, onion, lemon

juice, thyme, and salt, and mix together with a fork until the mixture is mostly smooth with some chunky bits.

4. To serve, garnish the dip with the radish or onion sprouts, and accompany with chips on the side.

SOFT AS VELVET:
THE SUMPTUOUS AVOCADO

ALTHOUGH THE AVOCADO has never garnered the fame of other native foods such as tomatoes, potatoes, squash, beans, and corn, the velvety green fruit is utterly American. Its native home is Mexico, probably initially the tropical southern part of the country. In the Aztec language, avocado was called *abuacatl,* meaning "testicle," in reference to its shape, and it is from the Aztec name that we, not realizing the meaning of the word, abstracted our own name, *avocado.*

Spanish conquistadores landing in Mexico reported trying the fruit; Hernando Cortés in particular noted that it was a staple of the Aztec diet. The Spanish also discovered they could milk the avocado's seed for a fluid they could use as ink.

In 1833, Judge Henry Perrine of Florida planted the first avocado in the United States. By 1856, cultivation of the avocado had begun in Los Angeles, California, though the first truly successful introduction didn't occur until 1871, when Judge R. B. Ord brought trees from Mexico and planted them in Santa Barbara.

In 1911, the owner of a major nursery in Altadena, California, Frederick O. Popenoe, sent an envoy to Mexico to seek outstanding avocados. When one of the trees he brought back survived the freeze of 1913, the avocado produced was named the Fuerte, Spanish for "strong." Then, in 1926, a pioneering avocado grower of Whittier, California, named A. R. Rideout, planted what he thought was a mistake, a tree that developed a heavy, blackish pebbly sort of fruit. Dismissing the tree, he sold the seeds to a postman named Rudolph Hass, who deemed the fruit no error. He used every dime he had to buy and plant the seeds. After some tries and some graftings, he had in hand the Hass avocado.

There are actually more than five hundred varieties of avocado, seven grown in California alone. Among them are the bacon, a midwinter green variety; the Gwen, a short, roundish sort; the Pinkerton, a long all-winter sort; the Reed, a summertime type, and the Zutano, a shiny, early September season opener. But in most markets only two are regularly featured, Fuertes and Hass. Smooth-skinned Fuertes has milder flavor than the creamy Hass, which most judge superior. California remains the largest producer of avocados, and in fact the original Hass avocado tree is still growing in La Habra, California.

CREAM CHEESE AND GRAPE LEAF DIP
WITH CRISP BAGEL ROUNDS

INGREDIENTS:

3 plain bagels, sliced into ¼-inch-thick rounds

6 jarred grape leaves, rinsed

1 cup good-quality cream cheese, at room temperature

2 tablespoons fresh lemon juice

4 oil-packed sundried tomatoes, drained and finely chopped

INVARIABLY THE BOWL OF DIP SURROUNDED BY CHIPS becomes a party's focal point. Finding a dip that's not the same-old, same-old is not unlike searching for a dropped football under a stack of scrambling players. But for both game watchers and partygoers, here's one that takes so few ingredients and is so speedy to make that it's a host's dream. The key is an unusual ingredient found near the olives and pickles in almost every store: grape leaves. As well as wrapping around Mediterranean dolmas and small birds for grilling, the shredded leaves add a scrumptious nip to a cream cheese dip. With a pinch of chopped sundried tomato on top, the dish offers pleasing visual and taste surprise.

1. Preheat the oven to 400°F.

2. Place the bagel rounds in one layer on a baking sheet and bake until lightly toasted, without turning, 7 minutes.

Use right away or store in an uncovered container at room temperature for up to 2 days.

3. To make the dip, place the grape leaves, cream cheese, and lemon juice in a food processor and process until smooth. Transfer to a bowl, sprinkle the sundried tomatoes across the top, and serve accompanied by the bagel rounds.

BEET, CHICKPEA, AND ALMOND DIP
WITH PITA CHIPS

APPETIZER TABLES FROM LEBANON TO EGYPT always include spreads and dips. A famous one combines beets, bread, garlic, and almonds; another is smoothed from beige chickpeas. Those made of chickpeas have so grabbed the American palate that stores offer them in a number of flavor variations. Here chickpeas are pureed and made more loamy and robust with the addition of beets. What emerges is a spread with a subtle sweetness and an anything-but-subtle, eye-catching magenta color.

MAKES ABOUT 2 CUPS

INGREDIENTS:

4 pitas, cut into 8 triangles each

1 large beet

1 cup cooked chickpeas

¾ cup extra virgin olive oil

5 cloves garlic, peeled

¼ cup slivered almonds

⅜ teaspoon kosher or fine sea salt

1½ tablespoons red wine vinegar

1. Preheat the oven to 400°F.

2. Spread the pita triangles out on a baking sheet without overlapping them. Bake, without turning, until light brown and crisp, 7 minutes. Use right away or store in an airtight container for up to 2 days.

3. Trim the beet and cut it into 8 chunks. Place the chunks in a saucepan, cover with water, and bring to a boil over high heat. Reduce the heat to maintain a simmer and cook until a fork easily pierces the center of a chunk, about 30 minutes. Drain, let cool enough to handle, and peel.

4. Place the beet chunks, chickpeas, olive oil, garlic, almonds, and salt in a food processor and process until smooth. Stir in the vinegar and transfer to a serving bowl. Serve the dip with the pita triangles on the side.

THE BOLD BEET

BEETS, CHARD, AND SPINACH all belong to the Chenopodiaceae, or goosefoot, family of plants. Undoubtedly the family got its name because the leaves of its members resemble the wide, thick, webbed feet of that ignoble squawker.

For years beets appeared in markets only in burgundy red, although seed catalogs call out the names of many varieties and hybrids. Among the types, all with alluring names, are Chioggia, Sangria, Kleine Bol, Monopoly, and Cylindra. Growing hidden in subterranean incubators, they issue forth in far more colors than red, crimson to aureate to ivory. In many countries the water they are cooked in also serves as a dye to turn onions pink and to stain Easter eggs red, meant to signify the blood of Christ.

EDAMAME BRUSCHETTA
WITH MINCED SCALLION, LEMON ZEST, AND BLACK SESAME SEEDS

MAKES ABOUT 24

INGREDIENTS:

2 cups frozen shelled edamame

½ cup extra virgin olive oil, plus more for brushing the bread

1 teaspoon kosher or fine sea salt

1 baguette, preferably a day old, cut diagonally into slices ¾ inch thick by 2½ inches long

2 large cloves garlic, smashed and peeled

2 tablespoons minced scallion, light green parts only

1 tablespoon minced lemon zest

2 teaspoons black sesame seeds, lightly toasted

EDAMAME ARE YOUNG, UNRIPENED SOYBEANS, relished as a snack and appetizer in Japan and now across the United States. Like fresh fava beans, their only European cousin, they need but a blanching to make them table ready. Edamame are usually served whole in the shell to accompany premeal drinks. They also enhance salads or, in more recent innovation, are mashed into a lively, soft green legumy spread to glorify bruschette. Packages of edamame, in the pod or shelled, are readily available in the frozen food section of most grocery stores, so get yourself a bag and prepare this elegant treat to begin a meal or augment the cocktail hour.

1. Bring a pot of salted water to a boil over high heat. Drop in the frozen edamame, bring the water back to a boil, and cook for 3 minutes. The edamame should be completely thawed and heated through. Drain them in a colander, then rinse under cool water until no longer warm. Shake the colander to dry the edamame a bit.

2. Combine the edamame, ½ cup olive oil, and salt in a food processor and process into a moist paste. At this point the edamame can be stored, covered, in the refrigerator for up to overnight. Remoisten with a little olive oil if necessary to make the paste spreadable, not clumpy, again.

3. Within 3 hours of serving, preheat the oven to 400°F.

4. Lightly brush one side of each bread slice with oil and arrange the slices in a layer, oil side up, on a baking sheet. Place in the oven and toast, turning once, until barely golden and still supple, 2 to 3 minutes total. Rub some of the garlic across the oiled side of each piece. Set aside at room temperature until ready to use.

5. When ready to serve, spread a generous tablespoon of the edamame paste across each bruschetta. Top with a pinch each of minced scallion and lemon zest and a light sprinkle of black sesame seeds.

FROM CANAPE TO BRUSCHETTA TO TOAST TO . . .

THE NOTION OF A ZESTY APPETIZER served on a small finger-friendly piece of bread came to America from France and Italy via Greece and England. Once adopted, Americans labeled them in our own inimitable way, as toasts, which is plain and declarative, although the tidbits on top are not so humble.

The term *canapé* refers to a small slice of bread, toast, or cracker crowned with a pat of cheese, meat, foie gras, salmon, a spread, or some other savory food. Originally from the Greek, *kounoupi,* it meant both "mosquito" and the curtain around a couch meant to keep mosquitoes away. Migrating to France, the word there became instead the term for "couch." French chefs of the time who had begun putting savory bits on bread thought the concoctions looked like little pillows on a sofa.

From the 1940s and '50s, countless canapés graced American home buffet tables for somewhat formal gatherings, weddings, graduations, and galas. But as time marched on to the '60s with their social changes, the term *appetizer* took over, with *hors d'oeuvres* still sometimes hanging on. Recently, however, both the term *canapé* and the canapé morsel have resurfaced to join their cousin *bruschetta*.

The Italian bruschetta is a crunchy starter or snack that consists of a spread or heap of creative tasties piled on a slice of toasted bread. It is larger and more heaped than the more delicate canapé.

The bruschetta and its thinner sister, the *crostino,* began their invasion of American restaurants and kitchens a few decades ago. Clearly no one minded the conquest. Quite the opposite, it proved a delightful kickoff to mollify the slightly peckish.

Our like of toast-based appetizers also derived from what became the lunch habit of hardworking Americans who needed to have a bite on a short midday break. Unlike Europeans' leisurely lunches, a very quick lunch, generally a fast sandwich, became the custom. To make that sandwich more satisfying, often the bread was crisped in concession to downing something that was at least warm.

A favorite American lunch, perhaps *the* favorite, became a toasted cheese sandwich, not unlike a Welsh rarebit. Tuna salad, deviled ham, even peanut butter sandwiches were spread on toast. The sandwiches then became more ornate, and it became an easy step to cut them smaller and make the toasts a tray for all sorts of appetizers. Now all three kinds of relish-topped bread adorn the starter menu: toasts, canapés, and bruschette.

ITALIAN AMERICANS AND THEIR COLOSSAL CULINARY CONTRIBUTION

Beyond America's early sweeping adoption of standard British cooking, no other cuisine has so influenced the American diet as has Italian. How many times a week is spaghetti cooked in the American home? Macaroni and cheese? How often is pizza delivered?

The story of Italians arriving in America is one of stops and starts: a first discovery, followed by a long lag and then a massive influx. With it came a vivacious, although at first insular people, bringing incredible customs, music, literature, and most of all food, food, food.

We all know how in the late 1400s Christopher Columbus, a young Italian sailor born in the seaport of Genoa, approached King Ferdinand and Queen Isabella of Spain with a scheme to reach Asia by sailing across the Atlantic. In 1492, he docked on an island in the Bahamas he named San Salvador. He was soon followed by other Italians: Giovanni Caboto (John Cabot), who arrived in Nova Scotia; Amerigo Vespucci, who reached South America; and Giovanni da Verrazzano, who sailed into New York Harbor.

AFTER THE NINA, PINTA, AND SANTA MARIA

In time, more Italians moored. Most were artisans—stonecutters, glassblowers, and woodworkers who came to help erect America's nascent cities. After the first small inroad of northern Italian artisans to American shores, practically no Italian immigrants followed for almost two centuries. However, in 1861, when Italy united into a single nation, matters changed abruptly and drastically. Many of the provinces, mostly in the South of Italy, were experiencing tremendous duress. From these, a massive immigration ensued. By 1920 more than four million Italians had entered the United States, 10 percent of America's entire population.

By this time, little land was left in America to homestead, so they took urban jobs in factories and groceries. They still did not think of themselves as Italians, but rather as Sicilians, Calabrians, Neapolitans, or Puglians. They clustered in cities and neighborhoods where their compatriots first settled. They established social clubs for members from their region, dedicated churches to their former patron saints, and opened eateries that served their regional food. The restaurants were family run; the food was inexpensive, warm, tasty, and filling.

ENCOUNTERS WITH PARMESAN

AMERICANS OF OTHER BACKGROUNDS discovered the restaurants. The dishes from Italy were quite different from what passed for dinner in America at the time. There was a parade of scrumptious preserved meats and rich cheeses. Flour paste was stretched into a hundred shapes, from long threads to fat tubes to bow ties to spirals, and served as beds for a mélange of sauces. They used garlic. They used a startling variety of fresh vegetables and fresh and dried herbs. They pounded meats thin and smothered them with wine, olives, and herbs. They grilled fresh fish until flaky. They started meals with a broad selection of appetizing savories.

By the late nineteenth century, tomatoes were just beginning to spread into Italy, but America had tons. In one of the most creative blendings, Italian Americans took an old tradition of spreading a sauce or cheese on a flat bread for a quick and inexpensive street food to New World heights. They flipped the flat bread into even larger circles, shellacked it with tomato sauce, topped it with cheese, pepperoni, sausage, peppers, onions, olives. They bestowed on us—pizza!

As more northern Italians began arriving in recent decades, their foods, somewhat more finespun, became part of the bill of fare. Plumped rice dishes, the rice especially developed in northern Italy to absorb more stock, pastas topped not with tomato but with pounded basil or arugula, pasta pockets filled with pumpkin, and tender potato dumplings all arrived in restaurants—adding to a cuisine of fresh, herbaceous, sparkling, sumptuous food.

PINTO BEANS AND GOAT CHEESE ON RAISIN BREAD CANAPES

INGREDIENTS:

1⅓ cups cooked pinto beans

2 tablespoons balsamic vinegar

1 teaspoon kosher or fine sea salt

½ teaspoon freshly ground black pepper

½ teaspoon ground cumin

8 slices raisin bread

1 cup (8 ounces) soft goat cheese

32 strips (½ inch long) bitter orange from a jar of marmalade

IN THE ARID SOUTHWEST OF THE UNITED STATES, many things come in mottled colors: sunsets, horses, beans. Since nicknames were the mode of the day when the region was settled, many names of objects invariably took on reference to their jumbled colors: paint, piebald, pinto, for example. That last came to be applied to the bean of choice in much of Southwestern cooking, as well as to horses. The wonderfully dappled, authentic pinto beans punched up with balsamic vinegar and cumin can be turned into a tangy finger food. Rather than on plain toasts, they are mounded on toasted squares of raisin bread with its winy sweetness, each swirled with a pungent goat cheese. In a final surprise, the whole arrangement is completed with strips of orange from a jar of marmalade. Not just unusual—delightful.

1. Preheat the oven to 400°F.

2. In a small baking dish, stir together the beans, vinegar, salt, pepper, and cumin. Spread the mixture evenly in the dish and bake, stirring once or twice, until the vinegar is absorbed and the beans are a rich brown, about 15 minutes. Remove and mash the beans slightly with a fork.

3. While the beans bake, place the bread on a baking sheet and toast lightly, turning once, about 5 minutes per side. Remove from the oven.

4. Spread each toast with a thin layer of goat cheese and cut into quarters. Top with about ½ tablespoon of the mashed beans. Garnish each with 1 orange strip and serve.

AMERICAN RAREBIT
WITH BOURBON, PICKLED SHALLOT, AND BACON BITS

UP UNTIL THE 1950s, Welsh rarebit was an expected, classic offering on the luncheon menus of private clubs and downtown restaurants that catered especially to ladies. Of British origin, there the rarebit was considered tavern fare, much like croque monsieur without the ham or pizza with cheese only. It is, after all, basically a grilled cheese sandwich, but made more savory with the addition of beer or port and mustard and more elegant, requiring a knife and fork to eat. Making it in small quantities means it can be enjoyed while the cheese is still molten. In keeping with the original spirit of casual but satiating fare, the toasts are topped with pickled shallot rings and crumbled bacon. Both punctuate the evolution of rarebit from British to American tables.

MAKES 16 PIECES

INGREDIENTS:

½ cup thinly sliced shallot rings, rings separated

1 tablespoon balsamic vinegar

¼ teaspoon kosher or fine sea salt

1 thick slice bacon, finely chopped

4 slices (about ½ inch thick) whole wheat bread

1 tablespoon butter

1 tablespoon bourbon

1 teaspoon sweet-hot mustard

8 ounces cheddar cheese, coarsely grated on a hand grater (about 3 cups lightly packed)

1. To make the pickled shallot rings, toss together the shallots, vinegar, and salt in a small bowl. Set aside until ready to use, up to several hours but not overnight.

2. To make the bacon bits, spread the chopped bacon on a microwave-safe plate lined with a paper towel or in an ungreased skillet. Microwave on high or fry over medium-high heat until crisp, 2 to 3 minutes. Set aside.

3. Toast the bread until dry but not crisp.

4. When ready to put the toasts together, heat the butter in a saucepan over medium-low heat until beginning to melt. Stir in the bourbon and mustard. Add the cheese and cook, stirring with a wooden spoon, until the cheese is melted. Right away, pour the molten cheese over the toasts and cut them diagonally into 4 triangles. Top each triangle with a pinch of shallots and another of bacon bits and serve.

HERBED QUESADILLAS WITH CANTALOUPE, ORANGE, AND ONION SALSA

INGREDIENTS:

Cantaloupe, Orange, and
   Onion Salsa (recipe
   follows), for serving

4 cups shredded melting
   cheese, such as Jack,
   cotija, cheddar, or a mix

¼ cup chopped scallion,
   light green parts only

1 teaspoon chopped fresh
   oregano leaves

1 teaspoon chopped fresh
   mint leaves

4 flour tortillas
   (8 inches in diameter)

Olive or canola oil,
   for frying

QUESADILLAS ARE AN AMALGAM OF New and Old World elements. The tortilla wrapper for the turnover is true New World. Cheese came to the New World from the Old, but it soon became the New World's own: supple Monterey Jack, ivory Mexican cotija, white to orange American cheddar. Besides being an amiable food merger, the quesadilla as snack offered speedy preparation for Americans who are nothing if not accelerated. Now quesadillas of all sorts delight diners. Once the quesadilla is filled with cheese, the salsa adds its own fun. Salsas are a New World sauce, but this one concocted of Old World melon and orange is both convivial and apt.

1. Make the salsa and set it aside.

2. Preheat the oven to 250°F.

3. Mix together the cheese, scallions, oregano, and mint. Spread 1 cup of the cheese mixture evenly over one half of each tortilla. Fold the empty side of the tortilla over the cheese mixture.

4. Heat oil to a depth of ⅛ inch in a large skillet set over medium-high heat. Place as many quesadillas in the pan as will fit without overlapping and fry, turning once, until the cheese has melted and the tortillas are golden and crisped on both sides, 2 to 3 minutes per side. Transfer to a baking sheet and place in the oven. Adding more oil to the skillet as needed, continue until all the quesadillas are fried.

5. Cut each quesadilla into 6 to 8 pie-shaped pieces. Place 1 tablespoon of the salsa on top of each piece and serve with the remaining salsa in a bowl on the side.

CANTALOUPE, ORANGE, AND ONION SALSA

ORANGES WERE BROUGHT TO THE NEW WORLD by Spanish conquistadores. Their cultivation spread so rapidly that by the time permanent settlers arrived to homestead in Central America, the Caribbean, and Florida, the natives were growing oranges and claiming them as their own. Christopher Columbus brought the first ancestor of the North American cantaloupe to America. The flavor and semifirm flesh of today's cantaloupes make them a favorite for fruit salad. In a mildly hot salsa, the orange adds lilt to the cantaloupe and smooths out the onion.

MAKES 1½ CUPS

1 cup chopped cantaloupe

¼ cup finely chopped peeled orange

¼ cup finely chopped red onion

½ teaspoon finely chopped jalapeño or serrano chile

2 tablespoons chopped fresh cilantro

2 tablespoons fresh lime juice

¼ teaspoon ground cumin

Pinch of kosher or fine sea salt

Mix all the ingredients together. Use right away or refrigerate for up to 4 hours (any longer and the brightness will fade). Serve chilled.

THE CULINARY GIFTS OF MEXICO AND MEXICAN AMERICANS

OTHER THAN ITALIAN CUISINE, perhaps none has so influenced American cooking and eating as that of Mexico and the Mexican Americans who lived in the United States even before the states were united. That the influence is so considerable stands to reason. Mexico is not only our immediate neighbor, sitting directly across the border to the south, but a number of our states were part of Mexico before that border was established.

Mexican Americans have been native to American soil for generations. Beyond what was already a local population, starting in the late 1800s another influx of Mexicans ensued, most fleeing upheaval and poverty in their country. The twentieth century then brought three further waves of Mexicans to America, the first taking place just after 1900, spurred by revolution in Mexico and a strong economy in the United States. By 1930 a million Mexican immigrants had come, streaming across the entire length of the open border. They worked on the railroads and in factories, began businesses, entered public life, became popular musicians, and exerted a massive cultural influence on American life.

Today 33 million people of Mexican origin live in America—one-tenth of the American population. Their importance in the melting pot of America is undeniable. They reside in every state and city, northern as well as southern, and across ranch and farmland from coast to coast. Spanish is the second-most-spoken language in the United States, and Mexican cuisine has seeped into every course in the American meal, from *taquitos* as appetizers to *sopapillas* as dessert. The people of the Southwest, Texas, California, and Florida were already cooking with the foods of native Mexico: corn, tomatoes, squash, beans, and capsicum peppers.

The contributions from Mexican cooking range from the crunchy hard tacos and sour creams of the northern provinces to the soft tacos and sweet cream toppings of the Yucatan. There's ruddy salsa, dotted with chile peppers from the desert, fresh *pico de gallo,* and tomatillo sweetness from the lush garden area of the central regions. The coasts have contributed garlic shrimp. The mountain area has given us its grilled and smoky beef *asada.* And from the South up to where Moctezuma once reigned comes one of the world's favorite foods, chocolate. Tortilla chips fill as much shelf space in grocers' as potato chips, along with jars of salsa of every sort. The list goes on and on. The debt we owe to Mexican Americans culinarily and culturally is incalculable.

CHICKEN LIVER TAQUITOS WITH RUBY GRAPEFRUIT PEANUT SALSA

INGREDIENTS:

Ruby Grapefruit Peanut Salsa
(recipe follows),
for serving

2 tablespoons extra virgin
olive oil, plus oil for
toasting the tortillas

8 whole chicken livers
(6 to 7 ounces), rinsed
and patted dry

½ cup dry sherry, such as
amontillado

4 corn or flour tortillas
(6 inches in diameter)

¼ cup (about 1 ounce) cotija,
queso fresco, or feta
cheese, crumbled

8 tender watercress sprigs

TACOS BEGAN AS HAND-HELD SAVORIES and remain pleasingly so. Their formula is a global one—fold something mouthwatering into an edible, usually bready, casing, and its purpose is clear: You can pick it up and eat it with no further ado. Tacos long ago crossed the border to become a mainstay across the United States. They have gone from lunch and dinner tables to the hors d'oeuvres one, here rolled into a small cylinder as a *taquito*. The filling is tender slices of chicken liver glistened with sherry, peppery watercress, and a wildly worldly salsa, mixing peanuts and citrus.

1. Make the salsa and set it aside.

2. Heat the olive oil in a sauté pan over medium-high heat. Add the chicken livers and sauté, turning once, until browned all around and cooked through but still moist, about 2 minutes per side. Add the sherry, increase the heat to high, and sauté until the liquid is bubbling and slightly reduced, about 2 minutes. Remove from the heat and set aside.

3. Lightly coat a large skillet with olive oil and heat over medium-high heat. Without crowding, toast the tortillas in batches until slightly crisp and golden on both sides, but still pliable, 2 to 3 minutes per side. Set them aside on a plate as you go.

4. Cut the chicken livers into bite-size slices. Place several slices on the edge of a tortilla. Drizzle a little of the sherry sauce from the pan over the slices. Spoon 1 to 2 tablespoons salsa over the slices. Sprinkle on 1 tablespoon of the cheese and set 2 watercress sprigs over all. Roll up the tortilla over the filling to make a thin tube. Repeat with the remaining ingredients. Cut the *taquitos* in half and nestle them together on a platter. Dollop each with more salsa and serve.

RUBY GRAPEFRUIT PEANUT SALSA

BOTH FRUIT AND NUTS have earned their status as honored members on the appetizer menu. Together, with a little chopped onion and a squirt of lime, they become an offbeat salsa, especially when the nut is roasted peanuts and the fruit that wake-up morning favorite, grapefruit. The salsa is downright divine for chicken, pork, or potato tacos, superb as a dip with soft pita chips, and indeed also good enough to spoon up on its own.

MAKES 1 CUP

1 small ruby grapefruit

⅓ cup finely chopped roasted salted peanuts

2 tablespoons fresh lime juice

1 tablespoon finely chopped red onion

2 teaspoons coarsely chopped fresh cilantro

Peel the grapefruit and separate it into sections. Cut away the white membrane around the outside of each section. Chop the sections into ¼- to ½-inch pieces and remove any seeds. Transfer the grapefruit to a bowl, add the remaining ingredients, and toss gently to mix. Use right away or set aside in the refrigerator for up to several hours.

HOW DID GRAPEFRUIT GO RUBY?

THE GRAPEFRUIT HAS A HISTORY of not just mystery but accident too. It is the only citrus fruit not from Southeast Asia, although one of its two forebears came from there. Apparently it showed up on the island of Barbados around 1700 as a spontaneous hybrid of sweet orange and Indonesian pomelo.

At first the strange interbreed was called by two names, *the forbidden fruit* and *shaddock* after the unwitting sea captain who had carried the pomelo seeds to the island. The fruit was not considered edible and its tree was used only as an ornamental shrub. Then someone of a different mind-set accidentally tasted the fruit, and from then on matters got juicy.

Once grapefruit was deemed tasty, American agronomist entrepreneurs jumped on its possibilities. Soon orchards of it were planted in Florida, Arizona, and California. One particular grower named John H. Shary thought the fruit could be the savior of the Texas economy (oil had not yet been discovered), so he planted sixteen thousand acres of it. Since the then-nameless fruit grew on its tree in clusters, much like grapes grow on a vine, despite its contradictions in size, color, and site of fruition, the growers nicknamed it for that habit, and the misleading misnomer stuck: the grapefruit.

In 1920 the first commercial shipment of grapefruit left the Rio Grande valley of South Texas, packed in onion crates. In a similar shipment nine years later, something odd was found: a grapefruit with a pink, rather than white, flesh. Apparently it had come from a rather pinkish tree. The rush to reproduce the pink grapefruit turned into a stampede. Soon several varieties were being grown, all for market appeal, enriching and dubbing the pink hue as "ruby." A short time later the Ruby Red grapefruit of Texas was granted a U.S. patent.

Ever the gamblers, Texas growers took the opportunity to eliminate all its white varieties and stake their entire grapefruit reputation on the Ruby. Shary's prediction proved accurate, albeit somewhat less than the billions produced by the state's liquid "black gold." The commercial success of the Texas Ruby Red grapefruit industry has been phenomenal, to the point that some consider it to be as much a symbol of Texas as the lone star and bluebell.

YOGURT CHEESE WITH RIVULETS OF GARLIC DILL OIL

INGREDIENTS:

1 teaspoon kosher or fine sea salt

1 quart plain Greek yogurt

3 tablespoons fruity extra virgin olive oil

1 large clove garlic, minced or pressed

1 teaspoon chopped fresh dill

1½ teaspoons chopped fresh chives

½ teaspoon Hungarian paprika, either hot or sweet

Pita triangles, Ak-Mak crackers, or matzo, for serving

YOGURT CHEESE IS A CONVERSATION OPENER for any appetizer spread. "You *made* your own cheese, from yogurt!?" Yes, and it's a cinch, requiring little more than a dense Greek yogurt to start, three days' untended time, and some refrigerator space. Traditionally the yogurt cheese is rolled into walnut-size balls before being doused with olive oil and dusted with paprika. To save effort and embolden the presentation, here it is merely spread into a thick, creviced layer and given a sheen with rivulets of herbed olive oil. As well as an eloquent snack, yogurt cheese without any frills makes a fine, low-calorie base for a bagel schmear or garnishing dollop on a side dish of lentils, lima beans, or chickpeas.

1. Line a colander with 3 layers of cheesecloth, leaving a generous overhang. Stir the salt into the yogurt and transfer to the colander. Set the colander in a bowl, making sure there is plenty of space between the bottom of the bowl and the bottom of the colander. Cover loosely with plastic wrap and set aside to drain in the refrigerator for 3 days, pouring off the whey whenever it reaches high enough to touch the bottom of the colander. The yogurt cheese is ready when it is thick enough to roll into small balls.

2. To serve, stir together the oil, garlic, dill, and chives. Spread a layer of yogurt cheese about ¾ inch thick on a platter. With a tablespoon, make three or four ¼-inch-deep indentations in the cheese and pour the oil mixture all across the top. Sprinkle with the paprika and serve with the pita or crackers.

CRISP BABY ARTICHOKES, FENNEL, AND LEMON ROUNDS

THERE ARE MULTITUDINOUS VARIATIONS on the theme of battered or breaded fried vegetables, fish, and chicken. The Japanese have their irresistible tempura creations; the Mediterraneans have their no less resistible deep-fried croquettes, East Indians their spice-battered vegetables, even Maryland's and Louisiana's battered and fried soft-shell crabs fit the bill. Among the most captivating is a bouquet of lusty vegetables and thin lemon rounds coated in a simple egg and flour wash. The crispy mix is so bright and finger-licking good, it's fun to invite guests into the kitchen to enjoy each piece hot off the stove.

1. Preheat the oven to 170°F. Line 2 baking sheets with paper towels.

2. Snap the hard outer leaves off the artichokes down to the tender, light green inner leaves. Trim off the stems and tops and cut the artichokes in half, or into quarters if they are more than an inch or so in diameter. Fill a bowl with water and add the lemon juice and the trimmed artichokes.

3. Trim the root end of the fennel and slice the bulb into ¼-inch-thick rounds. Set aside.

SERVES 4

INGREDIENTS:

- 12 baby artichokes
- 1½ tablespoons fresh lemon juice
- 1 medium-size fennel bulb
- 1½ cups all-purpose flour
- 1 large egg, lightly beaten
- ½ cup warm water
- Peanut, canola, or extra virgin olive oil, for frying
- 12 lemon rounds (⅛ inch thick)
- 12 large fresh parsley sprigs, including 1 inch or so of tender stem
- 2 tablespoons large capers, preferably salt-packed, rinsed and patted dry
- 20 kalamata or oil-cured black olives with pits
- Kosher or fine sea salt

4. Spread the flour on a plate. Whisk together the egg and warm water in a wide bowl. Set both the flour and egg mixture near the stove.

5. Pour oil to a depth of ¾ inch into a large skillet or sauté pan and heat over medium-high heat. Drain the artichokes and pat dry with paper towels.

6. When the oil is hot enough to sizzle a sprinkle of flour, begin frying. Dip the artichokes in the egg bowl and transfer, without shaking off the drip, to the plate with the flour. Turn to coat them and place them in the skillet. Fry as many pieces as will fit without overlapping (a little crowding is okay). Fry until golden and beginning to crisp, about 4 minutes. Use tongs to turn them gently, so as not to break the crust, and continue cooking until tender and crisp all around, about 4 minutes more. Transfer to a prepared baking sheet, set aside in the warm oven, and continue with another batch until all the artichokes are cooked.

7. Coat and fry the fennel in the same way. It will take about 4 minutes per side, turning once. Transfer the fennel to the baking sheet in the oven.

8. Continue with the lemon rounds and parsley sprigs, breading and frying them as described above. They will take about 1 minute per side, turning once. When you turn them, add the capers and olives without coating them. Transfer to a prepared baking sheet, lightly sprinkle salt over all the fried food, and serve right away, while still warm and crisp.

ARMENIA, AMERICA, AND YOGURT

THE FIRST AMERICAN YOGURT, Colombo Yogurt, was set in motion in 1929 by Rose and Sarkis Colombosian, immigrants from Armenia. They made yogurt as they had in the old country for family and friends. The yogurt caught on with those who had enjoyed it in their native cuisines, so they started a company to produce it on a large scale.

Slowly, but only slowly, did the skeptical descendants of northern Europeans, who had their own version of soured cream and who were averse to anything new and anything sour, deigned to try it. Eventually they did, and yogurt took off.

It was many years later that Dannon Yogurt was introduced in New York by a Swiss-born Spanish émigré, Joe Metzger, along with his son Jan and his other partner, Isaac Carasso, a Parisian yogurt maker. They set up their yogurt company in the Bronx. At first they turned out only two hundred eight-ounce jars a day, which they sold for 11 cents each, mostly to local ethnic markets. But their production increased yearly. By 1947 Dannon, now in Long Island City, had added a layer of strawberry on the bottom of yogurt cartons. In 1948, they offered a vanilla-flavored yogurt, which was followed by more flavors. Many companies then joined the craze, so that today yogurt comes in many sizes, various levels of full milk to less fat, and almost every flavor imaginable. In recent years the market has seen the arrival of ultra-thick Greek yogurt, some imported, but most made Greek-style here in America, among them: Fage (meaning in Greek "eat"), Chobani (meaning "shepherd"), and Oikos (meaning "household" or "family" by Dannon).

EGGPLANT HALF-MOONS

WITH RED BELL PEPPER SLICES, FETA, AND GREEN OLIVE CHOP

EGGPLANTS WERE ONCE KNOWN AS *LOVE APPLES* in England because they were thought to be an aphrodisiac. Half-moon slices of them trimmed with a border of red pepper and decorated with other colorful edibles make a beautiful and intriguing meal opener. Why does it taste so alluringly wonderful? The slices are softened with olive oil, which eggplant delights in. Underneath all, a leaf platter helps to neatly transport the seductive array from hand to mouth.

1. Trim the stem and bottom off the eggplant. Cut the eggplant crosswise into six ¾-inch-thick rounds. Cut the rounds in half to make 12 half-moons.

2. Cut the pepper in half lengthwise, remove the stem and seeds, and trim off the membrane. Slice each half crosswise into twelve ¼-inch-thick half-circle strips.

3. In a small bowl, mix together the olives and oregano and set aside.

MAKES 12 HALF-MOONS

INGREDIENTS:

1 globe eggplant (about 8 ounces)

1 small red bell pepper (4 to 6 ounces)

10 large green olives, such as Sicilian-style, Atalanti, Ionian, or cracked green, pitted and finely chopped

1 teaspoon chopped fresh oregano leaves

12 small inner butter lettuce leaves, flattened

Extra virgin olive oil, for sautéing the eggplant

¼ cup (about 1 ounce) crumbled feta cheese, mashed

4. Arrange the lettuce leaves on a platter and set aside.

5. Pour oil to a depth of ¼ inch into a large sauté pan and heat over medium heat. Add the eggplant half-moons in a single layer (work in batches if necessary) and sauté gently, turning once, until just cooked through (soft and slightly browned), 6 to 7 minutes on each side. Remove the pan from the heat.

6. Press a red pepper strip along the rounded edge of each eggplant half-moon. Press 1 teaspoon of the feta cheese on each half-moon, just beside each red pepper strip.

7. Return the sauté pan to the stovetop over low heat. Cover and cook until the feta melts, 3 to 4 minutes.

8. Place about 1 teaspoon of the green olive chop on top of each half-moon. Set each of the half-moons on a lettuce leaf and serve.

EGGPLANT:
THE GREAT PURPLE EGG

EGGPLANTS ARE TECHNICALLY a fruit, a member of the nightshade family, related to potatoes and tomatoes. They originated in India and were first recorded in an Egyptian papyrus from 1552 BCE. The first ones were small, white, and egg shaped, leading the English when they arrived there around the time of Henry VIII to call them *eggplant,* which now seems an incongruous name. The English cooked them in a rather bland manner, not yet understanding how eggplants welcome herbs, spices, and other vegetables.

Eggplants were introduced to America by the Spanish in 1808, although the English style of cooking them was presented by Eliza Leslie in her early American culinary guide *Directions for Cookery*. She recommended three ways: stewed, fried, and stuffed, all with bread crumbs. What really turned America on to eggplant was eggplant Parmesan, served in all the little Italian cafés and eateries that sprang up across the country. Added to that has been ratatouille, moussaka, eggplant salad, fried eggplant, baba ghanoush, and caponata. Eggplants can also be scooped out and filled with onion or meat, most often in combination with their distant cousin the tomato. They can be stir-fried with garlic and peppers, grilled crisp, baked, and sautéed. With eggplant the possibilities are virtually endless.

BUTTON MUSHROOMS WITH MARSALA WINE AND TARRAGON

LOAMY, SYLVAN BUTTON MUSHROOMS are a perfect all-in-one, hand-to-mouth bite. When poached in a sauce of tangy yet dulcet Marsala wine and tarragon with its iota of licorice flavor, they are satisfying bite after bite.

1. Heat the oil in a large nonreactive pot or sauté pan over medium heat. Add the mushrooms and turn to coat all around. Add the garlic, tarragon, wine, lemon juice, salt, and pepper and cook, continuing to turn, until the mushrooms are somewhat golden and the liquid is almost evaporated, about 7 minutes.

2. Transfer the mushrooms to a bowl, sprinkle the parsley over the top, and serve warm. Or refrigerate for up to several days, holding out the parsley. Reheat on the stovetop, sprinkle with the parsley, and serve.

INGREDIENTS:

- ¼ cup extra virgin olive oil
- 1 pound button mushrooms, stems trimmed, rinsed, and patted dry
- 2 cloves garlic, coarsely chopped
- 1 teaspoon chopped fresh tarragon or ½ teaspoon dried
- ½ cup Marsala wine
- 2 tablespoons fresh lemon juice
- ½ teaspoon kosher or fine sea salt
- ¼ teaspoon freshly ground black pepper
- 1 tablespoon chopped fresh flat-leaf parsley

ZUCCHINI FRITTERS
WITH WHITE CHEDDAR CHEESE AND FRIED PARSLEY TOPPING

MAKES 12 FRITTERS

INGREDIENTS:

Yogurt Lime Sauce
(recipe follows),
for serving

3 cups grated zucchini
(about 2 medium-size),
patted dry

¾ cup finely chopped yellow
or white onion

⅔ cup grated white cheddar
cheese

1 large egg, beaten

1 teaspoon dried marjoram

¾ to 1 cup all-purpose flour

1 teaspoon baking powder

1 teaspoon kosher or fine
sea salt

Extra virgin olive oil, for
frying the parsley and
fritters

12 fresh parsley sprigs,
preferably curly-leaf

THE GLORY OF ZUCCHINI IS MANY FACETED. They simmer, sauté, or grill to make a lovely side dish. Shaved they make an appealing vegetable salad ingredient. Across every Mediterranean country and many homes and restaurants in America, they are chopped into a highly likable fritter. To make the vegetable-intense fritters even more enticing, they are blended with a sharp American cheddar cheese.

1. Make the sauce and set it aside.

2. To prepare the fritters, combine the zucchini, onion, cheese, egg, marjoram, ¾ cup of the flour, the baking powder, and the salt in a large bowl. With your hands, knead the mixture until well blended, adding more flour as necessary to make a fairly dry batter. Form into patties 3 inches in diameter (about ¼ cup batter each). Transfer the patties to a plate as you go. Make sure the patties don't touch. Set aside for 10 to 30 minutes.

3. Pour oil to a depth of ¼ inch into a medium-size sauté pan and heat over medium-high heat. Add the parsley and fry, turning once with tongs, until crisp, 1 to 1½ minutes total. Transfer to paper towels to drain.

4. Add as many fritters to the pan as will fit without crowding and fry, turning once, until golden and crisp on both sides, about 2 minutes per side. (Reduce the heat if the oil becomes too hot and the fritters start to burn.) Transfer the fritters to paper towels to drain as you go. Continue with another batch, adding more oil as necessary, until all the fritters are fried.

5. Garnish each fritter with a dollop of the sauce and strew the parsley over all. Serve the remaining sauce on the side.

YOGURT LIME SAUCE

ZUCCHINI FRITTERS IN ITALY come topped with just a sprinkling of cheese. Corn fritters, with or without pecans and mint (page 28), would usually be served as plain as the country folk who first patted them. But tastes in contemporary America are for a little admixture of flavors, a little smack of moisture, and something to lighten the fritters. A drizzle of Yogurt Lime Sauce accomplishes both.

MAKES 1¼ CUPS

1 cup plain Greek yogurt

2 tablespoons fresh lime juice

1 teaspoon chopped fresh cilantro leaves or chives

Dash of Hungarian paprika, either hot or sweet

½ teaspoon kosher or fine sea salt

Combine all the ingredients in a small bowl and whisk to mix and smooth the yogurt. Set aside to mellow for 15 minutes or so before serving or store in the refrigerator up to overnight.

TIP: DON'T FORGET THE FLOWER. Zucchini and their squash cousins all bear beautiful edible flowers before the squash develops. Those flowers can also make a fritter. Wash the flowers carefully so as not to bruise their delicate petals. Gently pat them dry, then fill them with a pinch or two of grated or crumbled mild cheese, such as mozzarella, provolone, queso fresco, mild white cheddar, or Monterey Jack. Lightly batter the blossoms with egg and flour and fry them in oil at a depth of ½ inch over medium-high heat, turning once with tongs, until barely golden, only 3 to 5 minutes altogether. Arrange them on a platter, which will empty in less time than the squash flowers took to cook.

A PAIR OF FRITTERS IN YOGURT LIME SAUCE

A FRITTER IS A SMALL CAKE made of batter, often containing bits of fruit, vegetable, or fish, and sautéed or deep-fried. The name comes from the Latin word for "to fry." (It also means "to tear into pieces," which leads to the saying "to fritter away" time or money.) The appeal of fritters is manifold.

For starters, they are somewhat crunchy, combining bits of shredded foods, frequently an informal mix with herbs and especially with salt, the most popular of all spices.

Almost every cuisine includes fritters forged from a veritable garden of components. Potatoes are the foundation of both Ashkenazi latkes and Swedish potato pancakes. Haitians mash and fry patties of plantains. The Zapotecs of Mexico make a fritter of black beans. Others turn to chickpeas, chard, lentils, conch, cod, and cheese.

Sometimes fritters are sweet, like doughnuts, funnel cakes, beignets, and the various honey-soaked dough balls of the Near East. Fritters also figure as the traditional food of special holidays, like the pancakes of Shrove Tuesday, the last day before the Lenten fast; on Boxing Day, the day after Christmas in England; or the *zeppole* made for Saint Joseph's Day in Naples. Sometimes the name refers to a whole piece of fruit, such as a prune in Hungary or a vegetable dipped in batter, such as Japanese tempura, or the all-American onion ring.

Fritters turn the cook into a demigod: When making the fritters on this page and the next, your job is to stand before a pan and tend them as they sizzle to crisp perfection. Your guests will probably gather at the stove, ready to sample the fritters as soon as they are done.

CORN, PECAN, AND MINT FRITTERS

INGREDIENTS:

Yogurt Lime Sauce
(page 27), for serving

3 to 4 cups fresh corn kernels
(from 3 medium-size ears)
or frozen organic corn
kernels

½ cup pecans, finely
chopped

¼ cup finely chopped red
onion

¼ cup chopped fresh mint
leaves

1 teaspoon kosher or
fine sea salt

½ teaspoon freshly ground
black pepper

⅛ teaspoon grated nutmeg,
preferably freshly grated

1 large egg, lightly beaten

6 tablespoons all-purpose
flour, or more as needed

Vegetable oil, for frying

½ cup coarsely shredded
Monterey Jack cheese

OF THE FIVE TYPES OF CORN—dent, flint, pop, flour, and sweet—it is sweet corn hybrids that hold American hearts. We eat it off the cob dripping with melted butter and slice golden kernels from the ears to serve as a sunny vegetable side dish. We cream it and soup it. Corn also makes a splendid fritter, soft enough to sink teeth into, pebbled enough to be chewy and satisfying. A touch of mint and unexpected nutmeg bring these fritters to full fantastic.

1. Make the sauce and set aside.

2. Place the corn in a small bowl and add the pecans, onion, mint, salt, pepper, and nutmeg and stir to mix. Stir the egg into the corn mixture, then slowly whisk in enough flour to make a thick batter.

3. Pour oil to a depth of ¼ inch into a large skillet and heat over medium-high heat. With floured hands, take about 3 tablespoons of the fritter mixture and pat it into a patty 2 to 2½ inches in diameter. Place the patties in the skillet in a single uncrowded layer, working in batches if necessary. Fry, turning once, until crisp and brown on both sides, about 3 minutes per side.

4. Spread 1 teaspoon of the cheese on top of each patty. Cover the skillet, turn off the heat, and let sit until the cheese has melted, about 1 minute. Place on a platter and serve with the sauce on the side.

WHISKEY-SOAKED FIGS WITH MINT AND CURRANT PESTO

THERE ARE REASONS THAT FIGS ARE VENERATED. Their flavor inspires poetry and their form art. When charred a little on a grill or in a broiler and served as an appetizer, the result is an invitation to satisfaction. Should a bottle of rye not be at hand, a good bourbon will suffice.

1. Place the whiskey in a small pan or microwave-safe bowl and heat it until barely warm and not yet simmering. Place the figs in a bowl and pour the warm whiskey over them. Set aside to soak and soften for 30 minutes or so.

2. Make the pesto and set aside.

3. Preheat the broiler or prepare a medium-hot grill.

4. Lift the figs out of the whiskey and slit them lengthwise, just enough to open them slightly. Place them on a baking sheet or string them on a skewer. Broil or grill them, turning once, until soft and a little charred, 10 to 12 minutes.

5. Place a dab of the pesto in the opening of each fig. Arrange on a platter and serve.

MAKES 16 PIECES

INGREDIENTS:

1 cup rye or bourbon whiskey

16 dried Calimyrna figs

Mint and Currant Pesto (recipe follows)

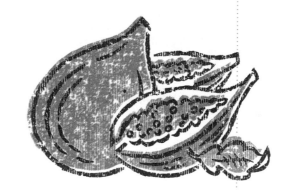

RYE WHISKEY, RYE WHISKEY

RYE WAS AMERICA'S MOST PREVALENT, most beloved whiskey until Prohibition, but after its repeal, rye never reclaimed its former rank. Instead, the nation's other darling whiskey, bourbon, surged ahead. Though both are whiskeys, rye is in some ways the more elegant of the two, smoother, more mellow. It is less sweet than bourbon and has a nuance of peppery tartness. As well as a soak for dried figs, either can be used for a steak sauce (page 76), sweetened and reduced for a dessert topping, or poured anywhere a splash of dark whiskey is wanted.

Bourbon may have gained on rye after Prohibition because bourbon's corn is much cheaper than grassy rye. To be called rye whiskey by American standards, the whiskey must be distilled from at least 51 percent rye grain. Rye's other 49 percent is most often made up of a blend of corn and malted barley. Once the grain mix, called a *mash,* is composed, rye is cooked to 160 proof, after which it is put to age in new but fire-charred barrels, where it sits for two years. Canada makes rye whiskey as well, but it contains only a fraction of and sometimes no rye. Interestingly, as long as the Canadian distiller matches the taste of rye whiskey, the product can be called rye.

Many of America's most famed cocktails originally were made with rye, namely the old-fashioned, the whiskey sour, and the Manhattan, the major rival of the ever-popular martini served in the very same sort of glass. Other old-time rye drinks include rock and rye, made with rye whiskey, bitters, and rock candy, and the Algonquin, made with rye whiskey, dry vermouth, and pineapple juice. Due to rye's current popularity, a number of contemporary cocktails employing it have emerged. There's the rye whiskey cocktail with powdered sugar, bitters, and a cherry; the boulevard, with dry vermouth and Grand Marnier; and the sneaky Pete, with coffee liqueur and milk.

A further note: One of the ryes made by the Anchor Distilling Company of San Francisco is named Hotaling's Rye in honor of the A. P. Hotaling & Company's warehouse on Jackson Street. It was filled with cases of rye whiskey when the 1906 earthquake struck; the whiskey survived.

MINT AND CURRANT PESTO

A DAINTY DAB of nose-tingling mint pesto adds a cooling green, yet robust bounce to whiskey figs. The pairing is historically grounded. Romans flavored wine sauce with mint and also seriously relished figs, so the combination would seem apt to them. In modern-day America, we cultivate huge amounts of mint, using it for gum, candy, and oil, as well as this pesto.

MAKES ABOUT 1 CUP

3 tablespoons dried currants
3 tablespoons warm water
⅔ cup fresh parsley leaves
½ cup fresh mint leaves
1 clove garlic, smashed and peeled
¼ cup pine nuts
¼ cup grated Parmesan cheese
⅓ cup extra virgin olive oil

1. Combine the currants and water in a small bowl and set aside to soften for 10 minutes or so.

2. Drain the currants and place them in a food processor along with all of the remaining ingredients. Process until almost smooth but still a little textured. Use right away or store in the refrigerator for up to overnight.

DATE, FETA, AND PROSCIUTTO ROLL-UPS

DATES WERE INTRODUCED TO AMERICA by the Spanish missionaries of Mission San Ignacio in Baja California around 1765. They were brought north by 1818 and further encouraged when in 1890 the U.S. Department of Agriculture sent explorers to collect offshoots of Babylonian and Arabian Medjool varieties. They didn't thrive all that well, but in 1912 the importation of the Deglet Noor variety turned the Coachella Valley of California into a veritable date oasis. When dried, date sugar condenses into a nugget of sweetness, and dates are eaten as a straightforward and fortifying treat. They may also be stuffed with almonds, walnuts, orange peel, and tahini.

MAKES 35 PIECES

INGREDIENTS:

35 (about 8 ounces) pitted dry dates

3 ounces (about ¾ cup) feta cheese, crumbled

1 to 2 tablespoons milk

4 to 5 ounces thinly sliced prosciutto, cut into strips 4 inches long and ½ inch wide

35 tender fresh cilantro sprigs

1. Heat an ungreased sauté pan large enough for the dates to fit in a single layer over medium heat. Add the dates and brown them, stirring constantly, until they are slightly crisped and no longer sticky, about 8 minutes. Remove from the heat and let cool enough to handle.

2. In a small bowl, place the cheese and milk and mash them together with a fork until the feta is smooth and moist.

3. Open the dates where they are split, or with a paring knife make a slit along one long side to open them. Place about ¼ teaspoon of the cheese mixture in the opening and press the sides together. The stuffing will come out a bit beyond the edges. Roll a strip of prosciutto around the date, placing a cilantro leaf under the last ½ inch of the prosciutto strip. Arrange on a platter and serve.

FETA: JUST A SLICE

FETA, GREECE'S MOST famous cheese, has become one of the world's most beloved. However, the word *feta* isn't actually the name of the cheese. It just means "slice." The cheese was already so desired by Byzantine times that when ordering it, people would just ask for "a slice."

Feta is a moist, crumbly sheep's or goat's milk cheese. Although the density ranges from very soft to almost hard, generally it comes medium-soft. It is a brined cheese which, shortly after firming, is placed in a saltwater solution to stop its ripening. Thus it retains its young, curdlike qualities. Readily available in almost any supermarket, it is lively and sweetly milky in flavor, making it a wonderful appetizer cheese, complement to salads, or addition to cheese mixtures.

LEEK, POTATO, AND DILL FILO PIE

MAKES ONE 9 x 13-INCH PIE

INGREDIENTS:

- 3 tablespoons extra virgin olive oil

- 3 to 4 medium-size leeks, white and light green parts only, rinsed, chopped, and drained

- 1 large egg

- 1 tablespoon milk

- 2 medium-size russet or Yukon gold potatoes (8 to 10 ounces each), peeled and coarsely grated

- ⅓ cup grated Parmesan cheese

- 3 tablespoons chopped pitted kalamata olives

- 2 tablespoons chopped fresh dill

- ¾ teaspoon kosher or fine sea salt

- Dash of cayenne pepper

- ½ cup extra virgin olive oil or 8 tablespoons (1 stick) butter, melted

- 12 sheets filo dough, cut to cover a 9-by-13-inch baking pan, at room temperature (see Tip)

ROOT VEGETABLES ARE AMONG THE MOST DIVINE in Eden's garden, with or without embellishment. The pie here contains two of the best: leeks, which are bulbs, and potatoes, which are tubers. Leeks are the mildest of onion kin, and potatoes are America's most relished comfort food. A commingling of them dotted with olives and cheese and layered within sheets of filo dough is a dish that can serve as starter or, with salad, as lunch or dinner.

1. Preheat the oven to 375°F.

2. Heat the 3 tablespoons olive oil in a large sauté pan over medium heat. Add the leeks and sauté until well wilted but still bright green, about 10 minutes. Transfer to a medium-size bowl and set aside to cool slightly.

3. Lightly beat together the egg and milk. Add to the leeks along with the potatoes, cheese, olives, dill, salt, and cayenne and stir to mix.

4. To assemble the pie, spread a thin coat of oil or melted butter on the bottom of a 9-by-13-inch baking pan. Work quickly or place a damp cloth over the filo sheets you are not yet working with. Brush the top of a sheet of filo with oil or butter and lay it across the pan. If 1 sheet is not enough to cover the pan, trim to size and overlap a second oiled sheet. One at a time, oil and lay 5 more sheets of filo on top of the first. Spread the leek and potato filling across the filo stack. Oil and place a filo sheet over the filling, then oil and top it with 5 more sheets.

5. Roll the edges of the filo toward the center to make a border and brush them with oil or butter. With a sharp knife, carefully score the first 2 or 3 layers of filo to mark out 12 equal rectangles.

6. Place the pie in the oven and bake until the top and edges are golden and crisp, 45 to 60 minutes. Remove and let cool slightly.

7. Cut through the score lines to make individual pieces and serve warm or at room temperature. The pie will keep in the refrigerator for 3 days. Gently reheat it in a 350°F oven.

⊙ **TIP: FILO FINESSE.** Filo dough can be found fresh at many ethnic grocers, and precut frozen filo, rolled into a cylinder between thin sheets of wax paper, is available in the freezer section of most supermarkets. To use, thaw the dough at room temperature, unroll the cylinder, and remove as many sheets of filo as you will need. Work quickly or cover these with a damp cloth to keep them from drying out as you work. Reroll the remaining sheets tightly into their wax paper and return to the freezer.

Filo sheets comes in various-size rectangles. Large ones will require trimming to size before use; small ones might require overlapping to make layers that completely cover a pan's dimensions. Don't throw away the trimmings. You can shred them, sprinkle them with chopped walnuts, pecans, or pistachios, drizzle lightly with honey and melted butter, and bake at 375°F, until golden and crisp, about 20 minutes.

SUNDRY SAVORY FILO PARCELS

THE HOST OF SAVORIES that come out of the oven in thin crisp sheets of paper-thin dough gives undeniable evidence to how engaging they are as a festive snack or ideal gateway to a meal. It matters not if the crust is replete with cheese, vegetable, meat, poultry, or fish. Filled-filo treats are never monotonous, and the best part is how easy they are to create. Despite rampant "fear of filo," the dough is a most forgiving pastry and it is premade. You can layer it into a pie, form it into an envelope, crenellate it into tiny or large cups, curve it into coils to hold almost any savory or sweet, traditional or novel. A baker's experienced hands aren't necessary to contrive a pretty edible. Razor straight or raggedy edged, the morsels maintain their choose-me appeal. The Leek, Potato, and Dill Pie; Mustard Greens, Fennel, and Feta in Crenellated Filo Cups; and Sherried Mushroom Coils are three brassy fillings in three filo styles. They can be mixed and matched or swapped around, depending on predilection and occasion for serving them.

MUSTARD GREENS, FENNEL, AND FETA
IN CRENELLATED FILO CUPS

**MAKES 12 MINI OR
6 LARGE FILO CUPS**

INGREDIENTS:

3 cups finely chopped tender mustard greens (from a 12-ounce bunch)

1 tablespoon extra virgin olive oil

1 small yellow or white onion, finely chopped (about ½ cup)

2 tablespoons chopped fresh fennel fronds, including some of the tender stalk

1 tablespoon chopped fresh dill

1 large egg, well beaten

½ cup (about 2 ounces) crumbled feta cheese

1 tablespoon fresh lemon juice

3 sheets filo dough, 12 to 13 inches by 15 to 17 inches each, or enough to make up the equivalent, at room temperature

3 tablespoons extra virgin olive oil or melted butter

USING MUSTARD GREENS AS A FILO FILLING is a variation of the classic spinach and feta cheese pie *spanakopita,* which has worked its way from immigrant Greek American tables to the American deli and popular cocktail fare. Here it is presented elegantly in individual filo cups, either mini or muffin size. One mini cup is a single bite, perfect for placing on an appetizer tray. Full muffin size is three or four bites, and so if offering those to standing guests, be sure to offer small plates or large napkins as well.

The cups are excellent served with ouzo, as the Greeks do with *spanakopita,* or any of ouzo's kin, such as anisette or Pernod, or another aperitif, such as sambuca or Campari, or a flinty white wine. You will need a muffin tin, either the mini sort that has twelve wells, or a regular one that has six larger wells.

1. Bring a pot of water to a boil over high heat. Add the mustard greens and cook until tender, 4 to 5 minutes. Drain in a colander, gently pressing down on the greens to rid them of excess moisture without pressing them dry. Transfer to a bowl and set aside.

2. Heat the 1 tablespoon oil in a large skillet over medium heat. Add the onion, fennel, and dill and sauté until the onion is soft, about 4 minutes.

Transfer to the bowl with the mustard greens. Add the egg, feta, and lemon juice and mix together.

3. Preheat the oven to 375°F.

4. To make the filo cups, lightly brush 1 filo sheet all the way to the edges with oil or melted butter. Work quickly or cover the sheets with a damp towel so they don't dry out. For mini cups, cut the sheet into quarters, then halve

the quarters. Lay one of the half-quarters crisscrossed over another. Using both hands, lift up the 2 crossed sheets and place them in a cup of an ungreased 12-well muffin tin, forming them upward without pinching them together, to make a cup. Do the same with the 2 remaining cut quarters of the first sheet.

For the larger muffin cups, follow the same process, only cut the oiled sheet into quarters. Lay 1 quarter crisscrossed over another quarter. Using both hands, lift up the 2 sheets and place them in a cup of an ungreased 6-well muffin tin, forming them upward without pinching them together to make a cup. Do the same with the remaining 2 quarters of the first sheet. Continue with the remaining 2 whole filo sheets, oiling or buttering and quartering them, until you have either 12 or 6 muffin wells lined with filo.

5. Gently place 2 tablespoons of the filling into each mini cup or ¼ cup of the filling into each larger cup. Lift up the edges of the filo to meet in the middle, tucking any pieces of filo that break off into the center. Bake until deep golden on top and crisp on the sides and bottom, 10 minutes for the mini cups, 15 minutes for the large cups. Remove from the oven and let rest for 5 minutes.

6. Serve warm or set aside for up to several hours and serve at room temperature or reheat the filo cups in a 350°F oven for 10 minutes.

SHERRIED
MUSHROOM COILS

MAKES 20 PIECES

INGREDIENTS:

6 ounces cremini (brown) mushrooms, stems trimmed

2 ounces shiitake mushrooms, stems removed and discarded

2 tablespoons extra virgin olive oil or butter

1 large shallot, finely chopped

1 teaspoon hot or sweet Hungarian paprika

½ teaspoon chopped fresh thyme

½ teaspoon kosher or fine sea salt

1 tablespoon dry sherry, such as amontillado

1½ teaspoons fresh lemon juice

1 tablespoon all-purpose flour

½ cup extra virgin olive oil or 8 tablespoons (1 stick) butter, melted

20 sheets filo dough, cut into approximately 8-by-11-inch rectangles, at room temperature

THERE ARE 1,841 KNOWN SPECIES OF EDIBLE MUSHROOMS. Many of the varieties spring up after summer rains in both lowland and high mountain regions of the United States. Mushroom festivals celebrate them, and often wild ones appear carefully identified in local markets. These in season can also slip between sheets of filo to bake up tastily. Soaked in sherry, rolled in flaky filo, and baked, mushrooms make attractive hors d'oeuvres, but muscats and other sweet wines can substitute for sherry, and the rolls can be formed into flutes or triangles.

1. Preheat the oven to 375°F. Lightly oil a baking sheet and set aside.

2. Rinse the mushrooms and pat them dry. Chop them very finely with a chef's knife (not a food processor, which will mash them). Set aside.

3. Heat the 2 tablespoons oil or melt the 2 tablespoons butter in a medium-size sauté pan over medium heat. Add the shallot, stir to mix, and cook until translucent, about 2 minutes. Stir in the mushrooms, paprika, thyme, salt, sherry, and lemon juice. Increase the heat to medium-high and cook until the juices are mostly evaporated, 3 to 4 minutes, depending on the dimensions of the pan. Sprinkle the flour over the top, stir to mix, and cook for 1 minute more. Remove from the heat and set aside to cool.

4. Oil or butter a whole rectangle of filo. Spread 1½ tablespoons of the mushroom mixture in a narrow line ½ inch in from the edge along a short side of the sheet. Roll the ½ inch of filo over the filling and continue rolling, forming a long, thin cylinder. Starting at one end, coil the cylinder around itself, tucking the end tip underneath. Repeat with the remaining oil or butter, filo sheets, and mushroom filling.

5. Place the coils, seam side down, on the prepared baking sheet. Lightly oil the tops of the coils and bake until the mushroom filling is hot and the filo is quite golden, 20 to 25 minutes. Serve warm or at room temperature. The coils will keep in the refrigerator for 3 days. Gently reheat it in a 350°F oven.

BUFFALO AND CAPER MEATBALLS

LITTLE WALNUT-SIZE MEATBALLS, often served pierced with a fancy toothpick, have so long been a standard on the appetizer table that they could be thought humdrum. But there is nothing boring about a meatball that's been updated. Rather than beef or pork, these are made with buffalo, America's own lean and flavorful indigenous meat, now available in many markets. Capers spruce up the meatballs. The toothpick remains, but the appetizer meatball has become a savory with a savor.

MAKES 35 TO 40 MEATBALLS

INGREDIENTS:

1 pound ground buffalo

½ medium-size onion, finely chopped

¼ cup capers, preferably salt-packed, rinsed and chopped

¼ cup bread crumbs, preferably homemade (page 41)

1 rounded tablespoon tomato paste

1 large egg

¼ teaspoon grated nutmeg, preferably freshly grated

¼ teaspoon freshly ground black pepper

Kosher or fine sea salt

Extra virgin olive oil, for sautéing the meatballs

¾ cup chopped fresh parsley

1. Mix together the meat, onion, capers, bread crumbs, tomato paste, egg, nutmeg, and pepper in a medium-size bowl. Season with salt to taste. Roll the mixture into walnut-size balls. Use right away or cover and refrigerate for up to 2 days.

2. To cook the meatballs, heat 1 tablespoon of oil in a large heavy skillet over medium-high heat. Working in batches, add as many meatballs as will fit in the skillet without crowding and stir to brown all around. Sauté, stirring occasionally, until cooked through, 10 to 12 minutes. Transfer to paper towels and continue with another batch, adding more oil as necessary, until all the meatballs are cooked.

3. Place the parsley on a plate and roll each meatball in the parsley, arranging them on a platter as you go. Serve right away, accompanied by toothpicks for picking them up.

MEATBALL MERRIMENT

AMERICAN INNOVATION has led to very interesting meatball concoctions. A prize winner at the Altus Grape Festival in Altus, Arkansas, was the Great Grape Meatball. Altus was settled by German and Swiss immigrants, who established a wine industry, and hence the festival's theme. The winning ground beef balls included red seedless grapes and grape jelly, along with cocktail, chili, or soy sauces. Well, why not?

PEANUT-CRUSTED CHICKEN WINGS WITH SOUTHEAST ASIAN DIPPING SAUCE

MAKES 16 PIECES

INGREDIENTS:

8 chicken wings or
   16 drumettes

¼ cup all-purpose flour

1 teaspoon kosher or fine
   sea salt

1 large egg

¼ cup water

¾ cup salted roasted
   peanuts, finely ground but
   not pulverized

Southeast Asian Dipping
   Sauce (recipe follows),
   for serving

2 tablespoons finely
   shredded fresh basil
   leaves

FROM THE EASTERN UNITED STATES CAME BUFFALO WINGS, named for their city of origin and making their debut at the family-owned Anchor Bar, where the vinegar and chili-coated wings served with blue cheese dip and celery sticks established them as an all-time American bar food.

From the Far East of the globe, however, came another sort of wings, those that are served as a starter in the Southeast Asian cuisines of Vietnam, Thailand, and Indonesia. They commonly come with a peanut or fish-based, spicy-tart dipping sauce. The version here tilts to Southeast Asia and combines the Asian pizzazz of the two sauces with a peanut crust on the wings and fish-based sauce for dipping them. A wing as starter helps any meal or event take flight.

1. Preheat the oven to 375°F. Lightly grease a baking sheet.

2. If using whole chicken wings, cut off the wing tips and reserve them for another purpose. Cut each wing in half at the joint, making 16 pieces. Pat them or the drumettes dry on paper towels. Set aside.

3. Mix together the flour and salt on a plate. In a wide bowl or dish, whisk together the egg and water. Spread the peanuts on a separate large plate.

4. Dust the chicken with the flour, turning to coat all around. Dip each piece in the egg mixture, transfer to the plate with the peanuts, and turn to coat all over.

5. Arrange the pieces on the prepared baking sheet so they don't touch one another and bake until the peanut coating is golden and almost crisp on the bottom, about 10 minutes. Turn over the pieces and continue baking until golden and crunchy on the top, about 12 minutes more.

6. While the chicken pieces are cooking, make the sauce.

7. Transfer the chicken pieces to a serving platter. Gather up any peanuts left on the baking sheet and scatter them, along with the basil, over the top. Serve warm or at room temperature, with the dipping sauce on the side.

SOUTHEAST ASIAN DIPPING SAUCE

RICE VINEGAR IS a specialty of Asian cooking. It is a low-acid vinegar that provides a gentle nudge, rather than a strong kick to myriad dipping sauces. Brown rice vinegar, in particular, augments the intriguing complexity (called *umami*) of the sauce. It is available in large supermarkets either in the Asian foods section or with the specialty vinegars. Regular, not seasoned, rice vinegar or an extra tablespoon of lime juice can substitute for it.

MAKES ABOUT 1 CUP

½ cup fish sauce, preferably Thai

2 tablespoons rice vinegar, preferably brown rice vinegar

2 tablespoons water

1 tablespoon fresh lime juice

2 tablespoons sugar, preferably light brown

1 large clove garlic, minced or pressed

2 teaspoons finely chopped small fresh chile, red or green, including seeds

2 tablespoons finely shredded fresh basil leaves

Place the fish sauce, rice vinegar, water, lime juice, sugar, garlic, and chile in a small bowl and mix until the sugar is dissolved. Add the basil right before serving. Use right away or store in the refrigerator for up to overnight. After that, the sauce loses its luster.

WHITEFISH CAKES WITH TARTAR SAUCE

INGREDIENTS:

1 pound whitefish fillets, such as walleye or other pike, halibut, sea bass, or cod, hand-chopped into ¼- to ⅓-inch bits

3 tablespoons finely chopped scallion, light green parts only

¼ teaspoon chopped fresh tarragon

2 large egg whites, lightly beaten

2 cups bread crumbs, preferably homemade (see Tip)

1 teaspoon kosher or fine sea salt

8 tablespoons (1 stick) butter, for frying the cakes

2 cups thinly shredded romaine heart or iceberg lettuce, for serving

Tartar Sauce (recipe follows), for serving

NO DOUBT MANY PEOPLE MADE CAKES of flaky fillets of fish, but a signature one that has joined the American meal as a first course comes from the Jewish tradition. And like the bagel, whitefish cakes have become everybody's food. The cakes can be made of fresh, not smoked, fish and prepared in many styles: Southwest (with jalapeños), French (with Dijon mustard), and Japanese (with panko crusting), to name a few. The cakes below are rather traditional but with a twist of tarragon and scallion. It's essential to hand-chop the fish, as a food processor will smash the delicate flesh and make it too soft. The cakes are exceptionally good accompanied by the classic English enhancement of tartar sauce.

1. Combine the fish, scallion, tarragon, egg whites, 1 cup of the bread crumbs, and the salt in a medium-size bowl and mix gently with your hands to blend the ingredients. Form into 12 patties, each about 2 inches in diameter.

2. Spread a small amount of the remaining 1 cup bread crumbs on a plate and coat both sides of each fish cake with the crumbs, adding more crumbs to the plate as necessary. Place the cakes as they are made on a separate plate, being sure they don't touch. Cover loosely with plastic wrap and refrigerate for at least 30 minutes and up to several hours.

3. To cook the fish cakes, melt 3 table-spoons of the butter in a sauté pan over medium heat until the butter begins to foam. Add as many cakes as will fit without crowding and fry, turning once, until golden and crispy on both sides, about 2 minutes per side. Transfer to paper towels and continue with another batch, adding more butter as necessary, until all the cakes are fried. The cooked cakes may be held in a warm oven on baking sheets lined with paper towels for up to 1 hour.

4. To serve, spread the lettuce on a platter. Set the fish cakes on the lettuce and top each with a dollop of tartar sauce. Serve while the cakes are still warm.

TARTAR SAUCE

TARTAR SAUCE NEVER becomes prosaic or banal. It is a perfect taste-enhancing, creamy yet plucky topping, and there's hardly a fish or vegetable that it doesn't embellish with flair. Also, it's an excellent dip for bread.

MAKES ABOUT 1 CUP

¾ cup mayonnaise

¼ cup packed chopped fresh flat-leaf parsley

1½ tablespoons finely chopped scallion, light green parts only

1½ tablespoons finely chopped cornichons

¼ teaspoon freshly ground black pepper

1 tablespoon fresh lemon juice

Combine all the ingredients in a small bowl and whisk to mix. Use right away or store in the refrigerator for up to 2 days.

⊙ TIP: HOMEMADE BREAD CRUMBS: YESTERDAY'S BREAD TODAY AND BEYOND. With a food processor and some day-old bread there's no reason to settle for the sorry excuse for bread crumbs available commercially. The best bread for all-purpose crumbs is batard, ciabatta, or similar French or Italian bread without seeds, walnuts, olives, or other embellishment.

To make bread crumbs, cut off most of the crust (leave a little on for texture) and then cut the bread into roughly 1-inch chunks. Put the chunks in a food processor up to the top of the blade knob—no higher, or the bread will turn into a glob rather than crumbs. Process until as fine as you like. Four cups of 1-inch chunks yields approximately 2½ cups of medium-fine crumbs. If you want extra-fine crumbs for coating food with an extra-crisp crust, before processing briefly dry the chunks further in a low oven until firm but not toasted. Let them cool before processing. Store any crumbs you won't be using within 2 or 3 days in the freezer.

FISH CAKES, CHOPPED LIVER, LOX, AND BAGELS

THE JEWS OF EASTERN EUROPE came to America driven by poverty, pogroms, and eventually genocide in a great wave lasting from the late 1800s until after World War II. As with all immigrants, they brought with them their familiar foods and food preparations. Like the dishes of other arriving groups, these ethnic edibles merged into the American melting pot and became simply American. Though others had smoked salmon, it is Jewish lox that gained supremacy. While some may eschew chopped liver, many are crazy for it. Whitefish purchased in a thick slice is turned into salads and cakes.

Lox and also whitefish are regularly accompanied by a particular bread—the bagel. Legend has it that in 1683 a Jewish baker wanted to thank the king of what later became Poland for protecting his people from Turkish invaders and so baked a special hard roll shaped like a riding stirrup for the king, who was an ardent horseman. Soon the stirrup became round and the bread evolved into a gift not just for a king but to give mothers in childbirth and babies as teething rings.

With the Eastern European Jews, the bagel immigrated to cities such as Toronto, Montreal, and New York. By 1907, bagels were being boiled and baked at such a rate that a union of bagel bakers was formed. Today bagels are so widely adopted that even airlines serve them for breakfast.

TUNA PEARLS IN BELGIAN ENDIVE BOATS WITH PONZU SAUCE

MAKES 12 PIECES

INGREDIENTS:

Ponzu Sauce (recipe follows)

3 to 4 Belgian endives, depending on size

4 ounces sushi-grade tuna, hand-cut into ¼-inch dice

1 teaspoon finely grated or minced peeled fresh ginger

1 teaspoon finely shredded fresh mint leaves, for serving

1 teaspoon chopped fresh chives, for serving

WHEN SUSHI APPEARED IN AMERICA IN THE 1970s, it caused a culinary tsunami. The delicacy of pristinely fresh fish won over palates until not only were sushi restaurants full, but home cooks were rolling sushi, slicing sashimi, and chopping raw fresh fish for hand rolls and fish tartars. Tuna tartar in particular became the new crown princess of openers. Here a toss of tuna "pearls," ever so lightly seasoned with ginger and mint and nestled into Belgian endive leaves, is an intercontinental appetizer delight.

As with the whitefish cakes, the key to turning this very simple composition into a picture of beauty is to carefully dice the tuna by hand. That way the pieces appear as small iridescent jewels rather than a mash. It is also important to keep the tuna refrigerated until ready to use to keep the individual bits firm.

1. Make the ponzu sauce and set it aside.

2. Cut off the bottoms of the endives just enough to free the large outer leaves, removing and discarding any wilted or blemished ones, until you have 12 large, pretty leaves.

3. To assemble the endive boats, spread about 2 teaspoons of the diced tuna across an endive leaf. Dot a minuscule pinch of ginger across the top of each. Moisten with a sprinkle of the ponzu sauce, dust lightly with mint and chives, and serve, with the remaining ponzu on the side to use as a dipping sauce.

PONZU SAUCE

PONZU IS A LIGHT, oil-free dressing or dipping sauce imported from Japanese cuisine. The Japanese serve it at the table alongside the dish rather than included within it. Widely used to enhance meat, fish, and vegetable dishes, it has now become popular with Western chefs who appreciate its clean, clear, slightly sweet, slightly salty citrus flavor that enriches without dominating. As well as the exotic citrus called *yuzu,* ponzu typically includes mirin, a Japanese sweet rice wine. Sake sweetened with a tinge of sugar delivers the same taste with a fresher nuance.

MAKES ⅔ CUP

¼ cup light soy sauce

¼ cup fresh yuzu juice or fresh citrus juice blend (see Tip)

1½ tablespoons sake

1 tablespoon rice vinegar, preferably brown rice vinegar

½ teaspoon sugar

Combine all the ingredients in a small saucepan and bring just to a boil over medium heat. Cool and use immediately or store covered in the refrigerator for up to 2 weeks.

➲**TIP: YUZU PERFUME.** Ponzu was based originally on the exotic citrus yuzu. Native to Asia, where it grows wild in Tibet and China, it later became cultivated, most notably in Japan. Yuzu carries an enigmatic, sensual fragrance and flavor that softly entices one to enjoy the heady waft and puzzle over how to define it.

Recently yuzu has appeared in Northern California markets, brought from nearby Asian growers who cater to a large population of Japanese consumers and a growing number of chefs and curious home cooks. It is still a rarefied ingredient, available only in scattered markets from late fall to early winter.

With no yuzu at hand, the question is, how to re-create its elusively attractive presence in a dish? A blend of other citruses seems the way to go, but opinions and solutions range widely. Should we use grapefruit or not, orange or not, lime or not, or just go with lemon?

To create ponzu sauce offering a *parfumerie* blend that simulates the elusive yuzu aroma and taste: Combine ¼ cup fresh lemon juice, preferably from Meyer lemons, 1½ teaspoons fresh lime juice, and 1½ teaspoons fresh grapefruit juice and swirl to mix. Use soon, while the esters are still drifting up and the juice is audaciously fresh.

SHRIMP WITH CANDIED PECANS
IN BUTTER LETTUCE LEAVES

MAKES 12 PIECES

INGREDIENTS:

½ cup Candied Pecans
(recipe follows)

12 jumbo shrimp
(about ½ pound),
peeled and deveined,
if necessary

1 teaspoon kosher or
fine sea salt

2 tablespoons mayonnaise

1 tablespoon chopped fresh
cilantro

12 small butter lettuce leaves

Cayenne pepper, for garnish

LEAVE IT TO THE INVENTIVE COOKS of the island of Hong Kong to come up with a pairing of shrimp with mayonnaise and candied nuts. Surrounded by water, lively Hong Kong is the epicurean center of Cantonese cooking, the first of many regional styles of Chinese cuisines to sweep across the United States. In such enclaves as San Francisco's and New York's Chinatowns, Cantonese remains the main manner of Chinese fare, one that includes such familiars as egg rolls, fried wontons, sweet and sour pork, and hoisin, plum, and oyster sauces. The mayonnaise blanketing the unique shrimp appetizer shows the influence of the English who held Hong Kong for ninety-nine years. But the candied pecans are a pure American spin on Hong Kong's usual walnuts. Curious as the dish may seem, it's a winner.

1. First make the candied pecans. When cool, coarsely chop them and set aside.

2. Place the shrimp in a medium-size sauté pan. Add the salt and enough water to barely cover them. Bring just to a boil over high heat. Drain off the water immediately and rinse the shrimp briefly under cool water. Pull off their tails and coarsely chop the meat.

3. Place the shrimp and pecans in a medium-size bowl, add the mayonnaise and cilantro, and toss to mix. Spread about 1½ tablespoons of the mixture in the center of a lettuce leaf and sprinkle ever so lightly with cayenne. Serve right away or refrigerate covered for up to 2 hours and serve cold.

CANDIED PECANS

CANDIED NUTS HAVE been a favorite for centuries, but no ancient mystery is involved in turning them out. Simply tossed with sugar and water, nuts can be glazed and toasted in an oven or microwave in minutes.

MAKES ½ CUP

½ cup shelled pecans

1½ teaspoons sugar

Pinch of cayenne pepper

1 tablespoon water

1. Preheat the oven to 425°F. Or, use a microwave set on high.

2. Place the pecans on a baking sheet or microwave-safe plate and sprinkle with the sugar and cayenne. Toss to mix. Sprinkle with water and spread out the nuts in an uncrowded layer.

3. Toast in the oven until gold and sizzling, about 5 minutes, or in the microwave, about 3 minutes. Remove and stir to break up the clumps. Set aside until the sugar coating hardens, about 3 minutes.

4. Use right away or store in an airtight container at room temperature for up to several weeks.

CANTONESE COOKING

IN 1849 AN EVENT OCCURRED that changed both Chinese and American history: the California Gold Rush. The district of Canton on the South China Sea had become economically distressed, and the news of gold in America spread like wildfire. Calling California "Gold Mountain," by 1851 twenty-five thousand Chinese, mostly men and largely from Canton, had come to America. They were soon working not only in the mines but on the railroad as well.

Although government acts were passed to exclude them from citizenship, they succeeded in enterprise, their forte. They opened haberdasheries, laundries, and restaurants.

In rapid course, Cantonese cooking spread from the West to every city and state across the nation. Chinese food became an alternative to American and Italian for the busy and time poor. It also became the "takeout" food of choice. With the clear popularity of such food, fancier, upscale establishments followed. The Cantonese tradition of a dim sum brunch showed up. Dinner menus became replete with a dizzying and exciting array of appetizers.

Shrimp and candied nuts with mayonnaise was one of them. How different, how pretty, and how intriguing as a prelude to a meal.

POTAGES THAT FILL

f anything epitomizes America's melting pot of people, it is America's simmering pot of soup.

Soup has been part of all cuisine since fire was tamed and cooking vessels were devised and placed over fire. The potpourri of foodstuffs, spices, and liquids that goes into a soup is as varied as the diverse people living in the world.

Just about all of the varieties have reached the cookstoves of America, and we have taken to them all. We think no more of sipping a sizzling rice soup than we do a minestrone, no more of ordering a bowl of borscht than of corn chowder, no more of cooking up a steaming miso than we do of cooling off with a refreshing gazpacho. Seafood bisque, cream of mushroom, lentil porridge, nourishing chicken, tomato, potato, hot and sour, coconut, consommé, Cuban shrimp, Egyptian sesame, vegetables of every sort, meat of every type, fish plucked from the cool sea and dunked into hot broth—all of them are ours.

Soups restore. The recuperative claims are true. To have a soup is to spring back from droopy to dynamic. Americans spoon up more than ten billion bowls of soup every year—thick or clear or creamy, rustic or sophisticated.

We love soup so much that all around the country countless food festivals celebrate it. The Alligator Festival in Boutte, Louisiana, often features Alligator and Sausage Jambalaya. At the Napa Valley Mustard Festival in California, attendees are feted with Artichoke Soup with Rock Shrimp. At North Carolina's Seafood Festival, Beaufort Bisque is a traditional offering, and at the Kansas Threshing Days Festival there is always Cherry Moose Soup. Following is a miscellany of warm and innovative soups that pour from our culinary pot.

SOUP AS METAPHOR

SO ESSENTIAL IS soup and so known that it shows up not only in its beloved bowl but also as a metaphor for many things:

❯ *Primordial soup* describes the churning mass from which the first life sprang.

❯ *Word soup* refers to any jumble of words that is incomprehensible to the listener or reader.

❯ *Duck soup* is a term that denotes a really easy task.

❯ *Pea soup* is a fog so thick, like the puree it refers to, that no one can see through it.

❯ *Soup legs* is used by athletes to describe their or someone else's legs gone liquid from fatigue.

❯ *Sop* is a word for a bribe and a reference to a spineless individual. The word *soup* comes from *sop*, first the bread used to soak up milk, then a stewlike dish that was eaten by sopping it up with bread. Now the sop is just the bread again.

HEIRLOOM TOMATO SOUP WITH LACY CHEESE CRISPS

FROM ABOUT 1830 when tomatoes were finally accepted as an edible for the American table, countless shapes, colors, and nuances of taste have been hybridized. The success of a rustic and simple tomato soup such as this one is determined by the tomatoes. For the outcome to be bracing, to be deeply flavored, the tomatoes should be full-summer-ripe, juicy with sugars developed until heady. If summer is yet to appear or has slipped away, to make it a year-round soup, choose the best hothouse tomatoes the grocery offers and amend with a dollop or two of good tomato paste stirred in. With lacy cheese crisps adding a special element, the soup is one that can start the meal elegantly or easily serve as the meal.

1. Core the tomatoes, quarter them, and pull out the seeds with your fingers. Cut the tomatoes into ¼-inch-wide strips and transfer them, along with their juices, to a bowl.

2. Heat the olive oil in a medium-size pot over medium heat. Add the onion and garlic and sauté until the onion is translucent and softened, about 3 minutes. Stir in the tomatoes and juices, the oregano, and the salt. Add the water and bring to a boil over high heat. Reduce the heat to maintain a gentle simmer and cook, uncovered, until the tomatoes are very soft and the bright red liquid is reduced to a rich brownish red, about 35 minutes.

3. While the soup simmers, make the cheese crisps and set aside.

4. To serve, ladle the soup into individual bowls. Sprinkle with the chives, prop a cheese crisp in each bowl, and serve warm.

SERVES 4

INGREDIENTS:

- 2½ pounds red tomatoes, preferably heirlooms or beefsteaks
- 2 tablespoons extra virgin olive oil
- 1 medium-size yellow or white onion, finely chopped
- 4 large cloves garlic, minced or pressed
- ½ teaspoon chopped fresh oregano or ¼ teaspoon dried
- ½ teaspoon kosher or fine sea salt, plus more to taste
- 6 cups water
- 1 tablespoon chopped fresh chives, for serving
- Lacy Cheese Crisps (recipe follows), for serving

LACY CHEESE CRISPS

CHEESE CRISPS ARE an inventive hand-me-over from Italy, where they are made with aged Montasio cheese. Equally stellar for making them is a dry Jack cheese. It has a slightly sharp, nutty flavor typical of Italian grana cheeses. The cheese crisps are a snap to make either on the stovetop or in the oven. The advantage to the stovetop is that they cook much more quickly but they can be cooked only one or two at a time. In the oven, four to eight can be baked at once, depending on how many baking pans you use.

MAKES 4 CRISPS

Vegetable oil, for coating the pan

1 cup coarsely shredded hard grating cheese, such as dry Jack, aged Asiago, or Parmesan cheese

1. *To cook on the stovetop:* Lightly film a medium-size sauté pan or skillet with oil and heat over medium heat until a few drops of water sprinkled into the pan sizzle. Sprinkle a generous ¼ cup of the cheese into the pan, making a 4-to-5-inch-wide circle. Cook without disturbing until light golden on the bottom and just barely melted across the top, 2 minutes, give or take a few seconds. As they're done, lift up the crisps with a metal spatula and transfer to a plate. Continue with another until all the cheese is used.

To cook in the oven: Preheat the oven to 375°F. Line a baking sheet with parchment paper (or use a non-stick baking sheet, which requires no lining). Sprinkle ¼-cup amounts of the cheese into circles as described above, leaving plenty of room between them so they can spread without getting stuck together as they cook. Cook until golden on the bottom, without turning, about 7 minutes.

2. Use the crisps right away or store in an open container; enclosing them will cause them to wilt.

⊃TIP: LACY CHEESE CRISP BOWLS. When they are just out of the pan and still warm and supple, the cheese crisp circles can be formed into edible bowls to hold all manner of nonliquid foods such as leafy salads, shrimp cocktails, scrambled eggs, appetizer-size servings of vegetable taco filling (page 253), eggplant stuffing for bell peppers (page 288), miniature meatballs (page 37), or almost anything else you can imagine.

To form crisps into bowls, undercook the circles ever-so-slightly. Quickly, while they're still malleable, lay the crisps, bottom side up, over an upside-down flat-bottomed drinking glass. The crisps will naturally drape down to form a bowl. It is best to use the stovetop method, as those baked in the oven run the risk of becoming too crispy. Use the cheese bowls right away or store as described in the main recipe, taking care to handle them extra-gently so they don't become cheese crumbles, though those are also delicious.

TOMATOES:
THE RUBY JEWEL OF THE AMERICAS

WHEN THE SEAFARING, gold-seeking European explorers of the fifteenth and sixteenth centuries crossed the Atlantic Ocean and stumbled onto the American continents, they unearthed a treasure chest of edibles ultimately more valuable than any of the riches they plundered. Its amazing contents included corn, potatoes, squashes, capsicum peppers, pineapple, avocado, chocolate, vanilla, almost every kind of bean, and tomatoes. Meanwhile, the newly arrived wayfarers brought along their own comestibles: rice, wheat, cows, pigs, and chickens. It was a grand time in the history of cuisine. The merger of the foods from the two hemispheres led to an explosive marriage of culinary innovation the likes of which has never been repeated.

The tomato was the crop that soon topped the list in terms of gastronomic importance. More than chocolate or vanilla, more than corn or beans, it was the alimental jewel.

Long before recorded history, the tomato had first sprouted in the Peru-Ecuador-Bolivia region of the Andes. It rapidly spread to Mexico, where it took a central place in Mayan and then Aztec cooking. But despite its appeal, at first the new settlers in America eschewed the strange orb. Many thought it was a new sort of apple, only to bite it and reject it. Others called it a *love apple*, but heeding Eve and another sort of love apple, they didn't dare sample it. Some thought it was poisonous. Thomas Jefferson and others thought it was a comely plant to have in a garden, but not something to eat.

Back in Europe, another sort of sentiment was forming. The Spanish and then the French and Italians were more open to trying the new discovery, and they had the perfect climates—rainy springs and hot, sunny summers—to nurture tomatoes.

Very soon, cooks were off and running: A little of this, a little of that, onion and garlic, walnut, cheese, and oregano. One early Italian writer called it *pomo Peruviana*, thinking it from Peru. Another called it *poma d'oro*, referring to yellow tomatoes. The Spanish called it *pome de Moro*, "Moor's apple," though it was not at all Moorish.

The first cookbook to mention tomatoes was published in Naples in 1692. By 1752, English cooks were singing its praises for flavoring soups. By 1800 tomatoes were showing up in European farmers' markets, and fifty years later they were being grown all over Italy, southern France, Spain, and Greece and were creeping into Turkey and around the Levant.

By early in the nineteenth century, the tomato made it back to the Western Hemisphere. The French and Spanish of New Orleans, who were accustomed to eating tomatoes, demanded them. Elsewhere doubts lingered about the safety of the tomato until 1820, when a certain Colonel Robert Gibbon Johnson announced he would eat a bushel of them in front of the Boston courthouse. Thousands came to witness his death, but he didn't die. George Washington Carver then advocated tomato consumption, along with peanuts and yams, to the southern poor. Soon more and more tomatoes, and more and more types of them, were being cultivated. With a long delayed "aha!" the tomato entered American salads and sauces and became the basis of what is probably our favorite soup.

Today it's hard to imagine how we could live without tomatoes. We are the world's top producer, and backyard gardeners from Rhode Island to California grow them. We stew them and stuff them, pair them as sauce with meats, bake them and grill them, chop them, dice them, slice them. They have become our true "love apple."

VEGETABLE SOUP WITH RED BELL PEPPER PESTO

INGREDIENTS:

Red Bell Pepper Pesto (recipe follows), for serving

¼ cup extra virgin olive oil

1 medium-size yellow or white onion, thinly sliced

2 cloves garlic, coarsely chopped

3 medium-size tomatoes, cored and coarsely chopped

1½ teaspoons kosher or fine sea salt, plus more to taste

8 cups water

1 tablespoon tomato paste

1 large carrot, cut into ¼-inch-thick rounds

6 ounces small summer squash, stem ends trimmed, squash halved or quartered, depending on size, flowers rinsed inside, if using

2 cups packed thinly sliced white-ribbed chard leaves and stems

2 cups cooked white beans, such as cannellini, flageolets, or navy beans

1 teaspoon chopped fresh thyme

1 cup fusilli, penne, or other small dried pasta

1½ teaspoons finely chopped fresh rosemary, for serving

NOTHING QUITE MATCHES A VEGETABLE SOUP so chock full of garden components it emerges like an earth-issued stew. Like Genoese-style Italian minestrone or *Provençal soupe au pistou,* such a soup turns extra filling, meal-like, and intercontinental with the inclusion of pasta and dried beans from the Americas. A small sprinkle of fresh rosemary and a swath of red bell pepper pesto swirled across the top supply additional pleasure.

1. First make the red bell pepper pesto.

2. Heat the olive oil in a large pot over medium heat. Add the onion and garlic and cook until wilted, about 3 minutes. Add the tomatoes and salt and continue cooking until the tomatoes are quite soft, about 10 minutes.

3. Add the water, tomato paste, carrot, squash, chard, beans, and thyme and bring to a boil over high heat. Reduce the heat to maintain a brisk simmer and cook, uncovered, until the carrots and squash are crisp tender, 20 minutes.

4. Add the fusilli and continue cooking until it is al dente, 12 minutes.

5. Adjust the salt seasoning and ladle the soup into individual bowls. Swirl a wide patch of red bell pepper pesto across the top and sprinkle with rosemary overall. Serve right away, with the remaining pesto on the side.

RED BELL PEPPER PESTO

RED BELL PEPPER PESTO was originally created as an appetizer for our first cookbook together, *Good &*

Plenty. That was almost thirty years ago, but our attachment to it is still going strong. In high summer, when red bell peppers are at their sweetest and not all that expensive, roasting and peeling some can provide for a stupendous pesto. It can then be used in assorted ways from hors d'oeuvres dip to pasta sauce, to topping for vegetables, fish, or poultry, wherever a bold stroke of red and flavor will glamorize an otherwise simple preparation. It is especially bewitching used to enliven a bracing vegetable soup.

MAKES ABOUT 1⅓ CUPS

2 large red bell peppers, roasted, peeled, and seeded (recipe follows)

2 large cloves garlic, coarsely chopped

2 tablespoons pine nuts

2 tablespoons freshly grated Parmesan cheese

¼ cup extra virgin olive oil

½ teaspoon kosher or fine sea salt

Place all the ingredients in a food processor and puree as finely as possible. Use right away or refrigerate covered for up to 3 days.

ROASTED BELL PEPPERS

MANY RECIPES CALLING for bell peppers specify roasted and peeled peppers. Thus prepared, they also can be sliced and used on their own, dressed with a little olive oil and vinegar and a sprinkle of salt, to serve as a side dish or bruschetta topping.

2 large bell peppers, any color

1. Preheat the oven to 400°F.

2. Place the peppers on a rack in the middle of the oven and roast, turning once, until charred all around, 20 to 30 minutes, depending on the size of the peppers. Transfer the peppers to a counter, cover them with a kitchen towel, and let cool for 15 minutes.

3. With your fingers and a paring knife, peel the peppers. Slit them open and remove the seeds and membranes. Cut up the peppers according to the size you want for the recipe you are using.

TIP: THE MANY COLORS OF CHARD. The leaves and ribs of tender young chard of any color can be chopped, sautéed, and presented as a side dish with perhaps a splash of lemon and a drizzle of fruity olive oil. Once mature the ribs of the more colorful varieties don't make particularly good fare as they don't cook into sweet tenderness. The white-ribbed variety of chard, on the other hand, offers more options. Normally the leaves are stripped off the stems and each part is cooked separately. In a bold vegetable soup, that step isn't necessary. Instead, thinly shred the chard through leaf and rib and cook them together in the pot.

POTATO AND YOUNG GARLIC SOUP

SERVES 4 TO 6

INGREDIENTS:

2 tablespoons butter

1 cup coarsely chopped young garlic

5 cups water

4 medium-size russet potatoes (about 2 pounds), peeled and cut into 1-inch chunks

2 large thyme sprigs, fresh or dried

2 teaspoons kosher or fine sea salt

½ teaspoon freshly ground white pepper, plus more for garnish (optional)

¼ to ⅓ cup heavy whipping cream, for serving

2 tablespoons chopped fresh chives, for garnish

A KITCHEN WITH A SIMMERING POT OF POTATO SOUP is like a sanctuary, snug and secure, a momentary respite from the travails of life. The soup provides a particularly assuring trinity: comfort, energy, and satiation. In March and April, when the warmth of potato soup is still wanted, the verve of young garlic can provide it with a spring persona. Produce and farmers' markets offer that fleeting treat: young, not fully developed garlic that looks more like a scallion than a garlic bulb. In place of young garlic, baby leeks do nicely.

1. Melt the butter in a large, heavy pot over medium-low heat. Add the garlic and 2 tablespoons of the water and cook, still on medium-low heat so the garlic doesn't burn or become bitter, until quite soft, about 5 minutes.

2. Add the potatoes, thyme sprigs, salt, pepper, and remaining water and bring to a boil over high heat. Reduce the heat to maintain a gentle boil and cook, uncovered, until the potatoes are quite mashable, about 20 minutes. Remove from the heat and let rest for at least 15 minutes and up to 2 hours.

3. Remove the thyme sprigs and with a potato masher or wire whisk break up the potatoes into a chunky "puree."

4. To serve, reheat the soup over medium-low heat just until steaming. Ladle into individual bowls and swirl a tablespoon of cream across the top of each bowl. Garnish with the chives and extra white pepper, if using, and serve right away.

SESAME SOUP
WITH KALAMATA OLIVES AND BASIL

SESAME SOUP IS A CLASSIC FAST-DAY DISH FOR ORTHODOX Christians throughout the eastern Mediterranean and Middle East. During those times religious dietary laws dictate that meat of any sort be eschewed, sometimes along with fish, dairy, and oil. What's a hungry person to do? A favored solution is sesame soup. A rosy one, enhanced and turned an appealing pink with tomato paste and dressed with olives and basil, fulfills piety and is a smart addition to today's menus.

1. Combine the rice, garlic, tomato paste, bay leaf, salt, and water in a large pot and bring to a boil over high heat. Reduce the heat to maintain a simmer and cook, uncovered, until the rice is tender, 20 to 22 minutes.

2. Whisk together the sesame paste and lemon juice in a medium-size bowl. Add 1 cup of the rice-cooking liquid, whisk to blend, and add the mixture to the rice pot. Whisk to mix and heat just until beginning to boil.

3. Remove the bay leaf and ladle the soup into individual bowls. Sprinkle the olives and basil over the top and serve right away.

SERVES 4

INGREDIENTS:

- ⅔ cup short-grain or risotto rice
- 1 clove garlic, minced or pressed
- 2 tablespoons tomato paste
- 1 bay leaf
- 1 teaspoon kosher or fine sea salt
- 2 quarts water
- 1 cup sesame paste
- ¼ cup fresh lemon juice
- 8 kalamata olives, pitted and coarsely chopped
- 1 tablespoon thinly shredded fresh basil leaves

SESAME PASTE:
AKA TAHINI

SESAME PASTE, ALSO known as *tahini,* refers to a buttery paste ground from sesame seeds. A staple throughout the eastern Mediterranean, Middle East, and all the way to Israel, tahini is something like peanut butter, though used more commonly as a cooking ingredient than as a spread. Like fresh peanut butter, tahini naturally separates as it stands, its solids sinking to the bottom and its oil rising to the top, and so it needs to be remixed before use. Two minutes oh high in the microwave, in a microwave-safe container, not the tin it usually comes in, softens sesame paste enough that it can be whisked back into a satiny emulsion. You can usually find it next to the peanut butter or in the international food section in most supermarkets, in health food stores, and in specialty markets that cater to the cuisines where it is commonly used.

LENTIL AND ROMAINE SOUP
WITH SALTED LEMON ROUNDS AND
FETA CHEESE

SERVES 4 TO 6

INGREDIENTS:

- 4 tablespoons (½ stick) butter
- 1 medium-size yellow or white onion, finely chopped
- 1 medium-size carrot, finely chopped
- 1 large clove garlic, finely chopped
- 6 cups water
- 1½ cups French green lentils
- 3 tablespoons tomato paste
- 1 bay leaf
- 1 teaspoon chopped fresh thyme
- 2 teaspoons kosher or fine sea salt
- ½ teaspoon freshly ground black pepper
- 3 packed cups thinly shredded tender inner romaine lettuce leaves
- 12 thinly sliced lemon rounds
- 3 tablespoons fresh lemon juice
- 2 tablespoons minced scallion, light green parts only
- ⅓ cup (about 1½ ounces) crumbled feta cheese

LENTILS—THE "PEASE" OF THE FAMOUS NURSERY RHYME "pease porridge hot, pease porridge cold"—were a staple of the Middle East, Near East, and Europe long before upstart potatoes arrived from the Americas. A soup of them, thick and as meaty as meatless can be, has long served as a workhorse porridge. On top of that, as it imparts nutrition, it conveys the values of moderation and simplicity. It's a humble soup yet prodigiously good. As they cook, lentils absorb all the flavors they are coupled with and change from meek to brawny. Here butter, onion, garlic, and thyme embolden their unassuming nature; tomato paste and lemon add a vivid element. Grassy romaine lettuce completes the taste profile.

1. Melt the butter in a large pot over medium heat. Add the onion, carrot, and garlic and cook, stirring frequently, until the vegetables wilt, about 3 minutes.

2. Add the water, lentils, tomato paste, bay leaf, thyme, 1½ teaspoons of the salt, and the pepper and bring to a boil over high heat. Reduce the heat to maintain a brisk simmer and

cook, uncovered, until the lentils are very soft but not mushy and the soup has thickened, about 25 minutes.

3. Add the romaine and cook until limp but still bright green, about 4 minutes.

4. While the soup cooks, spread the lemon rounds on a plate or paper towels and lightly sprinkle the top with the remaining ½ teaspoon salt. Set aside.

5. Just before serving, remove the bay leaf from the soup and stir in the lemon juice. Ladle the soup into individual bowls, float lemon rounds over the top of each, and sprinkle with scallions and feta over all. Serve right away.

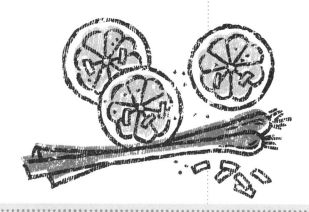

IN PRAISE OF

LENTILS

LEFTOVER LENTILS HAVE been found scattered on the ground where people lived thirteen thousand years ago and in buried clay pots as old as eight thousand years. They have played a role in parable: Esau gave up his birthright for a bowl of them. Throughout history they have been used to replenish overworked fields, returning nutrients to the soil. They have filled plates during Lent and satiated ranks of people from king to pauper.

Throughout time literally hundreds of varieties of lentils have been developed, as many as fifty or more meant solely for people to eat. They come large and small, in different colors, and processed with or without skins, whole or split. All look more or less like a flattened ball, or a lens, to which they owe their name. Yellow to orange lentils that come from southern Europe to the Near East are one of the oldest sorts. Egypt and India grow red lentils, from which a red-orange-hued porridge is made. The fields of France produce brownish green ones that retain their integrity and a bit of bite as they cook and are choice for making a resolute soup.

ALLIUMS

ALLIUMS, OTHERWISE KNOWN as the onion clan of the huge, wide-ranging lily family, could have come from anywhere since they developed from the bulbs of grasses. The ancestors of these we now eat probably sprouted in central Asia, but all were widespread as food by Egyptian times. Today alliums are consumed profusely from tenderlings to flowering stalks to bulbs and in their entire miscellany: chives, garlics, leeks, globe onions, and more. Slowly melted into a rich confit, thinly slivered for a finishing adornment, minced into a sauce, sprinkled across the top of a dish, alliums are edible from top to bottom and in every stage of growth. They are a glorious family that provides imagination to the cook as well as beauty and interest on the plate.

BROCCOLI AND PARSLEY SOUP
WITH FRIED BREAD

INGREDIENTS:

1¾ pounds broccoli

2 teaspoons kosher or
fine sea salt, plus more
as needed

½ cup packed fresh flat-leaf
parsley leaves

4 tablespoons (½ stick)
butter, plus more as
needed

8 slices (½ inch thick)
baguette

A PAIRING OF A BURLY INGREDIENT, such as broccoli, with a lacy one, such as parsley, offers an intricate intermixing of flavor even a discerning eater might not unravel. On the one hand there's authoritative punch, on the other something delicately faint. The beauty of broccoli is that it's a year-round vegetable, while equally year-round parsley imparts freshness even in the dead of winter. The key to bypassing broccoli's tendency to fade with cooking is to blanch it rapidly just until tender enough for a knife to pierce it. If then pureed while still hot, before it has time to overcook, broccoli will retain its dashing green color.

1. Cut the florets off the broccoli stems. Reserve the stems for another dish. Bring a medium-size pot of water to a rapid boil over high heat. Add the broccoli florets and salt and cook over medium-high heat until the broccoli is barely pierceable and still bright green, about 6 minutes. Stir in the parsley and drain right away, reserving the cooking liquid.

2. While still hot, puree the broccoli and parsley in a food processor in 2 batches, adding ½ cup of the cooking liquid to each batch before pureeing. Return the puree to the pot and thin with 1 cup or so more of the cooking liquid until you have a loose puree. Adjust the salt and set aside.

3. Melt the butter in a large sauté pan over medium-high heat. Add as many bread slices as will fit without crowding and sauté until light golden on both sides, about 2 minutes. Continue with another batch of bread, adding more butter as needed, until all the bread is fried.

4. To serve, reheat the soup, ladle into individual bowls, and garnish each with fried bread.

LAMB MEATBALL SOUP
WITH BABY GREEN BEANS AND
DILL BUTTER

THE LAMB MEATBALL SOUPS from the Mediterranean kitchen are among the most gratifying of meatball soups and inspired the one here. The tender meatballs, made pithy with the addition of crunchy bulgur wheat and ground walnuts, bubble gently along with tomato, green beans, and aromatic spices. That classic formula is followed here, topped by a beguiling, out-of-the-ordinary finish—a swirl of dill butter.

1. Combine the bulgur and water in a medium-size bowl and set aside to soak for 15 minutes.

2. To make the meatballs, place the soaked bulgur and lamb in a food processor and add the onion, walnuts, allspice, cinnamon, pepper, and 1½ teaspoons of the salt. Process until well blended and pasty, 2 minutes. Set aside in the refrigerator to chill and firm for at least 30 minutes. Form the chilled mixture into small balls, about 1 inch in diameter. Continue with the recipe or set aside, covered, in the refrigerator up to overnight.

3. When ready to cook the soup, combine the chicken broth, tomato paste, and remaining 1 teaspoon salt in a large saucepan and bring to a boil over medium-high heat. Add the meatballs and green beans and cook until the meatballs float to the top and the green beans are just tender, 4 to 5 minutes.

4. Meanwhile, melt the butter on the stovetop or in a microwave oven. Stir in the dill and set aside in a warm place.

5. To serve, ladle the soup into individual bowls. Swirl some dill butter across the top of each and serve right away.

SERVES 4

INGREDIENTS:

¾ cup bulgur

½ cup water

8 ounces lean ground lamb

1 small yellow or white onion, minced (about ¾ cup)

⅓ cup finely ground walnuts

¼ teaspoon ground allspice

Pinch of ground cinnamon

½ teaspoon freshly ground black pepper

2½ teaspoons kosher or fine sea salt

6 cups low-sodium chicken broth

3 tablespoons tomato paste

8 ounces thin green beans, stem ends pinched off

4 tablespoons (½ stick) butter

2 teaspoons chopped fresh dill

STEAK AND NOODLE SOUP WITH MOZZARELLA BALLS

INGREDIENTS:

- 2 tablespoons extra virgin olive oil
- 12 ounces flat-iron or boneless rib eye steak, cut into ½-inch-wide strips
- 10 cups water
- 2 small leeks, white and light green parts only, trimmed, sliced into ¼-inch-thick rings, and well rinsed (about 1½ cups)
- 1 medium-size red bell pepper, seeds removed, cut into ½-inch-wide-by-1-inch-long strips
- 1 cup roughly chopped drained oil-packed sundried tomatoes
- ½ teaspoon fresh thyme leaves
- 1 teaspoon kosher or fine sea salt, or more to taste
- ½ teaspoon freshly ground black pepper
- ½ cup dried cavatelli, orecchiette, or other small pasta
- 16 to 20 cherry-size mozzarella balls (ciliegine)

WITH BEEF BEING AMERICA'S FAVORITE MEAT, it follows that beef soups are a much-welcomed choice. They are thought of as he-man soups and preferred to be robust, but they can also be intriguingly playful. While a select cut of beefsteak provides a quick and intense stock and also offers tender morsels of beef, leeks and deeply flavorful sundried tomatoes give the more common onions and fresh tomatoes a new twist. The topper is the cheese, which is not a typical grated one but rather balls of soft, fresh mozzarella that melt across the middle of it all. Think of the whole concoction as a Philly cheese steak, Italian sub, or hoagie soup, only swimming in a rich, sippable broth.

1. Heat the oil in a large soup pot over medium-high heat. Add the meat and stir to brown all over, about 5 minutes.

2. Add the water to the pot and bring to a boil. Add the leeks, bell pepper, tomatoes, thyme, salt, and black pepper. Bring to a boil again, reduce the heat to low, and simmer, uncovered, until the meat is tender and the broth is beefy, 50 to 60 minutes.

3. Stir in the pasta and continue simmering until the noodles are soft, 12 to 15 minutes.

4. Add the mozzarella balls and stir until the balls are warmed through but not melted, 30 seconds. Remove the pot from the heat. Spoon the soup into bowls and serve right away.

SOUP AND SURVIVAL:
THE STORY OF THE SOUP KITCHEN

WHEN THE STOCK MARKET CRASHED IN 1929, the American economy went into a tailspin. By 1932, twelve million Americans, about 25 percent of the labor force, were out of work. With no income, families couldn't buy food, and in response an amazing phenomenon occurred: the rise of soup kitchens across the nation. These centers made gallons upon gallons of soup to feed the needy and stave off their hunger.

The first soup kitchens were run by churches and private charities. One of the early ones was the Capuchin Service Center in Detroit. From the onset, it fed from thirteen hundred to three thousand people a day. Over the next few years, more and bigger kitchens run by larger institutions, such as the Salvation Army, opened. As the Depression grew yet more dire, many semiprivate soup kitchens emerged with federal backing, such as those run by the Volunteers of America. Before long, people who were down-and-out came to rely on communal soup kitchens for subsistence.

During the Depression, as throughout the ages, soup provided a good answer to feeding masses. A few vegetables, a bit of meat only to enrich the broth, and any and every starch available could be added and cooked up with the one ingredient that was always available and abundant: water. It was enough to give sustenance and a bit of solace.

As the economy recovered and the Depression waned, the soup kitchens of the period, though they remain immortalized in song, poems, and novels, almost disappeared. The kitchens were but one example of a remarkable American cultural trait. Since everyone in America came from "somewhere else," early on, from about 1790, the country evolved an all-embracing feature that has been called "The Sympathetic State." Despite whatever notch and degree of difference, people aid people in troubled times.

CREAMY CHICKEN SOUP WITH CHANTERELLES AND EGG NOODLES

INGREDIENTS:

3 tablespoons butter

4 skinless, boneless chicken thighs (about 12 ounces), cut into ⅛-inch-wide strips

4 ounces chanterelles, stem ends trimmed, cut into halves or quarters, depending on size

1 large clove garlic, minced or pressed

1½ teaspoons hot or sweet Hungarian paprika

½ teaspoon freshly ground white pepper

2 tablespoons dry sherry, such as amontillado

6 cups low-sodium chicken broth

1 teaspoon kosher or fine sea salt, or more to taste

½ cup medium-width egg noodles

1½ cups heavy whipping cream

CHICKEN SOUP HAS FOR MILLENNIA been reputed to cure illness, restore energy, mend broken bones, and repair broken hearts. No one knows how these beliefs arose, but probably with the first chicken plunked into a pot of water and cooked into an uplifting elixir. Two basic versions of chicken soup developed: chicken soup with noodles or rice and cream of chicken soup. Here, in a bold amalgam of the two, the chicken and noodles float with chanterelle mushrooms in a rich broth of cream, sherry, and paprika. It is a salubrious tureen, generous enough to make a meal.

1. Melt the butter in a large pot over medium-high heat. Add the chicken, chanterelles, garlic, paprika, and pepper and sauté until the chicken is opaque and the chanterelles are wilted, 5 minutes. Stir in the sherry, bring to a boil, and transfer the mixture to a bowl.

2. Add the broth and salt to the pot and bring to a boil over high heat. Stir in the noodles and cook until barely al dente, 8 minutes. Return the chicken and chanterelles to the pot, along with the collected juices, and cook until the noodles are tender, 2 minutes more.

3. Stir in the cream and gently reheat without boiling. Serve right away.

M'M! M'M! GOOD:
JOSEPH CAMPBELL, DR. JOHN DORRANCE, AND CHICKEN NOODLE SOUP

IN 1869 IN CAMDEN, NEW JERSEY, what seemed an unlikely pair of men, a fruit merchant named Joseph Campbell and an icebox maker named Abraham Anderson, joined together to form an enterprise that was in neither's purview: a canned food company. It took only a few short years for the two to realize they had different visions. In 1877 Anderson left; Campbell bought out his share and changed the company's name to Joseph Campbell & Co. He also expanded the line to include ketchup, mustard, sauces, and salad dressing. In rapid time his Ready-to-Serve Beefsteak Tomato Soup became his best seller.

In 1894 Campbell retired and turned the company over to the general manager, Arthur Dorrance, who hired his nephew, John Dorrance. This proved an incalculable bonanza to both of them. John Dorrance had a bachelor's degree in chemistry from the Massachusetts Institute of Technology and a PhD from the University of Göttingen, Germany, and it did not take long for him to realize costs could be cut if he could figure out how to eliminate the water—the heaviest ingredient—from the soup. He invented a formula to condense soup, the first one in 1897 was tomato, and only Campbell had it.

AS SIMPLE AS 1 + 1

The result was explosive. One can of soup plus one can of water equaled brimming bowlsful. The company could package soups in cans one-third the size of cans produced by other companies, lowering the cost to the customer.

By 1904, the company was selling sixteen million cans of soup per year. By 1915, John Dorrance bought out his uncle and became sole owner and president of the company. His genius continued to express itself, and he developed the idea of using soup as an ingredient in recipes. Based on this innovation, the company's first cookbook, Helps for the Hostess, came out in 1916. Campbell's flagship soups, tomato, chicken noodle, and cream of mushroom, were launched in 1934. Cream of chicken hit the shelves in 1947. By the 1950s the company's sales had soared to $100 million.

Augmenting the sales were the company's distinctive red and white label, modeled on the colors of Cornell University, and the company's ear-catching jingle, introduced on the radio in 1930: "M'm, M'm good." It's a ditty that still invites humming along.

Campbell uses almost a million miles of noodles in its chicken noodle soup each year, enough to circle the equator more than forty times. Campbell's tomato, cream of chicken, and chicken noodle continue as the most popular canned soups, despite the many new brands now available. Americans eat about 2.5 billion bowls of the three favorites per year. The company is still located in Camden, New Jersey; the soups are sold worldwide; and by 2007, Dr. John Dorrance's little invention led to the Campbell Soup Company being one of the largest companies on the globe.

CHICKEN SOUP FROM MANY SOULS

SOME OF THE MANY KINDS OF CHICKEN SOUP that are served up steaming on American home and restaurant tables, soothing American lives, and delighting American palates are, in alphabetical order by ethnic origin:

BELGIAN: A famous soup from Gent is called *Gentse-waterzooi*, with chicken and vegetables, enriched with butter, egg yolks, and cream. Another called *booyah* is made from chicken simmered with cabbage and any number of other vegetables. It is popular in Wisconsin, where many Belgian Walloons settled and where it is nicknamed "Belgian penicillin."

BRAZILIAN: Known as *canja de galinha*, the soup is chicken broth with shredded chicken, rice, onions, garlic, cumin, and bay leaves.

BRITISH: A basic chicken broth soup, clear and watery, that usually includes traditional vegetables—carrots, celery, and onion. Considering the abundance of cream in the Isles, the British have also contributed fine versions of cream of chicken soup, such as Royal Velvet, sometimes with bits of chicken in, sometimes strained out.

BULGARIAN: In Bulgaria, the chicken soup is seasoned with vinegar.

BURMESE: Added to the chicken broth are coconut milk, cilantro, and lime juice and sometimes curry flavors.

CHINESE: There are many versions, usually made from older chickens for more flavor. Some contain wonton twists. Many are seasoned with ginger, scallions, star anise, soy sauce, rice wine,
and/or sesame oil. Sometimes the chicken pieces are in the soup.

COLOMBIAN: From Bogotá comes a famous chicken soup called *ajiaco*. It includes corn, potatoes, avocado, capers, *galinsoga* (a native, daisylike herb), and sour cream. Elsewhere around Colombia plantain is included, as is yucca or manioc.

FRENCH: The many chicken soups from France include clear consommé and soups that use thyme, white wine, garlic, cream, Calvados or apple cider.

GERMAN: Some chicken soups from Germany include noodles. Others are just a chicken broth with pickling spice.

GREEK: Called *avgolemono*, Greece's famous chicken soup is finished with a stir of lemon and eggs.

HUNGARIAN: A chicken soup might include carrots, celery, parsley root, bell peppers, tomato, onion, clove, and mace.

INDIAN: The chicken soups are heartily seasoned with ginger, cinnamon, cardamom, coriander, turmeric, cayenne, curry leaves, nutmeg, and clove.

ITALIAN: Called *pasta en brodo*, it is an uncomplicated soup with pasta, such as orzo, angel hair, or cappelletti in a rich chicken bouillon.

JEWISH: A chicken soup so famous it's called "Jewish penicillin," the soup is made from chicken—whole or almost any part—onions, carrots, celery, parsley, and dill, to which are added dumplings made of matzo meal, called *matzo balls*, a universal cure-all.

KENYAN: Here the soup is flavored with tamarind, pureed tomato, and clove.

KOREAN: To the soup are added ginseng, dried jujube fruit, garlic, ginger, and sticky rice.

MEXICAN: Besides the chicken soup with tortillas (see facing page), different versions include cabbage, avocado, and various other sorts of chile peppers, such as chipotle.

POLISH: The soup has ground almonds or dumplings made with almonds.

RUSSIAN: Some chicken soups are thickened with flour and egg. Some include chicken giblets, others spinach and one big dumpling.

UZBEKISTANIAN: Various versions include beets and turnips, rice and potatoes, and stuffed bell peppers.

ZAMBIAN: Along with the chicken, the soups hold onions, peanuts, okra, greens, and smoked fish.

CHICKEN SOUP
WITH TOASTED TORTILLA STRIPS
AND GOAT CHEESE

HOW MANY WAYS ARE THERE TO LOVE CHICKEN SOUP? The number would astound a poet. Countless versions make up the American bill of fare. A rendering from south of the border includes crisp strips of tortillas, chile peppers, and goat cheese, all layered in the bowl. The dried chile strips don't get cooked in the soup; rather, they are kept aside as a toasty garnish for each diner to add according to taste.

1. Heat the oil in a large, heavy pot over medium-high heat. Add as many tortilla strips as will fit in one uncrowded layer and fry, turning constantly, until crisp and golden, 1½ to 2 minutes. Transfer to paper towels to drain and continue with another batch until all the strips are crisped.

2. In the same pot, briefly fry the chile strips, 10 to 15 seconds. Transfer the strips to a paper towel to drain.

3. Reduce the heat to medium, add the garlic to the pot, and cook until lightly golden, 1 minute. Turn off the heat, but leave the pot on the stove. Transfer the garlic to a food processor, add the tomatoes, and puree until as smooth

as possible. Transfer the puree to the pot, add the marjoram, and cook over medium heat until slightly thickened, 4 to 5 minutes.

4. Stir the broth, chicken strips, and salt into the tomato mixture and bring to a boil over medium-high heat. Simmer until the chicken is cooked through, 5 minutes.

5. To serve, divide the tortilla strips among 4 individual large soup bowls. Add a generous tablespoon of the goat cheese to each and ladle in the soup. Garnish with a lime wedge and serve right away, with the toasted chile strips and remaining goat cheese on the side for each diner to add as desired.

SERVES 4

INGREDIENTS:

¼ cup extra virgin olive oil

4 fresh corn tortillas, cut into ½-inch-wide strips

1 large dried red chile, stemmed and cut into ½-inch-wide strips

3 cloves garlic, peeled

2 medium-size tomatoes, peeled, cored, and coarsely chopped

1 teaspoon chopped fresh marjoram or ½ teaspoon dried

5 cups low-sodium chicken broth

4 skinless, boneless chicken thighs, cut into ⅛- to ¼-inch-wide strips

1 teaspoon kosher or fine sea salt, or more to taste

4 ounces soft goat cheese, for serving

1 lime, quartered, for serving

CUBAN AMERICANS: HAIL TO THE CUBANS

Cubans, the people, the lifestyle, the food, have a long history as part of the American mix. Prior to the Louisiana Purchase, large areas of today's United States, including Louisiana and Florida, were part of a Spanish province ruled by the captain general of Cuba. As a consequence, as early as 1565, many from the island of Cuba had already moved into what later became part of America.

Then, when Saint Augustine, Florida, America's first city, was founded, hundreds of Cuban soldiers and their families settled there. Thousands more flocked to Louisiana and Texas, others to Key West and Tampa. When the United States claimed these territories from Spain in 1821, the Cubans became part of the American citizenry.

Many of the Cubans owned plantations and then farms. Others started businesses. In the late 1800s, an entrepreneur named Vicente Martinez-Ybor started a cigar-making factory in Ybor near Tampa. Cubans who knew the trade came to help in the factories. Their children's children are now fourth- or fifth-generation Americans.

In the mid-twentieth century, new waves came as a revolution swept their home country. A mere ninety miles away, and with a long history of Cuban citizenry, Florida naturally became the main destination for emigrating islanders, and Miami became the main city they flocked to, with Union City, New Jersey, ranking second.

Cuban assimilation into mainstream America has been profound and invigorating. The addition brought a cultural depth far deeper than just their island birth. Families had first come to Cuba from Catalan, Andalusia, Galicia, and Lebanon. A number were Jewish, mainly of Sephardic origin, with some from northern European Ashkenazi background. They also added their food to the American menu.

They brought the love of both tart and sweet plantains, falling-off-the-bone roasted pork, mounds of cassava root (yucca), fruit milkshakes, papayas, and guava paste. Their ground beef mix contains the usual tomato and peppers, but also garlic and green olives. Their staples of chicken with rice and rice with beans—called Moors and Christians, alluding to memories of Spain—feed masses of non-Cuban college students and city dwellers everywhere seeking filling, flavorful meals. The base giving punch to many of the dishes is a mix of onion, green pepper, tomato, garlic, oregano, cumin, and black pepper wilted in vegetable oil, called sofrito. Some foods are influenced by the African slaves and the many Chinese who came to the island; some suggest Basque herders. Then there is Cuban coffee, a small cup sweetened with a sugar foam called *espumita*, which emanated from Arab influence. Added to all are sodas of yerba mate, lemon lime, sour lime, and orange juice, and, of course, imaginative rum drinks aplenty.

To many the music and dancing are the reasons to head to the Cuban sections of Miami as well as Hialeah, Coral Gables, Palm Springs, Houston, New York City, and Union City. But even above the beat, the best contribution the Cubans have given America is memorable food.

CUBAN WHITEFISH CHOWDER WITH BLACK BEANS AND SWEET POTATO

SERVES 4

INGREDIENTS:

- 1 cup cooked black beans
- 1 large sweet potato (10 to 12 ounces), peeled and cut into ¾-inch chunks
- 3 cloves garlic, minced or pressed
- 2 jalapeño chiles, stemmed and cut lengthwise into thin slivers
- 6 cups low-sodium chicken broth
- 1½ teaspoons kosher or fine sea salt
- 1 pound thick whitefish fillets, such as sea bass, cod, or halibut, cut into 1½-inch chunks
- 10 ounces medium-size shrimp (about 20), peeled, tails removed, and deveined (if necessary)
- ⅓ cup (about 3 ounces) mascarpone cheese, for garnish
- 1 tablespoon coarsely chopped tender celery leaves, for garnish
- 1 tablespoon chopped fresh cilantro leaves, for garnish
- 1 lime, quartered, for garnish

CUBAN SEAFOOD CHOWDERS ARE AS JAZZY as the music wafting from Havana's Buena Vista Social Club or Miami's South Beach. Bubbling within a subtle baseline of chicken broth are morsels of fish and shellfish from close-by waters, legumy blasts of black beans, top notes of cilantro and garlic, and the hot beat of jalapeño pepper. Here a dollop of mascarpone cheese adds cool to the jazz.

1. Place the beans, sweet potato, garlic, jalapeños, broth, and salt in a large pot and bring to a boil over high heat. Reduce the heat to maintain a brisk simmer and cook until the sweet potato is tender, about 6 minutes.

2. Add the fish, cover, and continue cooking until it is barely cooked through, about 5 minutes. Add the shrimp and cook until barely firm and pink, 2 to 3 minutes.

3. Ladle the soup into bowls. Garnish each with a generous dollop of mascarpone, a sprinkle of celery leaves and cilantro, and a lime quarter. Serve right away.

➔TIP: **SWEET POTATOES OR YAMS?** In American cooking, especially that of the South, sweet potatoes are used in numerous ways, from morning biscuits to pureed soups to dinner pies to sweet potato fries to vegetable sides. Somewhere there even must be a sweet potato ice cream. Though sweet potatoes are often used interchangeably with yams, there are differences. The first is between New World sweet potatoes and yams, both members of the nightshade family, and Old World yams, or true yams, which are a member of the grass and lily family and rarely seen in our markets. More pertinent to daily cooking is how to choose between New World sweet potatoes and yams, which can be confusing. There are long, skinny sweet potatoes and wide, fat yams. There are sweet potatoes with a distinctly orange hue and yams with pallor. There are yams sweeter than sweet potatoes and vice versa.

The defining difference is in the texture. Sweet potatoes are mealier than yams, which are more pudding-like, spoonable rather than forkable when cooked. To complicate matters, grocers, perhaps not interested in the academics of the topic, often mark both sweet potatoes and yams as yams or else label them all as sweet potatoes. For serving as a baked potato, either will do. For dishes in which it matters that the vegetables remain in discrete pieces, such as salads, fries, casseroles, and soup, sweet potatoes are the first choice. They hold their shape better. For dishes that need a smooth texture, such as the Silken Yam Puree (page 124), yams are the way to go. For dishes in which just a bit of coarseness is desirable, such as sweet potato biscuits, mashed sweet potatoes, or sweet potato pie, sweet potatoes are the first choice, but either will do.

THE SANDWICH:
SOUP'S CONSTANT COMPANION

SINCE ALMOST FOREVER, bread has been a venerated companion for soup. It can act as a sponge to sop up the nourishing broth, and in fact it was that sop that gave soup its name. During the last few hundred years the bread sop evolved into something more: the sandwich, a cozy comrade in arms.

The invention of the sandwich is attributed to John Montagu, fourth Earl of Sandwich, a British statesman, rake, and gambler, who is said to have wanted his food sandwich style so he wouldn't have to leave the gambling table. The year was 1762, and the earl had been at the table for twenty-four hours. But in truth, putting a morsel of cheese, or meat, or vegetable between two slices of bread dates from biblical times.

Americans didn't start to call a sandwich a sandwich until well into the nineteenth century. As we moved our main meal from midday to evening, the appearance of the sandwich, often with soup, at the midday meal became more and more frequent and soon it became a lunchtime fixture. At first taverns and saloons offered them free to attract customers.

To partner with soup, the sandwich can be grilled cheese, roast beef, a Reuben, club, Dagwood, panino, submarine, BLT, hero, or hoagie. Whatever the bun, the filling, the melt, or the spread, the soup-and-sandwich combo retains its status as a tremendous lunch or light dinner option.

CROWDED
CHOWDER WITH COD, SHRIMP, AND CORN

CHOWDER WAS INTRODUCED IN NEWFOUNDLAND by Breton fishermen around 1750. The name comes from *chaudière,* the pot in which it was cooked. The original was a stew of cod (the provision that gained the fishermen their wages), salt pork, sometimes clams and potatoes, and milk. The chowder was thickened with flour or crushed crackers. The name migrated to other similar soups, to the point where neither seafood nor potatoes were necessarily included, though two of the most renowned American chowders—milky New England clam chowder and tomato-based Manhattan clam chowder—still have both. From the landlocked American heartland came a third venerated chowder, one featuring corn rather than potatoes. Here, Iowa and the Atlantic Ocean share the bowl in a sublime interecozone blend of cod, shrimp, and corn. For a true New England chowder, choose fresh cod or haddock, called *scrod* if small. On the Pacific coast, rock cod or halibut makes a fine chowder fish.

1. Peel and devein the shrimp, if necessary, retaining the shells. Combine the shrimp shells, broth, and wine in a medium-size saucepan and bring to a boil over high heat. Reduce the heat to maintain a brisk simmer and cook until the shells are quite pink, 5 minutes. Let cool for 1 to 2 minutes, then strain through a fine-mesh sieve into a bowl. Discard the shells and set the broth aside.

2. Cut the corn cobs in half crosswise. Holding the cob upright with the flat side down to steady it on the counter, shave off the kernels with a knife and place them in a bowl. Holding the cobs over the bowl, scrape them to collect their "milk" (see Tip). Set aside.

3. Melt the butter in a medium-size pot over medium-high heat. Add the onion and summer savory and sauté

SERVES 4

INGREDIENTS:

- 1 pound extra-large shrimp (26 to 30) with shells on
- 6 cups low-sodium chicken broth
- 1 cup white wine
- 3 medium-size ears corn
- 2 tablespoons butter
- 1 medium-size yellow or white onion, cut into ¼-inch dice
- 1 teaspoon chopped fresh summer savory or ½ teaspoon dried
- 1 pound cod or haddock fillets, cut into 1- to 1½-inch chunks
- 1 teaspoon kosher or fine sea salt
- ¼ teaspoon freshly ground black pepper
- ¾ cup heavy whipping cream
- 8 slices baguette, cut 1½ inches thick on the diagonal and toasted, for serving
- 1 lime, quartered, for serving

until the onion is translucent, about 2 minutes. Add the reserved shrimp shell broth, along with the cod, corn and its milk, salt, and pepper and bring to a boil, still over medium-high heat. Add the shrimp and cook until the cod is firm, the corn is tender, and the shrimp is barely pink and firm, about 4 minutes. Stir in the cream.

4. To serve, ladle the chowder into large individual bowls. Garnish each with baguette slices propped up in the bowl and a lime wedge. Serve right away.

➡ T I P : **CORN.** To remove corn from the cob, cooks have generally used a method called *scraping,* which not only cuts the kernels free but at the same time grates the cob to release and collect the starchy juices, called the *milk.* Adding the milk to many recipes lends them an extra-fresh, sweet sparkle. So routinely was scraped corn called for in older recipes that general housewares stores carried a special tool called a *corn scraper.* These days a chef's knife can substitute, for both cutting off the kernels and scraping the cobs.

To remove the kernels and scrape the cobs, cut a ½-inch-or-so piece off the bottom of each cob. Put the flat, cut end on a firm surface and, with a sharp knife or corn scraper, work down the cob to remove the kernels. Once the kernels are removed, give each cob a second pass with the knife, capturing the milk in a small bowl. In days gone by, scraped cobs were sometimes dried and carved into corn cob pipes, an American artifact now mostly relegated to archival shelves.

Furthering ingenuity and thriftiness, American cooks would boil the cobs to make a syrup, made golden and sweet with brown sugar. It's easy to make and perfect for topping pancakes, waffles, oatmeal, or ice cream. Here's how:

Place 3 scraped corn cobs and 5 cups water in a large saucepan and bring to a boil over medium-high heat. Cook briskly until the liquid is reduced to about 2 cups, 30 to 45 minutes. With a slotted spoon or wire strainer, remove and discard the cobs. Add 1 packed cup dark brown sugar and bring to a boil again, stirring to make sure the sugar dissolves. Reduce the heat to maintain a brisk simmer without boiling over and cook until the liquid is reduced to about ¾ cup and has the consistency of maple syrup, 10 to 20 minutes, depending on the dimensions of the pan. Use right away or cool and store in the refrigerator indefinitely.

COD:
THE FISH OF FORTUNE AND CHOWDER

SELDOM IN THE WORLD OF COMMERCE does there appear a natural commodity with a profit potential so huge that everyone wants to jump on the bandwagon to take it to market. Fish does not, as a rule, fall into this category, but there is one such fish: the Atlantic cod. Its commercial importance was enormous and remains so today. Cod has been called "the fish that changed the world."

Atlantic cod is a fish with a large family, including its equally desirable and lucrative cousins, haddock and pollack. But it is the so-called true cod, *Gadus morhua,* that has always been the prize catch. Until the twentieth century, when modern factory trawlers came along to pull cod from the ocean and the fish became distressed, prolific populations of them swam in the waters of the North Atlantic between Europe and America. Alexandre Dumas, famous French writer and gourmand, hyperbolized, "It has been calculated that if no accident prevented the hatching of the eggs and each egg reached maturity, it would take only three years to fill the sea so that you could walk across the Atlantic dry shod on the backs of cod."

Fishermen on the eastern side of the Atlantic Ocean had long fished for cod. Its commercial value came from salt-drying it because as long as it was kept dry it could be stored virtually forever. As such, it was a major food in Europe and beyond for daily consumption as well as for special purposes. For one, the Catholic Church considered it acceptable for the many year-round religious abstinence days—from every Friday to the whole of Lent—when meat could not be eaten. It was from the ocean and deemed a "cold" food, therefore not proscribed.

Equally important, as the age of exploration blossomed in the sixteenth century and the world was dizzy with seafaring, salt cod served as a staple protein provision on long voyages. When teeming schools of unimaginable, almost uncountable, numbers were found in the waters on the American side of the North Atlantic, particularly off the Grand Banks of what is now Newfoundland and the aptly named Cape Cod of Massachusetts, the economic benefits of cod fishing skyrocketed. Until then the source of supply had been restricted. Only the waters of the Bay of Biscay between Spain and France into the Arctic waters of Norway, Iceland, and Greenland contained the fish.

In Europe, cooks and seafarers had been using dried salt cod perhaps since as early as 800 CE for various stewlike preparations similar to future American chowders. The difference was that the later chowders, which first appear in early American recipes, called for fresh cod. With so much fresh catch at hand, cooks had no need to turn to dried. Today the choice can be either. Due to refrigeration and airplanes, fresh Atlantic cod is usually available in stores coast to coast, and salt cod can generally be found boxed in the fresh fish section or unboxed in large, irregularly shaped fillets in markets that cater to a Mediterranean clientele.

BIG MEATS BACK ON THE PLATE

YUM TASTY MIGHTY FINE NICE

MMM DELISH

Without question, the epicenter of the traditional American meal is meat. That prized pivot can also offer a serving of poultry or fish. Still, most often what Americans consider to be the true marrow of the meal is meat in its narrower sense: a serving of beef, lamb, or pork.

For eons, the continent and its first inhabitants had only wild game for meat, until later-arriving settlers brought with them cattle, sheep, and pigs, a trio of remarkable animals that could be husbanded rather than hunted. These animals were used as well for their milk, wool, and hide. In Europe, farms had been small and land for pasturing animals limited. A holding was rarely ample enough to produce both food for the table and animal feed. A well-off family had but a single cow, or perhaps a pair of lambs, or a sow and her brood. But the new hemisphere turned out to be so vast that it provided pasture and fodder galore, thus the possibility of meat every day. In due time meat became the heart of the American meal, the item that most demonstrated the plenitude of the new American life.

Meat became a custom so integral to the culture of the growing nation that no subsequent cuisine could daunt it. American Italian food, American French food, American Chinese food, American Every Cuisine's food has more meat in its dishes here than in their native lands.

With measureless grazing land, in particular herding cattle proliferated and beef became the primary American meat. Glorious roasts could decorate tables daily. Steak became both constantly available and affordable. Beef hamburgers became the national sandwich. The great grasslands also provided fodder for sheep, allowing Americans to turn from the mutton meat of older sheep to the steady pleasure of lamb. Meanwhile on thousands of farms, the pigs brought by the Spanish thrived. Pork became America's second-favorite meat. The recipes that follow feature all three meats, which are must-haves on the American dinner plate.

ABUNDANT, EXCELLENT: AMERICA'S BEEF

BEEF CATTLE WERE brought to America in 1521 when the Spanish introduced them to Mexico. Almost every arriving European group also brought a few on their immigrant ships. For the first two hundred years of American history, people continued to eat beef relatively rarely and then only locally raised beef since meat transported beyond a short distance would spoil. Most beef eaten was roasted in large cuts. Steak was almost unknown.

During the 1800s, several events occurred to enhance the American predilection toward beef. The Great Plains and Southwest were settled, providing huge amounts of pastureland, and a railroad line was stretched across the nation. Soon long cattle drives from Texas to the infamous railroad centers in Kansas, such as Abilene, emerged and the railroad lines were extended so they reached everywhere. Then a Detroit meatpacker named G. H. Hanharmand had the inspiration to send out refrigerator cars, and both the market for beef and American taste were transformed.

Centers for mass-marketing the meat, such as Chicago and Kansas City, sprang up, although they languished once beef could be brought by rail and eventually truck everywhere. Such was the accessibility that steak, hardly known before the Civil War, evolved into a favored meal, and a new, indigenous mythology emerged involving the cowboy, cowboy heroes, cowboy stories, movies, dress, and songs. Eating beef, so hugely available, affordable, and symbolic of the country and its citizenry's wealth, took on the iconography and the reality of what should be on the dinner plate. And it remains so.

We start with recipes for the esteemed steak, move on to beloved ground beef, follow with the Sunday centerpiece big cuts, and end with tender young beef, veal.

SEARCH-AND-RESCUE
STEAK WITH TOASTED GARLIC RUB

SEARCH-AND-RESCUE normally refers to the teams of people who search for unfortunate adventurers who somehow have become trapped or stranded. In our hectic and time-pressured lives, the term can also apply to our behavior when we get home at the end of the day: We search for food to rescue the family. That often leads to steak. Yet, even when hunger hovers and time is short, there's no reason plain steak can't be itself rescued, with an uncomplicated mix of searched-out seasonings. Spices, an herb, and toasted garlic rubbed into the steak turns it lively and makes for a successful deliverance from the day's exertions. Audacious in its forthright simplicity, the rub can also be used to perk up pork or chicken or as a soup seasoning. It's the trick of toasting the garlic that spins the rub to strikingly different.

1. To make the rub, heat a heavy skillet large enough to hold the steaks without crowding over high heat until it begins to smoke. Add the garlic and cook, using tongs to turn the cloves until charred in spots and toasty smelling, about 5 minutes. Remove the cloves and peel them. Mince or press them and place in a small bowl. Add the paprika, summer savory, salt, and the 1 tablespoon olive oil and blend together with a fork. Spread the rub on both sides of the steaks.

2. Lightly oil the skillet and heat over medium-high heat. Add the steaks and cook to taste, turning once, 3 to 4 minutes per side for medium-rare. Transfer the steaks to a platter, let rest for 5 minutes for the juices to settle, and then serve right away.

SERVES 4

INGREDIENTS:

16 cloves garlic, unpeeled

2 teaspoons hot Hungarian paprika

2 teaspoons dried summer savory

1 teaspoon kosher or fine sea salt

1 tablespoon extra virgin olive oil, plus more for oiling the skillet

4 steaks (8 to 10 ounces each), such as New York strip or rib eye, cut ¾ to 1 inch thick

SLOW-DOWN GRILLED STRIP STEAK

IN GENTLEMAN JACK PAN SAUCE

SERVES 4 TO 6

INGREDIENTS:

4 strip steaks (8 to 10 ounces each), cut ¾ to 1 inch thick

Kosher or fine sea salt and freshly ground black pepper

Gentleman Jack Pan Sauce (recipe follows), for serving

IT SEEMS THE LAST THING a busy person remembers is to slow down. But then evening comes, boots off, and a sigh can escape. What's called for is a nice grilled steak topped off with a sauce made from a "slow-down" beverage, Jack Daniel's wonderfully tempered Gentleman Jack Tennessee Whiskey. Strip steaks are a good choice because they're full of flavor, well marbled yet not too fatty, the kind of steak to chew on while decelerating. Grilling takes some time: no rushing permitted while the grill is prepared and the onion softens in the frying pan—the better to turn into a slow-down sauce.

1. Prepare a medium-hot grill or pre-heat the broiler.

2. Sprinkle both sides of the steaks with salt and pepper and set aside at room temperature while the grill heats.

3. Prepare the Gentleman Jack Pan Sauce.

4. To grill the steaks, place them on the rack directly over the heat or under the broiler. Cook to taste, turning once, 3 to 4 minutes per side for medium-rare. Transfer to a platter and set aside

in a warm place for 5 minutes for the juices to settle.

5. Pour the sauce over the steaks and serve.

GENTLEMAN JACK PAN SAUCE

WHETHER GENTLEMAN JACK is Jack Daniel's older brother is irrele-vant. He made his appearance in 1988, is twice aged, and is more debonair and cultivated than the other Jack. Lately Gentleman Jack has been given a modernized bottle, label, and cap. More important, he readily lends his elixir to a contemporary burnished steak sauce that can equally attire lamb, pork, and game but truly shines on that most elegant of entrées, a steak.

MAKES ENOUGH FOR 4 STEAKS

2 small yellow or white onions, halved top to bottom and sliced ¼ inch thick

Kosher or fine sea salt

¾ cup water

4 tablespoons (½ stick) butter, at room temperature

¾ cup Gentleman Jack or a good Kentucky bourbon

1. Spread the onions on a plate, sprinkle lightly with salt, and set aside until they begin to weep, 5 minutes. Without rinsing them, place the onions in a large sauté pan, add the water, and bring to a boil over medium-high heat. Cook until the onions are well wilted and the liquid is mostly evaporated, about 8 minutes.

2. Add 2 tablespoons of the butter and cook until the onions begin to brown, about 5 minutes. Add the whiskey and cook until the liquid is reduced by half and no longer "raw," about 2 minutes. Add the remaining 2 tablespoons butter and swirl the sauce with a wooden spoon until the butter is incorporated, about 2 minutes more. Use right away or set aside in a warm place for a few minutes and reheat before serving.

WHAT MAKES A WHISKEY NOT A BOURBON AND WHAT MAKES JACK A GENTLEMAN?

OVER IN HILLY TENNESSEE, away from the fame of Kentucky's bourbon, in 1866 a man in Lynchburg began to make a similar drink, but with a nice, smooth difference. He filtered his distilled product from the same corn, rye, and barley that makes Kentucky bourbon over a "rick" (stack) of ten feet of hard-packed charcoal. He made the charcoal from the sugar maple he cut from the woods and added water from a spring in a cave he knew (still named Water Cave Spring). He invented a square bottle for the drink and pronounced his potable, not a bourbon, but a Tennessee whiskey. His name was Jack Daniel.

The whiskey became one of America's most popular southern whiskeys, and it is made much the same today. A mash of grains is soured with yeast from the previous batch, just like a sourdough bread. It's fermented in copper stills, filtered for ten days through charcoal, which refines its spirit and provides a unique flavor, and then is aged in charred oak barrels to mellow and add color.

So popular was the whiskey that the company didn't offer any new version for more than a hundred years. But one day the folks at Jack Daniel's decided a more chivalrous drink was called for. In 1988 they created a whiskey still smoother, more refined, more courteous, and mannerly. They called it Gentleman Jack.

Indeed, Gentleman Jack is a polished drink, not quite the rough-and-tumble whiskey of before. It is filtered twice through the rick of sugar maple charcoal and twice mellowed. And Gentleman Jack has well-advertised mottos: "A gentleman knows naughty and nice." "A gentleman leaves the rat race to rats." "A gentleman shows up, not off." We think it suits today's steak with a terrifically gallant pan sauce.

Ironically, the town where the original Jack Daniel's and the new Gentleman Jack are made, Lynchburg, Tennessee, supports this major industry, but the county in which Lynchburg sits remains dry.

SIZZLING STEAK WITH AMERICAN BLUE CHEESE BUTTER AND SINGED ASPARAGUS

SERVES 4

INGREDIENTS:

Extra virgin olive oil, for oiling the pan if cooking on the stove and for coating the asparagus

Kosher or fine sea salt and freshly ground black pepper

4 T-bone, porterhouse, or bone-in rib eye steaks (12 to 16 ounces), cut ¾ to 1 inch thick

1 cup crumbled blue cheese, at room temperature

6 tablespoons butter (¾ stick), at room temperature

¼ cup finely chopped scallion, white and light green parts

1½ pounds medium-size to large asparagus, ends trimmed, stalks peeled if large

IN RECENT YEARS AMERICAN CHEESEMAKERS have developed blue cheese so scrumptious and toothy as to rival the acclaimed blue cheeses of Europe. Among the best are Buttermilk Blue or blue Brie from Wisconsin, Maytag Blue from Iowa, and Caveman Blue from Oregon. Buttermilk Blue is a great big cheese, made from raw milk and a secret blend of cultures. It is aged for two months to develop veins from yellow-green to deep blue. It has won a number of international competitions. Blue Brie is a blue-veined triple cream cheese. Maytag Blue is a forthright cheese and now widely available. Caveman Blue is a fruitier blue, highly creamy with a smatter-ing of crystals and nuances from hay to vanilla. Any of these kneaded into butter and topped on the steak makes the steak yet more luscious. Lacking an American blue, you can always turn to classic European ones, Stilton from England; Roquefort, Bleu d'Auvergne, or Saint Agur from France; Cambozola from Germany; Gorgonzola Dolce from Italy; Castello of Denmark; or Spanish Valdeón.

1. Prepare a medium-hot grill or lightly oil a large, heavy skillet and preheat it over medium-high heat.

2. Sprinkle salt and pepper over both sides of the steaks and set aside.

3. To make the blue cheese butter, combine the cheese, butter, and scallion in a small bowl and mash together with a fork until well mixed but still a little chunky. Set aside.

4. Toss the asparagus spears with olive oil and a little salt. Place them on the grill directly over the heat or in the prepared skillet. Cook, turning once or twice, until tender and singed all around, 5 to 10 minutes, depending on the size of the stalks. Transfer to a platter and set aside in a warm place.

5. To cook the steaks, place them on the grill directly over the heat or in the prepared skillet over medium-high heat. Cook to taste, turning once, 3 to 4 minutes per side for medium-rare. Transfer to a serving platter or 4 individual plates. Top each steak with 3 or 4 tablespoons of the butter mixture and set aside in a warm place for 5 minutes for the steak juices to settle as the butter melts. Arrange the asparagus to the side of the steaks and serve right away.

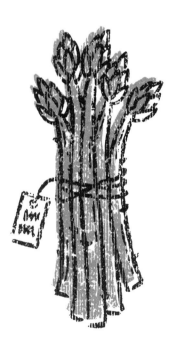

BUTTER:
FROM COW TO KITCHEN, A PACKAGED TRIP

FOR EONS BUTTER was usually made by farm wives, who churned it from milk. It can be made from sheep, goat, yak, and other milk, but in the West it has always been cow's milk butter that has reigned supreme. However, because of its consistency, the issue has never been how to make it, but rather how to keep it, pack it, and transport it. Packing it in leaves, mud, grass—all had been tried. It was only some years after it arrived in America that the conundrum was solved.

By 1791, farmers in the surrounds of New York City were making "dairy butter," which they collected in pats, balls, rolls, and rectangular cuts and brought by wagon or riverboat to the city. The farmers near Philadelphia, reputed to make the finest butter, molded theirs in lumps that sold for an outrageous dollar a pound. To get the butter to markets, all used wooden butter tubs that were made at water-powered sawmills.

Once ice-carrying ships came along, the pliant mass could now be kept relatively cool, but again only in some sort of contained form. For this the suppliers developed linen, rag, and cheesecloth wrappers in which to swath the butter. The customers would wash, iron, and return them. Where ice ships did not ply river waters, as in California, the solidified mass was wrapped in cambric cloth strips set in oblong cedar or redwood boxes, while the Elgin Butter Company of Elgin, Illinois, which became famous enough to give Elgin the title of "Butter Capital of the World," packed its product into fifty- or sixty-pound ash wood tubs and later repacked it into thin oval wood boxes. These methods produced the nationwide complaint that the butter tasted woody.

Then one of those amazing American innovations occurred: butter wrappers made of paper coated with paraffin or egg white and salt. These ended the woodiness but often left a waxy flavor or discolored the butter. Finally a long-lasting solution came along, the development of thin layers of vegetable parchment.

Cubes of butter are still wrapped in vegetable parchment. It is greaseproof, insoluble, odorless, and tasteless. All that remained was to switch the paraffin idea from wrapper to carton, for paraffin cartons seal out air and prevent spoilage. By 1900, such cartons were being produced, and soon machinery was developed to cut "prints" of butter in the long sticks weighing exactly a quarter pound. This is the way most butter comes to us today.

FILET MIGNON WITH TARRAGON SHALLOT BUTTER

SERVES 4

INGREDIENTS:

4 filet mignon steaks (6 to 8 ounces each), cut 1½ to 2 inches thick

Kosher or fine sea salt and freshly ground black pepper

1 cup white wine

2 tablespoons finely chopped shallot

½ teaspoon finely chopped fresh tarragon or ¼ teaspoon dried

8 tablespoons (1 stick) butter, at room temperature

1 tablespoon chopped fresh flat-leaf parsley

Extra virgin olive oil, for oiling the pan if cooking on the stove

THE FRENCH PAIRING OF FILET MIGNON and béarnaise sauce is an American steak house favorite. But the sublime béarnaise requires an aromatic reduction of shallot, white wine, and tarragon and an egg yolk base, a delicate procedure to accomplish without curdling the yolks before the butter is swirled in. In a less complicated version that preserves the spirit of béarnaise, the filets can be sauced with a simple butter sauce using the same aromatic base but without the egg yolks. It's a distinctive feature of new American home cooking, where a speedy finishing flourish turns an otherwise ordinary steak into an elegant preparation.

1. Sprinkle both sides of the steaks with salt and pepper and set aside. If grilling, prepare a medium-hot grill.

2. While the grill heats, make the butter. Combine the wine, shallot, and tarragon in a small saucepan and cook over high heat until reduced to about ⅓ cup, about 5 minutes. Reduce the heat to medium-low and gradually whisk in the butter, 1 tablespoon at a time. Stir in the parsley. Keep warm while cooking the steaks.

3. Place the filets on the grill or lightly oil a large, heavy skillet and preheat over medium-high heat; place the steaks in the skillet. Cook to taste, turning once, 6 to 8 minutes per side for medium-rare.

4. Place the filets on 4 individual plates. Pour the butter over them and serve.

FLANK STEAK ROLL-UPS IN POMEGRANATE MARINADE

SERVES 4

FLANK STEAK IS A COOK'S BOON for a quartet of reasons. Very lean, it is among the most flavorful of cuts and can be grilled or seared, cooked in its plank form or rolled and served in thick or thin slices. Unlike other cuts of beefsteak, it has a great deal of surface area, which means it can be plied with a diverse and inspired number of extras. Here is a mix that trips across the globe: American beef in a marinade of Middle East pomegranate and Asian soy sauce rolled around a stuffing of Mediterranean-style vegetables. The marinade is also an excellent precooking soak for chicken breasts or lamb shoulder steaks.

INGREDIENTS:

- ½ cup pomegranate juice
- 1 tablespoon light soy sauce
- ½ cup extra virgin olive oil
- 1 large clove garlic, minced or pressed
- Kosher or fine sea salt and freshly ground black pepper
- 1½ pounds flank steak
- 1 medium-size eggplant, ends trimmed, cut into ¼-inch-thick rounds
- 1 small red bell pepper, stemmed, seeded, and cut lengthwise into ¼-inch wide strips
- 20 fresh cilantro sprigs, tender tops only

1. To make the marinade, combine the pomegranate juice, soy sauce, 1 tablespoon of the olive oil, garlic, ¼ teaspoon salt, and ¼ teaspoon pepper in a dish large enough to hold the flank steak when it is opened out. Add the steak, turn to coat, and set aside at room temperature for 1 hour or in the refrigerator for up to 4 hours, turning 2 or 3 times.

2. If grilling, prepare a medium-hot grill.

3. Heat ¼ cup olive oil in a heavy skillet over medium-high heat. Add enough eggplant slices to fit in a single layer and cook, turning once, until soft, about 12 minutes. Transfer to a plate. Add more oil and continue with another batch until all the slices are soft. Set aside.

4. Lift the steak from the marinade, reserving the marinade, and place it on a work surface. Arrange the eggplant rounds in a single layer over the steak. Stack the pepper strips in a single row down the center on top of the eggplant.

RUBS AROUND THE WORLD

RUBS ARE COMPOUNDS made of spices, herbs, zests, or other flavorful tidbits. Originally they were developed not only for seasoning foods but as a way of sealing in juices and tenderizing. Influenced by the way other cultures treated and enlivened their foods, from Indian tandoori to Jamaican jerk, Mediterranean herb mixes, and beyond, rubs have entered the American culinary vocabulary. Applied to meat, poultry, or fish, they provide a facile way to satisfy a desire for extra pizzazz. Rubs can be dry, ground, powdered, or cracked herbs and spices sprinkled on much like salt before cooking, or wet, patted on as a thick paste. Favored ingredients for rub mixes around the world include:

- **JAMAICAN STYLE:** onion, allspice, clove, black pepper, cayenne, sugar, thyme

- **CHINESE STYLE:** five-spice, sugar, grated ginger

- **SOUTHWEST OR MEXICAN STYLE:** ground or whole seeds of dried chiles, achiote, cumin, or oregano

- **GREEK STYLE:** oregano, marjoram, thyme, savory, lemon juice, olive oil

- **BALKAN OR HUNGARIAN STYLE:** paprika, salt, celery seeds

- **FRENCH STYLE:** whole mustard seeds or prepared mustard, coarsely ground black pepper, or cracked green pepper

- **ITALIAN STYLE:** fennel seed, dried oregano, pressed garlic

- **NORTHERN EUROPEAN STYLE:** cider or cider vinegar, sage, tarragon, caraway seeds

- **NORTH AFRICAN STYLE:** turmeric, coriander, cumin

- **INDIAN STYLE:** cardamom, curry, powdered ginger

- **INDONESIAN STYLE:** ground peanuts, mace, chiles, ginger, lime juice

- **CAJUN STYLE:** garlic, cayenne, perhaps cinnamon, dried thyme

Stack the cilantro sprigs on top of the pepper and sprinkle salt and pepper over all. Roll up the steak from the bottom to the top, enclosing the filling and overlapping the edges, to make a single long roll. Secure the roll closed with toothpicks.

5. Place the steak roll on the grill directly over the heat or in a preheated lightly oiled heavy skillet over medium-high heat. Cook, turning several times so that all the sides are evenly browned, until done to taste, about 15 minutes total for medium-rare. Transfer to a plate and let rest for 5 minutes or so for the juices to settle.

6. While the steak cooks, if grilling, pour the reserved marinade into a small saucepan over medium-high heat. If pan-cooking, use the same pan the steak was cooked in. Bring to a boil and cook until reduced by half to a glaze, 3 to 5 minutes, depending on the pan's dimensions.

7. To serve, cut the steak roll into ½-inch-thick slices. Arrange the slices on a platter, pour the sauce glaze over the top, and serve right away.

STANDING RIB ROAST WITH MUSHROOMS, SHALLOTS, WALNUTS, AND RED WINE

IN DENVER, ONCE A RICH GOLD RUSH CITY and the terminus for many cattle drives, prime beef is revered. For generations, one of the city's greatest treats has been a meal at the Ship Tavern in the elegant Brown Palace Hotel. In the early days the only two dishes served were prime ribs of beef, wafting heavenly meat aromas across the room, and freshly caught and perfectly fried Rocky Mountain trout. Other choices now round out the menu, but those two standards remain forever engraved as the Ship's signature dishes. You can still get a cut from either end of the prime rib or a lovely rare one right from the middle. Restaurants like the Ship Tavern buy up most of the prime-grade beef these days, but a choice-grade standing rib is no mean substitute. The "Brown," as it is called locally, serves its prime rib au jus as of old with potatoes and beans. The innovations of wine-steeped walnuts, whole mushrooms, and shallots not only enhance the meat and serving plate but glamorize the rib roast with an evocation of a grand hotel and a bygone epoch. Be sure to count on at least fifteen to twenty minutes for the roast to rest after it is out of the oven. With such an elegant cut of beef like standing rib roast, or any other roast for that matter, it would be a pity to serve it at less than its succulent best, and that can only be attained if the meat is allowed standing time.

SERVES 4 TO 6

INGREDIENTS:

- 1 standing beef rib roast (2 bones, about 4 pounds)
- 2 cloves garlic, slivered
- Kosher or fine sea salt and freshly ground black pepper
- 16 medium-size white button mushrooms (about 12 ounces), stem ends trimmed, rinsed and patted dry
- 16 medium shallots, peeled
- ⅔ cup (about 6 ounces) walnut halves
- ¾ cup red wine
- ½ teaspoon chopped fresh thyme or ¼ teaspoon dried

1. Place the roast, bone side down, in a roasting pan that can go on the stove and is large enough to hold it with the shallots, mushrooms, and walnuts scattered around in a single crowded layer. With your fingers, push the garlic slivers into all the natural crevices in the top and sides of the roast. Sprinkle the meat all over with salt and pepper and set aside at room temperature while the oven heats. (The roast may be prepared and set aside at room temperature up to 2 hours in advance.)

2. When ready to cook the roast, preheat the oven to 475°F.

3. Place the roast in the oven and cook for 10 minutes. Reduce the heat to 350°F and continue cooking until the juices begin to sizzle and the meat begins to firm up, 40 to 45 minutes.

4. Scatter the mushrooms, shallots, and walnuts around the roast and cook until the vegetables and nuts are nicely browned, 20 minutes. Pour the wine around the roast, over the nuts and vegetables, and cook until done to taste, 20 to 30 minutes for medium-rare (130°F to 135°F on a meat thermometer).

5. Transfer the roast to a serving platter and set aside in a warm place for the juices to settle. Place the roasting pan with the nuts and vegetables on the stovetop, stir in the thyme, and cook over medium heat until almost all the liquid evaporates, about 10 minutes.

6. Carve the roast into ½- to ¾-inch-thick slices. Arrange the walnuts, mushrooms, and shallots around the meat and moisten with the liquid remaining in the pan. Add the bones on the side as a special treat and serve right away.

WALNUTS BY MANY ANOTHER NAME

THE WALNUT IS AN EAT-STRAIGHT-FROM-A-TREE FOOD that no doubt provided a ready meal for many early humans. Walnuts grow as a large green fruit with a thin edible but rather puckery flesh around a stone. Inside the stone is an inner core that is the nut. Walnuts are indigenous across a wide area from southeastern Europe and almost to China. Their value was such that as soon as man began to cultivate crops, walnuts were planted in orchards and used for both eating and their oil.

Mesopotamian inscriptions depict walnut orchards in the Hanging Gardens of Babylon, and the Code of Hammurabi circa 1795 BCE discusses the etiquette for eating them. Early Greeks cultivated a less plump sort of walnut and then discovered a nut grown by their neighbors and enemies, the Persians, that they called *Persian walnuts*. They also called them *bald nuts* for their shell, *helmet nuts* for their shape, and *royal nuts* for how much they were valued. That last name caught on with Romans, who called them the Royal Nut of Jove. The Armenians call them *four brains*.

North America has its own native walnut, the black walnut, indigenous to the East Coast. They have a more smoky, winy flavor than other walnuts, but such a hard shell that they are not widely grown commercially.

CROSS RIB ROAST WITH MUSTARD RUB AND MUSTARD GREENS

CONTEMPORARY CULINARY IDEAS have whisked roast beef from the unpolished crown jewel of a family get-together to a highly polished gem that honors family and guest like the royalty they are. The gilding applied to the roast can be of many varieties, but one that retains the classic bite of horseradish remains a prizewinner. In a similar fashion, a mix of Dijon mustard with mustard seeds, cumin seeds, and cracked black peppercorns gives beef roast verve. In addition, mustard greens, already with a nip of their own, salted and given a dash of lemon juice, offer a side dish just biting enough to awaken the tongue and provide a perky accompaniment. Cross rib roast (also called *English roll*) is a rather common sort of roast cut from the shoulder chuck area, but it is also uncommonly good, an inexpensive cut swank enough to serve both for tender oven roasts and succulent pot roasts. Tricked out in triple mustard, it's like Cinderella in a ball gown.

1. To make the rub, heat a small, heavy skillet over medium heat for 2 minutes. Add the mustard seeds and cumin seeds and cook, stirring frequently, until the mustard seeds are popping and the mixture smells toasty, 2 to 3 minutes. Place in a bowl and add the Dijon mustard and cracked peppercorns and stir to mix. Set aside.

2. Preheat the oven to 350°F.

3. With your fingers, press the garlic slivers into all the crevices you can find in the roast. Rub the top and sides of the roast with the mustard mixture and set aside at room temperature while the oven heats.

SERVES 6 TO 8

INGREDIENTS:

1 tablespoon mustard seeds

1 teaspoon cumin seeds

⅓ cup Dijon mustard

1 teaspoon black peppercorns, cracked with a mallet or coarsely ground

2 cloves garlic, slivered

1 cross rib roast (English roll) (2½ to 2¾ pounds)

4 cups stemmed and finely shredded mustard greens

2 tablespoons fresh lemon juice

½ teaspoon kosher or fine sea salt

MUSTARD:
SEED TO SAUCE AND SOME GREENS TOO

MUSTARD IN ANY OF ITS FORMS can save many a dish from the doldrums. As whole seeds or seeds pulverized to powder, the myriad prepared mustards available, and mustard greens, the plant's culinary offerings are beloved by spice aficionados and *Brassica* lovers around the world.

From its Mediterranean origins it traveled east, where in Japan mustard took on the form of a spicy paste for stirring into miso dressing. In China its leaves and stems became esteemed as a pickle to swirl into soups and to top rice. France and its exquisite Dijon region vaulted prepared table mustard to worldwide fame. In Germany a similar prepared mustard, this one including whole mustard seeds, makes a stellar topping for sausage. In England,

a clever cook, Mrs. Clements of Tewkesbury, in 1720 pounded mustard seeds into powder that could be mixed with water to make a seasoning paste. Jeremiah Colman then packed the powder into mustard-colored tins and sent it around the globe "by appointment to her majesty the queen" (or "his majesty the king"). In Italy, mustard is used to make an ages-old *mostarda* condiment. Scandinavians drizzle a dilled mustard sauce on their salmon gravlax.

In America the plant's piquant leaves headed south to become cherished as a cooked green, often including native pecans. And in its prepared form mustard took root in the arenas of America's national sport as the quotidian hot dog topping, day-glo yellow ballpark mustard.

4. Place the roast in the oven and cook until done as you like, 50 to 55 minutes for medium-rare in the center (130°F to 135°F on a meat thermometer). Remove and set aside in a warm place for the juices to settle for 10 to 15 minutes.

5. While the roast cooks, prepare the mustard greens. Bring a pot of water to boil over high heat. Add the mustard greens, pressing them down to submerge. As soon as the water boils again, drain the greens in a colander. Without squeezing them, shake the greens to dry a bit and transfer them to a bowl. Just before serving, toss with the lemon juice and salt.

6. To serve, carve the roast into ¼-inch-thick slices and arrange the slices on a serving platter. Garnish with the mustard greens and serve right away.

DUTCH OVEN POT ROAST WITH FENNEL, BUTTER LETTUCE, AND PANCETTA

A DUTCH OVEN, precursor of the slow cooking movement and herald of electric slow cookers, can move from stove to oven and make a dish crusty on the bottom, not just across the top. And it can also generate a rich broth. There is nothing like one for creating an excellent, juicy pot roast. The title *pot roast* may seem outmoded, but there is nothing passé about such a dish, especially when the surrounding ingredients are as modern and different as fennel, butter lettuce, and pancetta.

1. With a paring knife, make 4 small slits in each side of the roast and insert 1 garlic sliver in each slit. Sprinkle salt and pepper all over the roast.

2. Heat the olive oil in a Dutch oven or other heavy stew pot over medium-high heat. Add the roast and brown well on the top, bottom, and sides, about 6 minutes.

3. Add the water, fennel, lettuce, pancetta, marjoram, and ½ teaspoon salt to the pot and bring to a boil. Reduce the heat to maintain a gentle simmer, cover, and cook, turning the meat every half hour or so, until it is fork-tender, about 2½ hours.

4. Remove from the pot and let rest for 10 to 15 minutes for the juices to settle. Carve the meat into ¼- to ½-inch-thick slices and arrange them on a platter. Surround with the fennel and lettuce, pour the juices over all, and serve.

SERVES 4 OR 5

INGREDIENTS:

- 1 cross rib or chuck blade roast (English roll) (about 2½ pounds)
- 2 cloves garlic, each cut into 4 slivers
- Kosher or fine sea salt and freshly ground black pepper
- 2 tablespoons extra virgin olive oil
- 2 cups water
- 1 small fennel bulb (about 8 ounces), trimmed and cut into ¼-inch-thick half-rounds
- 1 head butter lettuce, leaves torn into 3-inch-wide strips
- 1½ ounces thinly sliced pancetta, cut crosswise into 1-inch-wide pieces
- 2 teaspoons chopped fresh marjoram or ½ teaspoon dried

WHY "DUTCH" OVEN?

THREE THEORIES SURROUND how the deep stew pot with its opposing "ears" and traditional swinging handle got the name *Dutch oven*. In one, the Dutch who settled in Pennsylvania brought the pots with them. In another, the Dutch traders who peddled goods from Pennsylvania's Pocono Mountains through New York's Catskills sold pots of that design. In the third, an Englishman named Abraham Darby traveled to Holland in 1704 to inspect how the Dutch cast metal in dry sand molds. Upon returning home, he reworked the method and soon began to make cast-iron cooking pots, which he called "Dutch" pots in reference to where he learned the method. The only trouble with this last theory is that the pots were already around about a century before Darby.

However the cooking vessel got its name, Dutch ovens were taken along by Lewis and Clark on their explorations. George Washington's mother so valued her Dutch pots she specifically bequeathed them in her will. Irish grandmothers cooking over open hearth fires had a bar upon which to hang the pot and swing it over the flames. Civil War supply wagons serving the soldiers carried them. Gold miners and settlers heading west depended on them. Chuck wagon cooks preparing big amounts of beans buried the pots in the cooking fire. Up until forty years or so ago, no kitchen was without one.

The shape of the ears has changed from time to time and from manufacturer to manufacturer. Some of the pots have a flat bottom, and some have three legs. Some have lips and some not; the swinging handle is sometimes thick, sometimes thin, and sometimes omitted altogether.

Nowadays the same design of lidded pot with ears is made of many materials other than cast iron and comes in many colors. In whatever shape or of whatever metal, the versatility of the pot is as undeniable as is its ability to produce deeply flavorful, succulent food. A Dutch oven can be used to make Irish soda bread and corn bread, pot omelets, long-simmered beans and pulses, and the most mellow of stews, especially when it comes to beef, which it braises to fall-apart tenderness.

NAPA VALLEY
POT ROAST WITH LEEKS AND CHARDONNAY

SERVES 4 OR 5

INGREDIENTS:

Kosher or fine sea salt and freshly ground black pepper

2½ pounds flat-iron or cross rib roast (English roll)

2 tablespoons butter

1 cup chardonnay

1 yellow or white onion, coarsely chopped

4 carrots, 1 coarsely chopped and 3 cut into ½-inch-thick ovals

2 medium-size tomatoes, chopped, or 1 cup canned crushed tomatoes

4 fresh thyme sprigs

4 fresh parsley sprigs

Leaves from 1 rib celery

1 cup low-sodium chicken broth

4 inner ribs celery, trimmed and cut into 2-inch lengths

3 small leeks, white and light green parts only, well rinsed and sliced into ¾-inch-thick rounds

1 teaspoon mustard seeds

A JOURNEY THROUGH CALIFORNIA'S NAPA VALLEY is a trek both sensory and surprising. A unique combination of earth movements, volcanoes, and erosion led to a hill-surrounded vale that is alternately rain-catching and sun-hot, ideal for gardens, orchards, and, most of all, grapes. Everywhere there are vineyards. As you wend up the roads, your eyes take in rows of staked vines stretching to the hilltops, reaching into gullies, lining river plains. More than 250 wineries and their tracts of vines divide the valley floor into a patchwork quilt of geographic beauty. At each tasting room stop, your palate meets wine from the valley's two ruling grape varietals: red cabernet sauvignon, the queen of hearts, and white chardonnay, the queen of diamonds. Customarily, the queen of hearts would assert her command over a beef pot roast, but the cuisine of Napa Valley is as strikingly distinct as its landscape. A Napa Valley pot roast simmered in chardonnay gives the diamond queen her due as she lends a crisp and sultry dash to the simmering sauce that sparkles around the meat and vegetables.

1. Generously salt and pepper the meat on both sides. Melt the butter in a large Dutch oven or stew pot over medium-high heat. Add the meat and brown lightly on both sides, 5 to 6 minutes altogether. Add the wine to the pot, then the onion, chopped carrot, and tomatoes, along with the thyme, parsley, and

celery leaves, and stir to mix. Pour in the broth and bring to a boil. Reduce the heat to maintain a gentle simmer, cover the pot, and cook until the meat is fork-tender, about 2½ hours.

2. Transfer the meat to a plate and set aside in a warm place. Strain the liquid through a fine-mesh sieve into a bowl and discard the solids. Let the liquid rest for a few minutes for the fat to rise to the top.

3. Skim and discard the fat from the liquid, return the liquid to the pot, and bring to a boil over medium-high heat. Add the celery ribs, leeks, sliced carrots, and mustard seeds and cook until the vegetables are just tender, about 20 minutes.

4. To serve, carve the meat into ¼- to ½-inch thick slices and arrange them on a serving platter. Pour the juices from the meat plate into the pot with the vegetables and stir gently to mix. Spoon the vegetables and liquid around the meat and serve right away.

➡ TIP: FLAT-IRON POT ROAST, A CUT ABOVE. Flat-iron roast used to be readily available in American markets. Every Yankee grandmother and every Jewish mother knew how to get one, namely, from the local butcher. The flat-iron cut, aka *blade chuck, top blade,* and *top chuck,* is taken from the top blade (bone) side of a thickly cut beef chuck shoulder roast. It's prized for pot roasting because when simmered in a casserole it cooks up as tender as a tenderloin steak. There are still butchers who can cut a flat-iron for that special pot-roast occasion if you call ahead. Without such a possibility, substitute a cross rib roast (English roll).

CHARDONNAY WINE

THE CHARDONNAY WINE GRAPE is the grape of many prized white wines of France's Burgundy, Chablis, and Champagne districts and also in countries from Argentina to Australia, Bulgaria, Yugoslavia, Canada, and Chile, near its original homeland in Israel, in England, and in many states across America. In the United States it most stunningly took root in California. It turns out that chardonnay loves the sun and soil of California, and California loves chardonnay. It has become the premier white grape of San Benito, Sonoma, Mendocino, and Monterey counties. But nowhere is it as celebrated as in the Napa Valley.

To say the white wines made from the chardonnay grape are big and full is perhaps an understatement, and the chardonnays of Napa Valley are particularly colossal. They are oaky, silken, and buttery. Depending on the particular soil and growing region, they carry notes of vanilla, nutmeg, hazelnut, honey, citrus, apricot, nectarine, peach, pineapple, pear, and more. When used in cooking, they impart resonant fragrance and taste to dishes from sautéed vegetables to stewed fruits and desserts and especially to a pot roast with a Napa Valley motif.

BRAISED BEEF SHANKS WITH TOMATO, ANCHOVY, AND CAPERS

AMONG MEAT SHANK COUSINS—LAMB, VEAL, AND BEEF—beef shanks are the least glorified. They are most often thought of as the big, bony cut best used for making beef broth. But, as is often the case, with some attention and dressing up, beef shanks can join the constellation of stars as the centerpiece on the table. In fact, they hold some of the most robustly flavorful beef, and, as a bonus, they harbor a rich marrow center equal to prized veal osso buco. Braised like a pot roast, they rival the best of such dishes. Here they are dressed up with some quite apparent frills: tomatoes, capers, and basil. But one is hidden like a provocative underslip: anchovy. Since humans have been fishing, small salted fish have been used to give depth to sauces and various dishes. They make braised shanks even richer. Since the anchovies entirely disintegrate into a sauce as the shanks cook, you don't have to explain a thing to the hold-the-anchovies crowd.

1. Heat the olive oil in a Dutch oven or other large, heavy pot over medium-high heat. Sprinkle the beef shanks on both sides with salt and pepper and add them to the pot. Cook, turning once, until the shanks are nicely browned on both sides, about 8 minutes. Transfer to a plate and set aside.

2. Add the wine to the pot, stirring to mix in the juices and browned bits from the bottom. Reduce the heat to medium, add the garlic, anchovies, tomatoes, and tomato paste, and stir to mix. Return the meat and collected juices to the pot and add the parsley sprigs and bay leaf. Cover and simmer gently until the meat is tender, 2 hours.

3. Turn off the heat and remove the parsley sprigs and bay leaf. Add the capers, cover, and let the shanks rest for 30 minutes, until the meat is falling off the bone. Reheat gently before serving.

SERVES 4

INGREDIENTS:

- 2 tablespoons extra virgin olive oil
- 4 cross-cut bone-in beef shanks (12 to 16 ounces each), cut 1½ to 2 inches thick
- Kosher or fine sea salt and freshly ground black pepper
- 2 cups red wine
- 8 cloves garlic, peeled
- 4 flat anchovy fillets, finely chopped, or ¾ teaspoon anchovy paste
- 2 cups canned crushed tomatoes
- ¼ cup tomato paste
- 8 fresh flat-leaf parsley sprigs
- 1 bay leaf
- 4 teaspoons large capers, preferably salt-packed, rinsed
- 2 tablespoons shredded fresh basil, for garnish

4. To serve, transfer the shanks to a serving platter and spoon the sauce over them. Garnish with the shredded basil and serve right away.

ANCHOVIES: TINY BUT BIG!

THERE THEY LIE, canned in an oily sea or crusted in salt like long-interred mummies needing a good brush-off. Yet they are one of the world's most numerous and economically important fish and have been so for eons. Though many sorts of small silvery fish are today called *anchovy,* the true anchovy comes from the southern European, Mediterranean, Aegean, and Black Sea coastlines. So potently sea- and salt-flavorful, they were the most desired ingredient the Romans relied on for their infamous Roman sauce, *garum.* From those early times until today they have also been served as a rousing salty appetizer snack and grilled for a nutritious main dish. Related to the herring, they are distinguished by a long mouth, almost always extending well beyond the eye, and a pointed snout. Other varieties of anchovy are found in tropical seas and in the Pacific Ocean off western South America. Today these tiny fish are generally filleted, salt-cured, and then canned in oil, either laid out flat or rolled around a caper, or layered in coarse sea salt. Plucked out and added to a culinary composition, they provide a burst of brininess to pizza, appear famously in Caesar salads, and also add a mysterious enrichment to brews of stews and sauces.

⊙TIP: **BRAISING VERSUS STEWING.** Both braising and stewing are methods of cooking food in liquid in a tightly covered pot, such as a Dutch oven, either on the stove or in the oven. But there's a difference. In braising, including pot roasting, large cuts are simmered in just enough liquid to come no more than an inch up the sides of the pan, whereas for stew, smaller pieces are immersed in liquid almost to cover. That means with braised dishes the liquid becomes intensely flavored and saucelike without necessarily requiring any thickeners or other techniques. In stewing, more liquid is used and although the liquid becomes quite flavored, it is more soup than saucelike and more of it remains in the final composition. To keep the liquid from disappearing while the meat cooks long enough to become tender in a braised dish, it should be cooked at the barest simmer. If the sauce threatens to reduce until none is left, or worse, burn on the bottom, turn off the heat and let the pot rest on the burner undisturbed for the last half hour. To keep the liquid from disappearing in a stew dish, just add a little more water, wine, or whatever liquid you are using.

OVEN BEEF STEW
WITH KALAMATA OLIVES
AND PAYLOADS OF GARLIC

FOR A LIVELY DISH, the joining of meat, garlic, and olives can't be beat. Here, in an oven beef stew, the olives are vivid, purple-black kalamatas and the garlic is increased to the point that whole cloves of them, turned silken soft as they stew, become not just a flavor element but a main component of the dish. Why kalamata olives? From the Kalamata region of the Peloponnesus in Greece, they are a fully ripened black olive of medium size and meaty texture with a dark and stirring flavor. They are so popular as to have gained the rank of a world favorite and now are grown not only in many other regions of Greece but also in Turkey, North Africa, Italy, Spain, and the United States. Why the garlic? When it comes to bold savor, you might as well ask, what else?

1. Preheat the oven to 425°F.

2. Heat the oil in a Dutch oven or other large stove-to-oven pot over medium-high heat. Add as many pieces of beef as will fit without crowding, sprinkle lightly with salt and pepper, and sauté until browned all over, about 5 minutes. Transfer the meat to a plate as you go and continue with another batch until all the beef is browned.

3. Add the garlic, olives, wine, tomato paste, and bay leaf to the pot and bring to a boil over high heat, stirring to dissolve the tomato paste. Add the beef and collected juices back to the pot, stir well, cover, and transfer to the oven. Cook until the beef is fork-tender and the liquid is reduced to a flavorful sauce, about 2 hours.

4. Remove the stew from the oven and let rest for at least 15 minutes or up to

SERVES 4

INGREDIENTS:

2 tablespoons extra virgin olive oil

2 pounds boneless beef chuck or cross rib roast (English roll), cut into 2-inch chunks

Kosher or fine sea salt and freshly ground black pepper

4 heads garlic, cloves separated and peeled

24 kalamata olives

2½ cups red wine

1 tablespoon tomato paste

1 bay leaf

¼ cup thinly shredded fresh basil, for garnish

2 tablespoons chopped fresh flat-leaf parsley, for garnish

OLIVES IN AMERICA:
A BRIEF HISTORY

THE FIRST OLIVES in the United States were carried to California by Spanish missionaries in the form of cuttings from Spanish trees, when they saw the area had a climate and landscape similar to their home. The cuttings were planted all along the road linking the many missions settled by Junipero Serra and his followers: San Diego, Los Angeles, San Juan Capistrano, San Gabriel, San Carlos up to San Francisco, San Rafael—twenty-one in all.

That the olives thrived in many of these locations and in the California sun is a vast understatement. By 1800, Mission San Diego alone had more than five hundred olive trees, and by 1875 there were close to fifteen thousand olive trees in the state. By 1976 there were almost forty-three thousand acres of commercially grown olive trees in California's Central Valley, producing eighty thousand tons of olives. California was not the only place the Spanish brought their olives. They also established them in Florida.

Unfortunately, the olive-processing companies, eager for profit, opted for quick-curing the olives with a particularly harsh lye treatment rather than adhering to the time-honored slow-curing methods followed in the Old World, which preserves the olives' essential flavor rather than sapping it. As a result, while enjoying the crop, for years Americans knew only a pallid version of the fruit. Recently, that questionable trade-off, speed versus quality, has seen a reversal by small olive producers, largely again in California. Today many sorts of olives are cultivated on American soil—green olives, black olives; large and plump, small and wrinkled—and they are cured as keenly as those in Europe, some in oil, some in brine, sometimes with herbs or spices, sometimes vinegared, sometimes stuffed with pimiento, almond, or jalapeño.

With the new bounty of American olives, the scope of excellent imported olives in our stores has expanded enormously. Many carry a wide variety of this lively food, often enticingly displayed in olive bars similar to the olive marts of Spain, Italy, and Greece, where barrels of the fruit beckon avid consumers to purchase a half kilo or so for snack alone or as cooking ingredient.

a few hours for the flavors to marry as the stew settles. Reheat before serving if necessary.

5. To serve, remove the bay leaf and season the sauce with salt to taste. Sprinkle with the basil and parsley and serve right away.

LAGER-BEER-BRAISED BEEF
WITH SWEET AMERICAN ONIONS

EARLY ON IT WAS DISCOVERED THAT, besides being good to eat raw, onions add tremendous depth to the flavor of all kinds of dishes. They are an almost given essential in producing a rich stew or sauce. Featuring them in a stew brewed with beer is derived from the Belgians and their traditional carbonnade but easily takes on a New World accent. In recent years America has been producing very special sweet onions. Taking the Belgian model into an American translation via sweet onions creates a beef stew surpassingly lush. In a nod to its origin and how well their rich beers steep a stew, try using a Belgian-style beer.

1. Sprinkle the beef all over with salt and pepper. Melt the butter in a large, heavy stew pot over medium-high heat. Add as many beef pieces as will fit without crowding and cook, turning, until lightly browned all over, 4 to 5 minutes per batch. Transfer to a plate and continue with another batch until all the meat is browned, reducing the heat if the butter starts to burn. Set the beef aside.

2. Add the onions to the pot and stir to coat the slices. Reduce the heat to medium and cook, stirring from time to time, until the onions are beginning to turn golden, 15 to 20 minutes.

3. Increase the heat to medium-high, pour in the beer, and stir to mix. Add the beef, collected juices, garlic, and thyme to the pot and bring to a boil. Adjust the heat to maintain a gentle simmer, cover the pot, and cook until the meat and onions are fork-tender, about 1½ hours. Remove from the heat and set aside to rest for 15 minutes; up to 1 hour is best.

4. When ready to serve, reheat the stew. Garnish with the parsley and serve right away.

SERVES 4 TO 6

INGREDIENTS:

- 3 pounds boneless or cross-cut beef short ribs, cut into 2-inch pieces
- Kosher or fine sea salt and freshly ground black pepper
- 4 tablespoons (½ stick) butter
- 6 medium-size sweet onions, such as Vidalia, Maui, or Walla Walla, halved top to bottom and sliced ¼ inch thick
- 2 bottles (about 3 cups) Belgian-style amber lager beer
- 4 large cloves garlic, minced or pressed
- 1 teaspoon chopped fresh thyme
- 2 tablespoons chopped fresh flat-leaf parsley

KOREAN AMERICANS: A STALWART PEOPLE AND THEIR VIGOROUS FOOD

In 2003, Korean Americans celebrated a red-letter day in their history, the one hundredth anniversary of Korean immigration to the United States. Though a few political exiles and students had ventured to our shores as early as 1885, shortly after the United States signed a treaty of peace, friendship, and commerce with Korea, it wasn't until 1903 that the first large wave of Koreans began adding their hearty food to the American melting pot. Koreans brought with them industriousness and a wealth of knock-down, dazzling food.

That first wave consisted of 7,500 people. They were brought to Hawaii in 1903 by a determined missionary named Horace Allen at the behest of the Hawaiian Sugar Planters' Association. Those who braved the voyage were searching for the same thing so many pioneers before them had sought, a better life. They must have been quite dazed at the climate change from frosty Korea to tropical Oahu.

The number of Koreans in America remained fairly small until the 1950s. Then nearly 100,000 Korean women came as brides of American soldiers. They were followed by 300,000 children adopted into American families in the ensuing years. Like other immigrant groups before them, they spread out and opened markets and restaurants downtown, in suburbs, on major avenues, on little side streets.

Their meat barbecues, called *bulgogi*, are deeply flavorful. Other irresistible dishes include *mandoo*, dumplings filled with bean sprouts, chile, and pork; *cho-ki kook*, clam soup; *go-chu-jeon*, fried stuffed green peppers; *juhn kol*, mixed broiled meats; *koon ko ki*, fried steak. To top them all was a meat and potato stew made with the New World favorite beef instead of pork and accompanied by the beloved kimchee.

MEAT AND POTATOES
KOREAN STYLE WITH
QUICK KIMCHEE

SERVES 4

INGREDIENTS:

Quick Kimchee (recipe follows), for serving

1 tablespoon peanut or canola oil

2 pounds boneless beef short ribs, cut into 1-inch chunks

1 small yellow or white onion, halved and sliced ¼ inch thick

2 cloves garlic, coarsely chopped

1 tablespoon minced peeled fresh ginger

½ jalapeño chile, finely chopped, or ½ teaspoon red chile flakes

2 tablespoons rice wine, dry white wine, or sake

2 tablespoons light soy sauce

1 teaspoon sugar

1 cup water

4 medium-size (about 1½ pounds) Yukon gold potatoes, scrubbed but not peeled, cut into ⅛-inch-thick rounds

4 scallions, white and light green parts only, trimmed and cut lengthwise into thin slivers, for garnish

12 tender fresh cilantro sprigs, for garnish

IN HILLY, ALMOST ARCTIC KOREA, swirling snow, frozen ground, and chilling winds for a good part of the year mean that the delicate garden vegetables that flourish in much of Asia are supplanted by hardy, cold-resistant sorts. Grilled and stewed meats replace the light compositions that mark other Asian cuisines. Cooked in a style more rustic than refined and decidedly piquant, Korean dishes of meats and vegetables together are steeped in boisterous seasonings—garlic, ginger, spice pastes of soybeans, chile, dried anchovy, and fish sauce. The meal, often cooked in a clay stewing pot known as a *Ddukbaegi,* is built around a mound of steamed rice and eaten with thin chopsticks. But fork and spoon and any sturdy pot will do for cooking up and dining upon meat and potatoes in Korean style.

1. Make the kimchee.

2. Heat the oil in a large, heavy pot over medium-high heat. Add as many pieces of beef as will fit without crowding and brown briefly all over, about 4 minutes. Transfer to a plate and continue with another round until all the pieces are browned.

3. Add the onion, garlic, ginger, and jalapeño and stir to mix. Add the wine, soy sauce, sugar, and water and stir to mix. Return the meat and collected juices to the pot and arrange the potato slices over the meat without stirring. Reduce the heat to maintain a simmer, cover, and cook until the meat and potatoes are tender, 45 to 60 minutes.

Remove from the heat and let rest for 5 to 10 minutes.

4. To serve, arrange the meat and potatoes on a platter or in individual bowls. Pour the juices over all, garnish with the scallions and cilantro, and serve with the kimchee on the side.

QUICK KIMCHEE

THE KOREAN TASTE for inward, in lieu of outward, warming can in part be attributed to the Portuguese, who brought chiles to Korean kitchens as they attempted, without success, to conquer the lands of the valiant Koreans. A signature result of that introduction is kimchee, which accompanies virtually every Korean meal. It's a spicy relish usually of fermented cabbage whose zestiness can range from simply warming to alarming. Here it is reproduced in speedy fashion, more as a spicy wilted salad rather than a long-fermented relish. After resting at room temperature for an hour, the kimchee may be transferred to another container, covered, and set aside in the refrigerator for up to two weeks, during which time it becomes less slawlike, more "pickled" and mellow. For an added, and customary, touch, include a cup of julienne strips or thin rounds of daikon radish in the cabbage mix.

MAKES ABOUT 3 CUPS

1 small or ½ large (12 to 14 ounces) napa cabbage

1 teaspoon kosher or fine sea salt

2 scallions, white and light green parts only, cut crosswise into 2-inch-long pieces, then cut lengthwise into thin strips

1 clove garlic, minced or pressed

½ teaspoon minced peeled fresh ginger

¼ teaspoon red chile flakes

¼ teaspoon pure chile powder

2 tablespoons hot water

1. Remove and discard the not-so-pretty outer leaves from the cabbage. Halve the cabbage lengthwise and cut out the core. Cut the halves lengthwise into ½- to ¾-inch-wide strips and place the strips in a large bowl. Add the salt and toss to mix, squeezing with your hands to break up the cabbage a bit.

2. Add the scallions, garlic, ginger, chile flakes, chile powder, and hot water and toss to mix. Cover loosely with plastic wrap and place a large, heavy unopened can or another bowl half-filled with water on top of the plastic to weight down and soften the cabbage. Set aside at room temperature for 1 hour to lightly pickle the cabbage before using.

BEEF AND SALT PORK STEW WITH THYME TOASTS

A TRIED AND TRUE, albeit for a while shunned, ingredient has returned to the adventuresome cook's repertoire: salt pork. The use of salted pork was brought to the New World by northern Europeans, whose impoverished diets had led them to preserving every scrap of meat from each slaughter for later nourishment. Scandinavians put minced salt pork in meatballs or pound beef cutlets thin to wrap around a toothsome chunk of salt pork. The French cut salt pork into thin strips to lay over pâtés for moisture during cooking. The English add it minced to their beloved meat pies. But when the fashion for meat without fat took over in American cooking, salt pork was rebuffed. Recently again, it has begun to show up as an emboldening ingredient, here featured in a strapping beef stew made all the more succulent by its inclusion. The thyme toasts round out the dish with an herby crunch and make it a meal.

1. Rinse the salt pork under running water then blanch it in boiling water to cover for 2 minutes. Pat dry with paper towels. Trim the skin off the blanched salt pork, reserving it. Cut the salt pork lengthwise into ¼- to ½-inch-thick slices, then cut the slices crosswise into 1- to 1½-inch-wide pieces.

2. Melt the butter in a Dutch oven or other large, heavy stew pot over medium-high heat. Add the salt pork and its reserved skin and sauté, stirring frequently, until rosy and slightly firm, about 3 minutes. With a slotted spoon, transfer the salt pork pieces and skin to a bowl.

3. Add as many pieces of beef as will fit in an uncrowded layer, sprinkle them liberally with pepper, and sauté, turning the pieces, until lightly browned all over, 4 minutes. Transfer the beef to the bowl with the salt pork and continue with another batch until all the beef is lightly browned.

4. Add the celery and onions to the pot and cook until the vegetables are wilted and beginning to soften, about

INGREDIENTS:

- 8 ounces salt pork, blanched
- 4 tablespoons (½ stick) butter, plus more if necessary
- 2 pounds boneless beef short ribs or beef chuck, cut into 1½- to 2-inch pieces
- Freshly ground black pepper
- 3 tender inner ribs celery, cut into ¼-inch pieces
- 2 medium-size yellow or white onions, cut into ¼-inch pieces
- 3 cups water
- 2 cups red wine
- ½ small celery root (5 to 6 ounces before halving), peeled and cut into ¼-inch dice
- 2 bay leaves
- 20 to 24 slices baguette, cut ¾ inch thick on the diagonal
- Extra virgin olive oil, for brushing on the bread
- 1 tablespoon chopped fresh thyme
- ¼ cup chopped fresh flat-leaf parsley leaves, for garnish

3 minutes. Transfer them to the bowl with the salt pork and beef.

5. Add the water and wine to the pot and stir to mix, scraping up the browned bits on the bottom. Return the meat, vegetables, and collected juices to the pot, along with the celery root and bay leaves, and bring to a boil over high heat. Reduce the heat to maintain a simmer and then skim the foam off the top. Partially cover the pot and simmer until the meat is almost tender, 1½ hours. Remove the cover and continue simmering until the meat is fork-tender and the liquid is reduced and saucy, about 30 minutes more. Remove the pot from the heat and set aside, partially covered, for at least 20 minutes and up to 2 hours for the meat to relax and absorb the juices.

6. While the stew is simmering, make the thyme toasts. Preheat the oven to 375°F or use a toaster oven.

7. Lightly brush each bread slice with olive oil. Toast until barely golden around the edges, 3 to 4 minutes. Turn over the slices and sprinkle the thyme over them. Return to the oven and continue toasting until nicely golden, 1 to 2 minutes more. Set aside at room temperature until ready to serve, for up to several hours.

8. To serve, remove the bay leaves and salt pork skin from the stew. Reheat the stew, sprinkle the parsley over the top, and garnish with the thyme toasts.

A LOOSE HISTORY OF THE SLOPPY JOE

WITHOUT A DOUBT, America's most famous "loose meat" concoction—a term that has gone the way of many of its Depression companions, such as hep-cat and apple annies—is the sloppy joe. It was called loose meat because the meat was cooked crumbled so it could be spread around and stretched with additions like bread crumbs, sweet peppers, onion, eggs, and cheese.

The sloppy joe recipes began appearing about 1930, but in truth no one knows exactly where the dish originated. Most sources claim that the "joe" is generic for "anyone" and the sloppy part is pretty obvious.

For history buffs who want facts, the Heinz Company in Pittsburgh, which as a ketchup maker has a vested interest in the sandwich, investigated the obscure beginnings of the slurry. They claim it was invented in a café in Sioux City, Iowa, in 1930 and was the creation of a cook named Joe. Others, however, demur, and say, while it indeed, was Sioux City, the dish was at first just called a *loose meat sandwich* and was spawned in 1934 at Ye Olde Tavern Inn by a couple named Abraham and Bertha. In its numerous versions, the dish quickly became a standard, a great American prototype, and as times improved, it hung on rather than going away. Now it appears at soccer celebrations, at birthday picnics, and as a cornerstone of dad's-night-to-cook.

UPSCALE STEAK
SLOPPY JOES

A GREAT AMERICAN CAMPFIRE and hard-times classic gets fresh, and goes gourmet. Without losing the essence of the saucy sloppy joe sandwich, here the meat becomes lean steak, the sauce is made from fresh tomatoes, and the toasted sourdough bread replaces the bun. Beer is often the accompaniment and remains the first choice to moisten the mix. The dish serves its original purpose of stretching meat into a satiating meal for many, but now taste and not the stretch is the aim.

1. Heat 2 tablespoons of the olive oil in a large sauté pan over medium-high heat. Add the onion, celery, and bell pepper and sauté until soft, about 10 minutes. Transfer the mixture to a bowl and set aside.

2. Place the steak in the same sauté pan and increase the heat to high. Cook the steak, turning once, until well seared on both sides, about 4 minutes per side. Transfer the steak to a plate and set aside.

3. Reduce the heat to medium-high and return the onion mixture to the pan. Add the tomatoes, jalapeño, tomato paste, beer, celery leaves, brown sugar, thyme, cumin, cinnamon, mustard, Worcestershire sauce, and vinegar and stir to mix. Cook until the tomatoes are softened and saucy, about 8 minutes.

4. While the sauce cooks, preheat an oven or toaster oven to 400°F. Drizzle the remaining 2 tablespoons olive oil over one side of the bread slices and toast, oiled sides up, until golden, about 3 minutes.

5. Cut the steak across the grain into ¼-inch-thick slices.

6. Add the steak slices and any collected juices to the sauce and stir until thoroughly covered with sauce and hot, 2 to 3 minutes.

7. To serve, place a slice of toasted bread on each of 4 plates. Mound the sloppy joe mixture over the bread and serve.

SERVES 4

INGREDIENTS:

- ¼ cup extra virgin olive oil
- 1 small white or yellow onion, chopped
- 1 large rib celery, chopped
- ½ medium-size yellow bell pepper, stemmed, seeded, and chopped (1 cup)
- 1 pound boneless rib eye steak or boneless beef short ribs
- 6 large plum tomatoes, chopped
- ½ to 1 jalapeño chile, to taste, chopped
- 3 tablespoons tomato paste
- ½ cup beer or water
- ½ cup celery leaves
- 2 tablespoons dark brown sugar
- 1 tablespoon fresh thyme leaves or ½ teaspoon dried
- ½ teaspoon ground cumin
- ½ teaspoon ground cinnamon
- ½ teaspoon mustard powder
- 1 tablespoon Worcestershire sauce
- 1 tablespoon cider vinegar
- 4 slices sourdough bread, cut from a large round loaf (about ½ inch thick each)

CHEDDAR CHEESE-STUFFED BURGERS

INGREDIENTS:

- 1½ to 2 pounds ground beef chuck or round
- ½ teaspoon kosher or fine sea salt
- ¼ teaspoon freshly ground black pepper
- ½ cup shredded sharp cheddar cheese
- 2 tablespoons minced red onion
- 2 teaspoons Dijon mustard
- 4 hamburger-size bakery buns
- Relishes of choice (page 106)

CHEDDAR CHEESE IS A HARD COW'S MILK CHEESE named for the district of its origin, the southwestern county of Somerset, England, called Cheddar. It is one of England's oldest cheeses, imported to the United States with the cattle that the English brought to their American colonies. In the traditional method of cheddar manufacture, the firm milk curd is cut, or "cheddared," into small bits to drain. They are then pressed into cylinders, wrapped in muslin and wax, and aged from three months to two years. As Vermont, New York, and Wisconsin evolved into dairy states, cheddar became one of the foremost cheeses made in America. So large is the demand, it is now largely factory produced, but the good news is artisanal cheddars have risen once again. Cheddar is the most common cheese used to create the proverbial cheeseburger. But when the cheese is tucked inside a hefty burger, Jack, fontina, feta, or another favorite melting cheese can also be used.

1. Combine the meat, salt, and pepper and mix gently with your hands to blend. Divide the meat into 4 portions and pat each into a ball.

2. Mix together the cheese, onion, and mustard in a small bowl.

3. With your thumb, press a well in each burger ball and place about 2 tablespoons of the stuffing mixture into it. Pinch together the meat to enclose the stuffing and press the balls into ¾- to 1-inch-thick patties. Set aside.

4. Prepare a medium-hot grill or heat a heavy skillet large enough to hold the patties in one uncrowded layer to medium-high.

5. Add the burgers and cook until beginning to brown on the underside, 3 to 4 minutes. Turn them over and cook until done as you like, 3 to 4 minutes more for medium-rare.

6. While the burgers cook, split the buns in half. Toast them, cut sides down, on the grill rack to the side of the burgers or in a toaster until lightly golden, 2 to 3 minutes.

7. Place each burger in a bun on individual plates and serve, surrounded with relishes.

WHO PUT THE PATTY IN THE BUN?

THE LEGENDS SURROUNDING the origin of hamburgers are almost as many as the burgers served in burger joints. One version has the meat coming from the merchant sailors from the seaport of Hamburg, Germany, bringing home the idea of raw chopped beef after a trading voyage to the Baltic Sea. A second story relates that cooks for the Hamburg America Line Company, which brought huge numbers of immigrants from Europe to America in the 1800s and early 1900s, had the inspiration to mince their provision of beef to stretch it over the long voyage. As it happened, the passengers took a liking to it and called the minced meat, often served as patties, after the shipping line where they first ate it. They continued making it in the New World.

How the hamburger became America's blue-ribbon sandwich has at least as many divergent claims. In the first account, a young concessionaire, Charles Nagreen, was plying food in 1885 at the Outagamie County Fair in Seymour, Wisconsin, when he found his sales increased if he slipped his butter-fried chopped meat between slices of bread so that his customers could take it with them. A second tale has another young concessionaire of beef steaks and sausage, Frank Menches, age twenty-seven, at the County Fair in Akron, Ohio, in 1892 running out of sausage, grinding the beefsteak he had remaining, and serving it as a patty. Curiously, it was the same year that H. J. Heinz (of later "57 Varieties" fame) decided to introduce for sale nationally at the Philadelphia fair the tomato sauce he had invented in 1876 and called *ketchup*. His sauce would become the all-time favorite hamburger relish and the leading product of his company. However, it seems that the hamburger was then invented again for the first time in 1900 in New Haven, Connecticut, when Louis Lassen ground up lean beef, broiled it, and served it plain between two slices of toast at his three-seat Louis Lunch diner.

What is sure is that the hamburger sandwich took off to celebrity at the 1904 St. Louis World's Fair. The beef patties, peddled by German immigrants in the city, were sizzled up and packaged between bread slices. It seems the beef and bread coupling was an idea that had reached its time and place. It surely met its market as well. Today almost nothing is as ubiquitous in the United States, or globally, as the widespread American hamburger.

AMERICA'S MEAT MARKET

IN 1673, FRENCH EXPLORER Louis Jolliet and French missionary Jacques Marquette both independently discovered the Chicago River and realized it connected to the Illinois River and from there to the Mississippi River and the Great Lakes. They were followed in the 1770s by a fur trader of African descent named Jean Baptiste Point du Sable, who founded a settlement on the north bank of the Chicago River. The outpost bordered on a verdant, somewhat fetid, marshland, and Point du Sable, without knowing the meaning, took the native name for the area, Eschikagou, which means "the stench of decaying onions," only he pronounced the word "Chicago."

Since the settlement sat on a hub of access, it soon increased in significance. By 1833, Chicago's population had burgeoned to four hundred residents, enough to call itself a town. But it was in 1848 that Chicago truly burst forth as a bustling center of both transportation and barter. That year an easily navigable canal was completed between the Chicago River at the southern tip of Lake Michigan to the Illinois River at a point that allowed access to the Mississippi. Once done, the canal afforded an unbroken inland waterway from the Atlantic Ocean to the Gulf of Mexico. It meant that at last the trade of livestock, grain, and lumber from the western frontier to the industrial East Coast became fluid and Chicago lay at the crossroad. Almost instantly the trade of commodities became vibrant, indeed raucous with over four hundred vessels filled with goods sailing in and out of the city per week. It became clear that an office to oversee the exchange of goods was vital, and a number of local businessmen acting to stabilize the booming trade established an institution that still influences the American diet, the Chicago Board of Trade.

To this day the city continues as the epicenter of commodities trading in the United States, a vast number of them the food we eat. To facilitate the huge amount of trade in goods, the city of Chicago erected enormous warehouses and stockyards filled with cattle and pigs. Railroads traveling east, west, north, and south arrived, making the city the nation's largest nucleus for the "iron horse." Meatpackers, corn brokers, even vegetable middlemen arrived. Wealth ebbed and flowed—but mostly flowed.

The fundamental importance of the city was highlighted in 1893 when its famous world's fair, called the World's Columbian Exposition, took place. Twenty-seven million people attended, almost half of the total population of the United States at the time. George Ferris loaded sixty people at a time on his new gimmick, the Ferris Wheel. Among other famous firsts featured at the fair were Aunt Jemima Syrup, Cracker Jack, Juicy Fruit gum, Shredded Wheat, and the ice-cream cone.

With all the action and the many people who streamed into the town, Chicago also grew into a lively center for arts and learning, inspiring architecture, jazz, blues, and food—deep-dish pizza, pike caught minutes earlier from Lake Michigan, and fittingly, impeccable prime beefsteaks. In 1999 the city initiated an outdoor art exhibit called "Cows on Parade" which featured delightful, nostalgic sculptures of cows seemingly grazing on downtown sidewalks, and Cows on Parade stores still boast cow paraphernalia. It has become unnecessary to have the cattle and pigs in nearby yards. Still, the Board of Trade by Internet and trading floor remains as keen as ever.

BLUE CHEESE-STUFFED BURGERS

STORY HAS IT THAT THE FIRST TIME blue cheese and beef were united was when Marie Louise, the daughter of Emperor Francis I of Austria, married Napoleon Bonaparte. Marie Louise had been trained in fine Austrian cooking, and when she went to France, she took with her a collection of Austrian recipes. Apparently she instinctively knew good food combinations and one day joined a wonderful find from her new home, French Roquefort cheese, with chopped beef. In fact, she pressed the chopped beef into a patty and stuffed it with the Roquefort. When Napoleon was a prisoner on St. Helena Island, his second, and more permanent, exile, he requested the Roquefort-stuffed beef burger at least once a week. His request was never granted. Nonetheless, the combination of beef and blue cheese remains spectacular. For an American big, bold burger, Maytag Blue serves as well as Roquefort, and mixed with chives and oregano, the stuffing turns the burger into something illustrious.

1. Combine the meat, salt, and pepper and mix gently with your hands to blend. Divide the meat into 4 portions and pat each into a ball.

2. Mix together the cheese, chives, and oregano in a small bowl.

3. With your thumb, press a well in each burger ball and place about 2 tablespoons of the stuffing mixture into it. Pinch together the meat to enclose the stuffing and press the balls into ¾- to 1-inch-thick patties. Set aside.

4. Prepare a medium-hot grill or heat a heavy skillet large enough to hold the patties in one uncrowded layer to medium-high.

5. Add the burgers and cook until beginning to brown on the bottom, 3 to 4 minutes. Turn them over and continue cooking until done as you like, 3 to 4 minutes more for medium-rare.

SERVES 4

INGREDIENTS:

- 1½ to 2 pounds ground beef chuck or round
- ½ teaspoon kosher or fine sea salt
- ¼ teaspoon freshly ground black pepper
- ½ cup crumbled blue cheese, such as Maytag Blue or Roquefort
- 2 tablespoons chopped fresh chives
- 2 teaspoons chopped fresh oregano
- 4 hamburger-size bakery buns
- Relishes of choice (see Tips)

CHEESE-STUFFED BURGERS TWO WAYS

SINCE ITS INCEPTION in the annals of American cooking, many things have been done to the paramount American sandwich, the hamburger. Bacon, mushrooms, avocado, Thousand Island dressing, and on and on have been added as a flourish, but nothing has ever vanquished the original fillip for the burger: cheese. When the cheese is tucked inside the patty instead of layered on top, cheesy curds infiltrate every meaty bite and the revered burger moves from prosaic to perfect. The cheese-stuffed burger can sit softly cosseted in a bun, as is the usual practice. It can also stand alone as a hamburger steak. The meat can be ground beef chuck or round as well as ground buffalo, now available at many food markets.

6. While the burgers cook, split the buns. Place the bun halves, cut sides down, on the grill rack to the side of the burgers or in a toaster and toast until lightly golden, 2 to 3 minutes.

7. Place each burger in a bun on individual plates and serve surrounded with relishes.

⊙TIPS:

RELISHING DESIGNER BURGERS. Yes, there's a classic set of burger toppings, but thinking outside the bun, a whole lot more possibilities pop up. The classics can be mixed with these neoclassics to give a burger a mix-and-match architecture and a mighty scrumptious smack.

THE CLASSICS. Ketchup, mustard, mayonnaise, tomato slices, onion slices, pickles or pickle relish, a leaf of iceberg lettuce.

THE NEOCLASSICS. Major Grey's mango chutney, bacon strips, guacamole, sautéed mushrooms, pickled jalapeño slices, barbecue sauce, Thousand Island dressing, salsa, salad greens (arugula, watercress, mizuna, for example), sautéed onions, Red Bell Pepper Marmalade (page 128).

Burgers also practically demand one or the other of two almost prescribed sides: A Haystack of Shoestring Fries (page 292) or French-Fried Onion Rings (page 284).

DOUBLE VEAL CHOPS WITH SHIITAKE MUSHROOM MARSALA CREAM SAUCE

VEAL, THE CENTERPIECE OF NUMEROUS ITALIAN ENTRÉES, is stellar in a Marsala wine sauce softened by the addition of cream. Firm, peppery shiitake mushrooms bring earth, spice, and texture to the dish and lift the mélange to a divine fusion of Far East and Italian American cooking. The shiitakes play a major role in the dish and so are more of a companion than an accent. The veal is luscious, the mushrooms velvet, the meld of the two masterful.

1. Lightly sprinkle the chops with salt and pepper on both sides. In a heavy sauté pan large enough to hold the chops in a single layer, melt 2 tablespoons of the butter over medium-high heat. Add the chops and cook, turning once, until medium-rare, about 12 minutes total. Reduce the heat if the butter starts to burn. Transfer the chops to a serving platter and set aside in a warm place while making the sauce.

2. Melt the remaining 2 tablespoons of butter in the same pan over medium heat. Add the mushrooms, shallot, and thyme and stir to mix. Cook, stirring from time to time, until the mushrooms are well wilted, about 5 minutes.

3. Increase the heat to high and add the Marsala followed by the cream. Cook, stirring, until reduced and thickened to saucy, 3 minutes.

4. Pour the sauce over the chops and serve right away.

SERVES 4

INGREDIENTS:

4 double-thick veal chops, each about 8 ounces and cut 1½ inches thick

Kosher or fine sea salt and freshly ground black pepper

4 tablespoons (½ stick) butter

8 ounces shiitake mushrooms, stems discarded, caps thinly sliced (about 5 cups)

¼ cup finely chopped shallot

4 teaspoons chopped fresh thyme

½ cup Marsala wine

2 cups heavy whipping cream

VEAL SCALOPPINE WITH GREEN OLIVES AND RADISHES

SERVES 4

INGREDIENTS:

12 to 16 red radishes, trimmed, leaving ½ inch of green top, and quartered

1 tablespoon butter

1 tablespoon extra virgin olive oil

All purpose flour, for dusting the scaloppine

1 pound veal scaloppine, pounded to ⅛ inch thick

2 cups low-sodium chicken broth

12 premium green olives, pitted and quartered

1 garlic clove, minced

1 teaspoon ground cumin

1 bay leaf

¼ teaspoon kosher or fine sea salt

¼ teaspoon freshly ground black pepper

¼ cup fresh parsley leaves

ONCE THOUGHT SO EXOTIC, the smells and flavors of Tunisia, Algeria, and Morocco have been steadily joining the American palate as North Africans ply diners with their saporous foods in charming rug-upholstered restaurants. In a veal scaloppine more commonly associated with Italy, the marvels of North Africa's pungent cumin together with the charm of green olives, the gentle bite of radish, and quick sauté brings the casbah to a kitchen several thousand miles away.

1. Bring a small saucepan of water to boil over medium-high heat. Add the radishes and blanch until the red has barely faded to pink, 30 to 60 seconds. Drain in a colander, rinse under cool water, and set aside.

2. Melt the butter in the oil in a large skillet over high heat. Dust the veal slices all over with flour. Place as many of them in the skillet as will fit without crowding and quickly brown them, turning once, until barely golden, 1 to 2 minutes per side. Transfer to a plate and set aside in a warm place. Continue with another batch until all the veal is cooked.

3. Reduce the heat to medium-high and add the broth, olives, garlic, cumin, bay leaf, salt, pepper, and radishes. Bring to a brisk simmer and cook until the liquid is thickened and reduced to about ¾ cup, 8 to 12 minutes.

4. Return the veal slices to the skillet and turn to coat them with the sauce on both sides. Place 2 or 3 scaloppine on each of 4 individual plates. Ladle the sauce and vegetables over them, sprinkle with the parsley leaves, and serve.

PARSLEY:
THE CURLY AND THE FLAT AND ITS PLACE ON THE AMERICAN PLATE

PARSLEY might be described as the universal herb. In western European cooking, it's a pervasive green seasoning or garnish. From Germany to Russia, it's prized not only for its leaves but also for its root. Farther east into China, Southeast Asia, Indochina, and, oddly, across the Pacific Ocean to Mexico and down to Central and South America, parsley maintains its status in all its guises—leaf, root, garnish, vegetable. In a more aromatic form, as leafy cilantro, also known as *Chinese parsley,* it grows all across the Mediterranean and throughout India, central Asia, and China.

The question is, considering its global use in cooking, when and how did parsley become an expected "decoration" on American plates, not necessarily to be eaten? In the 1950s, chefs and cooks, wanting to emulate Europe, came up with the notion that an elegant presentation deserved a touch of decoration. Parsley was pretty and abundant, available when few fresh herbs were. A sprig or two of the curly-leaf variety in those days became a routine fresh finesse on the plate. In fact, it became used so regularly that it faded into the shadows, barely noticeable and without culinary value. So it remained for twenty-five years or more.

Then came the food revolution, beginning in the early 1970s and still going full force today. The obligatory use of parsley as a garnish plunked on a plate without thought came into question. The trend, instead, turned to the innovative incorporation of fresh herbs as a seasoning in or on the dish. Concomitantly, as adoration for Italian cooking burgeoned, where parsley was the herb in either the cooking or the gilding of the dish, it had to be Italian flat-leaf parsley. Poor curly-leaf parsley, once so relied on, was relegated to unsophisticated country cousin status.

Ah, but once the heat of passion and revolution cooled to a more temperate degree, as it inevitably does in matters of love and cooking ingredients, the worth of curly parsley started creeping back, and this variety reappeared in numerous ways: in bouquets garnis, in vibrant and picante green sauces, as part of a crisp fried vegetable potpourri (page 21), and especially as topping, simply chopped or lightly dressed.

LEG OF LAMB WITH SPICY PECAN PESTO

INGREDIENTS:

1 bone-in leg of lamb
(6 to 8 pounds)

Kosher or fine sea salt and
freshly ground black
pepper

Spicy Pecan Pesto
(recipe follows),
for serving

TO DINE ON LEG OF LAMB HAS ALWAYS BEEN A TREAT. All sorts of accompaniments have been created for it with mustard, rosemary, garlic, mint, and fruits among the most venerated. The glory of a bone-in leg is that it offers a spectrum of succulent, done-to-taste slices from medium-rare in the center to moistly brown at the shank end. With a spicy pestolike pecan condiment, each slice becomes remarkably dazzling.

1. Prepare a medium-hot grill for indirect grilling or preheat the oven to 375°F. Sprinkle the lamb all over with salt and pepper and set it aside at room temperature.

2. *To grill the lamb:* Place the meat on the grill to the side of, not directly over, the heat source. Cover and cook, turning several times, until done as you like, 1 to 1½ hours, depending on the size, for medium-rare in the middle (130°F to 135°F on a meat thermometer), adding more charcoal as necessary.

   To cook the lamb in the oven: Place the meat in a roasting pan and cook, turning once, until done as you like, 1 to 1½ hours, depending on the size, for medium-rare in the middle.

3. While the lamb cooks, make the pesto.

4. When done, transfer the lamb to a platter and set aside in a warm place for the juices to settle for at least 20 minutes.

5. Carve the lamb and serve with the pecan pesto on the side.

SPICY PECAN PESTO

A BIT SOUTHERN, a bit southwestern, a bit Mediterranean, a New World nut and fresh chile are paired with Old World seasonings in a jewel of a pesto. As an American riff on an ancient theme, it plays well almost anywhere: as a condiment for meats, poultry, and game; as a topping enhancement for simply prepared potatoes, pasta, bruschette; or as a dip for pita triangles.

MAKES ABOUT 2 CUPS

2 cups pecan pieces

4 cloves garlic, peeled

2 jalapeño chiles, stemmed

2 teaspoons whole black peppercorns

½ teaspoon kosher or fine sea salt

1 cup walnut, peanut, or canola oil

2 teaspoons balsamic vinegar

Finely grind the pecans in a food processor. Add the garlic, jalapeños, peppercorns, salt, and the oil and process until pureed as fine as possible. Add the vinegar and process until blended in. Use right away or refrigerate for up to 2 days and bring to room temperature before serving.

THE BRAVURA OF GRASS-FED LAMB

LAMB IS THE CULINARY NAME for both young sheep and the meat from them. There are more than a thousand distinct sheep breeds of all different sizes, shapes, and colors, some bred for wool, some for wool and meat, some with hair and no wool. More than forty types are reared in the United States. Besides meat and wool, sheep provide a rarely recognized myriad of other products: skin for parchment, footwear, rugs; lanolin for lubrication and moisturizing; tallow for candles and soap; bone for dice and buttons; intestines for sausage casing and surgical thread; milk for cheese and yogurt; and even, mixed with pulp, droppings for paper. Besides for clothing, the wool is used for tennis ball and pool table covers, mattress filling, upholstery, and yarn and is the best material for cleaning up oil spills, from the kitchen to the sea.

But it is the meat of young sheep that is the species' crowning glory. Lamb is still the least-eaten meat in America—far more beef and pork are consumed—but for many lamb is considered the most sublime.

Sheep have never taken well to a diet of grain. They far prefer grass, and so raising the best of sheep and lambs takes lots of land with grassy fields, verdant meadow, and pasture. American lamb comes to the table grass-fed and from states famous for their grasslands—Vermont, Illinois, Colorado, California, Oregon.

The preferred cuts of lamb in America are the quick-cooking and steaklike chops cut from the loin, rib, and shoulders. Leg of lamb, so large it is often reserved for feeding a crowd, comes next, followed by crown ribs, the saddle, shoulder roasts, flank, and shanks.

All are expansive in taste and indulgent in tenderness, and we delight in recipes for every one. We take the selected cuts from a glaze of Coca-Cola to a pecan pesto, to grassily appropriate dandelion greens. The preferred degree to cook all, save shanks, which are long cooked, is medium-rare.

LAMB CHOPS
WITH SCALLIONS
IN COLA GLAZE

INGREDIENTS:

2 tablespoons extra virgin olive oil

8 lamb shoulder or sirloin chops

Kosher or fine sea salt and freshly ground black pepper

6 bunches scallions, white and light green parts only, cut lengthwise into thin strips

1½ cups regular Coca-Cola or Pepsi-Cola

3 teaspoons anise seeds

AMONG ALL THE WAYS TO PREPARE LAMB, is there a thoroughly American way that hasn't been done before? If not, here's a candidate, a glazing of lamb chops with an indigenous, ubiquitous, truly all-American product. Either Coca-Cola or Pepsi-Cola tenderizes as it both browns and coats the meat with sweet flavor. Scallions and the unusual use of anise seeds in the sauce lend a Chinese nuance. It's a dish of red, white, and blue surprise.

1. Heat the oil in a sauté pan large enough to hold the chops without crowding over medium-high heat. Sprinkle the chops on both sides with salt and pepper, add them to the pan, and sauté until browned on both sides, about 4 minutes per side.

2. Add the scallions, cola, and anise seeds to the pan and continue cooking, turning 3 times, until almost all the liquid disappears and the chops are glazed on both sides and still pink in the centers, about 8 minutes altogether.

3. To serve, arrange the chops on a platter, heap the scallions on top, and pour the remaining pan juices over all. Serve right away.

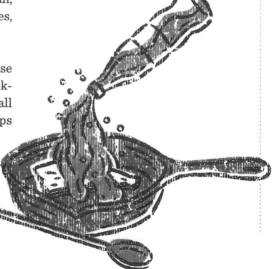

COCA-COLA (AND PEPSI, TOO)

NOT ONLY HAVE THE ETHNIC GROUPS that streamed into America influenced the making of the nation's cuisine, certain American foods have in turn influenced the world. As blue jeans and hamburgers were winging their way around the globe, another American product spread like wildfire: cola drinks, namely Coca-Cola and Pepsi-Cola.

Coca-Cola is the world's most popular drink. It was invented around 1884 by a pharmacist named John Stith Pemberton in Columbus, Georgia. He first called it "Pemberton's French Wine Coxa," and indeed he intended to imitate wine with a dollop of alcohol. He meant the brew to be headache medicine (though he at times also claimed it was a cure for dyspepsia, neurasthenia, impotence, and morphine addiction). The following year, however, his Georgia county passed a prohibition law, so Pemberton developed a nonalcoholic version. His business partner, Frank Robinson, then dubbed the drink with a name that declared the other ingredients in the mixture, the stimulant coca leaves and the flavoring of kola nuts, Coca-Cola. Robinson also created the drink's logo.

By 1887, Pemberton started looking for backers. He sold a stake in his new drink to several people, including Asa Candler, who incorporated the company and eventually solidified his ownership by burning all the early records of the company.

Candler was an aggressive marketer, and it was his methods that are perhaps most responsible for Coca-Cola's explosive and continuing growth. He gave out vouchers for free drinks, had Coca-Cola wall murals painted, and placed media advertisements. In due time the Coca-Cola Company put out painted Coke trays and inscribed drinking glasses. At first as the company grew, a number of different bottlers were distributing the drink in variously shaped bottles. The famous bottle in which Coke became sold exclusively, the contour bottle, also called the *hobble skirt* bottle, was fashioned in 1915 by a Swedish glassblower, Alexander Samuelson, who had immigrated to America some twenty years earlier. He meant to base the design on the kola nut or leaf since they were flavorings for the drink, but he delegated an underling to research the shape of the kola nut and leaf for him. The employee returned with sketches of the cacao pod, not the kola nut, and Samuelson founded his design on these. The mistake would prove invaluable. On this error Coca-Cola got what it wanted, a bottle so recognizable that even when broken it could be identified.

IT HITS THE SPOT

PEMBERTON wasn't the only pharmacist busily compounding a new health beverage. Miles away another druggist was concocting a brew with remarkably similar ingredients, ingredients that most pharmacists of the time believed were curatives for common aliments. So it was in 1893 in New Bern, North Carolina, that the druggist Caleb Bradham stirred together his own miscellany, including kola nuts, and possibly the stomach enzyme pepsin, a component that has never been confirmed. He first called the elixir Brad's Drink, but in 1898 he changed the name to Pepsi-Cola.

For quite a while, Bradham's drink struggled. Coca-Cola had grabbed domination of the cola market both at home and internationally and Pepsi-Cola had to declare bankruptcy twice. However, Pepsi jolted back. In 1906, when Congress passed the Pure Food Act, Coke had to clean up its coca leaves, while Pepsi didn't. Then, in 1934, in the midst of the Depression, Pepsi began to offer a twelve-ounce bottle for the same nickel that bought only a six-ounce bottle of Coke.

Other cola drinks popped onto the market, but America's Coke and Pepsi had established themselves as "the real thing." The two became huge competitive rivals, now lasting for more than a century. The remarkable thing, however, is how both came to impart an American image around the world. Everybody, everywhere, it seems, wants a Coke or a Pepsi.

RACK OF LAMB WITH STEWED BERRIES
AND SAVORY PEAR
BREAD PUDDING

SERVES 4 TO 6

INGREDIENTS:

Savory Pear Bread Pudding
(recipe follows),
for serving

2 racks of lamb, frenched

Extra virgin olive oil,
for coating the racks

Kosher or fine sea salt and
freshly ground black
pepper

Stewed Berries (page 116),
for serving

UNLIKE PORK RIBS, which are familiar as twelve-bone slabs of large spareribs or small baby back ribs, a rack of lamb stretches only to six or seven rib chops, sometimes eight, if the butcher includes the last small taste at the tip. Whether six, seven, or eight ribs long, a lamb rack is enough to serve two to three hearty eaters. It is best cooked simply, with no more seasoning than salt and pepper. Robust as is, extra flavor comes from surrounding postscripts, here the deeply fruity, complex-tasting though easy-to-make compote of fresh raspberry and dried cranberry, laced with a cabernet wine and a savory dried pear bread pudding. You can use the cooking technique, namely minimal seasoning and high heat, for any rack of lamb and surround it to suit yourself in other ways. Have the butcher trim the rack French style, meaning cut the extra fat off the top and between the ribs and crack the hard bone, called the *chine bone,* to which the ribs are attached. The rack now can easily be divided into chops for serving.

1. First make the bread pudding and set it aside in a warm place.

2. Preheat the oven to 450°F.

3. Rub the racks of lamb all over with a little olive oil and sprinkle them with salt and pepper on both sides. Heat a heavy ovenproof skillet large enough to hold the lamb without

CHURRO SHEEP:
AMERICA'S FIRST HERDS

WHEN, ON HIS SECOND VOYAGE WEST in 1493, Christopher Columbus established a residence on Hispaniola, he took along a number of sheep to provide him a "walking food supply." He was followed in 1504 by the conquistador Hernando Cortés, who took some descendants of Columbus's original sheep to mainland Mexico. Then, in 1540, yet a third Spanish conqueror who lived in Mexico, Francisco Coronado, heard tales of Seven Cities of Gold to the north and was determined to find them. He launched an overland expedition heading into what is now the Southwest and brought some of the Mexican sheep with him.

They were what the Spanish considered ordinary sheep, not valuable merinos, and they called them *churro,* meaning "scrub." The Spanish gave the sheep to the Natives of the Southwest, the Pueblo and the Diné, or Navajo, to herd and weave textiles.

While we dine on far different sheep, it is still the churro sheep that Pueblos and especially the Diné use for meat and also to weave their incredible and highly valued blankets. Churro fleece is composed of an inner coat of fine wool fibers and an outer coat of long coarse hair that repels snow and rain. The natural colors of the wool range from gray to brown to white. To these the Diné added vegetable dyes made from surrounding desert plants for rust, blue, and red pigments and formulated a set of traditional forms and patterns in their weaving. All the while, the mutton of the sheep for many decades kept the Diné from starving.

Though the history of their survival is tangled and at times bitter, America's first sheep live on in the locale where they were first imported. Indeed, the Navajo-Churro Sheep Association was formed in 1986 and continues to preserve and encourage the breed.

touching over medium-high heat. Place the lamb in the skillet, fat side down, and cook until browned on the bottom and beginning to sizzle, 3 to 4 minutes.

4. Turn the racks over and transfer the pan to the oven. Cook until done to taste, about 8 minutes for medium-rare (130°F to 135°F on a meat thermometer). Remove from the oven and set the racks aside, still in the pan, for 10 minutes to finish cooking and for the juices to settle.

5. While the racks cook, make the compote.

6. To serve, carve the racks into chops and accompany with the compote and bread pudding on the side.

SAVORY PEAR BREAD PUDDING

WHEN FACED WITH the cavity of a turkey, chicken, game hen, or other bird to fill, it's a common American custom to reach into the bread box for a somewhat dried-out leftover loaf. Cut into chunks, seasoned, moistened with butter, it can be turned into stuffing. A bread stuffing can soak up sumptuous meat juices as well, and when it comes to rack of lamb, it's time to think inside the box. A bread stuffing, especially one with dried fruit suspended in an egg custard, makes a stunning accompaniment to roast meat, absorbing all the sublime drippings. And, it has the added enticement of being a crossover bread pudding.

SERVES 6

3 tablespoons butter, plus a little extra for coating the baking dish

1 large rib celery, halved lengthwise and thinly sliced

½ medium-size yellow or white onion, chopped

2 dried pear halves, cut into ¼-inch dice (⅓ cup)

½ teaspoon chopped fresh sage leaves

3 large eggs

2 cups milk

¾ teaspoon kosher or fine sea salt

6 cups cubed (1-inch) day-old baguette or country-style bread with crust

1. Preheat the oven to 350°F. Lightly coat a 3-quart glass or ceramic dish with butter.

2. Melt the butter in a medium-size sauté pan over medium-high heat. Add the celery, onion, pear, and sage and stir to mix. Sauté until the vegetables wilt, 3 to 5 minutes.

3. Whisk together the eggs, milk, and salt in a large bowl. Add the bread and pear mixture and stir to mix. Pour the pudding into the prepared dish and bake until toasted on the top and a knife inserted in the center comes out clean, 40 to 45 minutes. Remove and let rest for at least 10 minutes and up to 30 minutes. Serve warm.

STEWED BERRIES

BERRY JOINED WITH berry makes a gala olio for meat, even more so when mediated with hearty red wine. As well as for lamb, the compote beguiles on game and pork.

MAKES ABOUT 2 CUPS

2 cups fresh raspberries

2 cups dried cranberries

2 cups cabernet sauvignon or other hearty red wine

Heaping ¼ cup sugar

Combine the raspberries, cranberries, wine, and sugar in a medium-size saucepan and bring to a boil over medium-high heat. Stir gently and cook until thick enough to coat a spoon, about 8 minutes. Remove from the heat and cool to room temperature. Serve at room temperature or chilled. The compote will keep, covered, in the refrigerator for up to several weeks.

GINGER-RUBBED LAMB CHOPS WITH PAPAYA AND PAPAYA SEED SALAD

THOUGH SHEEP ARE RAISED IN HAWAII and other places with sweltering climates, their warm coats more often make them the denizens of cooler climes, so a combination with tropical fruit is rather novel. Papayas provide judicious sweetness to lamb, and their peppery seeds, reminiscent of radish or watercress, provide a contrapuntal note. Add fresh ginger and the dish of wintry meat becomes positively tropical-spicy sultry.

SERVES 4

INGREDIENTS:

8 loin or rib lamb chops,
  cut 1 inch thick

2 teaspoons finely grated
  peeled fresh ginger

2 cloves garlic, minced or
  pressed

Kosher or fine sea salt

2 firm papayas

⅓ cup fresh orange juice

⅔ cup peanut or canola oil

2 tablespoons finely
  shredded fresh mint
  leaves

4 cups torn frisée

1. Rub the chops on both sides with the ginger, garlic, and a sprinkle of salt. Set aside at room temperature for up to 1 hour or refrigerate for up to several hours (remove from the refrigerator 30 minutes before cooking).

2. When ready to cook, prepare a medium-hot grill if grilling.

3. Peel the papayas, cut them in half lengthwise, and scoop out the seeds, reserving 1 tablespoon. Set the papaya halves aside.

4. To make the dressing, whisk together the orange juice and oil in a small bowl. Stir in the mint and reserved papaya seeds and set aside.

5. Place the chops on the grill directly over the heat or in a lightly greased heavy skillet over medium-high heat. Cook, turning once, until done as you like, 5 to 6 minutes per side for medium-rare.

6. Divide the frisée among 4 plates. Thinly slice the papaya and arrange the slices over the frisée on one side of each plate. Set the lamb chops alongside the papaya, drizzle the dressing over all, and serve.

LAMB SHANKS
WITH CHICKPEAS, BLACK OLIVES, AND GOLDEN RAISINS

SERVES 4

INGREDIENTS:

2 tablespoons extra virgin olive oil, plus extra for coating the noodles

4 large (1¼ pounds each) or 8 small (12 ounces each) lamb shanks (see Tip)

Kosher or fine sea salt and freshly ground black pepper

8 cloves garlic, minced or pressed

1 cup cooked chickpeas

1 cup canned tomato puree

⅓ cup pitted kalamata olives

¼ cup golden raisins

2 cups red wine

1 tablespoon balsamic vinegar

2 teaspoons chopped fresh summer savory or 1 teaspoon dried

12 ounces dried pappardelle or other big pasta

1 tablespoon very finely shredded fresh mint leaves, for garnish

NO MEAT IS MORE TENDER THAN THAT CLOSEST TO THE BONE. This is decidedly true of lamb shanks. Cooked until the meat is sliding off the bone, it shreds into tender morsels. Here chickpeas, both familiar and unexpected, round out the shanks. Chickpeas arrived in America as a staple with people from Uzbekistan to the Spanish Pyrenees, all sheep-herders in their native lands. They absorb the juices yet provide a nubbly texture. Added to the mix are salty olives and sweet golden raisins, two more elements of the mountain herder cuisines.

1. Preheat the oven to 350°F.

2. Heat the 2 tablespoons oil in a Dutch oven or other heavy, large ovenproof pot over medium-high heat. Sprinkle the lamb shanks with salt and pepper, place them in the pot, and, turning them once or twice, brown them all over, about 8 minutes.

3. Add the garlic, chickpeas, tomato puree, olives, raisins, wine, vinegar, and summer savory to the pot. Stir to mix and bring to a boil, still over medium-high heat. Cover the pot and place it in the oven. Cook until the shanks are fork-tender, 1½ to 2 hours, depending on the size of the shanks.

Remove the pot from the oven and set aside to rest for 10 to 15 minutes so the juices settle.

4. When the lamb is almost done, cook the pasta according to the package directions until al dente. Drain, coat lightly with oil, and set aside in a warm place.

5. To serve, divide the pasta among 4 dinner plates or place on one large platter. Top with the shanks and spoon the sauce all around. Garnish with the mint and serve right away, while still warm.

➲ TIP: **LAMB SHANKS, FORE AND AFT.** Lamb shanks come from either the forelegs or the hind legs of the animal. The hind leg shanks, about 1¼ pounds each, are larger and meatier because they do the push-pull work, which develops muscle and bulk. The foreleg shanks, about 12 ounces each, are used more for navigational work as the animal maneuvers through the fields, requiring less muscle work. Most meat counters carry the hind legs, which give more meat for the money. Ask the butcher to "crack" the shanks into halves or thirds for easy eating. The less meaty but more delicate forelegs don't need to be cracked; they're quite manageable whole. One whole hind leg or two forelegs make a generous serving.

AMERICA'S FIRST FRIEND: MOROCCO

THE FIRST COUNTRY TO RECOGNIZE THE UNITED STATES OF AMERICA as a nation was an unlikely one— the kingdom of Morocco. In the 1780s the two countries signed a treaty of peace and friendship. That treaty remains the longest unbroken one of its kind in all of history. The two countries have stood together, honoring freedom and diversity.

While that early Treaty of Friendship was signed by John Adams and Thomas Jefferson, Moroccan immigration to America was quite rare at first, although some say that Moroccan sailors may have trumped Columbus at arriving on American shores, and many Jewish Moroccans who first settled in South America came to the North American colonies in the 1600s. When far more Moroccans arrived much later, in the 1950s and on, they mostly came as small business owners and professionals and headed to California, Texas, and the cities of the East Coast.

Like others, they brought their truly vibrant cuisine to join in the great American assemblage: steaming dishes enhanced by cinnamon, ginger, turmeric, cumin, cayenne, saffron, anise, sesame seed, and native olives, brined spicier than European ones. Oranges, lemons, prickly pears, pomegranates, almonds, dates, walnuts, chestnuts, barley, melons, and cherries served as dessert. The arid Moroccan climate favors herds, and the sheepherding Berbers there savor a roast lamb dish. Other signature dishes feature chicken stuffed with rice and raisins and topped with dabs of honey; pigeon baked in a pie with sweetened almonds, the thin filo pastry top sprinkled with powdered sugar; and balls of grain and meat topped with eggs, which like their lamb and chicken stews are cooked in a tajine.

LAMB AND QUINCE TAJINE WITH DANDELION RAITA

INGREDIENTS:

1½ tablespoons peanut or canola oil

3 pounds lamb stew meat, preferably with bones, cut into 1½-inch pieces

Kosher or fine sea salt and freshly ground black pepper

1 medium-size onion, halved and sliced ¼ inch thick

1 teaspoon ground ginger

½ teaspoon ground turmeric

¼ teaspoon ground cinnamon

¼ teaspoon cayenne pepper

3 cups water

2 quinces (about 1 pound total), unpeeled, cored, and cut into 8 wedges each

Dandelion Raita (recipe follows), for serving

Raisin Couscous (page 260), for serving

1 tablespoon finely shredded fresh mint, for serving

NO DISH PUTS TOGETHER A MEDLEY of sweet, salty, sour, and bitter better than a Moroccan tajine. In them tastes encircle one another and coalesce in an astonishing harmony.

A tajine is not needed to make a fine tajine stew. A regular Dutch oven or other large lidded stovetop cooking pot will do. Here the tajine is sweetened and made rosy with quince, which happily doesn't require peeling, and is served, as is typical, atop couscous and counterposed with sassy condiments. For quinces, you must seize their season, late October to early winter. When they are not available, you can substitute green apple and a few dried apricots. Tajines also typically have fiery harissa as a side condiment (page 259) and a chutneylike fruit relish, such as Lemon Apricot Relish (page 259).

1. Heat the oil in a large, heavy pot over medium-high heat. Sprinkle the lamb with salt and pepper and place as many pieces in the pot as will fit without crowding. Cook, turning them once or twice, until brown all over, about 5 minutes. Transfer to a plate and continue with another batch until all the lamb is browned.

2. Return the lamb and collected juices to the pot, add the onion, and stir to mix. Add the ginger, turmeric, cinnamon, and cayenne and stir to mix again. Pour in the water and bring to a boil. Reduce the heat to maintain a simmer, cover, and cook until the lamb is tender but not yet falling off the bone, 1½ to 2 hours.

3. Add the quinces to the pot and continue cooking, uncovered, until the quinces are tender, the lamb is falling off the bone, and the liquid is reduced to a sauce, about 30 minutes.

4. While the tajine cooks, prepare the raita and couscous.

5. To serve, mound the couscous on a large platter. Ladle the tajine over the couscous, sprinkle the mint over all, and serve with the raita on the side.

DANDELION RAITA

A RAITA IN origin and name is a South Asian condiment, most typically served as a cooling punctuation to India's fiery fare. Since raitas are composed of foods also common to Morocco, it makes for an exotic twist to unite a raita with a tajine. Yogurt, garlic, and lively dandelion add both creamy rivulets and earthy green to a mouthful of tajine. If dandelion is not available, equally lively watercress sprigs will do.

MAKES 2½ CUPS

Large pinch of kosher or fine sea salt

2 cloves garlic, peeled

1 tablespoon peanut oil

1½ packed cups chopped tender dandelion greens

2 cups plain Greek yogurt

TAJINE: THE VESSEL

MANY OF THE DISHES WITH EXOTIC NAMES that have entered the ken and yen of American diners are, in their countries of origin, not romantically titled at all. They are simply named for the pot they are cooked in. Bouillabaisse is one of these. It is named after the cauldron sailors used to keep afire on their boats into which they threw scraps of their catch. Casseroles are another, as are Moroccan tajines. A tajine is not only the food in the vessel, it is also the vessel itself. A tajine is a heavy ceramic deep-lipped plate covered by a conical clay lid. Meat, some vegetables, often fruit, and heady spices are put on the plate and covered with the cone lid and then left to stew and steam over a low flame until everything inside is exquisitely plumped and blended. Many tajine pots are beautifully decorated; the prettiest come from the town of Safi, Morocco. The best ones for cooking, though, are the plain reddish brown earthenware ones from the town of Salé. Their porousness allows for well-timed braising.

1. Spread the salt on a cutting board. Place the garlic on top of the salt and mince it into the salt.

2. Heat the oil in a medium-size saucepan over medium-high heat. Add the garlic and salt mix, along with the dandelion greens, and stir them to combine. Sauté until the greens are quite wilted, about 2 minutes. Remove from the heat and set aside to cool.

3. Place the yogurt in a medium-size serving bowl and whisk it smooth. Stir in the dandelion greens and set aside at room temperature until ready to serve, up to 30 minutes, or refrigerate for up to 3 hours, bringing to room temperature before using.

CROWN ROAST OF PORK WITH THREE PUREES

SERVES 12

INGREDIENTS:

1 crown roast of pork
(16 ribs, 8 to 9 pounds)

6 cloves garlic, slivered

½ teaspoon chopped fresh
rosemary

Kosher or fine sea salt and
freshly ground black
pepper

Chunky Applesauce
(recipe follows),
for serving

Creamy Chestnut Mash
(facing page), for serving

Silken Yam Puree
(page 124), for serving

A CROWN ROAST OF PORK is contrived from the same cut as a bone-in pork loin roast (page 125) or chops, but it's a grand presentation of the whole slab of ribs. Actually, it requires a slab plus four, meaning sixteen ribs' worth, to form a circle that's tied into a crown. This is a job for the butcher, so order in advance. It's an extravagance worthy of a large group of friends or a special family get-together. Echoing bejeweled royal crowns, a crown roast of pork has rib bones rising up, which can be decorated with paper curlicues encircling a cap of tender meat. It demands bedecking, and here three purees made from apples, chestnuts, and yams, in three degrees of smoothness, provide that beautifully.

1. One or two hours before cooking, remove the roast from the refrigerator, place it on a baking sheet, and press the garlic slivers into the crevices between the chops. Sprinkle the top with the rosemary and a liberal amount of salt and pepper and set aside at room temperature.

2. When ready to cook, preheat the oven to 450°F.

3. Place the roast in the oven and cook for 15 minutes. Reduce the heat to 325°F and continue cooking until the juices are no longer running pink (162°F to 165°F on a meat thermometer), 2 to 2½ hours. Remove the roast from the oven and set aside in a warm place to rest and finish cooking for 15 to 20 minutes.

4. While the roast cooks, make the three purees.

5. Transfer the roast to a serving platter and carve into chops by cutting between the ribs. Serve right away, with the purees in separate bowls on the side.

CHUNKY APPLESAUCE

AMERICA IS A land of apples, apples, and more apples. Of the innumerable sorts, many are local only and never seen in stores. Still, markets do an admirable job of carrying a splendid array of apple varieties, red, yellow, and green. Some are eaters, some better for cider or jelly. Apples good for a chunky applesauce are ones that don't call for much extra sugar, such as Granny Smith, Golden Delicious, Braeburn, Winesap, and Fuji.

MAKES 4 CUPS

4 pounds sweet-tart cooking apples, peeled, cored, and cut into 1-inch chunks

½ cup sugar

¼ cup fresh lemon juice

⅛ teaspoon ground cloves, for garnish

1. Place the apple chunks in a large saucepan. Add the sugar and lemon juice and toss to mix. Cover and cook over medium-high heat until soft all the way through but still holding some shape, about 15 minutes.

2. Remove and let cool briefly, and then mash with a fork into a chunky sauce. Set aside until ready to use or cool completely and refrigerate for up to 1 week.

3. Serve warm or chilled with the cloves sprinkled over the top.

CREAMY CHESTNUT MASH

CHESTNUTS ARE a winter treat. The drawback to enjoying them is that the fresh ones are quite time-consuming and a pain in the thumbs

TANTALIZING AND VERSATILE PORK

HERNANDO DE SOTO brought the first pigs to the mainland of North America when he ferried a small drove to Tampa Bay, Florida, in 1539. By the time de Soto died a mere three years later, the original thirteen had grown to at least seven hundred, not including the ones he and his troops ate or the ones that escaped to become the ancestors of today's wild American boar. And although pigs in early America became such a nuisance that walls in nascent towns were built to keep pigs on one side and people on the other, pork comprised the main meat consumed, and over the nation's centuries its popularity has hardly ebbed. Pork is the second-most-devoured meat in the United States with farms across every state in the land raising pigs. Besides the roasts and chops and tenderloins we adore, pork provides us our often daily ham, bacon, and sausage.

Pork has a double culinary glory. The succulent and satisfying meat comes in a wide range of cuts so giving they can be treated to numerous ways of cooking—roast, sauté, barbecue, among others—and the meat is so mild it befriends a plethora of accompaniments. We exploit both cooking methods and myriad companions in this chapter.

to prepare. But now that freeze-dried or vacuum-wrapped chestnuts can be found in fancy food stores, already cooked and peeled, they're at hand any time of year. No denying that they're an extravagance, but a little goes a long way.

MAKES 3 CUPS

1½ pounds freeze-dried chestnuts

1 cup heavy whipping cream

½ teaspoon kosher or fine sea salt

1. Place the chestnuts in a medium-size saucepan and add enough water to barely cover. Bring to a boil over medium-high heat. Cook until the chestnuts are soft, about 5 minutes. Transfer to a food processor, along with 1 cup of the cooking liquid, and process until almost, but not quite, smooth. Return to the pot or a microwave bowl and stir in the cream and salt.

2. Reheat briefly on the stovetop or in a microwave oven and serve right away. Or cool, refrigerate for up to 5 days, and reheat before serving.

SILKEN YAM PUREE

FOR THIS SILKEN puree served in a triumvirate of sides for an elegant meal, the widely available Garnet yams, elongated in shape, deep orange inside, are a first choice.

MAKES 4½ CUPS

6 large yams, peeled and cut into 1-inch chunks

Kosher or fine sea salt

¼ teaspoon grated nutmeg, preferably freshly grated

1. Place the yams in a large saucepan and add enough water to cover by ¾ inch. Bring to a boil over high heat. Reduce the heat to maintain a brisk simmer and cook until the yams have collapsed, 18 to 20 minutes.

2. Puree the yams and whatever remaining cooking liquid there is together in a food processor until silky smooth. Add more water if necessary to achieve a moist puree. Season with salt to taste. Sprinkle the nutmeg over the top just before serving.

BONE-IN PORK ROAST
WITH SCOTCH-SOAKED PEACHES AND
SINGED ONION RINGS

SCOTCH WHISKEY IS a highly distinctive beverage. Whatever the type, single malt, vatted malt, blended, single grain, each is decidedly earthy and silken on the tongue, yet soothingly stirring. The beverage's savor, while esteemed as a drink, is a challenge for a cook. Rare is the culinary use for it. But the honeyed version of it, called Drambuie, gives a clue as to how and on what scotch might come into play, namely on something sweet and fruity. The proper companion should be equally lush, lest the scotch dominate rather than blend. A peach suits that call just fine: It's voluptuous, sweet, fruity, and easily intermingles with other tastes, and pork revels in such company.

INGREDIENTS:

¼ cup scotch whiskey

¼ cup packed dark brown sugar

⅛ teaspoon ground cloves

2 large, firm peaches, any fuzz washed off (but unpeeled), peaches cut into quarters and pitted

1 pork loin roast (3 ribs, 2¼ to 2½ pounds)

Kosher or fine sea salt and freshly ground black pepper

3 large cloves garlic, slivered

1 medium-size yellow or white onion, cut into ¼-inch-thick rings, rings separated

1. Preheat the oven to 375°F.

2. Combine the scotch, brown sugar, and ground cloves in a large dish and stir to mix. Add the peaches, turn to coat, and set aside.

3. Generously sprinkle the roast all over with salt and pepper, spread the garlic slivers across the top, and place in a roasting pan large enough to also hold the peaches and onions without crowding. Place in the oven and cook until the roast is firm but the juices are still running pink, 25 minutes.

4. Lift the peaches out of the scotch mixture, reserving the liquid. Arrange the peaches in a layer on one side of the roast and spread the onion rings on the other side. Pour the scotch mixture over the peaches and roast, leaving the onions dry. Cook for 10 minutes, stir the peaches, and continue cooking until the meat juices are no longer pink (162°F to 165°F on a meat thermometer), about 10 minutes more. Transfer the meat to a serving platter and set aside in a warm place to rest while the peaches finish cooking.

A PIG, A POTATO, AND A BONE OF CONTENTION

RARELY HAS A PIG BEEN A PIVOT POINT IN HISTORY, but one pig had the distinction. It started a war.

Known as the Pig War, the fray began on June 15, 1859, when Lyman Cutlar, an American settler on San Juan Island in what is now Washington State, shot and killed a trespassing pig belonging to British subject Charles Griffin of Hudson's Bay Company.

"It was eating my potatoes," said Cutlar, who had already warned Griffin about his masher-loving pig. Griffin's reply was that it was up to Cutlar to "keep your potatoes out of my pig."

Normally the shooting of a pig would not matter, but it so happened that relations between the Americans and the British were on a short fuse at that time. Both were claiming the San Juan Islands as their own, and tempers were primed to blow. When British authorities threatened to arrest the porcine executioner, Cutlar's fellow Americans called on the United States military for protection. In response, in marched the U.S. 9th Infantry.

In a clear demonstration of how one warlike act can lead to another, the British immediately dispatched three warships to the area. Americans then sent in more troops, to which the British doubled and redoubled, until Rear Admiral Baynes, of the British naval forces in the Pacific, declared, "I will not involve two great nations in a war over a squabble about a pig." Nonetheless, by August, American forces numbered close to five hundred and the British had four times as many. At this point President James Buchanan charged General Winfield Scott, commanding general of the U.S. Army, to defuse the situation.

The quarrel over the San Juan Islands continued throughout the Civil War until 1872, when the question of ownership was delegated to a third party, King Wilhelm I of Germany, to mediate. He declared the land north of the 49th parallel to be Canadian, the land to the south American, which meant the San Juan Islands indisputably fell to the Americans. The British departed within a month.

What recompense went to Cutlar for his potatoes or Griffin for his swine is not known, the matter having disappeared into the larger scope of history. And what might have happened had the singular sow's disposal led to further war is but a matter of speculation. What remains certain is that pork and potatoes go together, be the potatoes unwittingly bellicose whites or placatory sweets or yams.

5. Continue roasting the peaches and onions until the peaches are lightly glazed and easily pierced with a fork but still hold their shape, about 10 minutes.

6. Arrange the peaches and onion rings around the roast, pour the juices over all, and serve right away.

PORK SHOULDER ROAST WITH RED BELL PEPPER MARMALADE

PORK SHOULDER ROAST, also known as *Boston butt* or *picnic shoulder,* is among the most meltingly, falls-into-tender-slices pork roasts available, yet its richness has not always been recognized. There's a story to be told about that. Around the time of the American Revolution, some pork cuts were not as highly regarded as those considered "high on the hog," like the tenderloin or ham from the leg. Boston butchers cut the shoulder differently than in other regions, so pork shoulder roasts took on their first nickname, Boston butt. Also, since the cut was thought second grade, it was considered not quite appropriate for a fancy dinner, but rather more fitting a picnic, hence the second nickname, picnic shoulder. Following the theme of pork and beans, a combination well known in Boston, here an American bean known by the name of *lima,* after the capital city of its native Peru, is used fresh or frozen to replace the more usual dried beans of pork and beans.

1. To prepare the roast, combine the garlic, rosemary, fennel seeds, salt, and pepper in a small bowl. With your fingers, rub the mixture all over the roast, pressing it into any crevices you find. Place the roast in a dish, cover with plastic wrap, and refrigerate for at least 3 hours or overnight, which is better. Remove from the refrigerator 30 minutes before cooking.

2. Make the marmalade.

3. When ready to cook, preheat the oven to 350°F.

4. Place the roast, fat side up, in a roasting pan and roast until nicely golden on top, 1 hour. Turn the roast over and continue cooking until golden on the other side and just

SERVES 6

INGREDIENTS:

2 cloves garlic, minced

1 teaspoon chopped fresh rosemary

1 teaspoon fennel seeds

2 teaspoons kosher or fine sea salt

1 teaspoon freshly ground black pepper

1 boneless pork shoulder roast (2 to 2½ pounds), tied

Red Bell Pepper Marmalade (recipe follows), for serving

3 cups fresh or frozen lima beans

LITTLE-KNOWN PORKOLOGY

DURING THE WAR OF 1812, a boatload full of barrels of pork was shipped to America's fighting troops under government procurement from a New York pork packer named Sam Wilson. Each barrel was stamped *U.S.* The soldiers knew who sent the pork and thought the U.S. was for Uncle Sam, not United States. Thus "Uncle Sam" came to represent the government.

❯ In early New York City, the hogs owned by many settlers were allowed to range for food wherever they wanted. Some settlers, tired of losing their crops to these marauders, decided to build a wall to limit the hogs' roaming. The street along this border came to be known as Wall Street. Many would say the hogs still hang out there.

❯ In 1818, a man named Elisha Miles opened Cincinnati's first slaughterhouse, and within a decade the city was packing more barrels of brined pork, a food staple at the time, than any other city. So many barrels, in fact, that the city was soon nicknamed Porkopolis. Cincinnatians commonly began to refer to their home as Porkopolis, to the point that in 1839 one proud denizen invented a musical instrument termed the Porco-Forte. It was a keyboard instrument fashioned after a piano, but with a hammer action whereby pigs' tails are pricked as each key is struck, permitting a gradation of squealed notes depending on

the intonation of the pigs and which keys are struck and how hard.

❯ Early telegraph operators became so annoyed at the number of inept operators that they began to call the clumsy ones *hams* for their porky, bumbling fingers. The term carried over to early independent radio operators, thus ham radio.

❯ In eighteenth-century England, a shilling was called a *hog.* Thus a profligate person who spent a whole shilling on something was said to "go the whole hog."

❯ During the Middle Ages, metal was too pricey to use for pots. Instead, cooking vessels were made of a cheap clay called *pygg.* It was the habit of housewives to drop any coin saved into one of their less-used clay pots. They called this their *pygg bank.* In the nineteenth century, potters mistook the now obscure word pygg for "pig" and fashioned coin banks in the shape of the animal.

cooked through (162°F to 165°F on a meat thermometer), 30 to 40 minutes. Remove and set aside to rest in the pan for 10 to 15 minutes for the juices to settle.

5. While the roast cooks and rests, cook the lima beans. Bring a medium-size pot of water to a boil over high heat. Add the beans, reduce the heat to medium-high, and cook until just tender, about 8 minutes for either fresh or frozen limas, regardless of the package instructions. Drain in a colander and set aside.

6. Transfer the roast to a carving board. Add the lima beans to the roasting pan, stir to coat them with the pan juices, and spoon them along with the juices onto a serving platter. Carve the roast into ¼- to ½-inch-thick slices and set the slices atop the beans. Serve with the marmalade on the side.

RED BELL PEPPER MARMALADE

MARMALADE is the Portuguese name originally for a sweet, thick quince paste. In the fifteenth century the paste became known farther afield as both a luxurious sweet treat and as a medicine and was exported to England for both purposes. About the same time, lemons and bitter oranges were beginning to arrive in Tudor England, and as these were at first also turned into thick paste preserves, they too were called marmalades. Soon other fruits were turned into relatively solid confections, and in the 1700s these pastes slowly evolved into a looser jelly containing bits of fruit and fruit peel. The classic "marmalade" soon became the British spreadable jam made of bitter or Seville orange. This was all well before many New World foods, such as red bell peppers, infiltrated Old World cooking and expanded the concept of marmalade. Marmalade of red bell pepper, slightly sugar sweetened and vinegar tarted, makes a fine marmalade to couple with a pork roast.

2 medium-size red bell peppers, stemmed, quartered, seeded, and very thinly sliced

1 small yellow or white onion, halved and very thinly sliced

1½ teaspoons caraway seeds

⅓ cup sugar

⅛ teaspoon cayenne pepper

2½ cups apple juice

¼ cup apple cider vinegar

1. Bring a small pot of water to boil over high heat. Add the bell pepper and onion slices, let come to a boil again, and drain right away.

2. Toast the caraway seeds in an ungreased skillet over medium-high heat or microwave oven on high until starting to pop, 3 to 4 minutes either way.

3. Combine the peppers, onion, caraway seeds, sugar, cayenne, apple juice, and vinegar in a medium-size saucepan and bring to a boil over medium-high heat. Cook for 10 minutes, then reduce the heat to medium and cook, stirring from time to time, until the mixture is thickened and almost candylike but still liquid, about 25 minutes. Remove from the heat and cool slightly, then use right away. Or cool completely and store, covered, in the refrigerator for up to 3 months.

WINE-BRAISED PORK TENDERLOIN
IN ANY-JAM-YOU-CAN-GRAB SAUCE

SERVES 4 TO 6

INGREDIENTS:

2 pork tenderloins
(1 to 1¼ pounds each)

Kosher or fine sea salt and
freshly ground black
pepper

1½ tablespoons extra virgin
olive oil

1 medium-size yellow or
white onion, quartered
and sliced ¼ inch thick

8 cloves garlic, thinly sliced

1½ cups white wine

¼ cup sweet-hot mustard

¼ cup good fruit jam, such
as apricot, peach, currant,
or cherry

PORK AND JAM PRESERVED FROM RIPE SUMMER FRUIT plus some white wine for speedy, moist braising and some mustard for punch allow both the rural and urban cook to put together a meal in 20 minutes that has enough sauce to dollop on a side dish of potatoes or grain. It may not be haute cuisine, but the dish is always haute good.

1. Sprinkle the tenderloins with salt and pepper and cut them in half crosswise. Heat the oil in a heavy sauté pan large enough to hold the tenderloin halves without crowding over medium-high heat. Add the tenderloins to the pan and lightly brown them all over, about 4 minutes. Add the onion and garlic to the pan and continue cooking until they are nicely browned, 4 to 6 minutes.

2. Add the wine, reduce the heat to medium, and simmer, turning the tenderloins occasionally, until partially cooked but still rare in the thickest part, about 5 minutes.

3. Stir the mustard and jam into the pan, increase the heat to medium-high, and cook briskly, turning the tenderloins occasionally, until the meat is no longer pink in the center and the sauce is very thick, 8 to 10 minutes. Transfer the tenderloins to a plate and let rest for 5 minutes for the juices to settle.

4. Cut the tenderloins diagonally into ½-inch-thick slices. Arrange them on a serving platter or individual plates, spoon the sauce over the top, and serve right away.

PORK GYROS WITH RADISH TZATZIKI

PRACTICALLY NO FAST FOOD HAS SPUN AROUND THE WORLD as absolutely as Greece's upright juice-dripping gyros. Spinning as it cooks on myriad upright skewers, the tasty meat is sliced, wrapped in a pita, sauced, topped with onions and more, and ready to devour on the spot. The word *gyros* means "turn," and some say that the dish began with Alexander the Great's soldiers, who wrapped meat around their swords and cooked it by constantly spinning their swords over a fire. Called *souvlaki* in Greece, which still means "sword," stands peddling gyros have stood in every Greek city since Alexander's time, and as Greeks circumnavigated the world, the gyros went with them. Today gyros can be bought and savored in almost every city and town in America.

Traditionally gyros are made of minced lamb, herbs, and spices packed like an upright meat loaf, but in recent years, pork gyros have become the rage. Rather than the classic garlic, cucumber, yogurt *tzatziki* sauce that accompanies the lamb archetype, a radish sauce whirls pork gyros to audacious surprise.

SERVES 4 TO 6

INGREDIENTS:

¼ cup extra virgin olive oil

¼ cup red wine

3 cloves garlic, coarsely chopped

2 teaspoons fresh oregano leaves

1 bay leaf, crumbled

½ teaspoon kosher or fine sea salt

¼ teaspoon coarsely ground black pepper

2 pork tenderloins (1 to 1¼ pounds each)

Radish Tzatziki (recipe follows), for serving

Vegetable oil, for oiling the skillet if cooking on the stove

6 pita breads

1 large red onion, quartered and thinly sliced

2 medium-size tomatoes, thinly sliced

2 cups arugula leaves

1. Mix together the olive oil, wine, garlic, oregano, bay leaf, salt, and pepper in a large dish. Cut the tenderloins in half crosswise, put them in the marinade, turn to coat all around, and set aside in the refrigerator for several hours or up to overnight, turning occasionally. Bring to room temperature before cooking.

2. Make the tzatziki and set it aside.

3. When ready to cook the pork, prepare a medium-hot grill or heat a lightly greased large heavy skillet over medium-high heat.

4. Lift the tenderloins out of the marinade and place them on the grill or in the pan. Cook, turning to brown all around, until no longer pink in the thickest part, 20 to 25 minutes. Transfer to a plate and let sit for 5 minutes for the juices to settle.

THE PORK QUEEN OF IOWA

IOWA IS THE NATION'S NUMBER ONE pork-producing state. There are close to ninety thousand pig farms, and the state markets 25 million hogs annually, a quarter of the nation's total. Several decades ago the hog farmers decided that one of their daughters, in tiara and sash, would help promote their product, and so for fifty years or more, the state of Iowa elected a Pork Queen. The competition included no swimsuits or evening gowns. There was only one talent: pork showing. Questions were asked about only one topic: pigs and their raising. As the queen's job for a year was to represent the interests of the Iowa pork industry, she had to have speaking skills, be able to decode the ear notches that farmers use to tell pigs apart, know the market price for hogs both carcass and live, and have the wherewithal to show up at stores, ride on the hood of a Cadillac in parades, attend county fairs, zoos, and expositions, where often she would hand out samples of pork burgers and pork loins.

Behind the contest was an organization of women called the Porkettes. They organized the Pork Queen contest, promoted pig-related products, and ran a for-profit company called the Iowa Pigskin Sales Company.

The competition for Pork Queen was once lively, as was the competition for other farm titles, Beef Queen, Lamb Queen, Honey Queen, and queens of farm-grown fruits like peach, cherry, and melon. But today many of the crowns have been discontinued. Farmers' daughters have by and large turned their attention to other matters, and the contest has been discontinued.

The demise of the Pork Queen contest comes with a touch of irony. While fewer want to carry on the tradition or tiara, raising pork in Iowa and elsewhere is, in fact, growing tremendously. Americans are serving pork more and more because it is tender and flavorful. Alas, the pork queen may go, but anyone who makes the pork recipes in this chapter has a chance to win the title Queen of the Kitchen.

5. While the pork rests, lightly toast the pitas on the grill or in the pan, turning once, until soft and speckled golden on both sides, 1 to 2 minutes per side.

6. To serve, thinly slice the tenderloins crosswise and place 4 or 5 slices on each pita. Top with several onion and tomato slices. Spoon some of the tzatziki over them and finally top with arugula. Fold and serve with the remaining sauce on the side.

RADISH TZATZIKI

TZATZIKI IS PART SAUCE, part salad. It appears on every Greek and Near Eastern appetizer table and is drizzled over every gyros sandwich, spooned over pilafs, spread over dolmades, dolloped into soups, slathered on fritters. Classic tzatziki features chopped cucumber, but, like cucumbers, radishes have a crisp texture and a zesty juice. Since tzatziki benefits from both these qualities, radish is a natural and colorful twist as a variation on cucumber. While Greek cooks most often add dill to the mixture, mint contributes extra brightness. Either will do; cook's choice.

MAKES ABOUT 1½ CUPS

½ teaspoon kosher or fine sea salt

1 large clove garlic, peeled

1 cup plain Greek yogurt

8 large radishes, trimmed and finely chopped

2 teaspoons chopped fresh mint or dill

1. Spread the salt on a cutting board. Place the garlic on top of the salt and finely chop it into the salt.

2. Combine the yogurt, garlic and salt mix, radishes, and mint in a small bowl. Whisk to mix and smooth. Chill before using, but eat the tzatziki on the day that you make it.

SMOKE-TINGED PORK CHOPS WITH THAI PEANUT SAUCE

NEXT TO BEEFSTEAKS, pork chops have long been America's preferred quick, easy, and economical choice. Tender and tasty, they offer a worthy contrast to the "redness" of other meats. Their possibilities are legion. They can be cooked in a zesty Spanish style, creamy French, fruited Pacific, or jerked the Caribbean way, among others. Dotted with a sauce laced with another American favorite food, peanuts, they can also be turned out in the style of the Malaysian peninsula. Slow grilling gives the chops a smoky tinge, which boosts the island aura.

1. Prepare a medium-hot grill or heat a large heavy skillet to medium-hot.

2. Season the pork chops with salt and pepper on both sides. Place on the grill directly over the heat or in the skillet. Cover and cook, turning once, until just cooked through, about 20 minutes altogether. Transfer to a platter and set aside in a warm place.

3. While the chops cook, make the peanut sauce and set it aside.

4. To serve, place the pork chops on a platter or individual plates and spoon the sauce over all.

THAI PEANUT SAUCE

SPICY PEANUT SAUCE as a dip for skewered meat, chicken, or fish or as a dressing for salads and vegetables has taken America by storm. Coconut milk and a mixture of herbs and spices make the sauce both silky and stout.

INGREDIENTS:

4 pork loin chops (about 10 ounces each), cut 1 inch thick

Kosher or fine sea salt and freshly ground black pepper

Thai Peanut Sauce (recipe follows), for serving

PEANUTS:
THE NUT THAT'S NOT A NUT

DESPITE ITS PLACE on grocer shelves and on our tables, the peanut is not a nut. As its name indicates, it is a legume, in the same family as peas and beans. As the name also indicates, it is a legume with a particularly nutty flavor. From its first arrival in America, the peanut became such an important and popular food crop that it took on a number of appellations: *groundnut, ground pea, goober pea, monkey nut,* and *pinder* to name a few, some of these, like goober, being names of African tribal origin.

The peanut was a pilgrim to our shores. Like many immigrants, its journey here was circuitous and not entirely planned. It seems the peanut first grew in Peru or western Brazil. Though no fossil record traces of the wild peanut exist, the people of these lands have been making peanut-shaped clay jars for 3,500 years. When the Spanish vanquished Peru and the Portuguese conquered Brazil, they took the nourishing and rather curious legume back with them to Europe. They also took peanuts to Mexico and Haiti, and as both the Spanish and Portuguese had long plundered the African coasts, somewhere on one of these voyages the

peanut jumped ship to become an important African staple. From Africa it was brought by captured slaves to North America, in particular to the South, where initially it served as a garden crop and a familiar food that plantation slaves could raise for themselves. From its cultivation as slave food, plantation owners used it for oil and food and as a substitute for cocoa. George Washington Carver, a man born into slavery who became a botanist, improved the plant and invented peanut butter and many other uses for the peanut. The peanut continued its journey, eventually showing up as a highly popular snack and cooking ingredient. Today the largest crop of peanuts is grown in China, and it figures as an almost daily food in Southeast Asian cuisine.

We eat peanuts as a snack, but overwhelmingly we eat them as peanut butter. It is a signature dish of childhood—a peanut butter sandwich and a glass of milk provide 83 percent of a growing child's daily need for protein, and although we theoretically outgrow it, peanut butter remains a lifelong adoration for many.

½ cup salted roasted peanuts

1 cup coconut milk (regular, not low-fat)

2 tablespoons finely chopped scallion, white and light green parts only

1 tablespoon fish sauce, preferably Thai

2 teaspoons chopped fresh cilantro leaves

1 teaspoon finely chopped jalapeño chile

1 teaspoon chopped fresh mint leaves

Finely grind the peanuts in a food processor. Bring the coconut milk to a boil in a small saucepan over medium-high heat. Stir in the peanuts, scallion, fish sauce, cilantro, jalapeño, and mint and remove from the heat. Cool to room temperature and serve.

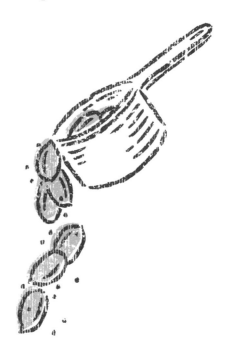

PINE-NUT-CRUSTED PORK SCHNITZELS WITH WILTED CHICORY AND GREEN APPLE

SCHNITZEL IS THE GERMAN WORD FOR MEAT CUTLETS, a much loved bistro and family fare from Germany to Austria, Switzerland, Hungary, Serbia, Croatia, and beyond. In their most recognized rendering, wiener schnitzel, a classic of Viennese cooking, the schnitzels are made from veal cutlets, or fillets, but schnitzels can also be forged from chicken or pork cutlets.

For schnitzels, the cutlets are pounded thin (although now very thin cutlets can be purchased), then dusted with flour, dipped in egg so they can hold a batter, and finally patted with a crusting, traditionally of fine bread crumbs. As the cutlets came to American cooking, brought by Germans and Austro-Hungarians, they kept their persona of refined but simple fare. Here the cutlets are newly dressed in a coat of pine nuts and made glittery with a garnish of bitter chicory and sweet-tart green apple wilted in a spiky balsamic vinaigrette.

1. Unless the cutlets are already very thin, pound them between sheets of plastic wrap or wax paper with a meat hammer or other pounding device until they are no more than ¼ inch thick. Spread the pine nuts out on a plate. Dust each cutlet on both sides with flour. Dip each briefly in the beaten egg and lightly sprinkle each side with salt and pepper. One at a time, pat pine nuts into both sides of each cutlet. Transfer the cutlets to another plate as you go.

2. In a heavy sauté pan large enough to hold the cutlets without crowding, melt the butter over medium heat until foaming. Add the cutlets and cook until golden on the bottom, 2 minutes. Turn the cutlets over and cook until golden

SERVES 4 TO 6

INGREDIENTS:

- 6 thin pork cutlets (about 1¼ pounds total)
- 1 cup pine nuts, finely ground
- All-purpose flour, for dusting the cutlets
- 1 large egg, beaten
- Kosher or fine sea salt and freshly ground white pepper
- 6 tablespoons butter
- 1 cup packed shredded chicory or escarole
- 1 Granny Smith or Pippin apple, quartered, cored, and grated through the large holes of a grater
- 1½ tablespoons extra virgin olive oil
- 1 tablespoon balsamic vinegar
- 2 teaspoons red wine
- 1 small clove garlic, minced or pressed

on the second side and just cooked through, 2 to 3 minutes more. If the butter starts to burn, reduce the heat slightly. Transfer to a serving platter or individual plates and set aside in a warm place.

3. Place the chicory and green apple in a bowl. Combine the olive oil, vinegar, red wine, and garlic in a small pan. Bring to a boil over high heat, then immediately pour the mixture over the chicory and apple. Toss gently to mix.

4. Arrange the chicory and apple to the side of the cutlets and serve right away.

THE BLIND PIGS OF DETROIT

SINCE ITS FOUNDING, Detroit, Michigan, has always been a city of many ethnic groups. Among the first were populations of Eastern Europe—the Czechs, Slovakians, Slovenians, Bohemians, Moravians, Polish, Ukrainians, and along with them Germans from Bavaria, Alsace, Silesia, and Prussia. All were from areas where pork was the mainstay meat, fresh and preserved, and all were devotees of the pounded, breaded pork known by the German term *schnitzel*. In Detroit eateries and households, pork dishes continued to be favored and served with the preferred beverage, beer. But the pigs that provided the pork to fill these plates were not Detroit's only pigs. For a goodly period of the city's history, there were also numerous "Blind Pigs."

On May 1, 1917, as part of a fervor that was sweeping the country, Michigan approved a statewide prohibition on the sale of beer, liquor, and wine, which was redoubled when in January 1919 the federal government, in the Volstead Act, prohibited all alcoholic drink nationwide. Michigan, however, occupied a unique location. The Detroit River that separated Michigan from Canada was in places less than a mile across, and along its twenty-eight-mile border were coves and rocky shoals aplenty. While Canada had also outlawed the retail sale of liquor, it hadn't outlawed *making* liquor. Indeed, in Ontario alone, just across from Detroit, there were forty-five distilleries and breweries. As a result, Detroit rapidly became a smuggler's as well as a drinker's haven.

In no time at all, cargoes of booze from Canada found their way first in boat holds and then even through a pipeline into a willing Detroit. Some of the beverage was quickly dispersed to other places around the country, but much found its way to secret watering holes around Detroit. *Speakeasy* was a common term for such hidden drinking establishments, but Detroit had its own term, too. The places were called *blind pigs*.

At one point more than twenty-five thousand blind pigs were operating in Detroit. They took the cover of private clubs, hidden taverns, restaurant back rooms, and storefronts. A customer could buy a shot of liquor from a car parked in the lot of an auto plant, and one man operated a blind pig directly across the street from police headquarters. Free lunches were common in blind pigs because they drew in the hungry as well as the thirsty.

Unfortunately, the enormity of the illegal liquor business and its profit spawned serious violence. Stray bullets and hijackings were not uncommon. Eventually an outraged U.S. citizenry tired of the absurd attempt at quenching a clearly unquenchable thirst and forced a repeal of the Volstead Act. The once blind pigs of Detroit were thrust again to visibility.

STUFFED CALIFORNIA
PORK ROLLS

THE FIRST DATE PALMS IN AMERICA were planted in California as seedlings by Franciscan and Jesuit missionaries in 1769; whole potted shoots of date trees from Egypt were brought around 1890. Agricultural entrepreneurs sought to create a native date market, and similar introductions were made to southern Arizona, particularly around Tempe and Phoenix. Much the same happened with the importation of almonds to America. Franciscan monks brought them to coastal missions, but it wasn't until farmers moved them from the coast to inland California that they flourished. Now California is the largest producer of almonds in the world. Early on, farmers used both dates and almonds to fatten pigs and make the meat more flavorful. That tradition is followed here in a truly California dish of thin pork cutlets rolled around a compound of dates and almonds with a dash of California's famous orange for gusto.

1. To make the stuffing, place the dates, orange, almonds, bread crumbs, lemon juice, tarragon leaves, ½ teaspoon salt, and allspice in a food processor and process until minced to a paste. Transfer to a bowl and set aside.

2. Spread the cutlets out on a work surface. Place 1½ to 2 tablespoons stuffing along the center of each cutlet. Roll the cutlet over the stuffing, taking care that no stuffing spills out the ends, overlap the meat at the top, and secure with a toothpick. Sprinkle each roll with salt and pepper.

3. In a sauté pan large enough to hold all the rolls in a single layer, melt the butter over medium-high heat. Place the rolls in the pan and brown all around, about 6 minutes. Add the wine, cover the skillet, and simmer until the meat is just done, about 8 minutes. Transfer the rolls to a platter and set aside in a warm place.

4. Increase the heat to high and continue simmering the sauce until thick enough to coat a spoon, 3 to 4 minutes.

5. Drizzle the sauce over the top of the rolls, sprinkle with the parsley leaves, and serve.

SERVES 4 TO 6

INGREDIENTS:

1 cup pitted dates, chopped

1 medium-size navel orange, peeled and separated into sections

½ cup slivered almonds

½ cup bread crumbs, preferably homemade (page 41)

1 tablespoon fresh lemon juice

2 teaspoons fresh tarragon leaves

½ teaspoon kosher or fine sea salt, plus more for sprinkling on the pork rolls

⅛ teaspoon ground allspice

12 boneless pork cutlets (about 2½ pounds total), cut or pounded ¼ inch thick

Freshly ground black pepper

4 tablespoons (½ stick) butter

1 cup white wine

2 tablespoons fresh parsley leaves

SWEET AND SPICY BABY BACK RIBS WITH APRICOT SOY GLAZE

SERVES 4 TO 6

INGREDIENTS:

½ cup apricot preserves

2 large cloves garlic, minced or pressed

¼ teaspoon cracked Sichuan pepper or white peppercorns

¼ cup fresh lime juice

¼ cup white wine

1 tablespoon light soy sauce

2 slabs pork baby back ribs (2½ to 3 pounds), each cut into thirds

Vegetable oil, for oiling the baking sheets if baking

10 to 12 fresh cilantro sprigs, for garnish

A WAVE OF POLYNESIAN-STYLE FOOD swept across America in the 1950s. It started with a small shack-style restaurant called Trader Vic's in Emeryville, California, not so far from the docks of San Francisco and the yawning Pacific Ocean. The popularity was almost instantaneous, not only because of the mainland's introduction to the different and delightful tastes, but also because the food evoked images of palm-tree-lined beaches and romantic island escapes. Since pork is the major meat of the Polynesian islands, many of the dishes featured it, among them always a pupu, or appetizer, of sweet and spicy ribs. A few little ribs may satisfy taste buds, but not the desire for a full plate. Here the serving has grown to platter size, and the Polynesian glaze with a little Asian-style twist is slightly sweetened with a European apricot accent. Sichuan pepper's fragrant spiciness adds an exceptional subtlety to the tender ribs; white peppercorns, less mature and nuttier than black ones, make a good substitute.

1. Stir together the apricot preserves, garlic, cracked pepper, lime juice, wine, and soy sauce in a small bowl. Place the ribs in a large dish, add the apricot mixture, and turn to coat the ribs all around. Set aside in the refrigerator for at least 1 hour, up to overnight.

2. When ready to cook the ribs, preheat the oven to 375°F or prepare a medium-hot grill.

3. Place the ribs on 2 lightly greased rimmed baking sheets large enough to hold them without crowding or on the grill directly over the heat. Bake or grill, turning 3 or 4 times to prevent sticking and burning, until the ribs are sizzling and cooked through, 30 to 40 minutes, depending on the size. Transfer to a platter, garnish with the cilantro sprigs, and serve right away.

PICKING FROM THE PECK OF PEPPERS

THE PEPPER THAT AMERICANS NORMALLY cook and season with is not the only sort of sprinkling pepper available. There are many kinds to add both heat and sapor. The one we grind or purchase already milled, in its various colors of black, white, and green, is true pepper, which comes from the *Piper nigrum* vine, native to India, though it is grown in many places nowadays. Once introduced, the pepper berry ultimately won the favor of the kitchens and tables of Europe and eventually much of the world. It developed into a major commodity in the spice route trade, actually prompting many of the early voyages of discovery, and was so valuable that rich people were known as *pepper pockets*. It remains the second-most-used spice after salt.

But there are other kinds of pepper used both in cooking and as a tabletop seasoning, and they are not at all the same, not even botanically. Sichuan pepper, commonly called *Chinese* or *brown pepper*, is not a true pepper berry. Rather it is the berry of a variety of prickly ash tree native to the Sichuan province in China. It is used in Chinese cooking to lend a sharp, somewhat woodsy note in the dish or as a component in the now-familiar Chinese five-spice blend.

Other table "peppers" include red peppercorns, actually the berries of a variety of sumac tree, and sansho, or Japanese pepper, which is the berry of a variety of prickly ash tree. Yet another type, long pepper, was the first kind to reach the Western world, and is now mostly used in its native South Asia, though American chefs flirt with it from time to time. Guinea pepper comes from the custard-apple family of western Africa. Cubeb pepper, from Indonesia, was once popular but later shunned for its roughness to the digestive tract. Others include drunk pepper, also from Indonesia and used in Polynesia; rose pepper, a berry from the Peruvian mastic tree; and melegueta pepper, a member of the ginger family. All are available in ethnic and online food stores and are worth trying.

The capsicum peppers, both bells of many colors and chiles from large to small, poblanos and Anaheims to jalapeños, serranos, and habaneros, to name but a few, come from the New World and are a plant of a different order. They gained the pepper name and entrance to the pepper clan from their bite, generally more forceful than peppercorns, and from the use of many of them in dried form either as flakes or powder, notably paprika, cayenne, and Aleppo. All are now used as much as *Piper nigrum* berries, sprinkled on foods around the globe.

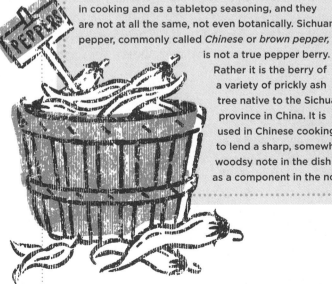

MESA-STYLE PORK AND CORN STEW WITH HERBED SOPAPILLAS

SERVES 4

INGREDIENTS:

¼ cup vegetable oil

2 pounds boneless pork butt or shoulder steaks, trimmed of fat and cut into 1½-inch pieces

Kosher or fine sea salt and freshly ground black pepper

2 yellow or white onions, finely chopped

1 quart water

2 tablespoons pure chile powder

Herbed Sopapillas (recipe follows), for serving

1 cup corn kernels, preferably fresh (from 2 small ears)

2 tablespoons fresh lime juice

8 tender fresh cilantro sprigs, for garnish

IN EVERY LAND WHERE PORK IS ENJOYED, a version of pork stew exists. In Jamaica, the dish has rum. In Indonesia, the stewing liquid is a curry. In Italy's Piedmont, white beans or pearly barley may be included. In the Caucasus mountain country of Georgia, the stew contains cilantro and marigold. But it's mesa-style pork stew from south of the border that American cooks favor over many others. Along with succulent chunks of pork are niblets of corn in a broth warmed with spicy but not too hot chile powder. With the stew come steamy tortilla puffs called *sopapillas*. Fresh and easy to make, sopapillas are basically flour tortillas leavened with baking powder so they puff up when fried. Here they are turned savory with summer savory, a mountain herb seasoning.

1. Heat 2 tablespoons of the oil in a large, heavy pot over medium-high heat. Season the pork with salt and pepper and put in as many pieces as will fit in the pot without crowding. Brown all over, 3 to 4 minutes, then transfer the pieces to a plate and set aside. Repeat with the remaining meat.

2. Reduce the heat to medium. Add the remaining 2 tablespoons oil and the onions to the pot, and cook, stirring occasionally, until wilted, 3 to 4 minutes. Return the pork and collected juices to the pot, add the water and chile powder, and stir to mix. Bring to a boil over high heat, then reduce the heat to maintain a gentle simmer. Cover and cook until the pork is fork-tender and the liquid is deep red-brown, 2 hours.

3. While the stew simmers, make the sopapillas.

4. Add the corn to the stew and cook over medium-high heat until the corn is soft, 3 to 5 minutes. Sprinkle with the lime juice and garnish with the cilantro. Serve right away, with the sopapillas on the side.

HERBED SOPAPILLAS

SOPAPILLAS ARE A typical treat of southwestern cooking, especially that of New Mexico, land of high mesas and chile plantations. There they are customarily served as a dessert dish, drizzled with honey or dusted with powdered sugar. Here they are seasoned aromatically and turned into a sauce sopper. To make them a sweet treat, eliminate the summer savory and add a teaspoon of sugar to the dough. When they are cooked, stream honey over them or dust them with powdered sugar.

MAKES 12

1½ cups all-purpose flour, plus flour for rolling out the dough

2 teaspoons baking powder

1 teaspoon dried summer savory

½ teaspoon kosher or fine sea salt

Peanut or canola oil

½ cup warm water

1. Combine the flour, baking powder, summer savory, and salt in a food processor and pulse briefly to mix. Add 3 tablespoons of oil and pulse until crumbly. Add the water and pulse until the mixture can be gathered into a ball. Transfer the mixture to a lightly floured surface and knead until the dough is smooth and elastic, about 3 minutes. Cover with a damp towel and set aside to rest for 30 minutes or up to 2 hours. Or wrap in plastic wrap and refrigerate for up to 2 days, bringing to room temperature before proceeding.

2. Roll out the dough into a 12-inch square about ⅛ inch thick. Cut it into 12 triangles.

3. Pour oil to a depth of 3 inches into a wide, deep, heavy pot and heat over medium-high heat until a piece of dough dropped in sizzles. A few at a time, add as many triangles as will fit without crowding and fry until puffed up and risen to the top, about 1 minute. Turn and continue frying until golden on the second side, about 30 seconds. Transfer to paper towels and continue with another batch until all the sopapillas are fried. Serve right away or set aside in a warm place for up to 30 minutes.

GAME: FOOD FROM THE WILD

All the first settlers who came to North America hunted game. The bounty of wild fauna from coast to coast was truly incomparable. Here they discovered venison, elk, moose, bear, wild birds, turtles, rabbits, raccoon, and, thriving by the millions, the great American bison called buffalo. Tracking down wildlife often meant survival. As the country lost its last frontiers, it left its wild ways and began raising great herds of cattle, sheep, and pigs. Game meat fell from eminence to rarity.

Still, that love of game has stayed with many Americans. In some families the custom of hunting and serving wild game has been passed down for generations. While hunting was once the only way to enjoy game, now game birds, rabbit, venison, buffalo, and elk are being farm-raised and

WHERE THE BUFFALO ROAMED— AND DO AGAIN

THE ANCESTORS OF THE AMERICAN BISON we call buffalo crossed from Asia to North America around 200,000 years ago. By the time people arrived, herds were thriving on the grasslands from the Adirondacks to the Ozarks, the Rockies to the Sierras. However, the Great Plains and prairie land of mid-America formed their perfect habitat. In their heyday, thirty to sixty million roamed there. With their rugged structure and dense coats, they were built to endure the plains' fierce winds, harsh winters, and burning summers. At one point, they were the most numerous grazing animal on earth, far surpassing the herds of the African savannas.

The sight of them must have been magnificent to behold. They were surprisingly agile and fast, able to run up to fifty miles per hour. Still, they were wild. Even today, ranch-raised buffalo aren't domesticated and can be lethal. Their wildness remains part of their magnificence.

At first Native Americans were able to hunt the buffalo only by collectively encircling on foot a few stragglers or by driving some over a cliff. When a number of tribes acquired and began to foster the horses brought by the Spanish, they were able to move to the plains and hunt buffalo as their main subsistence. The buffalo provided food and shelter, clothing from hides; rope from the rawhide; fuel from buffalo chips; jewelry, decorative beads, masks, and rattles from bones; cups and spoons from the horns. They were the objects of myth and lore.

Then came "the great slaughter" from 1872 to about 1885, when the animals were killed by the thousands for their valuable hides and not for food. As well, white hunters and settlers, encouraged by the American government, initiated a mass killing of the animals as a way to control the native tribes who survived on them.

If it had not been for a few concerned Americans late in the nineteenth century, the buffalo would have become extinct. When President Grover Cleveland made it illegal to kill buffalo in 1894, there were only three hundred left. But several farsighted and sentimental men who loved the Great Plains, such as Charles Goodnight and Samuel Walking Coyote, along with the National Park and Forest Services, came forward to save the magnificent animal. They secured and fostered the few remaining herds, and the great American buffalo was saved from the brink of extinction.

Now the buffalo are coming back. Herds again flourish in all fifty American states, and their numbers total close to 350,000. Buffalo are a source of nutritious, low-fat meat. They are easy and cheap to raise. Meanwhile, under careful stewardship they are returning to the prairie grasses on which they once thrived.

brought to butchers and grocery store meat cases everywhere.

We herald the homecoming with a round of recipes beginning with the king of American game, once almost lost to us, buffalo. The rich, beefy, lean meat dotes on gumptious accompaniments, and so we add onions, peppercorns, vinegar, and red wine to everything from steaks to chili. Venison and elk provide rich meat, too, and take to herbs, sour cherries, and zesty apple. The fine white meat of rabbit supports an arc of hearty flavors, from root vegetables to a stew bubbling with tomato and onion. And game birds from quail to squab to pheasant are so adaptable they can unite with homeland companions like corn bread and international fillips like grape leaves.

PAN-SEARED
BUFFALO STEAKS
WITH VINEGAR-GLAZED
ROASTED ONIONS

BUFFALO STEAKS BRING TO THE PLATE A WEALTH OF CHARAC-TER. The meat is lean and robust, like the lushest beef steak. Indeed the word *beefy* is buffalo's most apt description. Almost any way a good brawny beefsteak can be cooked applies as well to buffalo. The meat stands up to a bold herb such as marjoram and welcomes a bold red wine like cabernet contrasted with vinegar-glazed onions and the pungency of hand-cracked peppercorns.

1. Sprinkle both sides of the steaks with salt and set aside at room temperature.

2. Prepare the onions.

3. To cook the steaks, heat a lightly greased heavy sauté pan large enough to hold the steaks without crowding over medium-high heat until a drop of water sizzles on contact. Add the steaks and cook, turning once, for 8 to 12 minutes for medium-rare. Transfer the steaks to a platter and set aside in a warm place.

4. Add the marjoram, peppercorns, and wine to the sauté pan and stir to mix. Increase the heat to high and cook until the wine is reduced enough to lightly coat a spoon, about 6 minutes. Whisk in the butter pieces to make a smooth sauce. Pour over the steaks, garnish the platter with the onions, and serve.

INGREDIENTS:

4 buffalo steaks
(8 to 10 ounces each),
cut ½ to ¾ inch thick

Kosher or fine sea salt

Vinegar-Glazed Roasted
Onions (recipe follows),
for serving

Oil, for greasing the sauté
pan

1 tablespoon chopped fresh
marjoram leaves or
1½ teaspoons dried

2 teaspoons black
peppercorns, coarsely
cracked with a mallet

2 cups cabernet sauvignon

4 tablespoons (½ stick)
butter, cut up

WHO WAS BUFFALO BILL?

WILLIAM FREDERICK CODY, the man who came to be called Buffalo Bill, was born on February 26, 1846, in a frontier farmhouse in Le Claire, Iowa. Over the course of his lifetime he rose to become one of the most vibrant and charismatic figures of the Old West—a Pony Express rider, a soldier, a scout, and finally a flamboyant showman.

Cody's family was one of the intrepid early American sorts that kept moving west. When Cody was still a boy, they moved from Iowa farther west to Kansas. When his father died in 1857 and eleven-year old Cody was left to support the family, he took advantage of his frontier upbringing to provide for them.

At just fourteen, he became one of the renowned riders for the Pony Express, and after that scouted for the army. He participated in the great slaughter of the buffalo for their hides but in so doing took to supplying buffalo meat to the workers on the westward-moving railroad. It was for that he was dubbed Buffalo Bill.

As the Wild West was becoming no longer wild, Cody entered show business, capitalizing on what he knew. He put together a mix of western-themed spectacles, called it Buffalo Bill's Wild West Show, and took to the road.

The show opened in Omaha, Nebraska, in 1883. Cody performed sharpshooting exhibitions, both standing and riding his horse. He hired the country's most celebrated lady shooter, Annie Oakley, who could hit just about anything stationary or moving. He hired galloping horse riders who could spin themselves over and under a moving horse and reenacted stage coach holdups. He brought in famous Native American chiefs Red Cloud and, at times, the infamous Sitting Bull. He performed in London in honor of the Jubilee of Queen Victoria. He met Pope Leo XIII.

Bill Cody was the most famed celebrity of his time, and when he died in Denver on January 10, 1917, twenty thousand people attended his funeral. He is buried on Colorado's Lookout Mountain, one of his favorite places.

VINEGAR-GLAZED ROASTED ONIONS

THE BITE OF raw onion often disguises how dulcet onions can be and how readily they can turn into a sweet-sour treat. It only takes a dash of balsamic vinegar to buttress the onions' sweetness with a reviving tartness. Curious as it may seem, it also makes the onions more vegetable to the taste.

SERVES 4 TO 6

20 small boiling onions, peeled

2 teaspoons extra virgin olive oil

Kosher or fine sea salt and freshly ground black pepper

1½ tablespoons balsamic vinegar

1. Preheat the oven to 375°F.

2. Spread the onions out on a rimmed baking sheet, drizzle with the oil, sprinkle with salt and pepper, and turn to coat well. Place the baking sheet in the oven and roast the onions until they are tender all the way through, about 40 minutes. Sprinkle the vinegar over the onions and continue roasting uncovered until nicely glazed, about 5 minutes. Serve right away or set aside in a warm place for up to 30 minutes.

BUFFALO STEAKS WITH RED BELL PEPPER AND GREEN PEPPERCORN PUREE

FLAVOR IS WHAT BUFFALO STEAKS ARE ALL ABOUT, a remarkable asset in a meat that is leaner than beef, leaner than salmon, leaner than turkey! The taste is declarative and satisfying. Though beef steaks can well support an assertive sauce, the advantage lies with buffalo when it comes to accompanying a strapping steak with a stimulating topping such as a double-pepper puree. To have beef steaks in a pepper sauce or a pepper crust is rather classic. To feast on buffalo steak with a topping of two kinds of pepper, the corn and the capsicum both, is like turning a classic car into a rocket.

SERVES 4

INGREDIENTS:

4 buffalo steaks (8 to 10 ounces each), cut ½ to ¾ inch thick

Kosher or fine sea salt

1 medium-size red bell pepper, stemmed, seeded, and coarsely chopped

1 teaspoon green peppercorns

½ cup water

1. Prepare a medium-hot grill. Sprinkle both sides of the steaks with salt and set them aside at room temperature.

2. To make the puree, combine the bell pepper, peppercorns, ½ teaspoon salt, and the water in a small saucepan and bring to a boil over medium-high heat. Cover the pan and cook for 5 minutes, until the red pepper is somewhat soft. Continue cooking, uncovered, until the pepper is very soft and the liquid is almost gone, 5 minutes more. Remove the pan from the heat and set aside to cool for 10 minutes. Transfer the pepper mixture to a food processor and puree as fine as possible. Set aside at room temperature until ready to serve.

3. Place the steaks on the grill rack directly over the heat. Cook, turning once, for 8 to 12 minutes for medium-rare. Transfer to a platter and set aside for 5 minutes for the juices to settle.

4. Place a dollop of puree on each steak and serve with the remaining puree on the side.

BUFFALO CHILI WITH BLACK BEAN AND CORN SALSA

SERVES 4

INGREDIENTS:

2 tablespoons vegetable oil

1 large yellow or white onion, coarsely chopped

2 cloves garlic, coarsely chopped

1½ pounds ground buffalo

½ teaspoon kosher or fine sea salt

½ teaspoon freshly ground black pepper

2 tablespoons pure chile powder

1 teaspoon chopped fresh sage leaves or ½ teaspoon dried

1 teaspoon ground cumin

1½ cups chopped canned tomatoes with juices

2 cups water

Black Bean and Corn Salsa (recipe follows), for serving

8 to 12 flour tortillas, for serving

GROUND BUFFALO IS SHOWING UP IN MORE AND MORE supermarkets. It's lean, full of nutrients, and chunkily chopped. It offers rich, ruddy beef flavor and has a special advantage: It brings home the spirit of an Old West chuck wagon. Ground buffalo makes an ultra-hardy chili con carne, a dish that dates from frontier times and rates as a western classic. In essence, chili con carne is a meat stew, rounded out with onion, garlic, tomato, southwestern herbs and spices. The ingredient that makes it an iconic dish is pure chile powder. Sometime beans are included or, as here, they are mixed with corn and combined in a salsa to dollop on top.

1. Heat the oil in a large, heavy pot over medium-high heat. Add the onion and garlic and sauté until barely wilted, about 2 minutes. Add the meat, salt, and pepper and stir to mix, breaking up the meat as you go. Continue cooking until the meat is no longer red, about 5 minutes.

2. Stir in the chile powder, sage, and cumin. Mix in the tomatoes and water and bring to a boil. Reduce the heat to maintain a simmer, and cook, partially covered, until the meat is tender but still a little chewy and there is some liquid left in the pot, 1 hour.

3. Cover completely so more liquid doesn't evaporate and continue cooking until the chili is thick and saucy, about 30 minutes more. Remove the pot from the heat and let the chili rest for 15 minutes or set aside for up to several hours and reheat briefly before serving.

4. While the chili simmers, make the salsa.

5. Just before serving, warm the tortillas in a low oven or toaster oven.

6. To serve, ladle the chili into individual bowls. Place a large spoonful of the salsa on top and serve right away with the warm tortillas on the side.

BLACK BEAN AND CORN SALSA

FOR A COOK, a jar of salsa in the refrigerator is like money in the bank. For its expected zing plus a little crunch, the ingredients should be in small pieces rather than minced. Also, for salsa making, it's best to leave the seeds from peppers in the mix: They add soft spice to the life of the salsa.

MAKES ABOUT 2½ CUPS

1 cup cooked black beans

½ cup fresh corn kernels (about 1 medium-size ear)

1 medium-size tomato, cut into ¼-inch dice

1 small jalapeño chile, finely chopped

½ medium-size red bell pepper, stemmed, seeded, and cut into ¼-inch dice

½ medium-size green bell pepper, stemmed, seeded, and cut into ¼-inch dice

2 tablespoons fresh cilantro leaves

2 tablespoons fresh lime juice

2 tablespoons extra virgin olive oil

½ teaspoon kosher or fine sea salt

A CHILI HISTORY

CHILI STARTED AS A SOUTHWESTERN DISH made by the chuck wagon "cookie" to feed the hardworking, trail-weary wranglers on cattle drives. Along the long drives, buffalo, venison, antelope, and cattle furnished the meat. Chili was so well liked cowpokes wanted it even back in the bunkhouse. Soon so did ranchers, townspeople, and then city people, and so it spread from West to East until it became an American standard.

There is plain chili, a blend of stewed pinto beans and powdered chile, and then there is the same but with the addition of meat. The dish with meat is called *chili con carne,* which means "chile peppers with meat." By the 1880s, "chili queens," women who made a living selling chili, appeared on the squares of San Antonio, Texas. The 1893 Exposition in Chicago featured a San Antonio Chili Stand. In 1914, Fanny Farmer included the dish in her cookbook for home cooks.

Perhaps in reflection of the original cookies, somehow the dish became the province of men, and competitions between chili cooks led to a multitude of festive contests with men manning the stove. Chili mixes appeared under the names of those who claimed their own secret blend of spices. Two-Alarm Chili, created by Wick Fowler, a north Texas newsman, in 1970, was reputed to open eighteen sinus cavities unknown to the medical profession.

The versions today often use chili powder spice blends and sometimes fresh chiles. Other beans such as red kidney beans have been substituted for pinto beans. In short, there are almost as many variations of chili as there are bowls of it. But for the meat, why not go back to at least one early Old West element? Use buffalo.

Place the beans, corn, tomato, chile, bell peppers, cilantro, lime juice, olive oil, and salt in a large bowl and gently stir to mix. Set aside at room temperature for 1 to 2 hours for the flavors to blend or refrigerate for up to 2 days.

ROAST LOIN OF VENISON
WITH THYME-FOR-WINE SAUCE

INGREDIENTS:

1 carrot, coarsely chopped

1 rib celery, coarsely chopped

1 small yellow or white onion, coarsely chopped

1 large clove garlic, coarsely chopped

6 fresh thyme sprigs

3 whole cloves

2 teaspoons black peppercorns, cracked with a mallet

1 bay leaf, crumbled

1 teaspoon kosher or fine sea salt

¼ cup extra virgin olive oil

1 venison roast (2 pounds) from the loin or upper haunch

2 strips bacon

3 cups red wine

6 tablespoons (¾ stick) butter

EVEN WHEN FARM-RAISED, the flavor of venison touches on the wild and sylvan, recalling the ferns, bark, grasses, and garden flowers that the deer forage on. Venison is increasingly available in supermarkets and butcher shops. The cuts are many—steaks, rib racks, flank, medallions, shanks, saddles, stew meat, shoulder roast, and tenderloin. When choosing a cut, consider that the farther from the head and feet, the more tender the meat and the faster the cooking. Closer to the head and feet, the cuts are better treated with marinating and then slow cooking. All merit fun to fancy to hardy accents to accentuate the forest bouquet.

1. Combine the carrot, celery, onion, garlic, thyme, cloves, peppercorns, bay leaf, salt, and olive oil in a large, deep dish. Add the venison and turn to coat all around. Cover with plastic wrap and set aside in the refrigerator for at least 4 hours or up to overnight, turning once or twice. Remove from the refrigerator 30 minutes before cooking.

2. When ready to cook, preheat the oven to 375°F.

3. Transfer the venison and marinade to a Dutch oven or other heavy pot. Drape the bacon slices at equal intervals across the top of the venison, place the pot in the oven, and roast until done to your liking, 45 to 55 minutes for medium-rare (130°F to 135°F on a meat thermometer), depending on the thickness of the cut.

4. When the roast is done, remove and discard the bacon slices, transfer the roast to a serving platter, and set aside in a warm place. Pour the marinade, including the vegetables and herbs, into a wide, heavy saucepan. Add the wine and bring to a boil over high heat. Reduce the heat to maintain a brisk simmer and reduce the sauce by half, about 15 minutes. Using a wire strainer, lift out and discard the solid ingredients and continue cooking until the sauce is thick and bubbly, about 10 minutes more. Slowly whisk in the butter to make a thick, glossy sauce. Pour over the roast and serve right away.

RACK OF VENISON
WITH SOUR CHERRY SAUCE

RACKS OF four to eight ribs of venison make for a great company dinner. The thin layer of fat on the very lean meat adds a crisp and moist coating, while the bone, as always, invites transfixed nibbling. Fruit of all sorts provides an artful saucing for venison, sour cherries in particular. Fresh sour cherries have a short season at the beginning of summer, starting just before the sweet cherries come in. At other times, dried tart cherries are a fine substitute. Bold herbs, bay, thyme, and juniper berries round out the saucing.

1. In a large roasting pan, stir together the wine, vinegar, onion, juniper berries, garlic, bay leaves, thyme, salt, and pepper. Add the venison, turn to coat, and set aside in the refrigerator to marinate for 2 hours or so but not overnight.

2. Preheat the oven to 400°F.

3. When ready to cook, remove the venison from the refrigerator and lift out of the marinade, reserving the marinade. Heat a lightly greased large, heavy ovenproof skillet over medium-high heat. Add the venison and sear until brown on both sides, 3 to 4 minutes per side, finishing with the racks meat side down. Transfer the skillet to the oven and cook until still lightly pink in the center, about 20 minutes.

4. While the venison cooks, strain the marinade into a saucepan and bring it to a boil over high heat. Add the cherries, sugar, and allspice, reduce the heat to maintain a brisk simmer, and cook until reduced to a thickened sauce, about 18 minutes. Set aside.

5. Remove the venison from the oven and set aside in a warm place for the juices to settle, 10 to 15 minutes.

6. Place the venison on a cutting surface and cut into portions of 2 ribs each. Arrange the ribs on a platter. Add any juices that have accumulated in the baking pan to the sauce and spoon some over the meat. Serve with the remaining sauce on the side.

SERVES 4

INGREDIENTS:

1½ cups red wine

¼ cup balsamic vinegar

1 medium-size yellow or white onion, coarsely chopped

8 juniper berries, smashed with a mallet

2 cloves garlic, finely chopped

2 bay leaves, crumbled

4 large fresh thyme sprigs or ¾ teaspoon dried

½ teaspoon kosher or fine sea salt

½ teaspoon freshly ground black pepper

1 or 2 racks (8 ribs, about 2½ pounds total) venison

Extra virgin olive oil, for greasing the skillet

1½ cups fresh sour cherries, pitted, or dried tart cherries

¼ cup sugar

Dash of ground allspice

PECAN-CRUSTED ELK MEDALLIONS WITH APPLE JALAPENO JAM

SERVES 4

INGREDIENTS:

Apple Jalapeño Jam
(recipe follows),
for serving

½ cup pecans

4 elk medallions
(about 4 ounces each),
cut ¾ to 1 inch thick

1 to 1½ tablespoons Dijon
mustard

AMERICAN ELK (also called *wapiti*) is the finest of game meat. Sweet, mild, and not in the least gamy, it is a wonderful, and far leaner, alternative to beef. Luckily, like venison, elk is being farm-raised more and more and is sometimes available at a butcher shop or online. It comes in the same cuts as venison, with steaks like New York cut and medallions like filet mignons. The fineness of its flavor lends itself well to nut crusting, and the Native American pecan is the most complementary. A bit of mustard around the edge of the medallion keeps the pecans in place and at the same time adds a little bite to the meat.

1. Make the jam first so it can chill.

2. Heat a small skillet over medium heat. Add the pecans and lightly toast them, stirring constantly, 3 to 5 minutes. Remove the pecans from the pan and spread them on a plate. When cool, finely chop them.

3. To cook the medallions, prepare a medium-hot grill or set a large, heavy skillet over medium-high heat. With a pastry brush, lightly brush a thin layer of mustard all around the sides of the medallions. Roll the coated sides in the chopped pecans to crust them. Place the medallions on the grill or in the skillet and cook, turning once, 6 minutes per side for medium-rare.

4. Transfer the medallions to a platter and set aside for the juices to settle, about 8 minutes. Serve with the jam on the side.

APPLE JALAPENO JAM

IN THE WILD there are three subspecies of elk, the Rocky Mountain, Tule, and Roosevelt, all of them living in the West, so it seems apt to sauce elk in a western-inspired jam. Apples abound in the Pacific Northwest, as do the Roosevelt elk. Jalapeño peppers grow all through California and around the Rocky Mountains, where the Tule and the Rocky Mountain elk roam. A splash of apple juice and apple cider vinegar sharpens the jam.

MAKES ¾ CUP

⅔ cup apple juice

3 tablespoons apple cider vinegar

½ cup sugar

1 to 2 medium-size jalapeño chiles, sliced into strips ⅛ inch wide by ½ inch long

½ tart green apple, such as a Pippin, unpeeled, cored, and cut in ½-inch chunks

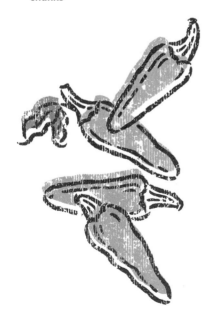

CHOICE GAME

WAPITI

WAPITI is increasingly the term applied to American elk to ensure their distinction from European moose. The term comes from the Shawnee language and means "white rump." Either hunted wild—only one is allowed per hunter per year—or farm-raised, elk meat is as lean and tasty as very lean beef. Elk steaks come as New York strip, tenderloin tip, sirloin, T-bone, rib eye, and flat-iron. Besides the steaks, also available are larger cuts: whole tenderloin, standing butt, rib racks, round roast, whole leg, and more for roasting. All the cuts, including also kebab and stew meat, are available at butcher shops that carry game and online. In addition, some grocery stores now offer ground elk, which makes a particularly rich spaghetti sauce.

AMERICAN VENISON

TWO MAIN SPECIES of deer roam wild in america: The white-tailed deer inhabits almost every state, and the big-eared mule deer thrives throughout the American West. The meat of both is lean, sometimes mild, other times slightly pungent. Deer are also raised domestically to provide the market with venison.

Farm-raised deer don't have to work as hard for their food and are consequently more tender. The steaks often don't need marinating, but roasts, shanks, and ribs of wild- or farm-raised deer and wild venison steaks all become more succulent if presoaked in a marinade.

1. Combine the juice, vinegar, and sugar in a small saucepan and stir to mix. Bring to a boil over medium-high heat, then reduce the heat to maintain a brisk simmer and cook until the mixture thickly coats a spoon, about 15 minutes.

2. Add the jalapeños and apple and continue simmering until the apples are soft, 15 minutes more. Transfer to a bowl and let cool to room temperature. Chill before using. The jam will keep in the refrigerator for up to several weeks.

RABBIT FRICASSEE
WITH HAM, TURNIPS, AND
BERRY COMPOTE

INGREDIENTS:

1 rabbit (about 2½ pounds),
   cut into 6 pieces
   (see page 157)

All-purpose flour, for dusting
   the rabbit

Kosher or fine sea salt and
   freshly ground black pepper

3 tablespoons butter

2 slices thinly sliced Danish
   ham, cut into 2-by-1-inch
   strips

2 cloves garlic, coarsely
   chopped

1 teaspoon chopped fresh
   rosemary or ½ teaspoon
   dried

1½ cups low-sodium chicken
   broth

2 small turnips, peeled
   and cut into 1-inch-wide
   wedges

Berry Compote (recipe
   follows), for serving

1 cup heavy whipping cream

2 tablespoons chopped fresh
   parsley, for serving

FOR EARLY ARRIVERS AND LATER SETTLERS IN AMERICA, one of the chief ways of hunting was to set snares for small game, which meant that rabbit, or actually wild hare, was one of their main foods. Though the names are used almost interchangeably, the two are actually different. Hares are larger and sport longer hind legs and ears. They live in the open country, where they must hear every footfall and snap of a twig, and those back legs must power them rapidly to find cover. Rabbits are not the long-distance runners that hares are, but they have equally fine-tasting meat and are America's most devoured game animal. They are also farm-bred. Their meat, like most game, is very lean and takes to almost any culinary company. It accepts equally vegetables and fruit, sour and sweet, finds a friend with any herb, and nestles down on any sort of bedding. Here it is in a fricassee plied with cream and a side of berry compote.

1. Lightly dust the rabbit pieces with flour and sprinkle with salt and pepper. Melt the butter in a large, heavy pot or sauté pan over medium-high heat. Add the rabbit and sauté until lightly golden on both sides, 5 to 6 minutes total. Transfer the rabbit to a plate.

2. Add the ham, garlic, and rosemary to the pan, stir to mix, and pour in the broth. Return the rabbit and collected juices to the pan and place the turnips on top. Bring to a boil, reduce the heat to maintain a gentle simmer, cover the pan, and cook until the rabbit is tender, 1 hour and 30 minutes.

3. While the rabbit cooks, make the berry compote.

4. To finish the dish, stir the cream into the pan with the rabbit and bring

it to a boil over high heat. Reduce the heat to maintain a gentle boil and cook until the sauce is thickened and creamy, about 10 minutes.

5. Garnish the fricassee with the parsley and serve right away with the berry compote on the side.

BERRY COMPOTE

A COMPOTE IS a fresh or cooked mix, often of fruit, used as counterpoint and relish to a main dish. The cranberry sauce that is served with Thanksgiving turkey, for example, is really a compote, not a sauce. As with that Thanksgiving turkey, which was wild when first feasted on, compotes, especially those of fruit, serve as a perfect accompaniment to game. Fruit is refreshing and also invokes the taste of nature. To provide a spirited companion to rabbit, the fruit of berry vines, so thorny yet poignant, is ideal.

MAKES ABOUT 2½ CUPS

2 heaping cups fresh raspberries, blackberries, marionberries, or cranberries

1½ cups full-bodied red wine

1½ tablespoons raspberry vinegar

1 tablespoon finely chopped shallot

1. Set aside 1 cup of the berries, then combine the wine, vinegar, shallot, and remaining 1 cup berries in a small saucepan. Bring to a boil over medium-high heat, reduce the heat, and cook at a brisk simmer until the mixture is thick and reduced by half, about 10 minutes.

2. Stir in the reserved berries, bring to a boil again, and remove from the heat right away. Use warm or cool and store in the refrigerator for up to 5 days.

CRANBERRIES:
RUBIES OF THE BOG

BY RIGHTS, the cranberry should be designated the all-American fruit. A true native, the large cranberry, traditionally seen in markets in late autumn and associated with winter feasts, grows only in North America, though a smaller cousin is indigenous to Scandinavia. Native Americans of what is now New England ground cranberries with dried meat and fat to make their life-sustaining pemmican. They also mixed the berries with honey for a sauce and mashed them into a poultice believed to treat blood poisoning and other ailments. Later, colonists devised their own recipes for cranberries, turning them into vinegar, candles, soap, and an elixir to prevent scurvy on long sea voyages.

Cranberry cultivation began around Cape Cod early in the eighteenth century. Today cranberries are grown along both North American shores from the United States into Canada, where wet and sandy marshes provide a natural habitat. Cranberry gathering occurs in late September to early October, when the fruit takes on its distinctive red color. Though the season to purchase them fresh is short, in recent years they have appeared in stores in the frozen fruit section year-round. Dried cranberries also are wildly popular and always available to put in salads, muffins and breads, puddings, compotes, and treated as a snack akin to raisins.

BAKED RABBIT WITH PRUNES AND SNOWY PARSNIP PUREE

SERVES 4

INGREDIENTS:

1 rabbit (about 2½ pounds),
   cut into 6 pieces, with
   kidneys and liver
   (see Tip)

Kosher or fine sea salt and
   freshly ground black
   pepper

12 pitted prunes

1 medium-size yellow or
   white onion, halved and
   sliced ¼ inch thick

2 cups white wine

⅔ cup low-sodium chicken
   broth

1 bay leaf

Snowy Parsnip Puree
   (recipe follows),
   for serving

2 tablespoons chopped fresh
   parsley, for garnish

BAKED RABBIT WITH PRUNES nested on a bank of parsnip puree made snowy with potato is a magical dish. It requires very few ingredients and no turning once in the oven. It is one of the tenderest ways to cook rabbit, and is a real audience pleaser.

1. Preheat the oven to 350°F.

2. Place the rabbit pieces, meaty back sides up, in a Dutch oven or other pot large enough to hold them in a slightly overlapping layer. Sprinkle with salt and pepper. Spread the prunes and onion slices over the top, pour in the wine and broth, and tuck in the bay leaf. Cover, place in the oven, and bake until the juices are bubbling and the rabbit is almost tender, 1 hour.

3. While the rabbit cooks, make the parsnip puree.

4. Remove the Dutch oven cover and continue baking until the rabbit is fork-tender and the juices are reduced, 30 minutes more. Remove

from the oven and let sit for 10 minutes while the juices settle.

5. To serve, remove the bay leaf from the casserole. Arrange the rabbit, prunes, and onions on a large platter or 4 individual plates and pour the juices over the top. Mound the parsnip puree to the side and sprinkle the parsley over all. Serve right away.

SNOWY PARSNIP PUREE

RABBITS, GARDEN RAIDERS that they are, are known to seek out root vegetables. The cartoon classic portrayal of rabbits munching carrots derives from eyewitness reports. As cooks discovered long ago, rabbit and root vegetables are equally well matched in a pot. Parsnips, the earnest cousin of turnips, beets, rutabaga, water chestnuts, potatoes, and carrots, are wonderfully compatible with rabbit. Like carrots, they are a dulcet vegetable, only instead of grassy, they are woody and earthy. Potatoes add a milky top note.

MAKES ABOUT 6 CUPS

6 medium-size parsnips, peeled and cut into ½-inch pieces

2 medium-size russet potatoes, peeled and cut into ½-inch pieces

Kosher or fine sea salt

6 tablespoons (¾ stick) butter, at room temperature

1 cup heavy whipping cream

1. Combine the parsnips and potatoes in a large pot. Add a large pinch of salt and water to cover by 1½ inches and bring to a boil over high heat. Cook until the parsnips and potatoes are fork-tender but not collapsing, 10 to 12 minutes. Drain briefly and return to the pot.

2. Add the butter and, with a potato masher or sturdy wire whisk, mash the parsnips and potatoes with the butter. Add the cream and continue mashing until you have a fluffy, almost smooth puree with a few chunks of parsnip. Season with salt, cover, and set aside in a warm place until ready to serve, up to 45 minutes.

OTHER SMALL GAME ON THE AMERICAN HISTORY MENU

THE MANY SETTLERS WHO CAME TO AMERICA and hunted did not limit themselves to the large game of the continent. Rabbit was but one of what there was to snare for eating. The land was teeming with small game, some of which we still eat, some we now look askance at. On the wild plate were:

Armadillo, beaver (some are being farm-raised now), bobcat, frog, muskrat, opossum, porcupine, prairie dog, raccoon (remember Daniel Boone?), rattlesnake, squirrel (still much hunted), turtle (easy for people to catch), and woodchuck (also in the West known as marmots and in the Mid-Atlantic as groundhogs).

Other big game animals also on the menu:

Alligator, antelope (also called pronghorn), bear, boar (though its ancestors were brought to America by the Spaniards and turned feral), caribou, moose, mountain goat, mountain sheep, and musk ox.

⊙ TIP: Dividing a rabbit into six pieces means one rabbit can serve four. The two hind leg pieces make one serving each, and the two saddle pieces along with a foreleg each make for two more.

Rabbit kidneys and liver are found within the rabbit carcass. Just pluck them away with your fingers, including as much of the savory fat surrounding the kidneys as there is. If the liver is rosy and firm, keep it too. If not, discard it.

To cook rabbit kidneys and liver, melt 2 tablespoons of butter in a small sauté pan over medium-high heat, add the kidneys and liver, and sauté, turning often, until firm to the touch and medium-rare, about four minutes. Transfer to a plate and sprinkle with salt and pepper. Cut the kidneys into quarters and thinly slice the liver. Serve with warm toasted baguette slices, lightly buttered.

THE FIRST TO ARRIVE: NATIVE AMERICANS

For eons after most of the rest of the world saw human habitation, the Americas remained an unoccupied Eden. Eventually as people wandered farther around the globe, they crossed over land and ice bridges that connected Asia with Alaska, and some drifted into the Americas. At least six waves of the first immigrants, each speaking unrelated languages, arrived. Others sailed across the Pacific to Hawaii. Today we call them Native Americans.

THE PUEBLO PEOPLE

THE OCCUPANTS OF THE MANY Pueblo villages of the American Southwest are thought possibly the descendants of the very earliest to arrive, the Clovis people. At first they hunted deer, elk, bighorn sheep, and rabbit, but by about 1000 BCE they also began to farm corn, beans, and squash and build permanent villages. They include, among others, the Towa, Acoma, Taos, Zuni, and Hopi.

THE ALGONQUIN SPEAKERS

SOME OF THE FIRST PEOPLE TO DRIFT into North America settled into the woodlands from Labrador down the Atlantic seaboard to the Great Lakes and down into the Mississippi Valley. The Algonquin speakers became among the most populous and widespread of the Native Americans. Most lived by hunting, although some took up agriculture. It is from their language that American English gained such food words as squash, succotash, hominy, and moose, and the terms *papoose, tomahawk,* and *wampum.* Among the tribes are Mohegans, the Ojibwa, Potawatomi, Cree, Shawnee, Kickapoo, Miami, Arapaho, Blackfoot, and Cheyenne. Their main game was caribou, moose, deer, beaver, birds, fish, and sometimes whales and seals. They also gathered wild rice.

THE IROQUOIS NATIONS

THE NEXT GROUP TO ENTER split the Algonquins apart. They were the Iroquois, among the most legendary of Native Americans. Although they still hunted deer and small game and collected shellfish, in time most adopted agriculture. A number of the tribes in the North united in a confederacy known as the League of Five Nations. They included the Seneca, Cayuga, Onondaga, Oneida, and Mohawk. Other groups in the North were the Kickapoo, Choctaw, Creek, Shawnee, and Huron. To the south a number of Iroquois tribes formed another great alliance, joining together in an illustrious union, the Creek, Chickasaw, Choctaw, Seminole, and the renowned Cherokee.

THE SIOUAN PEOPLE

TO MANY, the reigning image of the Native Americans is that of a warrior dressed in beaded vest, fringed leggings, war paint, galloping bareback with a lance aimed at a buffalo, living on the Great Plains in tepees. These iconic images do not tell the whole story of the Siouan speakers, for at first almost all lived east of the Mississippi and grew crops. Only occasionally did they hunt buffalo. Then came the horse. Seizing the opportunity to pursue the vast herds, a number of the tribes abandoned their crops, moved west and, on horseback, became full-time nomadic buffalo hunters. Among the Sioux are the Biloxi, Winnebago, Crow, Oglala, Dakota, Lakota, Missouri, Omaha, Kansa, and Wichita.

THE UTO-AZTECAN SPEAKERS

AT SOME TIME AROUND or before 1000 CE a new set of loosely connected hunting people began to appear in the West of North America, speaking tongues of a new family of languages, Uto-Aztecan. By 1100 some had drifted to Mexico, and by 1325 had taken over from the Mayans to establish the Aztec Empire. Others remained north where they existed on cattails, pickleweed, pine nuts, and sedge, rabbit, birds, lizards, and perhaps an occasional antelope. Among them are the Utes, Shoshone, Paiute, Bannock, Nez Perce, Flathead, Yakima, and Comanche.

THE ATHABASCAN PEOPLE

THE LAST WAVE of Native American arrivals entering as European settlers were already crossing the country in Conestoga wagons were the Athabascan-speaking tribes known as the Navajo and Apache. They were following the buffalo. Some scattered groups remained in Alaska. Of the two main groups, the Navajo was eager to adapt to a settled life and took up farming and sheepherding. The other group, the Apache, did not care to settle and continued raiding and hunting. Both call themselves Diné.

THE PACIFIC COASTAL AND ALASKAN TRIBES

WEST OF THE GREAT BASIN, across the Sierra Mountains, along the Pacific seacoast, and in Alaska live a medley of tribes speaking a number of different languages. To name a few along the West Coast, there are the Yuma, Mojave, Washo, Cahuilla, Chumash, Salinan, Miwok, Pomo, Yurok, Klamath, Modoc, Chinook, Suquamish. Along the coast of California most of the peoples lived on shellfish. In the coastal mountains, acorns were the staple. Farther north into the redwood forests, the great fish-filled rivers provided enough for wealth to be stockpiled. In Alaska are the sea-hunting Aleuts, the Eskimo-speaking Inupiaq and Yupic, and some Athabascan-speaking people, such as the Tlingit, who continue hunting moose, caribou, salmon, whale, walrus, seal, and duck along with gathering bird eggs and berries.

THE HAWAIIANS

ON THE CHAIN OF ISLANDS in the Pacific Ocean that became the nation's last state, there were native inhabitants of Polynesian descent. They came over an extended time in two waves, one from the Marqueses Islands and then another from Tahiti. They came with chickens, pigs, taro root, sweet potato, banana, coconut, and even sugarcane, but to this day they supplement their diet with seafood.

Today restaurants serving the foods of Native Americans have sprung up across the nation. Also increasingly available in grocers, specialty stores, reservation stores, online, and at roadside stands are the foods still hunted and gathered by tribes, among them Algonquin wild rice, Shoshone hand-gathered pine nuts, elk jerky, and the Northeast's famous pemmican compounds of berries, chokecherry, game meat, and suet for all of us to utilize. Among dishes that have as well entered daily cuisine are fried and stewed cactus paddles, four-leaf clover salads, various succotashes, corn soups, pumpkin from dried to baked, dishes of Anasazi and tepary beans, fire-smoked salmon, elk steaks, buffalo stews, smoked quail and wild turkey, squash blossom dumplings, moose meat summer sausage, and always in the movies and in front of the television, Native American popcorn.

RABBIT STEW
WITH PEARL ONIONS, SHALLOTS, RED WINE, AND VINEGAR

SERVES 4

INGREDIENTS:

½ cup extra virgin olive oil

1 rabbit (about 2¼ pounds), cut into 6 pieces (see page 157)

12 ounces pearl onions, peeled

8 ounces small shallots, peeled

3 cloves garlic, coarsely chopped

2 tablespoons tomato paste

1 cup red wine

⅓ cup balsamic vinegar

2 small bay leaves

2 whole cloves

1 piece (1½ inches) cinnamon stick

½ teaspoon kosher or fine sea salt

¼ teaspoon freshly ground black pepper

THERE WERE TWO WAYS FOR A HUNTER in the wilderness to cook a wild rabbit: Skewer it on a stick and roast it over the open flames of a campfire or take out a cast-iron swing-handled pot, hang the pot on an arm fashioned from a branch over the fire, put in the rabbit, and stew it. In the old days, stewing probably was the more common, for a few onions and other seasonings could be thrown in for flavor. Stewing is still one of the most widespread ways to cook rabbit even in domestic circumstances. It's practiced in almost every cuisine, from Italian *cacciatore* to French *lapin à la cocotte,* South American rabbit stew with coconut, and the Pueblo rabbit, squash, and juniper berry stew. Here the take is on Greece's famous wild rabbit *stifado,* rich with tomatoes and sweet pearl onions and spiced with cinnamon and bay leaf.

1. Heat the oil in a large nonreactive pot over medium-high heat. Add the rabbit pieces in an uncrowded layer and brown on both sides, about 5 minutes.

2. Add the onions, shallots, garlic, tomato paste, wine, vinegar, bay leaves, cloves, cinnamon stick, salt, and pepper, mix well, and bring to a boil. Reduce the heat, cover, and simmer, stirring once or twice, until the rabbit is tender, about 1½ hours.

3. Remove the bay leaves, cinnamon stick, and cloves. Serve in the pot.

SAUTEED QUAIL
WITH CRISP CARROT AND PARSNIP RIBBONS

NOT ONLY HAVE LARGE AND SMALL GAME ANIMALS long figured in the American diet, from the earliest days of hunting to today's butcher counter, game birds have as well. Dove to duck, goose to grouse, guinea hen, partridge, pheasant, pigeon, snipe, turkey, woodcock, blackbirds, marsh birds, and quail were all enjoyed. It seems everyone still sometimes desires a touch of the wild, and quail remain an avidly relished dish, as appetizer and entrée. By far the most succulent way to cook quail is to grill it over high heat or quickly sauté it as here. Seared in hot oil, its juices are sealed in and the lean meat stays moist and tender. The touch of honey in the marinade lends a warm golden glow to the quail.

INGREDIENTS:

- 6 quail (about 5½ ounces each)
- ¼ cup white wine
- ¼ cup extra virgin olive oil, plus oil for greasing the skillet
- 1 tablespoon honey
- 1 tablespoon chopped orange zest
- 1 tablespoon finely shredded fresh sage leaves
- ½ teaspoon kosher or fine sea salt
- ½ teaspoon freshly ground black pepper
- Crisp Carrot and Parsnip Ribbons (recipe follows), for serving

1. To prepare the quail, remove the backbones by cutting along each side of them and rinse and pat the quail dry. Combine the wine, ¼ cup oil, the honey, orange zest, sage, and salt and pepper in a dish large enough to hold the birds opened out in a slightly overlapping layer. Add the quail and turn to coat. Set aside to marinate, covered, in the refrigerator for 1 hour or up to 3 hours.

2. When ready to cook the quail, preheat the oven to 450°F and make the carrot and parsnip ribbons.

3. Lightly grease a heavy ovenproof skillet large enough to hold the quail opened out without overlapping and heat it over high heat until very hot. Lift the quail out of the marinade, shaking off the excess without wiping them, and place them breast side down in the skillet. Reduce the heat to medium-high and cook until barely golden on the bottom, 3 minutes. Turn them breast side up and transfer the skillet to the oven. Cook until the juices are no longer red but the breast is still rare to medium-rare, 2 to 3 minutes. Transfer the birds to a platter and set aside to rest for 3 minutes.

4. Garnish the quail platter with a handful of vegetable ribbons at each end and serve right away, with the remaining ribbons on the side.

CRISP CARROT AND PARSNIP RIBBONS

THE SAME PEELER that takes the skin off carrots and parsnips can continue its run and shred a curly heap of thin vegetable ribbons. Delicate yet flavorfully robust and crunchy, they are brightly pretty as well. To keep them crisp, the ribbons should be made soon before serving. They will hold in a warm place for up to 45 minutes. Besides being a fine ornament and side with quail, they can top chops, potatoes, and salad.

SERVES 3 OR 4

3 large carrots, peeled

3 medium-size parsnips, peeled

Peanut or canola oil, for deep-frying

Kosher or fine sea salt

1. Using a vegetable peeler, shave the carrots and parsnips lengthwise all around into ribbons, stopping at the core.

2. Pour oil to a depth of 2 inches into a deep pot and heat over high heat until a ribbon sizzles. Reduce the heat to medium-high and add as many of the ribbons as will fit without crowding. Fry until the ribbons are golden and have risen to the top, about 1½ minutes. Transfer to paper towels and continue with another batch. Sprinkle with salt and set aside in a warm place until ready to serve.

BRINGING BACK THE QUAIL AND THEIR FELLOWS

QUAIL IS THE NAME of several wide-ranging, plump, seed-eating, small to midsize birds. The European branch, Phasianidae, includes pheasants and partridges. The American branch, only distantly related, are from the family Odontophoridae, meaning "tooth carrying"—odd since they don't have teeth but rather serrated jaws. Some are long-tailed, some buff-crowned, some black-eared, banded, or spot-bellied. Most sport a fetching feather on their crown, larger for the males, smaller for the females. They are terrestrial, living on the ground and, except for a short burst when threatened, don't fly. They hang out in coveys, finding safety in numbers. Perhaps the most well known of the American branch is the famed bobwhite, a name derived from its characteristic whistling call, which sounds as if it is saying "bob white" and is much imitated in bird-whistling contests.

Although quail are farmed extensively in many nations, both for the bird itself and for its intensely tasty eggs, in the wild quail and other game birds are diminishing in number, the result of the destruction of habitat. The new policy of many states' game associations is: If the loss of their habitat is the reason they're decreasing, let's restore their habitat.

GRILLED QUAIL WRAPPED IN GRAPE LEAVES WITH GRAPE KEBABS

A SINGLE QUAIL IS SO SMALL it offers but a few bites of meat, best garnered by picking the bird up and eating it with your hands. The perfect cooking escorts are herbs such as thyme or sage, which echo the brush and scraggly bushes under which they nest. Wrapping them in grape leaves prior to grilling fashions an innovative pairing and results in birds that are heavenly succulent with an unexpected, almost citruslike gusto. Skewers of grapes complement the birds and leaf. The color of the grapes doesn't matter, nor whether they have seeds. The commonly found seedless green Thompsons and Red Flames are fine, but, if you care to venture farther, try the very tasty, large green muscats or wine-dark and winy-tasting Ribiers. Once cooked, the seeds add a pleasing crunch.

1. To prepare the quail, remove the backbones by cutting along each side of them with kitchen scissors. Open the quails out and rinse and pat them dry.

2. Combine the lemon zest, thyme, salt, pepper, and olive oil in a dish large enough to hold the quail in an opened-out slightly overlapping layer. Add the quail and turn to coat all around. Set aside to marinate in the refrigerator for 3 to 6 hours.

3. When ready to cook the quail, prepare a medium-low grill. Lift the quail out of the marinade and, without wiping them off, wrap each quail in grape leaves, using as many leaves as it takes to wrap each generously. Set aside at room temperature until the grill is ready.

4. String the grapes on 4 bamboo skewers and set aside.

SERVES 4 TO 6

INGREDIENTS:

- 8 quail (about 5½ ounces each)
- 1½ tablespoons coarsely chopped lemon zest
- 1½ teaspoons chopped fresh thyme
- 1½ teaspoons kosher or fine sea salt
- ½ teaspoon freshly ground black pepper
- 1½ tablespoons extra virgin olive oil
- 16 to 32 grape leaves, depending on size (enough to fully wrap each quail)
- 20 red or white grapes

HOW THE GREEKS SAILED TO AMERICA

CONSIDERING THEIR LONG HISTORY of seafaring, it is not surprising that the first Greek to arrive in America came as part of a Spanish exploratory voyage 250 years before the Declaration of Independence. His name was Don Theodoro, and he landed in 1528 in what was to become Florida. Many more Greeks arrived within two hundred years, well before the United States declared its independence. Among them, in 1768, was a group from Crete, Mani, and Smyrna who settled in Florida and formed a town they named New Smyrna.

By 1866, so many Greeks had sailed into the thriving American seaport of New Orleans that demand was enough to establish both a Greek consulate and the first Greek Orthodox church.

The New Orleans Greeks were followed by many more. The majority settled in the cities of the Northeast and Midwest, but some became miners or sought to farm in the American West as they had at home. In California they planted orchards and gardens of the fruit, nuts, and vegetables they loved. Others became sheep ranchers in western Colorado, again duplicating their heritage. In cities and small towns alike, many rapidly reconstituted another long-standing cultural tradition: They opened restaurants. In all their venues customers tasted moussaka, stuffed eggplant and grape leaves, baklava, and fell in love with sizzling, skewered, and gyrating thin shavings of lamb, chicken, or pork sauced in yogurt, wrapped in pita.

5. Place the quail on the grill directly over the heat and cook, uncovered, until the grape leaves are lightly charred on the bottom, 7 to 8 minutes. Turn and cook until the grape leaves are charred on the second side and the quail are firm to the touch, about 7 minutes more. Transfer to a platter and set aside in a warm place.

6. Place the grape kebabs on the grill rack directly over the heat and cook, turning once, until lightly charred and a little shriveled, about 6 minutes. Add the kebabs to the platter with the quail and serve, accompanied by a debris bowl to hold the grape leaves as they are peeled away.

MOLASSES-MARINATED SQUAB WITH SKILLET CORN BREAD

OFTEN MALIGNED IN THE TOWN SQUARE, where they strut boldly, leaving their tracings on everything from cars to streetlights to building facades, pigeons have also endeared themselves to city dwellers who enjoy them as urban wildlife and encourage their presence with a constant stream of bread crumbs. On the wing, pigeons are venerated for their role as stalwart messengers, avian angels who will travel for miles to deliver a note, carried in the beak all the way. But it is perhaps on the plate they are most highly prized. Young pigeons are called *squab* to distinguish them from either urban wildlife or hearty workhorse. They are small, tender, with a taste somewhat between quail and Cornish hen, mildly gamy in a white meat way. Unlike quail, which take somewhere between one and two per person, depending on the appetite of the eaters, or game hens, which can serve up to two, one squab per person is just the right size for a serving. Here they are glazed with a sugar derivative pairing of rum and molasses tinged with lemon, thyme, and balsamic vinegar.

1. To prepare the squabs, remove and discard the backbones by cutting along each side of them with kitchen scissors. Open the squabs out and rinse and pat them dry.

2. Combine the rum, molasses, lemon zest, thyme, salt, and pepper in a dish large enough to hold the squabs opened out. Place the squabs in the dish and turn to coat all around. Set aside to marinate in the refrigerator for 1 hour or up to 3 hours.

SERVES 4

INGREDIENTS:

4 squabs (12 to 16 ounces each)

½ cup dark rum

½ cup unsulfured molasses

6 tablespoons coarsely chopped lemon zest

2 teaspoons chopped fresh thyme

1 teaspoon kosher or fine sea salt

½ teaspoon freshly ground black pepper

Skillet Corn Bread (recipe follows), for serving

Extra virgin olive oil, for greasing the skillet

2 cups arugula

1 teaspoon balsamic vinegar

THE CORN CAKE CLAN

CORNMEAL was much more available than flour to African Americans in slave quarters. Breads made from cornmeal became part of a meal, a treat, even dessert. Several types of corn bread of varying textures, depending on how much, if any, wheat is included, developed in the South: hoecakes, cornpone, and hush puppies. Additional ingredients, such as onion, whole-kernel corn, hominy, jalapeños, cheese, onions, scallions, bacon, ham, and even oysters became regional distinctions. Most developed from cooks in the South, from slaves and their free descendants in the West with the discovery of Pueblo Indian corn and Mexican chile. New Englanders joined in when it came to corn bread, theirs being johnnycakes and Shawnee cakes.

3. While the squab marinates, make the corn bread and set it aside in a warm place.

4. When ready to cook the squabs, preheat the oven to 425°F.

5. Lightly grease an ovenproof skillet large enough to hold the squabs opened out without crowding and heat it over medium-high heat. (Use 2 skillets if necessary.) Lift the squabs out of the marinade and, without wiping them off, place them breast side down in the hot skillet. Cook until golden on the bottom, about 3 minutes.

6. Turn the squabs breast side up and transfer the skillet to the oven. Cook until the skin is golden and crispy and the breast meat is medium-rare, 9 to 11 minutes. Transfer to a platter and set aside in a warm place for 5 minutes for the juices to settle.

7. Toss the arugula with the balsamic vinegar and divide it among 4 individual plates. Set a squab on top of each and serve with the corn bread in its skillet on the side.

SKILLET CORN BREAD

NATIVE AMERICANS WERE growing corn long before Europeans arrived. Although the earliest settlers cultivated corn, the first colonists looked upon it with a jaundiced eye. Impelled by hunger, they tried it. They liked it, and when food supplied from their homelands became scarce, they took to growing it and cooking with it. As longtime bread lovers, these transplanted Europeans soon ground corn into meal for making loaves. Corn bread was an instant hit. As well as being tasty, it was easy to make in a skillet. The tradition has continued; skillet corn bread, simple and wholesome and appropriately corny in flavor, not only

rises, but in the pan the underside gets even crispier than the crust.

MAKES ONE 9-INCH ROUND CORN BREAD

1 cup yellow cornmeal

½ cup all-purpose flour

2 teaspoons baking powder

1 large egg

½ cup milk

¼ cup water

Pinch of kosher or fine sea salt

¼ cup extra virgin olive or peanut oil

1. Preheat the oven to 350°F.

2. Whisk together the cornmeal, flour, baking powder, egg, milk, water, and salt in a large bowl.

3. Heat the oil in a 9-inch cast-iron or other stovetop-to-oven skillet over high heat. Pour in the corn bread batter and cook until beginning to brown on the bottom, 5 minutes. Cover the skillet and transfer it to the oven. Cook until a knife inserted in the middle comes out almost clean, with a little moist batter still clinging, about 20 minutes. Set aside to cool slightly before cutting.

MOLASSES AND THE AMERICAN REVOLUTION

AS FAR BACK AS REVOLUTIONARY DAYS, when molasses was an important part of the American diet, it was a centerpiece of British trade. Home cooks used it as a sauce for beans, added it to bourbon, and swirled it into vegetables. They used it in puddings and pastries and glazed the wild game they hunted, especially the birds, with it. Up until the 1880s, molasses continued to be the primary sweetener used in America because it was much cheaper than refined sugar.

It was only after the end of World War I, when the price of refined sugar dropped drastically, that consumers abandoned molasses for crystallized sugar, which measure for measure is sweeter than molasses. By 1919, U.S. per-capita consumption of white sugar was twice what it was in 1880. Still, up through World War II, most households had molasses in the pantry and continued to use it in cooking. It was—and still is—an ingredient in barbecue sauce and ketchup, a flavoring for bacon, a sweetener for gingerbread, and a syrup for pancakes. Commercially it is also used to cure tobacco, as an ingredient in cattle feed, and to make yeast. And of course, distilling it makes rum. The home use of molasses has dwindled but is recalled in nostalgic recipes. So the thick, slow-running sugar that the British call *treacle* stays on our shelves.

To this day, molasses remains particularly American. It provides a more subtle, but deeper, dulcet flavor than processed sugar. Molasses comes in three grades: unsulfured, sulfured, and blackstrap. The designations have to do with the ripeness of the sugarcane when it is pressed into molasses and how far from the first pressing the outcome product is. The categories are as follows:

❯ UNSULFURED MOLASSES is the first press from ripe sugarcane. It is considered the finest.

❯ SULFURED MOLASSES, both light and dark, is the second glean, a by-product of crystal sugar making. Light sulfured molasses is from the first boiling of the by-product. Dark sulfured molasses is from the second boiling.

❯ BLACKSTRAP MOLASSES is the third boil from the cane sugar reduction. Some find its flavor too pronounced, dark, and somewhat bitter. Yet, in the process of being reduced to this extent, its beneficial iron content increases, and so while most is relegated to animal feed, some is used to add iron to human diets.

PHEASANT SALMI WITH RED WINE AND COCOA SAUCE

INGREDIENTS:

1 pheasant (about 3 pounds)

Kosher or fine sea salt and freshly ground black pepper

3 tablespoons butter

1 small yellow or white onion, chopped

1 clove garlic, chopped

2 fresh thyme sprigs

1 bay leaf

1 whole clove

2 cups low-sodium chicken broth

1 cup red wine

2 teaspoons good-quality unsweetened cocoa powder

½ teaspoon chopped fresh sage leaves

THOMAS JEFFERSON AND HIS FLOCK OF PHEASANTS inspires a very American interpretation of salmi, starring the regal bird. Pheasants now thrive all over North America. In addition to those running wild, ten million or more are raised every year on farms, on game preserves, and sometimes in residential backyards. Since the meat is very lean, dry roasting can leave the bird rather stringy and tough. Instead, choose an American-spirited salmi—a spiced stew most often of wild game birds—with wine and pancetta.

1. Remove the giblets and neck bone from the cavity of the pheasant and set aside in a dish. Cut off the first and second joints of the wings, leaving the drumettes attached to the breast, and set them aside with the giblets. Remove the backbone and ribs from the breasts and add them to the bowl with the giblets.

2. Cut the 2 whole leg (drumstick and thigh) pieces away from the breast. Cut the breast in half lengthwise down the breastbone, yielding two split breast pieces with drumettes attached. Sprinkle the breast pieces and the leg pieces with salt and pepper and set

them aside in a separate dish at room temperature for up to 1 hour or refrigerate for up to overnight.

3. Melt the butter in a large saucepan with high sides over medium-high heat. Add the breast and leg pieces and sauté them until lightly browned all over, 5 minutes. Transfer the pieces to a plate and set aside.

4. Place the backbone, wing tips, giblets, neck bone, onion, and garlic in the pan. Cook until the onion is translucent and slightly wilted, 2 to 3 minutes. Return the breast and leg pieces to the pan. Add the thyme, bay leaf, clove, and chicken broth and bring to a boil over high heat. Reduce the heat to maintain a gentle simmer, and cook, partially covered, until the leg pieces are almost, but not quite fork pierce-able and the breast pieces are still pink in the center, about 12 minutes. Transfer the breast and leg pieces to a dish again and set aside in a warm place, leaving the backbone, wing tips, giblets, and neck bone in the pan.

5. To make the sauce, add the wine and cocoa powder to the pan, stir, and bring to a boil over high heat. Reduce the heat to maintain a brisk simmer and cook, uncovered, until the sauce is a deep brown color and the consistency of a gravy, 25 to 30 minutes, depending on the diameter of the pan. Strain the sauce through a fine mesh sieve into a small bowl. Discard the solids and set the strained sauce aside for the fat to rise to the top while finishing the recipe.

6. To finish the salmi, preheat the oven to 425°F.

7. Place the breasts and leg pieces skin side up in a roasting pan and roast until the skin is nicely golden and the breasts are still medium rare, about 18 minutes. Remove the pan from the oven, place the pheasant pieces on a serving dish, and let stand in a warm place for the juices to settle.

THE SALMI(S) AND THE PHEASANT

ACCORDING TO the *Oxford English Dictionary, salmi* is a shortened term for salmagundi, which means a dish of chopped meats, anchovies, eggs, onions, and more. The diminutive *salmi,* however, returns to cookery specifics and describes a ragout of roasted game that is then stewed with wine, bread, condiments, and such. By the beginning of the twentieth century, famed chef and cookbook encyclopedist August Escoffier met the topic head on and expressed his issue with it. In *The Escoffier Cookbook,* he passionately opined:

"Salmis [it's with an *s* in French] is perhaps the most delicate and most perfect of the game preparations given us by old fashioned cookery. If it is less highly esteemed nowadays, it is owing to the fact that this recipe has been literally spoiled by the haphazard fashion in which it has been applied right and left to game already cooked, and cooked again for the purpose. A speedy preparation and a simple method of serving, which hastens the service and permit the Salmis being eaten hot, are the only necessary conditions. Moreover, the richness of this preparation is such as to make it independent of an ornate method of serving."

To wit, a salmis is not really a ragout, at least not a long-cooked one. The game must be seared quickly to brown it, then simmered just long enough to finish cooking it to tenderness. But for pheasant, and going Escoffier one better, the classic can be turned topsy-turvy with a stellar result. First the pheasant is simmered in an aromatic broth, then it is roasted separately from the sauce, which is reduced. This way the bird comes out an appealing ruddy-brown color with a crispy skin and the sauce is rich without the meat becoming stringy.

8. Skim the fat off the top of the sauce (there should be about 1 cup of liquid after skimming), and reheat in the microwave or in a saucepan over medium-high heat. Pour the sauce over the pheasant, sprinkle the sage over all, and serve.

POULTRY
IN MOTION

While there were domesticated fowl in parts of South America, keeping birds was not a practice in North America. When European settlers arrived, this changed. The English, Spanish, Dutch, and Swedish immediately introduced the farm birds they knew and we still savor, chicken and ducks at first and eventually geese. Every ship commissioned to sail to the new land brought some. The early colonists also domesticated a native game bird, rather a large grouse, that they mistakenly called *turkey.*

In due time, domestic birds spurred both a major industry and a culinary explosion. As much as their meat was relished, at first the continuing supply of eggs was valued most. Eggs could provide many a meal, and when a hen stopped laying, or extra roosters were engendered, that bird would be served on a platter.

Eggs left to mature could replace the entrée. Up until the time Herbert Hoover gave his famous 1928 campaign promise of "A Chicken in Every Pot and a Car in Every Garage," eggs continued to be a larger part of the American diet than the bird itself. In short, in America what came first was the sunny side, not the drumstick.

After World War II, poultry farming burst from a small farm enterprise to a major industry. Chicken on the dinner plate was almost quotidian fare for Americans. It's hard to say, à la chicken and egg, whether availability spurred demand or demand availability, but by the 1950s America's chicken industry had expanded sevenfold. A decade later chicken had come to rival meats as the most featured hub on the dinner plate, and today it can be purchased not just whole as was once the only selection but cut up, or by just certain parts.

Noting the arrival of chicken in every pot, the entrepreneurs of the turkey industry launched the bird from holiday treat to everyday pleasure, and it, as well as chicken, has become a daily offering, either as whole bird or, more often, in parts or as ground meat. Domestic game hens, duck, and geese remain a special treat.

FROM PILGRIM TO PLATE: THE POULTRY TALE

IF THE PILGRIMS DIDN'T HAVE turkeys for that first Thanksgiving, they probably had chickens and other birds. Indeed for 150 years after the Pilgrims landed, there was no Thanksgiving Day. The movement to have such a holiday came from George Washington in 1789, who set the date of October 2 as a "day to celebrate the constitution," but turkey wasn't mentioned. John Adams changed the date to May 9. Thomas Jefferson opposed the idea completely, saying that setting aside days for national holidays was what kings did, and so there was no Thanksgiving or turkey day at all for sixty more years. Only the thirty-year efforts and pleas of Sara Josepha Hale, writer and editor of a woman's magazine, who was influential in American cultural life, convinced Abraham Lincoln, in 1863, to declare a day of Thanksgiving. Still no turkey, until Fannie Farmer in her 1896 cookbook suggested the day include "Pilgrim foods."

That advice coordinated well with Lincoln's holiday, which itself coincidentally fell at the time that the now many turkey farmers of America slaughtered their flocks of turkeys, and so the birds were available fresh late in the fall. Yet it was even longer before the turkey became the quintessential dish for the autumn holidays. Too many pinfeathers to pick, complained housewives, from what was still a dark-meat bird. So in 1947, a cadre of farmers got together to develop a light-meat, more appealing turkey, called the bird a "Beltsville white," and began presenting one to the standing president as a centerpiece for the Thanksgiving holiday. It was with that, a bird with more white meat and the presidential seal, that the popularity of the native bird was finally launched.

Turkey consumption doubled between 1950 and 1960 and grew sixfold by the 1990s. Now Americans on average eat about eighteen pounds of turkey per year. Ben Franklin wanted to make the turkey, rather than the eagle, the national bird of the country. And in some ways we finally have.

GARLIC-SOUSED CHICKEN

CHICKEN IS ONE OF THE QUINTESSENTIAL QUICK FOODS a time-starved cook can prepare. It can be roasted whole in an hour, stewed in pieces even faster, fried rapidly, or sautéed in 25 minutes or less. And should the cook desire big, bold taste along with rapidity, chicken once again fills the bill. Sousing the bird with lots of garlic and cooking it in a sputtering bath of aromatic olive oil is not only a spectacular way to gild it, but a facile one. The dish needles the nostrils, arouses the appetite, and satisfies the yen for gumption. The preparation goes with just about anything, so almost any item you can scavenge from the larder with equal speed can serve splendidly as a plate companion.

1. Heat the oil in a heavy skillet large enough to hold the chicken without crowding over medium-high heat. Add the chicken pieces, skin side down, and sprinkle them with salt and pepper. Cook until lightly golden on the bottom, about 10 minutes. Turn the pieces over, sprinkle salt and pepper on the second side, and add the garlic. Cook, basting the pieces from time to time with the pan juices, until the chicken is almost done but the juices still run slightly pink in the centers, about 5 minutes.

2. Stir in the wine and tarragon and continue cooking until the chicken is done all the way through, about 5 minutes more for wing and breast pieces, 10 minutes more for legs and thighs. Transfer the pieces to a platter as they're done.

3. Pour the sauce from the pan over all and serve right away.

SERVES 4

INGREDIENTS:

¼ cup extra virgin olive oil

1 large chicken (4 to 4½ pounds), cut into 8 pieces, or the same amount of assorted chicken pieces

Kosher or fine sea salt and freshly ground black pepper

12 cloves garlic, coarsely chopped

1 cup red wine

2 teaspoons coarsely chopped fresh tarragon or ¾ teaspoon dried

MAJOR PLAYERS IN THE AMERICAN COOP

A CHICKEN IN EVERY POT

IN 1607, the Jamestown settlers brought with them five hundred chickens, which they kept for eggs but allowed to run around unpenned, thereby losing quite a number of eggs in hidden nests they could not locate and to egg predators. The Plymouth colonists in 1620 also brought European chickens with them, which flourished to the point that they gave the birds as gifts of friendship to their native neighbors. The surrounding tribes quickly caught on to the chicken and golden egg idea, and rather than kill the birds for dinner, they too kept the chickens and collected the resulting eggs for succeeding meals.

Over time Americans raised many breeds of chicken: Plymouth Rocks exhibited at America's first poultry show in Boston in 1829; Wyandottes from New York State; Javas developed in the United States from Asian stock; Rhode Island Reds and Whites; Jersey Giants; Lamonas, a government experimental breed from Maryland; Hollands; some of Asian origin such as Brahmas, Malays, Sumatras, and Chinese Langshans; some of English origin such as Dorkings, Redcaps, and Cornish; Mediterranean Leghorns, Minorcas, and Blue Andalusians; Campines from Belgium; French Houdans; and miniature Asian bantams, to name just a few.

Prior to about 1930, chickens were raised primarily on family farms, and chicken was primarily a Sunday or special-occasion dish. As urban populations and demand increased, and as poultry farming changed so that thousands of birds could be produced, chicken became a daily and inexpensive way to feed a family. Today the chicken breed that lays the most eggs eaten in America is the Single-Comb Leghorn, a scrambled name derived from the bird's native city in Italy—Livorno, mispronounced as Leghorn—and the physical feature of one red comb on the chicken's head. The breeds most commonly eaten are the Cornish and White Rock. More than 23 billion chickens are raised annually, and now faddishly in urban backyards, and 3.36 billion pounds of these are reared for consumption in America.

NOT-SO-WILD CORNISH GAME HENS

THOUGH WE NOW CALL the popular small eating bird Cornish game hens, their original name was Rock Cornish game hens. And despite how familiar we are with them, they have actually been around for only a little over fifty years. They are also a true American innovation and not a game bird.

Sometime in the twentieth century, an artist and engraver named Jacques Makowsky and his wife, Therese, emigrated from Russia, first to France and then to America. After several years in New York City, the two retired to a farm in Connecticut, named for their leisure and the landscape, Idle Wild. They didn't remain idle long; they decided to raise poultry. Loving fine things as they did, they wanted only gourmet birds. They first raised guinea hens and then, after a number of years experimenting, tried a crossbreed of Cornish game cocks and Plymouth rock hens. The result was a small, chubby bird with almost all white meat.

The delectable Cornish game hen, growing only to 14 to 16 ounces, was introduced to the market in 1950. Its appeal is its size, its plump breast, and the fact that its meat retains a goodly hint of wild game bird.

Like a woodsy chicken, Cornish game hens can be roasted, stuffed, or sautéed, but they are also small enough to be deep-fried whole. Their petiteness plus flavor makes them ideal for a meal for one or two.

IF IT QUACKS LIKE A DUCK

MANY SPECIES OF DUCK EXIST in the wild around the world, and many species were domesticated for food early on. The one bred by early Americans is called Muscovy, and it is indigenous to Central and South America; it is tame and friendly and so heavy that the males can hardly fly. Native people of the lower Americas had long tamed and relished Muscovy ducks.

Legend gives three origins for the ducks' name. One is that the name derives from the Russian Muscovy Trading Company, which was operating up and down the Pacific coast and vigorously traded the ducks, although not to Russia. Another story says the name emanates from the Muisca people of Colombia, and another one claims they were named for the Miskito people of Central America. The ducks were indigenous to both areas.

All other American domestic ducks are descendants of the wild mallard, which seemingly originated in the Arctic. The steps in that domestication are obscure, but even the Chinese breeds, as well as the European ones, come from the cold-water paddler. And it was a late-arriving Chinese duck that changed American duck eating and farming: the Pekin duck.

The first white Pekin, or Peking, ducks arrived in America aboard a Yankee clipper in 1873. In 1874 an advertisement in *Poultry World Magazine,* formerly called *Fancier's Gazette,* offered for sale a few pairs of "Imperial Pekin Ducks." The same year a firm called Fogg and Co. negotiated duck trade with Japan and China. Nine ducks were brought to Long Island, and the subsequent breeding of them there became so illustrious that they acquired the revamped all-American name Long Island duck. Today the two most enjoyed ducks in America rivaling one another, the Peking and the Long Island, are in fact the same breed.

Since ducks are an active bird, their meat is dark and flavorful. Mostly it's ducklings under eight weeks of age that are savored. They weigh between three and five pounds and are very tender. Almost every nation has a way of treating duck, in a salmi (stew) in the eastern Mediterranean, with cabbage in Poland, with caraway in Czechoslovakia, and braised with walnut and pomegranate sauce in central Asia and dried, then roasted, hung in an oven, as in Chinese cuisine. All, including wild ducks, have happily been brought into American cuisine.

IT'S REALLY NOT A TURKEY

A TREMENDOUS VARIETY OF EDIBLE FOWL thrived in indigenous America. The most curious was America's scrawny-necked, barely flying, good-tasting large grouse, now called a turkey. The European settlers thought it was a type of guinea fowl, some of which they had acquired from Turkey and actually brought with them as early as 1620 (so the difference must have been apparent!). They had dubbed the guinea fowl with the nickname "turkey" for the country where they got it, and applied the same nickname to the American bird.

The value of America's turkeys as a highly available meal for struggling settlers was immediately apparent, to the point that wild turkeys became almost extinct. By 1930 they were living in only the most inaccessible habitats. The restoration of the wild turkey was achieved only around 1960.

So many generations of turkeys have been bred on farms that now the domestic turkeys, though clearly related in feature and feather to their wild ancestors, are quite a different bird. It is the domestic ones that we eat, though for some, the wild ones are still considered the ideal centerpiece of a banquet.

BIRDS OF OTHER FEATHERS

WE ALSO ENJOY GOOSE, another long-bred bird, especially at holiday time. As for swans and peacocks, they have flown away from our culinary repertoire.

SPATCHCOCKED CHICKEN WITH MOZZARELLA AND BABY BEETS

SERVES 4

INGREDIENTS:

Roasted Baby Beets (recipe follows)

Greens from 12 baby beets

Extra virgin olive oil

1 cup finely chopped mushrooms, such as cremini, shiitake, or button (about 8)

1 large clove garlic, minced

1 cup chopped (½-inch pieces) buffalo mozzarella

1 tablespoon large capers, preferably salt-packed, rinsed and coarsely chopped

½ teaspoon kosher or fine sea salt, plus extra for sprinkling on the chicken

Freshly ground black pepper

1 tablespoon chopped fresh dill

2 small chickens (2¼ to 2½ pounds each)

FROM TIME TO TIME, inspiration to create a dish can come merely from a rediscovered culinary term. Such a word is *spatchcock*. It means to split open a chicken or other fowl along the backside so it can be spread out "butterflied" and grilled or roasted with even surface heat on its two sides. The word and its technique offer double-barreled fun. Not only is *spatchcock* amusing and impressive to say, but spatchcocking allows, even invites, an under-the-skin stuffing. As the spatchcocked bird roasts, its workhorse filling of greens, mushrooms, and cheese melts into a sumptuous, hidden sauce that provides two times the "Aha!"

1. Preheat the oven to 375°F.

2. Begin roasting the baby beets.

3. To make the stuffing, sort through the beet greens, discarding all but the tender leaves and stems. Cut them crosswise into thin strips, wash them in plenty of water, and transfer to a colander to drip dry. (You should have about 2½ cups of prepared greens.) Heat 2 tablespoons of oil in a medium-size sauté pan over medium-high heat. Add the mushrooms and garlic and sauté until wilted, about 1 minute. Add the greens and continue sautéing until the greens are wilted, about 1 minute more. Transfer the vegetables to a bowl. Add the cheese, capers, salt, ¼ teaspoon pepper, and 1½ teaspoons of the dill and mix them together.

4. Split the chickens along one side of the backbone. Open them out and set them on a work surface skin side up. Press on the breastbones to flatten the chickens. Gently pull the skin away from the breasts and top part of

the legs. Stuff the beet green mixture under the skin. Place the chickens breast side up on a rimmed baking sheet large enough to hold them without touching. Drizzle oil across the top, sprinkle lightly with salt and pepper, and bake until the breasts are golden across the top, the meat is no longer pink between the leg and thigh, and the cheese is melted to oozing, 40 to 50 minutes.

5. Transfer the chickens to a platter, arrange the beets all around, and sprinkle the remaining dill over them.

ROASTED BABY BEETS

BEETS LOVE VINEGAR. They make a sublime soup served hot or cold and both adorn and satisfy as a simmered or roasted vegetable. The leaves, which early beet lovers gathered long before they esteemed the root, provide an earthy and nourishing green. Together they provide a great complement to meat and poultry.

SERVES 4

12 baby beets (about 2 inches in diameter), leaves removed and reserved, about ½ inch of stem still attached to the beets

1 tablespoon extra virgin olive oil

Kosher or fine sea salt and freshly ground black pepper

2 tablespoons balsamic vinegar

1. Preheat the oven to 375°F.

2. Place the beets in a baking dish. Add the oil, a sprinkle each of salt and pepper, and a splash of water and turn to coat all around. Cover the dish and bake until the beets can be pierced easily with a fork, 45 to 60 minutes.

3. Let the beets cool enough to be handled and, while still warm, rub off the skin with your hands, leaving the stem intact. Toss with the vinegar and set aside at room temperature until ready to use.

➥ **TIP: SPATCHCOCKED AND STUFFED IN SMALL PARTS.**
When it's more convenient to prepare smaller cuts of chicken, rather than a whole bird, bone-in, nonsplit, full chicken breast is the optimum choice for spatchcocking and stuffing. The cut is already spatchcocked, that is, split along the backbone and butterflied, so no effort there. You can then prepare a stuffing, such as the one for the whole chicken, and push it under the skin of each side of the breast. Roast as described; the timing is about the same.

CHICKEN BREASTS
IN COFFEE, VANILLA, SUNDRIED TOMATO, AND CURRANT CREAM

SERVES 4

INGREDIENTS:

3 tablespoons extra virgin olive oil

4 large bone-in chicken breast halves (about 12 ounces each)

Kosher or fine sea salt and freshly ground black pepper

2 cups heavy whipping cream

3 tablespoons strong brewed coffee

½ cup oil-packed sundried tomatoes, drained and chopped

3 tablespoons currants

½ teaspoon honey

½ teaspoon minced vanilla bean seeds and pod

¼ teaspoon ground cinnamon

¼ teaspoon grated nutmeg, preferably freshly grated

THE COMBINATION OF COFFEE AND CREAMY MILK, a revered combination on its own, also provides an alluring and somewhat wild foundation for a sauce to blanket chicken breasts. Coffee 'n' cream in color, rich in body, the sauce is completed with ingredients intense enough to stand up to its stalwart base: sundried tomatoes, currants sun-baked winy on the vine, and a bouquet of spices often found in company with coffee— Old World cinnamon and nutmeg with New World vanilla, all brought to fruition with a kiss of honey.

1. Heat the oil in a large sauté pan over medium-high heat. Sprinkle the breasts with salt and pepper on both sides and place them in the pan, skin side down. Sauté, turning once, until the breasts are done all the way through but still moist in the center and crisp on both sides, about 12 minutes per side.

2. While the breasts cook, mix together the cream, coffee, sundried tomatoes, currants, honey, vanilla bean, cinnamon, and nutmeg in a small bowl and set aside.

3. When the breasts are done, transfer them to a platter and set aside in a warm place. Pour the cream mixture into the pan and bring to a boil. Cook, stirring continuously, until thickened and gravylike, about 3 minutes.

4. Spoon the sauce over the top of the breasts and serve right away.

CHICKEN WITH SHALLOTS, VINEGAR, CAPERS, AND SAGE

FROM GEORGIA TO GIBRALTAR, BABYLON TO BILBAO, all those who knew of wine from early on enjoyed cooking a bird not only in that elixir but also in its sharp derivative, wine vinegar. To this day, vinegar is an essential part of virtually every larder, and combining it with tomatoes makes for an intriguing and double-good approach to cooking chicken. It's just the kind of contemporary, pizzazzy taste fancied nowadays. Sage is added, an herb able to meet the flavor phalanx head on.

1. Heat the oil in a large, heavy skillet over medium-high heat. Place the chicken pieces, skin side down, and the shallots in the pan and sprinkle with the salt and pepper. Cook, stirring and turning, until the chicken is lightly browned, 10 to 12 minutes.

2. Stir in the wine, vinegar, capers, tomatoes, and sage and bring to a boil. Reduce the heat to maintain a brisk simmer, cover the pan, and cook for 15 minutes. Turn the chicken pieces to coat all around, increase the heat to medium-high, and cook, uncovered, turning one more time until the chicken is tender and the liquid is thickened and saucelike, 10 minutes.

3. Sprinkle the parsley over the top and serve right away.

SERVES 4

INGREDIENTS:

- ¼ cup extra virgin olive oil

- 1 large chicken (4 to 4½ pounds), cut into 8 pieces, or the same amount of assorted chicken pieces

- 8 medium or 4 large shallots, cut in half if large

- ¾ teaspoon kosher or fine sea salt

- ½ teaspoon freshly ground black pepper

- ⅓ cup red wine

- ⅓ cup balsamic vinegar

- ¼ cup large capers, preferably salt-packed, rinsed

- 3 medium tomatoes, coarsely chopped

- 1 teaspoon chopped fresh sage leaves or ½ teaspoon dried

- ¼ cup chopped fresh parsley, for garnish

MOCK CHICKEN MOLE WITH TOASTED PUMPKIN SEEDS AND ANCHO CHILE PASTE

SERVES 4

INGREDIENTS:

1 tablespoon extra virgin olive oil, plus extra for toasting the pumpkin seeds

½ cup hulled raw green pumpkin seeds

1 large chicken (4 to 4½ pounds), cut into 8 pieces, or the same amount of assorted chicken pieces

Kosher or fine sea salt and freshly ground black pepper

1 medium-size yellow or white onion, finely chopped

3 cloves garlic, minced or pressed

¼ teaspoon anise seeds

2 cups low-sodium chicken broth

1 cup fresh orange juice

½ cup dry sherry, such as amontillado

2 tablespoons tomato paste

1 bay leaf

Ancho Chile Paste (recipe follows), for serving

1 cup fresh cilantro sprigs

½ teaspoon sherry or cider vinegar

3 ounces (1 bar) 85 percent or higher dark chocolate

¼ teaspoon ground cinnamon

MOLE, LIKE A PESTO, is a pounded sauce or paste and is the way the native people of Mexico and Central America sauce and spice many dishes, generally poultry. The word *mole* in Nahuatl means "mix" or "compound." There are many sorts of mole: guacamole (pounded avocado), mole verde (pounded pumpkin seeds), and the most famous one, mole poblano (pounded chocolate), named for the state of Puebla, where it originated. Mole poblano is considered so sublime and ingenious that it has come to be called simply *mole*. It is perhaps one of America's first fusion dishes, for early on the Spanish married it with the spices from their own cuisine. To Mexico's chocolate they added cumin, anise seeds, bay leaf, and sometimes a touch of sherry vinegar. Here is a simplified version of what is now a pan-Latino treat, popular throughout Central America, Spain, Portugal, and all across the American Southwest. The dried chile paste situates the version squarely in Mexico, as does the garnish of pumpkin seeds. But those seeds can be replaced with the almonds the Spanish adore and would choose instead. Depending also on region, the dish can be served with steamed white rice, polenta, tortillas, or bulgur to absorb every speck of chocolate sauce.

1. To toast the pumpkin seeds, lightly oil a heavy sauté pan large enough to hold the seeds in one layer with olive oil and heat over medium-high heat. Add the seeds and cook, stirring frequently, until plump and golden, about 5 minutes. Cool slightly and then use right away or store at room temperature for up to 2 weeks.

2. Heat 1 tablespoon of oil in the same pan over medium-high heat. Lightly sprinkle the chicken pieces with salt and pepper. Place them in the pan, skin side down, and cook, turning once, until lightly golden, 3 minutes per side.

3. Add the onion, garlic, and anise seeds to the pan and stir to mix. Sauté until the onion wilts slightly, about 2 minutes, then stir in the broth, orange juice, sherry, tomato paste, and bay leaf and bring the mixture to a boil. Reduce the heat to maintain a simmer, turn the chicken once to coat all around, cover the pot, and cook until the chicken is tender, about 30 minutes.

4. While the chicken simmers, prepare the chile paste.

5. Toss together the cilantro sprigs, vinegar, and a small pinch of salt. Set aside at room temperature.

6. When the chicken is done, transfer the pieces to a plate and set aside. Add the chocolate and cinnamon to the liquid in the pan and increase the heat to medium-high. Cook, stirring gently, until the chocolate is melted and incorporated and the liquid is slightly thickened into a sauce, about 15 minutes. Return the chicken to the pan, turn to coat all around, and cook until heated through, 3 minutes more.

MEXICAN CHOCOLATE:
A STORY BEGINNING WITH GREED AND ENDING WITH SPICE

THE CHOCOLATE BEAN HAS LONG NURTURED DESIRE and possessiveness. The avarice began when Quetzalcoatl, the great god of light of the Mayans and Aztecs of Mexico, stole the chocolate plant from his fellow gods and gave it to lowly humans. Quetzalcoatl planted the chocolate shrub in the fields of Tula, then a huge city in eastern Mexico, and asked Tlaloc, the god of the earth, for rain. When the small bush produced fruit, he collected the pods, toasted them, and showed the women of Tula how to grind the seeds with water to obtain the chocolate to eat and drink. A special tool was used for mixing the chocolate into a drink, which, until the Spanish brought sugar, was unsweetened. Indeed, the word *chocolate* is a Mayan compound term for "bitter water," *xococ* for "sour" or "bitter" and *atl* for "water" or "drink." The people also pounded chocolate into a sauce. With Quetzalcoatl's secret the humans became happy and wealthy.

But Quetzalcoatl's fellow gods grew envious of how happy humans were and discovered that these inferior beings somehow had gotten possession of their sacred chocolate. In revenge, the gods enticed Quetzalcoatl to get drunk and make a fool of himself. In shame, he took the chocolate plants from the humans and fled, leaving only a few seeds in the lowlands of Tabasco.

Luckily for all, the plants survived.

When the Spanish arrived in Mexico and came upon chocolate, they began to tinker with it. To it, they added sugar, Old World sweet spices, and nuts. Today's Mexican chocolate echoes the compound the Spanish concocted. It is tinged with cinnamon, almonds, and Mexico's own vanilla. It is sold shaped as hexagonal disks, wrapped in paper, and stacked in bright, tall boxes.

7. Transfer the chicken to a platter. Remove the bay leaf from the sauce and spoon a little over the chicken. Strew the pumpkin seeds and cilantro over the top and serve right away with the chile paste and remaining sauce on the side.

PARSING THE LARGE DRIED CHILES

AS WITH FRESH CHILES, dried chiles range widely in their heat ranking. Following is a rundown on the three kinds of large dried red chiles generally available, and their heat level, on a scale of 1 to 4, with 4 being the hottest.

ANCHO: Supple and aromatic, anchos are a staple in the cuisine of central Mexico. They are the dried version of poblano chiles and are used whole for stuffing, pureed into mole sauces, ground into a prized version of pure chile powder, and toasted to garnish tortilla soup. While not up there with the top-of-the-totem chiles on the heat scale, they nonetheless provide a brisk bite on the tongue. Heat level: 2 to 3.

NEW MEXICO: This is a varietal developed in New Mexico, now widely grown in Colorado and California and often marketed under the name *Colorado* or *California chile*s. Somewhat mild, relatively speaking, these chiles are used for red chile sauces, red chile flakes, and ground into chile powder. Heat level: 2 to 3.

PASILLA: Similar to anchos, pasillas are thinner skinned, less supple, and available in markets, Latino or otherwise, that carry packets of large dried chiles. They are key in the mole sauces of central Mexico and also a typical choice for chile powder. Heat level: 3 to 4.

ANCHO CHILE PASTE

POBLANO CHILES, WHEN dried, turn into large heart-shaped mahogany-colored wrinkled pods called *anchos*. Anchos are not really hot, just spicy; they have all the flavors of chile without excessive heat. Besides being an essential ingredient in mole, ancho chiles are used in adobo sauce and to spice tamales. A paste of them also makes a kicky dab for pork, beef, fish, and vegetable, as well as poultry, preparations.

MAKES ABOUT ½ CUP

2 large ancho chiles, stemmed and torn into small pieces

1 cup water

Kosher or fine sea salt

1. Place the ancho chile pieces in a small saucepan, add the water, and bring to a boil over medium-high heat. Cook until the chiles are quite soft, 5 minutes. Remove the pan from the heat and let the chiles cool slightly.

2. Puree the chiles, along with ½ cup of their cooking liquid, in a food processor. Season with salt to taste. The chile paste may be used as is, or if a smoother paste is desired, pass the puree through a fine-mesh sieve to extract the chile skins and seeds. The paste will keep in the refrigerator for up to 1 week or freeze for longer.

CRISPY OVEN CHICKEN
WITH POTATO AND
BROCCOLINI SALAD

THE FIRST SETTLERS in the Shenandoah Valley were Scotch-Irish, English, and overwhelmingly German. On the fertile land, they established dairy and poultry farms, all of which gave them scrumptious ingredients. Among them, buttermilk. Used as a soak, it adds tangy moisture and ensures crispy chicken. Oven-baked rather than fried, this dish is both dinner and picnic worthy.

SERVES 4

INGREDIENTS:

1 large chicken (4 to 4½ pounds), cut into 8 pieces, or the same amount of assorted chicken pieces

1 cup buttermilk

Butter, for greasing the baking sheet

1 cup all-purpose flour

1 teaspoon kosher or fine sea salt

½ teaspoon hot Hungarian paprika

Potato and Broccolini Salad (recipe follows), for serving

1. Place the chicken pieces in a dish large enough to hold them in one tightly packed layer. Pour the buttermilk over them, cover, and set aside in the refrigerator to marinate for at least 2 hours and up to 4 hours.

2. When ready to cook, remove the chicken from the refrigerator and let it come to room temperature.

3. Preheat the oven to 350°F. Lightly grease a rimmed baking sheet with butter.

4. Place the flour, salt, and paprika on a large plate and stir with a fork to mix. Lift the chicken pieces out of the buttermilk, gently shaking off the excess. Coat each piece all over with the flour mixture. Place the pieces skin side down without touching each other on the baking sheet as you go.

5. Place the chicken in the oven and cook until lightly golden on the bottom, 20 minutes. Turn the pieces over and continue baking until golden on the bottom again, 15 minutes. Turn the pieces once more and cook, skin side up, until golden crisp and sizzling, 5 minutes. Transfer to a serving platter.

6. While the chicken cooks, make the salad.

7. Transfer the chicken to a platter and serve with the salad on the side.

POTATO AND BROCCOLINI SALAD

LIKE A BRIDE, crispy chicken is frequently escorted by a well-dressed attendant: potato salad. Broccolini is a kissing cousin of broccoli, with long thin stems topped with a blossoming of small florets. It makes an appealing addition to a French/German-style potato salad, where the potatoes are dressed while still warm so they easily absorb the flavors of the dressing.

SERVES 4

4 broccolini stalks, cut into 2-inch lengths

3 medium-size russet, Yukon gold, or Kennebec potatoes, cut into ¼-inch-thick rounds

2 tablespoons finely chopped shallot

2 tablespoons extra virgin olive oil

1 tablespoon Dijon mustard

1 tablespoon large capers, preferably salt-packed, rinsed

1 tablespoon fresh lemon juice

¾ teaspoon ground green peppercorns

1 teaspoon kosher or fine sea salt

1. Bring a medium-size pot of water to a boil over medium-high heat. Add the broccolini and cook until they can barely be pierced and are still bright green, about 3 minutes. With a slotted spoon, transfer to a colander and set aside.

2. Add the potatoes and cook until barely tender, about 8 minutes. Drain into the colander with the broccolini and set aside briefly to drip dry.

3. Combine the shallot, oil, mustard, capers, lemon juice, peppercorns, and salt in a small bowl and whisk to mix.

4. While still warm, transfer the potatoes and broccolini to a bowl. Pour the dressing over them and mix gently. Serve warm or at room temperature.

RIVER CHANTEYS:
AN AMERICAN TRADITION

CHANTEYS, OR SHANTIES, refer originally to the songs of sailors at sea, working in unison and singing in rhythm and harmony to aid that work. Always sung at sea, never on shore, there were different sorts of chanteys: ones for hauling in the ropes to hoist the sails, ones for raising the anchor, some for crews of big ships, some for pumping water on leaky ships. Some were sung by all straight through. Some were call-and-response songs, with one voice singing a line of the story, followed by a chorus of all chanting a recurring pattern of words or syllables. The songs flourished from the fifteenth century into the days of the steam ships in England as well as France. They were led by a chantey-man, a self-appointed singing leader who would determine the song and start it. A good shanty man was highly valued and respected.

A new sort of chantey developed in America, the river chantey. America offered enormous resources of lumber, crops, minerals, meat, and fish, but the expanse of land was great and roads poor. The landscape, however, was crisscrossed with deep and wide rivers like the Shenandoah that were used to transport goods. There developed an industry of flatboats that plied the rivers carrying commodities. Along with the industry came flatboat men, who toiled on the boats and adopted the habit of singing to give rhythm and distract from repetitive chores.

White settlers were not the only ones to sing river chanteys. Crews of slaves from Africa, who already had a deep-rooted singing tradition, were also employed to man riverboats and sang songs that were noted as early as the 1800s. Their purpose was the same, to ease the heavy, reiterative labor and promote teamwork.

Today chanteys of sea and river are no longer sung by laborers, but rather by choirs and at folk fests.

PARMESAN AND CRACKER-CRUSTED CHICKEN WITH LEMON CREAM

SALTINE OR SODA CRACKERS are thin and flaky, sprinkled with semicoarse salt and perforated along the top and bottom. Saltines' distinct friability leads to many uses. Among them, legend says, Maryland cooks, looking for a crunchy way to revamp fried chicken, crush the crackers and use them to make an admirably crispy fried chicken. Here the cracker crumbs are intermixed with tantalizing grated Parmesan cheese, a combination well matched with a lemon cream sauce instead of classic gravy.

SERVES 4

INGREDIENTS:

¼ cup extra virgin olive oil, plus extra for greasing the baking sheet

1 cup saltine cracker crumbs (about 30 saltines)

½ cup finely grated Parmesan cheese

¾ teaspoon kosher or fine sea salt

1 large chicken (4 to 4½ pounds), cut into 8 pieces, or the same amount of assorted chicken pieces

1 large egg, beaten

4 tablespoons (½ stick) butter, melted

½ cup fresh lemon juice

1 cup heavy whipping cream

2 teaspoons finely chopped lemon zest

1. Lightly oil a rimmed baking sheet large enough to hold the chicken pieces without touching. Combine the cracker crumbs, Parmesan cheese, and ½ teaspoon of the salt on a plate and mix together with a fork.

2. Dip each chicken piece in the egg, then roll it in the cracker mixture, placing the pieces on the baking sheet as you go. Set aside at room temperature to dry and firm the crust for 20 to 30 minutes.

3. Preheat the oven to 350°F.

4. Place the chicken in the oven and bake until golden and crispy on the bottom, 30 minutes. Turn the pieces over and pour the butter over them. Continue baking until golden and crispy all around, about 20 minutes more.

5. While the chicken bakes, combine the lemon juice and ¼ cup oil in a small saucepan and bring to a boil over high heat. Reduce the heat to medium and whisk in the cream, zest, and remaining ¼ teaspoon salt. Cook until bubbly and thickened, 3 to 5 minutes.

6. Arrange the chicken on a platter. Pour the sauce over the top and serve.

BEER-BATTERED CHICKEN WITH CUMBERLAND GAP JELLY

SERVES 4

INGREDIENTS:

1 cup flat lager beer

1 large egg

1 cup all-purpose flour

Cumberland Gap Jelly (recipe follows), for serving

Peanut or canola oil or solid vegetable shortening, for frying

1 large chicken (4 to 4½ pounds), cut into 8 pieces, or the same amount of assorted chicken pieces

Kosher or fine sea salt

IN 1750 A DOCTOR AND EXPLORER NAMED THOMAS WALKER discovered a break in the foreboding Appalachians just north of where the states of Tennessee, Virginia, and Kentucky now meet. He named it the Cumberland Gap after the Duke of Cumberland. But the man who made the passageway famous was Daniel Boone, who marked the path with ax cuts. Settlers called it the Wilderness Trail, and it enabled people at last to set up farms throughout the inland South. Their homemade beer was the focus of their hospitality, barn dances, and evening respite from a hardscrabble life, and their way with their simple ingredients became the basis of southern cooking. One of their innovations was to combine the beer with the flour they ground and use it to coat chicken pieces, which they fried up crisp. Salt and a good dash of pepper in the flour and the grainy savor of beer were, and still are, the only seasoning needed. Lots of southern folks still add beer as in olden days to make the batter for their southern fried chicken. Here a companion sauce named for Cumberland, accented with port, citrus, and mustard, recalls those who first traversed the gap.

1. Whisk together the beer and egg in a large bowl, then slowly whisk in the flour. Set the batter aside in the refrigerator. Remove the batter from the refrigerator a few minutes before you're ready to cook the chicken.

2. Make the jelly.

3. Pour oil to a depth of about ¾ inch into a large, deep sauté pan and heat over medium-high heat. When a drop of batter sizzles and immediately rises to the top, dip the chicken pieces

into the batter, completely covering them with the batter. Dip only as many as will fit in the pan without crowding. Add the chicken to the pan and fry, turning twice, until dark golden, crisp, and cooked through, 15 to 20 minutes for the breast and wing pieces, 20 to 25 minutes for the legs and thighs. Transfer to paper towels to drain and sprinkle with salt. Continue with another batch until all the chicken is fried.

4. Serve right away, while still warm and crisp, with the jelly on the side.

CUMBERLAND GAP JELLY

THE ORIGINAL CUMBERLAND SAUCE calls for a tingling blend of tart red currants, the bite of yellow mustard, and the sweetness of port wine. As citrus fruit became available, cooks added a little flowery orange to the mixture. Cumberland sauce on chicken rather than game was a signature dish at the now defunct Maples Hotel in Florida. In a Floridian flair, here the well-traveled sauce joins grapefruit juice with the classic orange.

MAKES ABOUT 1¼ CUPS

1 cup red currant jelly
½ cup tawny port
¼ cup orange juice

FROM CUMBERLAND TO CUMBERLAND GAP

CUMBERLAND HISTORICALLY was an area in the far northwest of England abutting Northumberland and Westmorland with Scotland lying directly to the north. It was one of England's traditional thirty-nine counties, and Cumberland's clans fought fiercely against Roman invasions until the emperor Hadrian built a wall across northern England to protect his soldiers from them. Eventually the poor and rough land was subdued and came under the control of the English royalty. Dukes and earls would travel there to hunt. To sauce the bounty, a cook with ties to Hanover, Germany, concocted an English version of a German one and named it for the Duke of Cumberland. The sauce became a quintessential English condiment for game and cold meats such as ham and so was often served cold, slightly jellied.

The many immigrants from that rocky, abject countryside who settled along the Eastern Seaboard brought the game sauce they knew from their homeland and applied it to a dish of the domestic fowl they raised, namely chicken.

2 tablespoons fresh grapefruit juice
1 tablespoon grated orange zest
½ teaspoon dry mustard
Pinch of cayenne pepper

Combine the currant jelly, port, orange juice, grapefruit juice, orange zest, dry mustard, and cayenne in a medium-size saucepan over high heat and bring to a boil while gently whisking to mix. Reduce the heat to maintain a brisk simmer and cook until thickened just enough to very lightly coat a spoon, 15 to 20 minutes. Remove, cool, and use right away. Or cool completely and refrigerate for up to 3 months.

ROAST CHICKEN WITH WALNUT PESTO AND SHREDDED BASIL

INGREDIENTS:

Walnut Pesto
   (recipe follows)

1 whole chicken
   (3½ to 4 pounds)

Kosher or fine sea salt and
   freshly ground black
   pepper

1 lemon, coarsely cut up

2 small onions,
   coarsely cut up

2 tablespoons shredded
   fresh basil

THE CRAFT REQUIRED TO TURN OUT A PERFECT ROAST CHICKEN is actually quite uncomplicated. Start by stuffing the bird with lemon and onion to lend aroma and moisture from within. Roast it at a fairly high heat so that the skin crisps and renders its fat to moisturize the bird from without. Then, to take it beyond the everyday and transform it to resplendent, embellish it with a pesto sauce of walnuts, garlic, bread crumbs, and olive oil. Topped with such a concoction, it's a truly regal roast chicken!

1. Preheat the oven to 475°F.

2. Make the walnut pesto.

3. Sprinkle the chicken inside and out with salt and pepper. Stuff the chicken cavity with the lemon and onions, place the chicken breast side up in a baking dish just large enough to hold it, and roast it for 45 minutes. Spread some of the walnut pesto over the breasts and legs and continue roasting until the juices run golden and the legs easily separate from the thighs when wiggled, 10 to 15 minutes more.

4. Transfer the chicken to a serving platter, sprinkle the basil over the top, and serve with the remaining pesto on the side.

WALNUT PESTO

CALLED *BAZHA* **AND** *SATSIVI* in Caucasus Georgia, *tarator* in Turkey and Lebanon, and *salsa karydia* in Greece, a pounded walnut pesto originally from Lydia, Croesus's realm, is a golden and traditional augmentation for poultry, baked or fried fish, fried eggplant, and cooked vegetables like beets, green beans, and cauliflower. With a food processor and walnuts, bread, olive oil, garlic, and vinegar for the acid element, the pesto is facile to spin up, and you can use it for just about anything that sprouts, swims, or cackles.

MAKES ABOUT 1 CUP

2 cups coarsely cut-up crustless baguette

½ cup water

¾ cup walnut halves or pieces

¼ teaspoon kosher or fine sea salt

1 large clove garlic, peeled

¼ cup extra virgin olive oil

1 teaspoon red wine vinegar

1. Combine the bread and water in a small bowl and set aside to soak until the bread is thoroughly saturated, 1 or 2 minutes.

2. Pulverize the walnuts in a food processor. Squeeze the soaked bread almost, but not completely, dry and add it to the processor. Spread the salt on a cutting surface and finely chop the garlic in the salt. Add the garlic, salt, and oil to the processor and puree. Add the vinegar and puree as fine as possible. Set aside at room temperature until ready to use, up to 4 hours. Or refrigerate for up to 3 days.

THE GREATER PRAIRIE CHICKEN

THE GREATER PRAIRIE CHICKEN is unique to the grasslands of North America. It is a stout, medium-size grouse, approximately eighteen inches in length with a fine-lined but distinct striped barring across its entire body. The wings alternate dark brown with a pale beige. The feet are completely feathered down to the toes, and the prairie chicken's throat, lower cheeks, the area between the eyes, and down to the bill are tawny. Its bill is short and black.

Prairie chickens are beautiful birds to behold.

Except when the males are courting the females in spring, the gender of a bird is hard to determine. But mating season brings about a major turn of events. Males possess large black and buff-colored pinnae feathers on the backs of their necks, and when pursuing a mate, they raise these features vertically above their heads. To add to their virile display, they inflate bright yellow-orange throat sacs and reveal yellow-orange eyebrows.

Anywhere from eight to seventy males congregate before dawn, and over the next several hours they stamp their feet, strut, shake their wings, fan their tails, extend their feathers, and pump out their throats. They jump in the air and stick each other with their feet, wings, and bill. They hoot out a low, booming sound propelled by their air sacs, which can be heard for more than two miles. The fights are for territory, which is called their *booming ground,* and the winners gain the rights to breed. This, say their devotees, is truly a site to see.

At one time virtually millions of these glorious native "chickens" flocked across the nation, but they attracted hunters for both food and sport so that by 1853 shipments of them to city markets measured in the tons. Other encroachments endangered them. Forests were cleared, and grasslands were plowed for agriculture. Their cousin, the heath hen, did not survive. The greater prairie chicken proved more resistant, but barely. In 1905 and 1907 the first laws were passed restricting hunting to short periods, and finally in 1955 some states, like Wisconsin, banned their hunting altogether.

In Wisconsin, at least, America's prairie chickens have undergone a miraculous comeback. Due to several individuals, preserves of their habitat that include grass, shrubs, and swamps have been established to protect them, and they are once again thriving. At least seven generations of Americans have been awed by the greater prairie chicken, and more will be able to delight in them in days to come.

ROAST CHICKEN STUFFED WITH BULGUR, YELLOW SQUASH, AND BELL PEPPER PILAF

SERVES 3 OR 4

INGREDIENTS:

Bulgur, Yellow Squash,
and Bell Pepper Pilaf
(recipe follows)

1 large whole chicken
(4 to 4½ pounds)

Kosher or fine sea salt and
freshly ground black
pepper

CALL IT PROVINCIAL, CALL IT PEASANT, EVEN CALL IT BUCOLIC: there's little more gratifying than humble rustic fare. Bursting with natural goodness, such dishes are cooked straightforwardly without much fuss, with little ornament, and brought to the table without further ado. Juicy roast chicken stuffed with bulgur pilaf and stalwart garden vegetables is a paean to country cooking, a meal elysian in the most essential manner.

1. First, make the pilaf.

2. Preheat the oven to 400°F.

3. Lightly sprinkle the chicken inside and out with salt and pepper. Stuff the chest and neck cavities of the chicken with the bulgur mixture, pressing it in firmly so it all fits. Set the chicken breast side up in a roasting pan and roast until golden across the top and the juices run golden when the thigh is pricked, 1 hour and 10 minutes. Remove the chicken from the oven and set aside for 5 to 10 minutes for the juices to settle.

4. Scoop out the stuffing, transfer to a bowl along with any that has oozed out of the cavity during roasting, and moisten it with some of the cooking juices. Transfer the chicken to a serving platter. Carve at the table and serve with the stuffing on the side.

BULGUR, YELLOW SQUASH, AND BELL PEPPER PILAF

RATHER THAN GROUND into flour, left in whole berries, or rendered for its inner germ, bulgur is made from whole wheat berries that are boiled until they swell open. They are then drained and spread out to dry, often in the sun. Once dried, the precooked berries are crushed into small golden irregular-shaped nutty, earthy-tasting pebbles that make a homey plain pilaf. Studded with vegetables, the pilaf intertwines field and garden. Bulgur comes in three grinds: fine, medium, and coarse. For pilaf, coarse or medium is best. The dish can also be served as a humble side dish.

MAKES ABOUT 3 CUPS

2 tablespoons extra virgin olive oil, butter, or a combination

¾ cup bulgur wheat

1 large yellow crookneck squash, cut into ¼- to ½-inch pieces

1 medium-size red bell pepper, stemmed, seeded, cut into ¼- to ½-inch pieces

1 rib celery, chopped

2 tablespoons chopped shallot

2 teaspoons chopped fresh marjoram leaves

1½ teaspoons kosher or fine sea salt

1½ cups low-sodium chicken broth or water

1. Heat the oil in a large sauté pan over medium-high heat. Add the bulgur, squash, red pepper, celery, shallot, marjoram, and salt and stir to mix. Sauté until the vegetables begin to wilt and the bulgur becomes a little toasty, about 5 minutes.

2. Add the broth and bring to a boil over high heat. Reduce the heat to low, cover the pan, and simmer until the bulgur is fluffy and soft all through,

AMERICA'S FIRST CHICKEN BREED: THE RARE DOMINIQUE

STARTING WITH THE CHICKENS Columbus brought to the New World, all the initial breeds of the bird introduced were what is called *barred* in their markings. That is, rather than pure white or bronze, the feathers alternated in a repetitive rippling of white and gray or another color. Around 1750, among the barred chickens one was developed with a "rose" comb, flat and fleshy, terminating in a spike. In 1849, this distinctive American breed became known as Dominique, although farmers called the bird the *dominicker*. So popular and important to early chicken farmers was the breed that by the mid-1880s the American Poultry Association, formed in 1873, had laid out standards determining the size and appearance of the chicken.

It is a pretty chicken. Its feathers are full, fluffy, and look like waves with their alternating almost-black and almost-white color bars. The rose-shaped comb stands up in contrast like a pinkish red tiara and necklace combination, rather like a wimple head scarf. For a chicken, a bird that can get quite scrappy, the Dominique is calm and nonaggressive. Still, it is also a hardy bird, known for the ability to scratch up its own food, so it doesn't need the attention that more human-dependent breeds do. Dominiques can thrive outside in the wild or in barns in the winter cold. Their plumage blankets them, yet is soft enough for pillows. Their eggs are brown, and the hens will produce them even in adverse conditions.

In the 1900s Asian chickens came to America and gained economic importance so rapidly that the Dominique almost disappeared. For a while they were on the brink of extinction, with fewer than five hundred hens existing. They became listed as, and remain, critical under the American Livestock Breeds Conservancy of endangered breeds. Great efforts are being made to save Dominiques. Some devoted farmers continue to engender them, and their popularity is growing again. A trip to the local zoo is a good way to see America's first chicken breed, pretty as they are and happily strutting around.

about 22 minutes. Remove from the heat and set aside until cool enough to handle.

GIFTS FROM INDIA

The first person to arrive in America from India came in 1790 as a maritime worker, followed by a stream of émigrés until 1917, when Congress overrode President Wilson's veto and barred all Asian newcomers. Then a subsequent ruling in 1923 banned those already here from citizenship. By 1943, a number of prominent Americans, including President Roosevelt, called for an end to the discrimination against Indians and allowed them to obtain citizenship.

During the years they were restricted, Indians, both immigrants and those born here, were culling honors and prizes for America in everything from letters to sciences. Their contribution to America's well-being is enormous.

Yet to use the term *Indian* is to blanket these citizens under a massive umbrella. India itself is a composite of peoples, as interwoven as the fabrics spun there, and the Indians of America represent every thread. They came not only from the many varied parts of the Indian subcontinent but as well from other nations with large, established Indian populations.

A PANOPLY OF FOODS

AS A RESULT, the inventory of flavors and dishes Indian immigrants have contributed to the American rainbow of foods is extensive. From India come eggplant, sesame, mustard, cardamom, and pepper. Though the particular renditions differ by cooking technique, region, religion, social class, and the influence of the people who colonized different locales, all share a common thread of ingredients: rice, dried legumes, and wheat; coriander seeds, cinnamon, cardamom, ginger, chiles, and mustard seeds to name a few spices; onion, garlic, lentils, spinach sauces, and yogurt to ameliorate the spices. All love fritters: Samosas, batter-wrapped,

fried spicy dumplings filled with potato, peas, and other vegetables are probably the favorite pan-Indian snack.

South Indian foods, extending through Sri Lanka and including Kerala and Goa on the West Coast, feature coconut, curry leaves, and tamarind to augment chicken and vegetable dishes and, along the seashore, a miscellany of fish dishes.

North Indian foods reflect the culinary impact of the Moguls, the later-arriving invaders from the North who long reigned on the subcontinent and erected many of the massive palaces and palatial complexes, such as the Taj Mahal. Northern cuisine includes many dairy products, particularly a solid clarified butter called *ghee,* used as a cooking medium; a simple cow's milk cheese called *paneer,* and an array of milky sweets. These are joined by cashews and poppy seeds; mint instead of cilantro as the fresh herb; and a plethora of pickles from limes to gooseberries to cauliflower and carrots. Northern Indian fare is also famous for tandoor ovens in which people bake their universally appealing wheaty naan flat breads.

As for beverages, India, of course, is far famed for its teas, in particular Darjeeling, Assam, and all sorts of spicy chais that have of late overrun American coffee bars. Their beers, too, are loved; India pale ale is a hot seller in bars and brasseries west from England to Canada and America.

TANDOORI-STYLE
BEER-CAN CHICKEN

A LIAISON OF CUISINES AND PEOPLE can lead to strikingly imaginative dishes—for example, a cross-brewed (not bred, but really brewed!) barbecue! Here Indian-style barbecue, called *tandoori,* meets the American backyard grill, all propped up on a beer can, a traditional beverage in both cultures. Indians barbecue in a tandoor, a large clay pot, almost like an oven. A backyard grill can simulate a tandoor and produce the same succulent outcome. The key to the cojoined cooking is the Indian seasoning. Rather than a ketchupy barbecue sauce or a salting, the tandoori seasoning is softly spicy with a friendly punch from paprika. The paprika also lends a tinge of red to the chicken coating, mimicking the red food dye Indian cooks traditionally use when barbecuing. Inexpensive pop-top beer is fine for the cooking. It's the can itself and the malty steam that are key. For the beverage to serve along with the chicken, though, offer an India pale ale in the bottle.

1. Mix together the cumin, curry powder, ginger, paprika, cardamom seeds, salt, cayenne, garlic, yogurt, and lemon juice in a small bowl. Rub the chicken inside and out, including the neck cavity, with the mixture. Set the chicken aside in the refrigerator for at least 2 hours and up to overnight.

2. When ready to cook, prepare a medium-hot grill. Remove the chicken from the refrigerator.

3. Pop the tab on the beer can. With a "church key," punch 2 more holes in the top of the can. Holding the chicken upright, position its cavity on top of the beer can and press down to secure

the can within the cavity. (The can will fit most of the way into the cavity, but there will be an inch or two of can exposed.) Pull the chicken's legs forward to create a stable tripod configuration with the bottom of the beer can as the third leg.

4. Set the beer can chicken upright on the grill to the side, not directly over, the heat. Cover the grill and cook until the juices run golden when the chicken is pierced at the leg and thigh joint, about 1 hour and 10 minutes.

5. Using 2 sets of tongs, carefully lift the chicken off the beer can and place it on a platter. Carve and serve.

INGREDIENTS:

1 teaspoon ground cumin

1 teaspoon curry powder

1 teaspoon ground ginger

1 teaspoon hot Hungarian paprika

½ teaspoon cardamom seeds

½ teaspoon kosher or fine sea salt

¼ teaspoon cayenne pepper

1 clove garlic, peeled and minced or pressed

2 tablespoons plain Greek yogurt

1 tablespoon fresh lemon juice

1 whole chicken (3½ to 4 pounds)

1 can (12 ounces) beer

CHICKEN POTPIE UNDER FILO CRUST

SERVES 4

INGREDIENTS:

3 tablespoons butter

2 skinless, boneless chicken breasts, cut crosswise into 1-inch-wide strips

Kosher or fine sea salt and freshly ground black pepper

2 shallots, thinly sliced

1 small parsnip, peeled and cut into ½-inch pieces

¼ medium-size celery root, peeled and cut into ½ inch-pieces (about 1 cup)

2 ounces fresh mushrooms, such as shiitake or button, trimmed and thinly sliced (about ½ cup)

1 teaspoon chopped fresh thyme

2 tablespoons brandy

2 ounces unsmoked ham, coarsely chopped (about ⅓ cup)

1 tablespoon chopped fresh chives

2 teaspoons fresh lemon juice

1 cup heavy whipping cream

4 sheets filo dough

3 tablespoons melted butter

FOR MANY, chicken potpie is one of those foods that, whether from grandmother's kitchen or a homey nearby diner, spells comfort. Making the consoling pies from scratch dwindled during the 1950s, and frozen chicken potpies entered the culinary scene. They are serviceable but can't replace the homemade. It's true, a made-from-scratch replica of that memorable pie takes some time, but when the pie is crusted only on top, with already made, ultra-flaky filo dough, the time commitment is not that exacting. It's even possible to exchange the customary carrots and peas for an exciting mélange of shallot, parsnip, celery root, and mushrooms, and commingle them with cooked-on-the-spot chicken breast pieces. Eschewing the floury binding sauce, the pie embraces brandy and cream for thickening. The payoff is a pie that's soothing as ever, but oh so urbane.

1. Preheat the oven to 425°F.

2. Melt 2 tablespoons of the butter in a large sauté pan over medium-high heat. Sprinkle the chicken strips with salt and pepper; add them to the pan, and sauté until firm and no longer pink, about 3 minutes. Transfer the strips to an 8-inch square or round baking dish. Set aside.

3. Melt the remaining 1 tablespoon butter in the sauté pan and add the shallots, parsnip, celery root, mushrooms, and thyme and stir to mix. Reduce the heat to medium and sauté until the vegetables are wilted, 3 minutes. Increase the heat to medium-high, stir in the brandy, and cook until the liquid is mostly evaporated, 2 minutes. Add the ham, chives, and lemon juice, stir to mix, then stir in the cream. Bring to a boil and immediately pour the vegetables over the chicken in the dish. Set aside to cool to room temperature.

4. To assemble the pie: Cut each sheet of filo into a 9-inch square. Place 1 square on top of the chicken mixture.

With a pastry brush, brush it lightly with the melted butter. Lay another square on top of the first and brush it with butter. Repeat 2 more times, winding up with the top layer of filo brushed with butter. Tuck the edges into the pan and bake until the crust is golden and crispy and the juices underneath are bubbling up, about 30 minutes.

5. Remove the pie from the oven, let it cool for 5 minutes, then serve.

A MELTING POT OF ETHNIC CHICKEN DISHES THAT ARE REALLY AMERICAN

IN FOOD FORAYS TO ETHNIC RESTAURANTS, we Americans have often taken to particular dishes that are not ethnic at all but are, in fact, American inventions. Among these are some we think of as French, Italian, Chinese, or Indian. They include:

CHICKEN DIVAN: a casserole dish featuring chicken with broccoli and either Mornay or hollandaise sauce. It was created in the Divan Parisienne in New York City and became so popular that it turned into the restaurant's signature dish, to be much imitated in French restaurants across the country.

CHICKEN TETRAZZINI: a chicken inspiration created by a San Francisco chef. In the nineteenth century, it was an American tradition to name dishes after stars of the day (and also to attract said stars to the establishments). Luisa Tetrazzini was a highly admired diva at the San Francisco Opera. She doted on the meal named for her.

GENERAL TSO'S CHICKEN: fried dark-meat chicken served with vegetables and whole dried chile peppers in a mild hot sauce. Rather than in China, the dish was invented by Taiwanese immigrants to the United States and was named for General Zuo Zongtang, of the Manchu Dynasty. He was so hot-tempered that just mentioning his name was threatening enough to scare off enemies.

COUNTRY CAPTAIN CHICKEN: an India-style chicken dish, spiced with curry, topped with golden raisins and toasted almonds.

Created in Georgia in the early 1800s, it became a great southern favorite, dating from when Savannah was a major port for the American spice trade. According to Indian journalists, the term Country Captain was not known there. It perhaps comes from ship captains who wanted to curry favor.

CHICKEN BOOYAH: a thick, filling chicken stew that comes from Wisconsin, not Belgium. The Belgian immigrants of the area who spoke Walloon pronounce the French bouillon "bouyah" and called their soupy American innovation the same.

CHICKEN À LA KING: a dish with a more or less French name and more than one story of origin. In one it was fashioned by Chef Ranhofer of Delmonico's in New York City for the silver-spoon scion of a Wall Street tycoon, named James R. Keene, and was first called Chicken à la Keene. After his demise, it became a meal for a king, not a Keene.

CHICKEN ROCHAMBEAU: a Louisiana Creole dish with ham and a Rochambeau sauce of chicken stock with brown sugar. The combination gained widespread fame for the version served at Antoine's restaurant in New Orleans.

YELLOW CURRY CHICKEN WITH GREEN BEANS, COCONUT SPICE, AND SAFFRON RICE

SERVES 4

INGREDIENTS:

¾ cup unsweetened coconut flakes, plus ⅓ cup toasted (see Tip)

3 large shallots, peeled

¾ teaspoon ground cumin

¼ teaspoon ground turmeric

Pinch of cayenne pepper

Saffron Rice (recipe follows)

8 ounces haricots verts or other green beans

2 tablespoons peanut or canola oil

4 large skinless, boneless, chicken breast halves (about 2 pounds), cut into ½-inch pieces

1 jalapeño or serrano chile, finely chopped

2 cups coconut milk

2 cups low-sodium chicken broth

1 teaspoon kosher or fine sea salt

2 tablespoons whole fresh cilantro leaves

1 lime, cut into 4 wedges

INTERPOSED BETWEEN THE LANDS AND PEOPLE OF INDIA and those of Southeast Asia lies Myanmar, once known as Burma. Its food displays its betwixt position. From the eastern side of the country comes the influence of Manipur, India, and the Bay of Bengal, which bring the spice mixes of masala and curry. From the west comes the taste for fish sauce and coconut milk, the former showing up as the most familiar Myanmar sauce, the latter as the most common cooking liquid. As in India, chile peppers are favored, and as in Southeast Asia, cilantro and basil are a frequent garnish. Here a coconut-spice mixture as a topping to a Myanmar-style coconut milk curry intertwines both culinary customs, tossing together the flakes of the coconut fruit of Southeast Asia with the cumin and turmeric of Mother India.

1. Combine the ¾ cup coconut flakes, shallots, cumin, turmeric, and cayenne in a food processor and chop finely. Set aside.

2. Make the saffron rice.

3. If using haricots verts, leave them whole. If using other green beans, cut them crosswise into 1½- to 2-inch pieces. Set aside.

4. To make the curry, heat the oil in a large, heavy sauté pan over medium-high heat. Add the chicken and stir-fry until slightly firmed up, about 3 minutes. Add the coconut-spice mixture and the chile and stir to mix.

Stir in the green beans and cook until the beans begin to get limp, about 3 minutes. Stir in the coconut milk, chicken broth, and salt and bring to a boil. Reduce the heat to maintain a simmer and cook, uncovered, until the beans are al dente, 4 to 5 minutes more.

5. To serve, place a mound of rice in each of 4 individual bowls. Ladle the curry over the rice and garnish with the toasted coconut flakes, cilantro, and lime wedges.

SAFFRON RICE

OUNCE FOR OUNCE, measure for measure, saffron is one of the most expensive commodities in the world. It comes from the delicate stamens of the saffron crocus and must be painstakingly picked by hand. The saffron crocus blooms fleetingly in the fall of the year only, when the blossoms glow with vivid purple to violet to lavender petals that gorgeously contrast with the saffron yellow of their stamens. In spite of the cost, the unique color and aroma that saffron imparts to a dish make it exceptional. Those characteristics unfold beautifully in a pairing with rice, from risotto to paella to rice pudding, and more.

SERVES 4

1½ cups basmati or jasmine rice

3 cups water

Large pinch of saffron threads

1. Combine the rice, water, and saffron in a medium-size, heavy pot and bring to a boil over medium-high heat. Reduce the heat to low, cover, and cook without disturbing for 22 minutes.

2. Turn off the heat and let the rice sit for 10 minutes to finish steaming dry. Stir to fluff and serve right away or set aside in a warm place for up to 1 hour.

TIP: TOASTING COCONUT FLAKES. Unsweetened coconut flakes (larger than shreds, more like shavings of coconut) are available in health food and produce stores that sport bulk bins. They are worth seeking out for their crunchy, crispy texture. When toasted, they top curries, cakes, and pies with a golden hue. Here are the options for toasting coconut flakes:

In the microwave: Spread the flakes on a plate and microwave on high for 5 minutes, stirring once halfway through.

On the stovetop: Place the flakes in an ungreased medium-size sauté pan over medium-high heat and cook, stirring frequently, for 5 minutes.

In the oven: Preheat the oven to 375°F. Spread the flakes on a baking sheet, place in the oven, and cook for 5 minutes.

Once toasted, the coconut flakes will keep in an airtight jar in the cupboard for up to a week.

CORNISH GAME HENS BAKED WITH EGGPLANT AND GREEN OLIVES

INGREDIENTS:

- 1 medium-size eggplant, cut into 1-inch cubes
- 12 large cloves garlic, peeled
- ½ cup pitted Italian, French, or Greek green olives
- 2 tablespoons extra virgin olive oil
- 2 teaspoons fresh thyme leaves or ½ teaspoon dried
- 1 teaspoon kosher or fine sea salt
- 2 Cornish game hens, split in half
- 1 bay leaf, crumbled
- ½ teaspoon freshly ground black pepper
- 2 tablespoons chopped fresh flat-leaf parsley, for garnish
- 2 teaspoons finely chopped lemon zest, for garnish

IN THE ALL-SURROUNDING HEAT OF THE OVEN, Cornish game hens plump up to chubby and juicy and marry with dozens of ingredients and flavors surrounding them in the pot. Take green olives as one. Smooth and briny out of the container, their flavors are concentrated by roasting. Eggplant is another. Softened from baking, its texture becomes velvety and mellow. Together with thyme, the result is an amazing and unusual convergence of tastes, smooth yet spirited, rustic yet distinguished.

1. Preheat the oven to 450°F.

2. Toss together the eggplant, garlic, olives, olive oil, 1 teaspoon of the thyme, and ½ teaspoon of the salt in a large clay pot or Dutch oven or other ovenproof pot. Arrange the game hen halves skin side up in one tight layer over the vegetables. Sprinkle the bay leaf, pepper, and remaining thyme and salt over the top. Cover and bake until the eggplant is soft and the bird pieces are almost done, 40 minutes.

3. Stir gently, loosening the vegetables from the bottom, and continue baking uncovered until the hens are lightly browned and very tender, about 10 minutes more.

4. Garnish with the parsley and lemon zest and serve.

CORNISH GAME HENS STUFFED WITH DRIED RASPBERRIES AND SUNFLOWER SEEDS

THE NUMBER OF PERSONS WE FEED AT OUR DINNER TABLES is getting smaller. Often the table settings are only for two, and a holiday meal may be for four, too few for even the smallest turkey. Considering the alternatives, a smaller bird, such as a goose, is a little too rarefied; duck a bit complex. But Cornish game hens offer an ideal solution. They are charming in size and decidedly more special than a chicken for a festive meal. And they have a cavity made for stuffing. Cornish hens present a great opportunity to modernize and embellish a stuffing with a few new frills. Here fresh mushrooms give an earthiness, while dried raspberries add a touch of sweet fruit and roasted sunflower seeds give it some crunch. Using rich red wine makes a gravy that's a bit highfalutin.

1. Preheat the oven to 400°F.

2. Rinse and pat the hens dry and set aside at room temperature.

3. Melt the butter in a large skillet over medium-high heat. Add the onion and celery and sauté until the onion is transparent, about 3 minutes. Stir in the mushrooms, raspberries, sunflower seeds, thyme, salt, and pepper and sauté until the raspberries are soft, 4 to 5 minutes. Remove the skillet from the heat and let cool enough to handle.

4. Place the bread in a bowl. Add the mushroom and raspberry mixture to the bowl and, with a spoon or your hands, mix them together.

5. Press the stuffing mixture together and stuff it tightly into the belly cavity and under the neck skin of the hens. Place them breast side up in a flame-proof roasting pan. Bake for 15 minutes, reduce the heat to 350°F, and continue baking until the juice runs clear when the thigh of the hen is pierced and the skin is golden brown,

SERVES 4

INGREDIENTS:

4 Cornish game hens (1 to 1¼ pounds each)

8 tablespoons (1 stick) butter

1 small yellow or white onion, chopped

2 ribs celery, chopped

1 cup chopped fresh mushrooms

½ cup (6 ounces) dried raspberries

3 tablespoons roasted and salted sunflower seeds

2 tablespoons fresh thyme leaves

1 teaspoon kosher or fine sea salt

½ teaspoon freshly ground black pepper

6 ounces baguette or other good white bread, cut into 1-inch pieces (about 4½ cups) and lightly toasted

1½ cups red wine

another 45 to 55 minutes. Remove the hens from the pan and set them aside in a warm place to let their juices settle.

6. Place the roasting pan on a stovetop burner over medium heat. Pour in the wine and bring to a simmer, scraping up the brown bits into the wine. Reduce until thick enough to coat a spoon, about 5 minutes.

7. Place the hens on a platter or individual plates, glaze with the wine sauce, and serve.

THE PAPAYA AND THE COCONUT

THE PAPAYA

PAPAYAS ARE GROWN in a wide swath of tropical regions that range from their home in Central America to the Tropic of Cancer and on to the Tropic of Capricorn. The plant is not a true fruit, but rather a large herb growing up to thirty feet in height. Wherever it landed, the papaya developed to suit local preference for size, shape, color, firmness, and taste. The fruit ranges from the pear-shaped one most common to American markets, to ball-shaped, and the small, still-green ones beloved in Southeast Asia. The ones preferred in Mexico and Hawaii are ripe and sweet, perfect for their salsas and fruit drinks. Not only is papaya good to eat, but because of the papain it contains, it is used as a meat tenderizer, leather softener, a pre-dye for wool and silk, medicine, cosmetics, and shampoos.

THE COCONUT

THE COCONUT PALM, with its roundish fruit, bobbed across the water following almost the same belt as the papaya. It started its voyage so early, no one knows exactly where it originated, but the islands of the western Pacific are likely. From there it floated in one direction to the eastern Pacific, Central and South America and in another direction to Southeast Asia, India, the Seychelles, and Mauritius. Eventually it ventured to the Red Sea, Madagascar, and up East Africa to Egypt and the Mediterranean. It wandered so far because the beach-loving tree's fronds often extended over water, allowing the fruit easy access to a method of travel. In many of its new homes, it became more than an essential food. The fronds as well were used in building, the oil in soap, the milk provided a drink, and the husks turned into eating vessels. The name coconut comes from the Spanish for "goblin" because the three dots on the husk look like a comic face.

CRISPY THAI CORNISH GAME HENS

WITH PAPAYA AND COCONUT GARNISH

SERVES 4

INGREDIENTS:

4 cloves garlic, minced or pressed

¼ cup grated peeled fresh ginger

1 teaspoon ground turmeric

1 teaspoon red chile flakes

1 teaspoon kosher or fine sea salt

¼ cup light soy sauce

2 Cornish game hens (1 to 1¼ pounds each)

Peanut or canola oil, for frying

¼ cup sugar

2 tablespoons fresh lime juice

¼ cup coarsely chopped fresh cilantro leaves, for garnish

¼ cup fresh basil leaves, preferably Thai basil, for garnish

Ripe papaya slices, for garnish (optional)

Toasted coconut (see Tip, page 197), for garnish (optional)

MANY CHICKEN DISHES CAME TO AMERICAN PLATES via Southeast Asia from the regions now known as Thailand, Vietnam, the Malay Peninsula, and Indonesia. Arriving in the United States, the people from these places, with their distinctive cuisine and their passion for fowl, came upon a new bird: the Cornish hen. Tender, meaty, just the right size for the wok, the little hens were a natural. The Southeast Asian cooks' technique is a marvel: wok-frying them whole so they turn out entirely crunchy and saucing them in exotic ginger and soy. Unique indeed. A large, deep skillet or sauté pan can also be used.

1. Combine the garlic, ginger, turmeric, red chile flakes, salt, and soy sauce in a dish large enough to hold the game hens side by side. Press down firmly on the hen breasts to flatten the birds and add them to the dish. Turn to coat all around with the spice mixture and set aside in the refrigerator to marinate for at least 1 hour and up to 3 hours.

2. Pour oil to a depth of ¾ inch into a wok or heavy deep skillet large enough to hold the game hens without crowding. Heat over medium-high heat until a drop of water sizzles upon hitting the oil. Lift the Cornish hens out

THE ASIAN CAJUNS

LOUISIANA HAS BEEN HOME to Asian immigrants since 1763, with the first recorded settlement of Filipinos in America. The enslaved Filipinos had jumped ship in New Orleans and fled into the bayous to hide out among the Cajuns. They were followed in the 1860s by Chinese immigrants who came to work the sugar fields. Upon arriving in Louisiana, they, too, formed settlements in the swamplands near the fields where they worked. Lured by climate, the agriculture, the thriving shipping port, and river cities, over the next century many Japanese arrived. Koreans, as well, found the southern climate, commerce, and hospitality of Louisiana accommodating.

The numbers of Asian Cajuns in the state grew steadily. Then, in the spring of 1975, right after the fall of Saigon, Louisiana underwent a major influx of Asian settlers, largely Vietnamese. Once a French colony, Louisiana had always had a French consulate, and, as Vietnam also had been a French colony, many Vietnamese felt more at home there than in other states. In addition, as the government of Laos fell, Laotians arrived. Large numbers of Thai came, too, enough so that the government of Thailand set up a permanent consular office in New Orleans.

Many of the Asian immigrants in New Orleans launched small businesses. But many were from rural areas, both agricultural and with sea and river fishing economies. Louisiana's lush rice-growing lands, lucrative seashore, and the many lakes and rivers drew them. Many already experienced in shrimping bought boats and entered the fishing and shrimping industries. Still others brought their traditional joy of gardening to the vast bayous and urban Garden District alike. Others, as so many immigrant groups before them, opened restaurants.

Some of the most thriving eateries of New Orleans, Baton Rouge, Lafayette, and Shreveport are Asian, and in the bayous the mix with both Cajun folk and Cajun food has been a happy union. Some have even named their cafés Asian-Cajun. Both cuisines are replete with rice-based, spicy fare with tasty sauces. Seafood, pork, and poultry, especially fried chicken, predominate. As well as food, the Asian Cajuns have added their holidays and their ceremonial costumes to Louisiana's folkways, and also their music to Louisiana's distinguished musical scene. But the keystone is the food, and once again, the coming together at table triumphs.

of the marinade and carefully place them breast down in the pan. Discard the marinade. Reduce the heat to medium-low and fry until light golden on the bottom, 8 minutes. Turn and fry until light brown on the other side, 8 to 10 minutes. Increase the heat to medium-high and continue cooking, turning twice more, until deep golden all around and the thigh juices run golden, 3 minutes per side. Increase the heat to high and cook for 1 minute more on each side to crisp. Transfer the game hens to paper towels to drain.

3. Remove all but 2 tablespoons of oil from the wok. Add the sugar and cook, stirring gently, over medium heat until the sugar dissolves and the mixture thickens, about 5 minutes. Stir in the lime juice and bring to a boil.

4. Transfer the game hens to a serving platter and pour the sauce from the pan over them. Sprinkle the cilantro and basil over the hens, garnish with the papaya and toasted coconut, if using, and serve right away.

➤ TIP: SEMIDEEP-FRYING. A trick to successfully semideep-frying small hens or fowl is to flatten the pieces so that they aren't roly-poly, can be turned easily, and become evenly golden all around without a deep-fat fryer or the expense of a lot of oil. A second trick is to fry the hens relatively slowly and turn them often for most of the cooking time so that they don't burn before they're done.

DUCK LEGS BRAISED WITH RED WINE AND BELGIAN ENDIVES

DUCK IS MOST COMMONLY ROASTED, but duck pieces sautéed and then simmered in a winy broth offer a warm and easy-to-cook change. Duck meat is flavor absorbent, especially the bulbous, ruddy legs. In the sauté pan they glean the fruity essence from the wine, while the Belgian endive gives leafy company to both the legs and the broth. The slow simmering further allows every iota of wine and verdant taste to be drawn in.

1. Sprinkle the duck legs with salt and pepper. Heat the oil in a large, heavy sauté pan over medium-high heat. Add the duck, skin side down, and sauté until lightly browned, about 4 minutes. Turn the pieces over so they're skin side up, add the wine, broth, and thyme, and bring to a boil over high heat. Reduce the heat to maintain a brisk simmer, cover, and cook until the duck is medium-rare, about 30 minutes.

2. Place the endive quarters on top of the duck, cover again, and continue cooking over medium-high heat until the duck is deep reddish brown all around and fork-tender and the endive is quite limp but still a little crunchy, 10 to 15 minutes. Transfer the duck and endive to a serving platter and set aside in a warm place.

3. Bring the liquid in the pan to a boil over high heat and cook until reduced and thickened, 5 to 7 minutes. Pour the sauce over the duck and serve right away.

SERVES 4

INGREDIENTS:

4 duck legs
  (about 8 ounces each)

Kosher or fine sea salt and
  freshly ground black
  pepper

1 tablespoon extra virgin
  olive oil

1 cup red wine

1 cup low-sodium chicken
  broth

2 teaspoons chopped fresh
  thyme

4 Belgian endives, cut
  lengthwise into quarters

ROAST DUCK LEGS AND PARSNIPS WITH CINNAMON OUZO ORANGE SAUCE

INGREDIENTS:

½ cup ouzo

¾ cup fresh orange juice

2 tablespoons extra virgin olive oil

2 tablespoons finely chopped orange zest

2 bay leaves

½ teaspoon freshly ground white pepper

⅛ teaspoon ground cinnamon

4 duck legs (about 8 ounces each)

3 parsnips, peeled and cut into pieces that are 2 inches long by ¼ inch wide and ¼ inch thick

1 cup low-sodium chicken broth

12 tender watercress sprigs, for garnish

AROUND THE GLOBE, ducks are glazed with pomegranate, doused with cognac, and combined with walnuts, honey, olives, orange, caraway, sesame, and more. In one of the most famous treatments, a classic French one, they are sauced with orange. It's a refined theme to follow, but the dulcet saucing could use some bounce. The dash of Greece's beloved ouzo, a clear cognaclike beverage with an animated potpourri of spices, donates just that dynamism, while extra cinnamon adds a candied turn (remember Red Hots?). Such a renovation of duck à l'orange to duck with orange and ouzo makes for a distinct dish. The parsnip, with its tinge of sweet, is key to keeping it on an even keel, meaning ritzy but down-to-earth.

1. Preheat the oven to 375°F.

2. Combine the ouzo, orange juice, 1 tablespoon of the oil, orange zest, bay leaves, pepper, and cinnamon in a dish large enough to hold the duck pieces in a single layer. Add the duck, turn to coat all around with the mixture, and set aside at room temperature to marinate for at least 30 minutes and up to 1 hour.

3. Heat the remaining tablespoon of oil in a large sauté pan over medium-high heat. Lift the duck pieces out of the marinade, reserving the marinade, and place them, skin side down, in the pan. Cook until golden brown on the bottom, reducing the heat if necessary to keep them from burning, 8 minutes. Transfer them skin side up to a rimmed baking sheet and set aside.

4. Add the parsnips to the sauté pan and cook until they begin to turn golden, 2 minutes. Transfer them to the baking sheet with the duck, place in the oven, and roast until the duck is browned and crispy on top and the

parsnips are cooked through and golden, 30 minutes.

5. While the duck and parsnips roast, make the sauce. Pour the chicken broth into the sauté pan, stir, and cook over high heat until reduced to ½ cup, about 10 minutes. Stir in the reserved marinade and continue cooking over high heat until the mixture is thick enough to coat a spoon heavily, about 5 minutes.

6. Arrange the duck and parsnips on a large platter or individual plates. Spoon some sauce over each piece of duck, garnish with the watercress, and serve.

OUZO

ALL ACROSS GREECE, people sip an anise-flavored aperitif called *ouzo.* Although it is a latecomer on the beverage scene—it was first developed toward the end of the nineteenth century—it has deep roots in Greece.

What exactly is this compelling drink? Ouzo is distilled from grapes, figs, or raisins, with various sugars added later. Each brand is flavored according to each maker's secret recipe with an assembly of spices and herbs. Among the predominant flavorings are anise, coriander, mastic, and lime. Even more than coffee, in Greece ouzo is the beverage of community and conversation. It mediates the lazy afternoon chat, eases the late-evening repose when friends gather, refreshes the summer afternoon, and warms the winter get-together.

As well as being a tantalizing tipple, ouzo can invigorate many dishes. It gives an exotic touch to a sauce for poultry, fish, and snails, makes a pungent bath for steaming mussels, and renders jams and sweet syrups mesmerizing.

ROAST DUCK WITH HONEY-RUM GLAZE ON BRAISED RED CABBAGE

SERVES 3 OR 4

INGREDIENTS:

1 duck (about 4½ pounds)

Kosher or fine sea salt and freshly ground black pepper

1 tablespoon peanut or extra virgin olive oil

¼ cup honey

2 tablespoons dark rum

2 tablespoons Dijon mustard

2 teaspoons sesame seeds

½ head red cabbage (about 1¼ pounds), cored and thinly sliced

2 tablespoons balsamic vinegar

½ cup chopped fresh flat-leaf parsley

THE DUSKY FLAVOR OF DUCK often leads cooks to counter the meat with a sweet glazing. The usual choice has been fruit: cherries or peaches or citrus. Honey has also often been lavished on duck, but honey alone can cloy. If honey is swirled with an infusion of warm, candescent liquor, its sugariness is subdued. Rum has always been appreciated for its heating quality and adds a touch of that glow as well as an opaque mystery to foods. While eschewed as old hat for a while, rum has reappeared as a modern cocktail beverage and vindicated culinary enhancement. It's a perfect companion to honey in a duck-cloaking veneer.

1. Preheat the oven to 375°F.

2. Sprinkle the inside and outside of the duck with salt and pepper. Heat the oil in a large, heavy sauté pan over medium heat. Place the duck in the pan, breast side down, and cook until lightly golden, 4 minutes. Continue cooking and turning the duck several times until it is browned all around, 4 minutes per turn. (Use the side of the pan to prop up the duck when browning the wing sides.)

3. Transfer the duck breast side up to a roasting pan and pour off all but 2 tablespoons of fat from the sauté pan. Set the sauté pan aside. Place the duck in the oven and roast until sizzling and beginning to turn a darker golden brown, 30 minutes.

4. Mix together the honey, rum, mustard, and sesame seeds in a small bowl. Pour the mixture over the duck and continue roasting, basting with the glaze 3 times at 5-minute intervals, until the skin is crisp, 15 minutes.

5. While the duck roasts, bring a large pot of water to a boil over high heat. Place the cabbage in a colander set in the sink and pour the boiling water over it. Shake the cabbage dry and set aside.

6. Just before serving, heat the reserved duck fat in the sauté pan over high heat. Add the cabbage and stir, tossing to mix, until well coated, warm, and wilted. Add the balsamic vinegar, parsley, and salt and pepper to taste and stir just until the cabbage turns a vivid purple-red, 2 minutes. Set aside in a warm place.

7. To serve, carve the duck into sections—2 drumsticks, 2 thighs, and ¼-inch-thick breast slices. Spread the cabbage on a large serving platter and arrange the duck on top of the cabbage. Pour the collected juices from the duck roasting pan over all and serve right away.

RUM

RUM WAS THE MAJOR ALCOHOLIC BEVERAGE of early American settlers. It is distilled from the by-products of processing sugarcane into sugar. It also had a causal place in the slave trade since slaves were brought from Africa to the West Indies to grow sugar and make rum in the early sixteenth century.

Most rum is made from molasses, the residue remaining after sugar has been crystallized from sugarcane juice. It can also be distilled straight from the juice. Since sugar is already present, there is no need to add it to ferment rum. Distillation takes place after the fermentation and produces a clear white liquid. The golden to brown color of rum comes from aging it in oak casks. The specific flavors come from the yeast, whether attracted from exposure to the air or added; the distillation method; the aging; and the blending. Rums of different degrees of aging may be mixed. Spices are sometimes added.

The heavy, dark, full-bodied rums are the oldest type and have a heady molasses flavor. They are made primarily in Jamaica, Barbados, and Guyana. Besides molasses, they often include the skimmings from the sugar vats. Jamaican rums are always blended and are aged for five to seven years, generally in casks that have previously held bourbon. Often caramel is added to boost the color. Production of drier, light-bodied golden rums began in the late nineteenth century and is mostly done in Puerto Rico and the Virgin Islands. Brazilian cachaça is also a light-bodied and colored rum. To it, yeast is added and the rum is distilled in more modern methods using stainless-steel casks.

Rum is part of the potent mix of many cocktails—mai tais, piña coladas, hurricanes, Cuba libres, and more. It is the powerful uncolored white rum that gives the punch to mojitos. In the last few decades rum has undergone a huge surge in popularity. Citrus, coconut, and mango-flavored rums, spiced rums, and premium rums are available. But in addition, wonderful, molassesy, tropical-tasting rum is a frequently used and bold enhancement to meat and poultry glazes and to dessert and other sorts of sauces. To meet the mettle of stately duck, try a dark one.

CARAWAY-CRUSTED ROAST DUCK
WITH BALSAMIC-GLAZED PEARS

SERVES 4

INGREDIENTS:

1 duck (about 4½ pounds)

2 teaspoons caraway seeds

1 tablespoon chopped fresh thyme or 1 teaspoon dried

1½ teaspoons kosher or fine sea salt

¾ teaspoon freshly ground black pepper

1 tablespoon brandy

2 firm pears, preferably Anjou or Bartlett, quartered and cored but not peeled

1 tablespoon balsamic vinegar

1 teaspoon extra virgin olive oil

CARAWAY IS AN AUDACIOUS HERB that has long been fancied in Eastern Europe, and when people from those countries flocked to the great industrial cities of middle America, they brought with them the ways of caraway. One of these is as a companion to duck meat. The duet takes on a contemporary touch when joined with mahogany-hued, tangy, balsamic roasted pears. As well as a distinct accent on this charmer of a bird, the caraway crust is good on chicken and pork.

1. Cut the duck along one side of the backbone. Open the duck out, pressing down on the breast to flatten it. Place the duck, breast side up, in a dish large enough to hold it out flat. Combine the caraway, thyme, salt, pepper, and brandy in a small bowl and spread the mixture over the entire outside of the duck. Cover with plastic wrap, and set aside in the refrigerator to marinate for at least 4 hours and up to overnight. Remove from the refrigerator 30 minutes before cooking.

2. When ready to cook, preheat the oven to 400°F.

3. Place the pears in an ovenproof dish large enough to hold them in a single layer. Sprinkle with the vinegar and oil, turn to coat, and roast until the pears can be pierced with a fork but are still firm, 25 minutes.

4. As the pears cook, heat a large, heavy, ovenproof skillet over medium-high heat. Cook the duck, skin side down, until browned on the bottom, about 5 minutes. Turn the duck over and transfer the pan to the oven. Cook until the duck is medium-rare in the thigh, 11 to 14 minutes. Remove and set aside in a warm place for 5 minutes for the juices to settle.

5. To serve, cut the duck into leg and thigh pieces and slice the breast about ¼ inch thick. Arrange the duck pieces on a platter and garnish with the pears.

TURKEY AND PISTACHIO MEATBALLS
IN GORGONZOLA BASIL CREAM SAUCE

THE GREAT AMERICAN TURKEY historically has been thought of as the entrée for a holiday extravaganza and a bird to roast whole. But now you can find half turkeys, breasts, and legs—year-round. One of the most versatile cuts is ground turkey, which substitutes successfully for beef in the ever winsome meatball. A dash of pistachio and Parmesan cheese readies the turkey for rolling. When the meatballs are then nestled within an irresistible cream sauce laced with earthy, pungent Gorgonzola cheese and fragrant fresh basil...heaven. Serve the meatballs solo or set the sauce and balls atop a steaming bowl of pasta; everyone will clamor for seconds.

1. Combine the turkey, garlic, onion, pistachios, ½ teaspoon salt, ¼ teaspoon pepper, the egg, and the Parmesan cheese in a medium-size bowl. Knead with your hands until well blended. In heaping tablespoon amounts, form the mixture into balls, placing them without touching on a plate. You should wind up with about 28 meatballs. Use right away or cover and refrigerate for up to overnight.

2. Heat the oil in a large sauté pan over medium-high heat. Add the meatballs and sauté, turning to brown all over, until firm and cooked through but not hard, about 10 minutes.

3. While the meatballs finish cooking, combine the tomatoes, cream, and Gorgonzola in a small saucepan and stir gently until the cream is warm and the cheese melts, about 3 minutes. Stir in ½ cup of the basil leaves.

4. Place the meatballs in a deep serving dish or over pasta and pour the sauce over them. Sprinkle the remaining ½ cup basil over all and serve.

PAVO TACOS WITH CHIVE, MINT, AND CILANTRO SALSA AND QUESO FRESCO

INGREDIENTS:

Chive, Mint, and Cilantro
Salsa (recipe follows),
for serving

¼ cup peanut or extra virgin
olive oil

2 medium-size yellow onions,
finely chopped

2 large cloves garlic,
minced or pressed

4 cups finely diced roasted
turkey or 1½ pounds
ground turkey

4 medium-size tomatoes,
2 finely chopped and
2 coarsely chopped

⅔ cup white wine

¾ teaspoon kosher or
fine sea salt

12 corn tortillas, for serving

4 cups torn sturdy lettuce,
such as romaine or
iceberg, or a mix

2 cups crumbled queso
fresco or feta cheese

1½ cups sour cream

PAVO IS THE WORD FOR "TURKEY" IN SPANISH. As the large, gawky New World fowl rarely flies—never more than a few hundred feet at a time and not unless frightened—and more or less ambles through the day, scratching about for food, it may have partly earned the name *pavo,* meaning dolt.

Often a lot of the meat is left over from Thanksgiving or other festive meals. In that case, turkey tacos are one of the very best ways to use them, or if there aren't any leftovers, ground turkey makes a terrific and facile taco filling. Seasoning, such as the chive, mint, and cilantro salsa with chiles, adds an herbaceous punch to the turkey tacos. Finish them off with a crumbling of queso fresco, a Mexican semisoft cow's milk cheese, that thanks to the Hispanic population is widely available.

1. First make the salsa and set it aside.

2. Preheat the oven to 300°F.

3. Heat the oil in a large skillet over medium heat. Add the onions and garlic and cook, stirring frequently, until the onions are wilted, about 5 minutes. Add the turkey, increase the heat to medium-high, and stir the leftover turkey to heat through, about 5 minutes, or mash the ground turkey with a fork to break up the chunks and cook until browned, about 10 minutes. Stir in the finely chopped tomatoes, wine, salt, and 6 tablespoons of the salsa and cook until most of the liquid is absorbed, 10 to 12 minutes.

4. Meanwhile, wrap the tortillas in aluminum foil and place them in the oven to warm.

5. To serve, present the turkey filling, coarsely chopped tomatoes, lettuce, cheese, sour cream, and remaining salsa in separate dishes, along with the tortillas wrapped in a cloth to keep them warm. The tacos are assembled by each diner, according to taste, with this general guideline: ⅓ cup of the turkey filling spread in the middle of a tortilla, topped with a dollop of salsa, chopped tomatoes, lettuce, queso fresco, sour cream, and finally more salsa if desired.

CHIVE, MINT, AND CILANTRO SALSA

CHOPPED CHILES, vegetables, and aromatics originated with the Incas, Maya, and Aztecs. Although the concoction was more of a relish or chutney, in 1571, Alfonso de Molina, an early historian of the Spanish voyages to the New World, dubbed it the Spanish for "sauce," *salsa*. And salsa it has remained. Salsa can be compounded of many sorts of ingredients, often tomatoes; usually hot chiles, onions, garlic; sometimes other vegetables; sometimes fruit. Meant to add flavor as well as a decided dash to the foods they accompany, salsas have been taken to the heart of American cooking, and their variations nowadays are legion. Here a mix of chives instead of onions, with radish, garlic, and two south-of-the-border favorite herbs, cilantro and mint, is right in line with the salsa paradigm. It packs a punch on the heat scale. If that is not to your liking, use fewer chile peppers.

MAKES ABOUT 2 CUPS

6 jalapeño or serrano chiles or a mixture, stemmed and coarsely chopped

4 radishes, trimmed and coarsely chopped

2 large cloves garlic, coarsely chopped

2 cups coarsely chopped fresh chives

1 cup fresh cilantro leaves

¼ cup coarsely chopped fresh mint leaves

1 cup water

¾ teaspoon kosher or fine sea salt

Combine the chiles, radishes, garlic, chives, cilantro, and mint in a food processor and pulse to chop somewhat finely without mincing. Add the water and salt and pulse to mix. Use right away or store in the refrigerator for up to 3 days.

SHIMMERING FARE FROM AMERICAN WATERS

America has what few other countries have, a vast ocean on two sides teeming with fish and shellfish and great warm gulfs splashing up its southern borders. Each of the bodies of water offers up a platter of incomparable variety: salmon to cod, halibut to mackerel, ray to shark, tuna to mahimahi, grey snapper to red snapper, littleneck to razor clams, Wellfleet to Gulf to Kumamoto oysters, Dungeness to king to blue crabs, and, of course, lobster. To cap this plethora, within the continent rivers offer up bass, catfish, crayfish, trout, and even eel. Lakes, some modest, some as large as small seas, abound in pike, perch, sunfish, and sturgeon. Native Americans harvested from the sea, river, and lake with wicker baskets and twig dams. They plucked so much shellfish great mounds of cast-off shells stacked up. Those who followed found lobster so plentiful that families ate it until they were literally fed up. Swarms of shad swam up the waterways and were savored for roe and meat. Southern gulf waters yielded oysters and snapper. In the West, salmon leaped roaring cascades to spawn. Crab scurried up on beaches, later to be sold mounded in paper cups on fisherman's wharfs.

Fish have a number of incomparable advantages as provender, and the many peoples of America to this day exploit them all. Because water supports their weight, they need less bone structure and provide considerable edible meat for their size. Unlike land animals, over 90 percent of fish and shellfish varieties are edible. In fact, the assortment of comestible fish and shellfish is so great that not all have yet been tasted. Best of all, both swimmer and shell-housed accommodate so many ways of cooking, embrace so many kinds of flavors, and accede to so many ethnic styles that they spin America's new culinary melting pot into the most splendid fish stews.

On the menu are not just trout with almonds, but trout with Hawaiian macadamia nuts. Not only mackerel baked with lemon, but mackerel with rosy watermelon and lime-green tomatillos; traditional shrimp with vermouth Italian style, except on grits; lobster with drawn butter, yes, but also lobster tacos.

Fish and shellfish remain a major part of our diet and our pleasure, and now we espouse almost as many ways to cook the fish as fish exist.

FISHY FACTS

APPROXIMATELY 27,000 KNOWN SPECIES of fish swim in the world's waters, making them the most diverse form of vertebrates in the animal world, and there are probably thousands of species yet unnetted and unknown.

❯ In Texas it is illegal to have sex with a fish, and in Florida it is illegal to get a fish drunk. Since North Carolina has both laws, it begs the question of what the citizens are doing with drunk fish.

❯ The age of a fish can be determined by its ear growth rings.

❯ In 1999, a heron dropped a goldfish down a London chimney and the fish survived. No one knows where the heron caught the goldfish.

❯ A shrimp's heart is in its head, perhaps an apt placement for sensible romance.

❯ Catfish have more than 27,000 taste buds, which seems to give the term *bottom feeder* epicurean status.

❯ If there were no other reason for America to rebel against British rule, it might have been to eat luscious sturgeon. To this day all sturgeon, from which the most precious caviar comes, caught in British waters belong to the queen.

CRAB-STUFFED TROUT
WITH SHAVED FENNEL
AND ARUGULA

OPENED AND CLEANED, a whole fish offers a yawning packet to fill with bold herbs, tidbits like bacon, or jaunty greens like spinach or arugula. An intriguing path is to enliven one seafood creature with accents of a second. Here a freshwater swimmer is punctuated with a dash of saltwater denizen and the whole parcel is set on a bed of a bright salad.

1. Preheat the broiler or lightly grease a skillet that's large enough to hold the trout in a single layer (use 2 skillets if necessary).

2. Sprinkle the trout inside and out with about 2 teaspoons of the lemon juice and some salt. Set aside at room temperature for up to 45 minutes or refrigerate for up to several hours.

3. Combine the fennel, 2 more teaspoons of lemon juice, and ⅛ teaspoon salt in a bowl and toss to mix. Set aside at room temperature.

4. To make the stuffing, combine the crabmeat, bread crumbs, parsley, bell pepper, mayonnaise, and remaining 2 teaspoons lemon juice in a small bowl.

5. Divide the stuffing among the 4 trout cavities and secure closed with toothpicks. Place the trout under the broiler or heat the prepared skillet or skillets over medium-high heat, then add the trout. Cook until golden on one side, 4 minutes. Carefully turn and continue cooking until golden on the second side and the flesh along the backbone is firm but still a little pink, about 4 minutes more.

6. Spread the arugula on 4 individual plates. Set the trout on top of the arugula and garnish each with a mound of the fennel and a lemon wedge and serve.

SERVES 4

INGREDIENTS:

Extra virgin olive oil for greasing the skillet (optional)

4 boneless medium-size whole trout without heads, tails intact (10 to 12 ounces each)

2 tablespoons fresh lemon juice

Kosher or fine sea salt

1 medium-size fennel bulb, tops and bruised outer layers trimmed off, thinly sliced (about 2 cups)

6 ounces lump crabmeat, picked over

1½ tablespoons bread crumbs, preferably homemade, lightly toasted (page 41)

1 tablespoon chopped fresh flat-leaf parsley

2 teaspoons chopped red bell pepper

1 tablespoon mayonnaise

2 cups arugula leaves and tender stems, for serving

1 lemon, quartered, for serving

CATSKILL-STYLE BUTTER-FRIED TROUT
CRUSTED IN CORNMEAL

SERVES 4

INGREDIENTS:

2 large (about 1 pound each) or 4 small (about 12 ounces each) whole bone-in trout, cleaned

1 to 2 tablespoons fresh lemon juice

Kosher or fine sea salt

½ cup yellow cornmeal

8 tablespoons (1 stick) butter

THE EUROPEANS HAD LONG TIED FLIES onto a hook, knotted that hook to a line, strung that line along a long rod, and skimmed the fly across the water in the hopes of luring stream-dwelling fish. The Americans, especially those who settled in the famed Catskill Mountains of New York State, designed better fishing rods, superior line, ingenious reels to hold yards and yards of line, and techniques for casting upstream in the tumbling mountain waters. These developments made the Catskills famous as the center of American fly fishing. Anglers often hunkered down to fry the catch, and since butter was a main product of the Catskill dairy farms, the fish hit the fishing camp's cast-iron skillet in a splatter of that flavorful melted gold. One of the crispiest grains to dust the trout and make the skin crunchy turned out to be the fine meal of native corn. That Catskill combination cannot be improved upon. It is simple, succulent, and sublime, so glorious on its own that no innovation is needed.

1. Rub the trout inside and out with lemon juice and a sprinkling of salt. Coat the outside of each fish with cornmeal.

2. Melt the butter in a large skillet or heavy sauté pan. Add the trout and fry, turning once or twice, until the cornmeal coating is golden and crusty and the meat along the backbone is no longer pink, 12 to 16 minutes altogether, depending on the size of the fish. Transfer the fish to a platter or individual plates and serve right away.

THE CATSKILL SCHOOL OF FLY FISHING

IN AMERICA, three types of trout are native: brook, cutthroat, and rainbow trout. Rivers and streams offered new settlers abundant places to cast lines and ample edible fish to lure with real or pseudo flies. Early on, New York's Catskill Mountains emerged as America's fly-fishing heart and soul. It was here that American anglers started employing better American equipment and American fishermen discovered that the patterns for making flies in Europe did not correspond to American insects or what American fish were feasting on. Catskill anglers started developing their own fly-fishing style and also writing about their fishing.

One of the men most important to the development of American fly fishing and the preeminence of what became known as the "Catskill School of Fly Fishing" was Theodore Gordon. He had settled on New York's Neversink River in order to spend full time tying flies, fishing, and, while not fishing, writing articles on fishing for several journals—a single-purpose man. He was followed by George LaBranche, who created techniques for fly fishing in America's rapid-running mountain streams. Edward Hewitt, writing between World War I and World War II, promoted the now thoroughly embraced triad theme of American fly fishing: catch as many fish as possible, catch fish as big as possible, and reel in fish as difficult to catch as possible.

Two main Catskill streams, the Beaverkill and Willowemoc Creek, arose as the nucleus of America's fly-fishing sport. To this day the junction pool in Roscoe, New York, where the Willowemoc flows into the Beaverkill, is the hub of an annual pilgrimage every April 1 when the fishing season begins. The original Catskill fishing motifs remain: sparse rather than overly patterned flies, a certain way of fly presentation, and a passion for fishing. They have spread to all of America's fly-fishing areas, promoted by the search for challenge combined with leisure, trophy to display, and talk (true and untrue), and today's "catch and release" motto conserving the supply of fish. Millions of Americans engage in fly fishing, and the sport is ever growing.

PARMESAN AND CILANTRO-STUFFED MACKEREL WITH WATERMELON AND TOMATILLO SALSA

SERVES 4

INGREDIENTS:

2 Spanish mackerel
(1¼ to 1½ pounds each),
cleaned

Kosher or fine sea salt

⅓ cup finely grated
Parmesan cheese

⅓ cup fresh cilantro leaves,
coarsely chopped

Watermelon and Tomatillo
Salsa (recipe follows),
for serving

MANY VARIETIES OF MACKEREL SWIM IN OPEN WATERS not too far offshore of the Atlantic and Pacific Oceans, and the Mediterranean Sea. They are a prolific species, related to tuna and prized in a wide range of cuisines. Here in America, the popular fish stands out barbecued and grilled whole, or fresh and smoked in salad amalgams and fish cakes. It is seen in compositions reflective of its popularity in Central American cuisines, such as vinegared and semiraw *en escabeche.* Of all the varieties, Spanish mackerel, also called *Atlantic mackerel,* is the most culinarily admired because its meat comes out particularly firm, flaky, and mild all the way through, perfect as a wrap around a cheese and herb stuffing.

1. Sprinkle the mackerel inside and out with salt. Toss the cheese and cilantro together in a small bowl. Fill the cavities of the fish with the cheese mixture and set them aside at room temperature.

2. Make the salsa.

3. When ready to cook, prepare a medium-hot grill for indirect grilling or preheat the broiler.

4. Place the fish on the grill to the side of, not directly over, the heat or under the broiler. Partially cover the grill and cook, turning once, until firm and flaky and no longer pink along the backbone, about 7 minutes per side.

5. Transfer the fish to a platter and serve with the salsa on the side.

WATERMELON AND TOMATILLO SALSA

A SPARKLING, JUICY SALSA combines sweet watermelon with tart tomatillos, which look like little green tomatoes and add a punch. The salsa works equally well for other grilled fish or grilled poultry. It should be served the day it's made; it loses luster if kept overnight.

MAKES 2 CUPS

- 4 medium-size tomatillos, papery husks removed
- 2 cups chopped seedless red watermelon
- ⅓ cup finely chopped red onion
- 2 tablespoons coarsely chopped radish
- 2 tablespoons chopped fresh cilantro
- 2 tablespoons fresh lime juice
- 1 tablespoon finely chopped jalapeño chile
- ½ teaspoon kosher or fine sea salt

1. Bring a small pot of water to a boil over high heat. Add the tomatillos and blanch them for 2 minutes Drain, let cool enough to handle, then coarsely chop them and transfer to a bowl.

FROM A PLACE WITH NO WATER, THE WATERMELON

VERY FEW FOODS, particularly ones that spread to avid devotees worldwide, can claim a desert birthplace, especially from a zone as remote and harsh as the Kalahari Desert in southwestern Africa. But watermelon does, and not just from the fringes of the Kalahari but from deep in the heart of that parched land.

Perhaps the watery flesh of the melon learned to hold on to every drop of moisture so it could survive, becoming its own internal oasis. Whatever prompted its contrary evolution, the fruit became a source of water for tribes and travelers crossing those sandy stretches. It soon spread with wanderers, who sold the melon's seeds throughout Africa and along ancient trade routes that traversed the Mediterranean to the Far East. By 1600 CE the fruit reached England, where it received its highly literal English name, *watermelon,* just as England was colonizing America and the first African slaves were brought to American shores.

The rosy thirst-quencher was most likely brought to America with the slave ships and followed the settlement of Africans, already familiar with it, across the cotton and rice lands they tilled throughout the South. When the importation of sugar to the southern states was embargoed during the Civil War, Confederate soldiers boiled down watermelon as a source of sweetener. Though forty-four states grow watermelon today, three southern states are among the leaders: Georgia, Florida, and Texas. The attachment to certain foods survives long in cultures. Watermelon in Latin countries, as with the ancient Egyptians, lives on as a food of the Day of the Dead. More so than the Georgia peach, watermelon persists as a signature southern food.

2. Add the watermelon, onion, radish, cilantro, lime juice, jalapeño, and salt and stir gently to mix. Set aside at room temperature for up to 1 hour or refrigerate for up to 6 hours.

SALMON WITH WATERCRESS CREAM, SMOKED SALMON, AND ALMONDS

SERVES 4

INGREDIENTS:

Peanut or canola oil, for greasing the baking sheet

4 skinless wild salmon fillets (6 to 8 ounces each), ¾ to 1 inch thick

2 tablespoons fresh lemon juice

Kosher or fine sea salt

¼ cup sliced almonds

½ cup heavy whipping cream

1 cup watercress leaves, finely chopped

2 slices good-quality smoked salmon, cut into ⅛-inch-wide strips (see facing page)

SALMON HAS BECOME SO POPULAR that salmon steaks or fillets are featured prominently in markets daily. Luckily, the fish lends itself to so many glorious treatments you can indulge in whimsy with your dinner. Watercress, an aquatic plant of the mustard family, pairs naturally with salmon, lending harmony with the rich fish. Almonds add crunch, and cream smooths the triad into triumph.

1. Lightly grease a baking sheet with oil and place the salmon fillets on it. Season the fillets on both sides with 1 tablespoon of the lemon juice and a sprinkling of salt. Set aside at room temperature for up to 45 minutes or refrigerate for up to several hours.

2. Preheat the broiler or the oven to 500°F.

3. Toast the almonds in an ungreased skillet over medium-high heat or in a microwave oven on high until lightly golden, 4 to 5 minutes either way. Stir

them once or twice as they toast. Set aside.

4. Place the salmon under the broiler or in the oven and cook, without turning, until white curds form across the top and the flesh is firm, 6 to 8 minutes for medium-rare. Transfer the fillets to a platter and set aside for the juices to settle while making the watercress cream.

5. Put the cream in a small saucepan over medium-high heat. Bring to a boil, stir in the watercress and the remaining 1 tablespoon lemon juice, and remove from the heat right away.

6. Spoon the sauce over the salmon and top each piece with smoked salmon and almonds. Serve right away.

TYPES OF SMOKED SALMON
(ONE OF WHICH IS NOT SMOKED AT ALL)

THERE ARE A NUMBER OF WAYS and degrees to which salmon is smoked. On the West Coast, king salmon is generally used, although sometimes paler-fleshed chum is. On the East Coast, it's often farmed Atlantic salmon, though more and more smoked wild salmon can be purchased. For smoking, all the salmon are split, boned, and filleted. Then the variations begin.

There are two processes for smoking salmon: hot-smoking and cold-smoking. In hot-smoking, the fish is smoked for 6 to 12 hours in temperatures ranging from 120°F to 180°F. The time and temperature depend on how large the fish, how close to the fire, and how strong a smoky flavor is desired. In cold-smoking, the fish is kept in a storehouse at a temperature of 70°F to 90°F for 1 day to 3 weeks.

A roster of names describes the process.

❯ **SMOKED SALMON** is the generic term referring to any sort of smoking, regardless of the specific process.

❯ **LOX (OR BELLY LOX)** is probably the most famous smoked salmon, but oddly, when the word lox alone is used to describe the salmon, it is not smoked at all, but rather has only been cured in a salty brine.

❯ **NOVA** (sometimes called nova lox) has received a mild smoking and a mild brine that includes the addition of brown sugar. Nova is usually cured for 5 days and then cold-smoked for 10 to 12 hours. It is less salty and more subtle in flavor than lox.

❯ **INDIAN SMOKE** is first brined and then cold-smoked for up to 2 weeks. The end result is a sort of salmon jerky.

❯ **KIPPERED SALMON** is mildly brined, then hot-smoked and often dyed red.

❯ **SCOTCH SMOKED, IRISH SMOKED, AND DANISH SMOKED** are all unbrined cold-smoked Atlantic salmon.

❯ **SQUAW CANDY,** developed in Alaska, is strips of salmon that have been cured in a salt and sugar brine and then dried or hot-smoked. It, too, is essentially a salmon jerky.

NORTHERN LIGHTS INSPIRED
SALMON WITH CHIVE MINT OIL

SERVES 6 TO 8

INGREDIENTS:

- 1 tablespoon fresh lemon juice
- 1 piece (2½ to 3 pounds) skin-on wild salmon fillet, about 1½ inches thick
- Kosher or fine sea salt
- 1 small white onion, thinly sliced into rings, rings separated
- 2 lemons, sliced into thin rounds
- 1 cup coarsely chopped fresh chives (2 to 4 bunches)
- 2 tablespoons coarsely chopped fresh mint leaves
- ½ cup extra virgin olive oil

FIVE SPECIES OF SALMON SWIM IN THE GELID WATERS OF ALASKA: the sockeye, the king or chinook, the coho, the chum, and the pink. All are anadromous, meaning that they migrate upstream from the sea to breed in fresh water. They spend most of their growing in schools and feeding in the open sea, until once in their lives they return to the very up-cascading river where they were born to spawn the next generation. The beauty of Alaskan salmon in particular is how protected they are in their habitat. Alaskan fishery managers take advantage of their anadromous behavior to count them and ensure that they remain plentiful. They prohibit harvests from too far offshore or too close to shore where the fish cluster, and limit the harvest to licensed fishermen and specific plentiful areas.

The result brings to the diner the taste of salmon as it has been, unchanged, throughout the eons: firm, full-bodied, and pristinely briny. A large fillet, grilled and served in a slick of chive and leafy herb oil, retains that wild, cold-water flavor, enhanced as if by the moss and lichen of shore and riverside. Grilling the salmon fillet with skin on protects the bottom from burning so that the fish can cook without being turned, and that way the onion and lemon rings, which are part of the taste of the dish, don't fall away. A large fillet feeds many; it's a company dish.

1. Splash the lemon juice over the cut side of the salmon and sprinkle lightly with ½ teaspoon salt. Spread the onion rings and lemon rounds over the salmon and sprinkle lightly with more salt.

2. Prepare a medium-hot grill or preheat the broiler.

3. Bring a small pot of water to a boil. Line a colander or strainer with paper towels. Drop the chives into the boiling water, then drain them right away in the colander and rinse them with cool water. Gather up the paper towels and gently squeeze out any excess moisture. Transfer the chives to a food processor, add the mint, oil, and ¼ teaspoon salt and process until blended and almost smooth, about 2 minutes.

4. Place the salmon skin side down on the grill rack directly over the heat and cover the grill or place the salmon under the broiler. The onion rings and lemon rounds should still be on top of the fish. Cook without turning until white curds form across the top and the flesh is firm, 11 to 12 minutes for

medium-rare. Transfer the salmon to a large platter, keeping the onion and lemon rounds on top, and set aside for 10 minutes for the juices to settle.

5. To serve, drizzle some of the chive oil across the salmon and over the lemon and onion rings. Serve right away with the extra chive oil on the side.

GRILLED SALMON WITH SPINACH, PAN BROTH, AND CRISP GINGER TOPPING

SERVES 4

INGREDIENTS:

4 skin-on wild salmon fillets
(6 to 8 ounces each),
¾ to 1 inch thick

2 tablespoons fresh lemon
juice

Kosher or fine sea salt

¼ cup peanut or canola oil

¼ cup finely chopped peeled
fresh ginger

8 cups baby spinach, rinsed
and drained

¼ cup light soy sauce

¼ cup water

2 tablespoons rice vinegar,
preferably brown rice

ASIAN-INFLUENCED PACIFIC RIM DISHES did not stay on the Pacific Rim for long once their style was introduced to American cuisine. They were espoused with almost the speed of the sun's transit from state to state, city to city, and certainly from their first coast to the opposite one. Here a Pacific Rim favorite fish, salmon, stands out in its sophistication. Among the outstanding features are an unexpected mix of Asian American flavors combining a double contrast of textures, soft and crisp, leaf with liquid. The salmon's skin echoes of sushi, and the ginger topping acts like spicy crumbled chips.

1. Sprinkle the salmon all over with the lemon juice and some salt and set aside at room temperature for up to 45 minutes.

2. Prepare a medium-hot grill or preheat the broiler.

3. Heat the oil in a large sauté pan over medium-high heat. Add the ginger and cook, stirring, until crisp and golden, about 5 minutes. With a slotted spoon, transfer the ginger to paper towels. Set aside.

4. Pour off the oil from the skillet, but don't wipe it clean. Add the spinach and stir over medium-high heat until barely wilted, about 1 minute. With a slotted spoon, transfer the spinach to a colander, leaving whatever liquid the spinach has rendered in the skillet. Set the spinach aside.

5. Add the soy sauce, water, and vinegar to the skillet and bring to a boil over high heat. Remove from the heat and set aside in a warm place. If necessary, reheat briefly before serving.

6. To cook the salmon, place the fillets on the grill rack directly over the heat or under the broiler. Cook without turning until white curds form across the top, the flesh is firm, and the skin is crisp, 6 to 8 minutes for medium-rare, depending on the thickness.

7. To serve, mound the spinach on a large platter or 4 individual plates. Set the salmon on the spinach and spoon the pan broth all around. Sprinkle the ginger over the top and serve right away.

SPINACH:
THE LEAF CALLED THE *GREEN HAND*

SPINACH, which due to its shape means "green hands," and its cousins first sprang up in ancient Persia and got a ride around the world. The ships that took it worldwide and made it a gastronomic hit were the vessels of Arabia. Once the Arabs discovered the dense green leaf, they embraced it with such ardor that they titled it the "prince of vegetables." As they sailed to the Far East and conquered the lands around the Mediterranean, they introduced the leaf.

To people foot-weary of scavenging for wild greens, spinach came as a boon: It was easy to grow, at hand in the garden without foraging, and oh so palatable. Mild, yet intensely green and leafy in taste, it was less sharp than watercress, softer than orach, daintier than purslane, and it swept the competition under the sod. It grows to harvest in as little as 36 days and can be eaten raw or cooked. In medieval recipes, in both Europe and the Far East, it was married with egg, honey, almonds, and spices in sweet dishes and used in savory pies and flans. As an echo of that, to this day spinach is often flavored with nutmeg, especially when creamed. It plumps up nicely in Byzantine filo dough and European puff pastry, sweetly kissing any cheese or egg stirred with it. It takes thick cream and stands up to lemon and soy. As for winter's bacon and ham, from Holland to Hunan, it adds an ideal leafy complement.

Indeed, no traveler ever shook hands so easily and naturally with all the foreign cuisines it met.

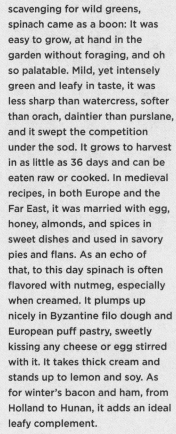

SEARED TUNA WITH WHITE BEANS AND SAUTEED CHERRY TOMATOES

SERVES 4

INGREDIENTS:

2½ tablespoons butter or extra virgin olive oil

⅓ cup bread crumbs, preferably homemade (page 41)

24 small cherry tomatoes

2 large cloves garlic, minced or pressed

4 tuna fillets (5 to 6 ounces each), ¾ inch thick

Kosher or fine sea salt and freshly ground black pepper

4 cups cooked white beans, such as great northern or Italian cannellini

¼ cup thinly shredded fresh basil leaves

¼ cup extra virgin olive oil

NO FISH IN TODAY'S MARKET, on restaurant menus, or on the cook's stove more personifies—or fishifies—a "You've come a long way, baby" story. There simply wasn't any fresh tuna to be had in American markets a generation or so ago. It was always canned and was presented only for eating mixed cold in tuna salad or hot in tuna casserole. Now it gleams fresh on ice in fish displays, ready to take home and sear as a centerpiece, singed and tossed in salads, thinly sliced or minced raw for sushi and tartars. It is looked for on restaurant menus as one of the day's special fresh fish entrées. Resting on a bed of white beans, cherry tomatoes, garlic, and basil, tuna fillets bring a still saladlike miscellany home, only now hot.

1. Melt 1 tablespoon of the butter in a medium-size sauté pan over medium-high heat. Add the bread crumbs and cook, stirring, until golden and toasty, about 5 minutes. Remove from the pan and set aside at room temperature.

2. Melt the remaining butter in the same pan over medium-high heat. Add the tomatoes and sauté until softened and wrinkled, 3 to 5 minutes, depending on their size. Stir in the garlic and set aside.

3. Heat an ungreased heavy skillet large enough to hold the tuna fillets in 1 layer without crowding over medium-high heat until a drop of water sprinkled in sizzles. Sprinkle the tuna with salt and pepper on both sides, place in the skillet, and cook, turning once, until well seared on the outside but still quite rare in the middle, about 2 minutes per side. Remove from the heat and set aside for 15 minutes for the flesh to firm before slicing.

4. Place the beans in the sauté pan with the tomatoes. Place the pan over medium heat and bring to a simmer. Cook until heated through, about 5 minutes. Divide among 4 dinner plates and sprinkle the toasted bread crumbs across the top. Slice the tuna steaks about ½ inch thick and set the slices over the beans and bread crumbs. Sprinkle the basil over the tuna and drizzle olive oil over all. Serve right away.

THE CATTLEMEN OF HAWAII (NOT A FISH STORY!)

IN 1832 A SAILOR turned cattle rancher named Parker found he didn't have enough experienced help on his cattle ranch on Hawaii's big island. With the help of his friend (and one could have a pal no higher), King Kamehameha, he brought in a troop of Mexican vaqueros with plenty of horse riding and cattle herding experience to train the Hawaiians in the arts of roping and riding. The vaqueros came with boots, saddles, a new language, and a flamboyance not seen before, including a new sort of music and dancing and a smallish sort-of-guitar the Hawaiians came to call ukulele. The Hawaiians dubbed the vaqueros "Paniolas" from "Espanola" or Spaniard. The Paniolas also brought their foods, which they integrated with Hawaiian cuisine. Hawaiians wrapped food in banana leaves, the Paniolas in corn husks; the Hawaiians offered ginger; the Paniolas brought tomatoes. Beverages morphed from tequila to rum mixtures, which you can still get, as before, in mason jars in isolated saloons near old ranching sites around the islands.

Cattle ranching eventually declined, but the taste for the island's fish did not. Fish farms rim the shallow shores and deep waters around where the cattle ranches were, and Hawaiian tuna is one of the prized catches.

NORI-TOPPED SEARED TUNA
WITH GINGER CARROT PUREE

INGREDIENTS:

1 pound carrots, cut into 1-inch chunks

2 tablespoons peeled and coarsely chopped fresh ginger

4 tuna fillets (5 to 6 ounces each), ¾ inch thick

Kosher or fine sea salt and freshly ground black pepper

½ sheet nori

1 tablespoon chopped fresh chives

Asian sesame oil, for moistening the tuna

1 lime, quartered

TAKING A CUE FROM JAPANESE COOKING, quickly seared tuna steaks, barren of any marinade or seasoning save salt and pepper, are clean yet vivid. Set alongside another minimalist element, a puree of carrots and ginger, the naked flavors thrum with lucidity. A confetti topping of nori, a crisp sea vegetable usually used to wrap sushi, caps the fish.

1. Combine the carrots and ginger in a medium-size saucepan, add water to cover completely, and bring to a boil over high heat. Reduce the heat to maintain a gentle boil, cover, and cook until the carrots are easily pierced with a fork, about 15 minutes. Uncover the pot and continue boiling until the carrots are mashable, about 3 minutes more. Remove from the heat and cool for a minute or two. Transfer the carrots, along with the ginger and remaining liquid, to a food processor and puree until as smooth as possible. Set aside in a warm place.

2. Heat an ungreased large, heavy skillet over medium-high heat until a drop of water sprinkled in sizzles. Sprinkle the tuna on both sides with salt and pepper. Place the tuna steaks in the skillet and cook, turning once, until well seared on the outside but still quite rare in the middle, about 2 minutes per side. Remove from the heat and set aside for 15 minutes for the flesh to firm before slicing.

3. Using tongs, hold the nori over a gas or electric burner and toast lightly until crisp.

4. Spread the ginger carrot puree on 4 individual plates and sprinkle with the chives. Slice the tuna steaks about ½ inch thick and arrange the slices over the puree. Dot the tuna with 2 or 3 drops of sesame oil and crumble the nori across the top. Garnish with a lime wedge and serve.

GRILLED HALIBUT WITH GRAPE LEAF SALSA

THE NORTHEAST COAST OF AMERICA was thick with wild grape-vines, and a few of the earliest colonies, most notably Jamestown, were established in the hope of producing wine. The fruit is not the only culi-narily useful part of the grapevine. Grape leaves had long been used as a food wrap and as you would an herb. But wild grapes are quite different from domesticated ones—their fruit is very sour, and their leaves tough to chew, so the colonists' hopes for a wine industry didn't come to pass until much later when cultivated vines were brought to America. Then, in upstate New York, California, and other areas, the leaves were part of the bounty. The taste of domestic grape leaves has no ready comparison; they are tart but not sour, a little sharp, and very verdant. Their use has dimin-ished in modern times; they are now recognized primarily as the wrapping for dolmas. Bringing them back into their many possibilities can provide a delightful surprise. Here, in such an offbeat salsa, grape leaves bring a new world of taste to halibut.

SERVES 4

INGREDIENTS:

- 2 pounds halibut steaks or fillets, 1 inch thick, cut into 4 portions
- 1 tablespoon fresh lemon juice
- Kosher or fine sea salt
- 2 tablespoons extra virgin olive oil
- 1 medium-size tomato, cut into ¼-inch dice
- ¼ cup packed thinly shredded jarred grape leaves
- 2 tablespoons chopped lemon zest
- 2 tablespoons chopped kalamata olives

1. Prepare a medium-hot grill or pre-heat the broiler. Season the halibut on both sides with the lemon juice and salt. Set aside at room temperature while the grill heats.

2. To make the salsa, warm the olive oil in a small saucepan over medium heat. Stir in the tomato, grape leaves, lemon zest, and olives, mixing well, and remove from the heat. Set aside.

3. To cook the halibut, place the steaks or fillets on the grill rack directly over the heat or under the broiler. Cook, covered if grilling, without turning, until flaky but not dry, 8 to 10 minutes for either method.

4. Transfer the halibut to a platter or individual plates. Top with the salsa and serve right away.

PANKO-CRUSTED MAHIMAHI WITH POLYNESIAN MANGO CHUTNEY

INGREDIENTS:

Polynesian Mango Chutney
  (recipe follows),
  for serving

1 cup panko (see facing
  page)

2 teaspoons black sesame
  seeds

4 mahimahi steaks
  (1½ to 2 pounds total),
  1 inch thick

1 large egg, lightly beaten

Peanut or extra virgin olive
  oil, for sautéing the fish

THE INTRODUCTION OF HAWAII'S NOTEWORTHY and scrumptious seafood to land-bound markets has been a boon to the fish lover. One island fish that quickly earned favored status was meaty and amenable mahimahi. While it's ready for many a culinary treatment, staying island style, with a few twists, remains among the best. Today, with the influx of new cuisines, crusting choices have mushroomed. As well as a plethora of nuts such as almonds, pine nuts, macadamias, and pistachios, there are the seeds, such as fennel and sesame. From Japan comes another new option, a captivating version of bread crumbs, called *panko*. Light, airy, and crunchy, panko stays resolutely crisp, and when tossed with earthy black sesame seeds, the two together provide both the exotica and crunch to make the dish remarkable. Halibut will do in place of mahimahi, and white sesame seeds can step in for black. The chutney transports it back to Polynesia.

1. Make the chutney and set it aside.

2. Mix together the panko and sesame seeds on a large plate. Dip each mahimahi piece in the beaten egg, turning to cover both sides, then coat all around with the panko mixture. Set aside briefly.

3. Pour oil to a depth of ¼ inch into a heavy sauté pan large enough to hold the pieces without crowding and heat over high heat. Add the fish and cook until it begins to turn golden on the bottom, 1 to 2 minutes. Turn the fish over and cook on the second side, 1 to 2 minutes more. Reduce the heat to medium-low and continue cooking and turning every 2 to 3 minutes, until the crust is golden and crispy all around and the fish is cooked through but still moist in the center, 7 to 8 minutes more.

4. Transfer the fish to individual plates and spoon some of the chutney over the top. Serve right away.

POLYNESIAN MANGO CHUTNEY

FRUITS FROM HAWAII have brought about a riot of color and divergent taste selections to America's culinary amalgamation. Pineapple, an island native, was the first fruit to merit veneration. Then came the mango, an immigrant welcomed with open arms to Hawaii's tropical gardens. Chopped and combined with pineapple juice and other major flavors from the islands' unique menu, it makes a refreshing chutney.

MAKES ABOUT 2 CUPS

1 ripe mango, peeled, cut off the pit, and cut into ¼- to ½-inch chunks

1 medium-size yellow or white onion, finely chopped but not minced

1 jalapeño chile, stemmed and halved

1 piece (2 inches) peeled fresh ginger, cut crosswise into thirds

½ cup sugar

½ cup unsweetened pineapple juice

½ cup fresh lime juice

PANKO:
A CRUMB OF ANOTHER TEXTURE

THE PORTUGUESE ACCIDENTALLY brought the first bread to Japan in 1543 when one of their ships came ashore during a storm. The Japanese saw the sailors eating bread, in time adapting it and its Portuguese name, *pan*, into their cuisine. Panko is the Japanese cook's version of crumbs, used to make a crisp coating for fried foods, in particular seafood such as fish fillets and shrimp, but also chicken and even pork cutlets.

Added to the borrowed name *pan* is the Japanese suffix *ko*, meaning "child of" or "derived from," so in essence "little breads." Panko's crumbs are coarser than what American cooks recognize as the almost sandy bread crumbs commercially available. Restaurant chefs esteem panko crumbs for their stay-crisp power under heat and on the plate; they don't get soggy unless moistened. Home cooks have begun to embrace panko for the same reasons, especially since it has become common packaged and ready to use on supermarket shelves.

Combine the mango, onion, jalapeño, ginger, sugar, and pineapple and lime juices in a medium-size nonreactive saucepan and bring to a boil over medium heat. Reduce the heat to maintain a simmer, cover, and cook until beginning to thicken, 15 minutes. Uncover and continue cooking until the mango is collapsing into a puree and the liquid is quite thick, 15 minutes more. Remove from the heat and remove and discard the jalapeño and ginger pieces. Use right away or cool completely and refrigerate for up to 3 days. Reheat before using, if desired.

WHITEFISH FILLETS
WITH LEEK, KUMQUATS, AND
SWEET WINE

SERVES 4

INGREDIENTS:

4 whitefish fillets
(6 to 8 ounces each),
such as halibut, or sea
bass, ¾ to 1 inch thick

2 tablespoons fresh lemon
juice

Kosher or fine sea salt

1½ tablespoons extra virgin
olive oil

1 medium-size leek,
white and light green
parts, cut into 2-inch-
long shreds, rinsed, and
drained

6 kumquats or 1 Seville
orange, thinly sliced

¼ cup sweet muscat wine

2 tablespoons fresh orange
juice

1 bay leaf

1 tablespoon chopped fresh
chives, for garnish

Freshly ground black pepper,
for garnish

BY AND LARGE, TRADITIONAL FISH-COOKING CUSTOM decrees that the only fruit to apply on fish is lemon; the only wine a dry, white one, never a touch of sweet. Contemporary cooking, taking a cue from all the ethnic tributaries in the new culinary sea, has found those provisos to be limiting. In a rule-breaking combination of surprises, here whitefish is splashed with sweet, mildly tangy muscat wine. The ordinary onion is replaced with its kin the leek. And along with lemon, the citrus is orange. Not your common sweet orange, but rather the sour, more astringent kumquat or alternatively, Seville orange, whose tartness adds an unexpected shade to the dish. Both kumquats and Seville oranges make only seasonal appearances in markets, so finding them can be a challenge, limited to late fall and early winter. In lieu of them, the next best choice is blood orange, also seasonal. After that, use navel slices; their peel cooks up toothsome and delicious, if not as pleasantly bitter.

1. Place the fillets in a baking dish large enough to hold them in 1 layer and sprinkle them on both sides with the lemon juice and salt. Set aside in the refrigerator until ready to cook, up to 2 hours.

2. When ready to cook the fish, preheat the oven to 450°F.

3. Heat the oil in a heavy skillet over medium heat. Add the leek and kumquats and cook until barely wilted, 1 minute. Stir in the wine, orange juice, and bay leaf and bring to a boil, still over medium heat. Cook until the leek and kumquats are well wilted, 2 minutes. Pour over the fish, spreading the leek and kumquats out evenly. Place the dish in the oven and bake until the

liquid is bubbling and the fish flakes easily when pierced with a fork, about 15 minutes.

4. Remove the bay leaf and serve right away, garnished with the chives and a sprinkle of black pepper.

A FEW OTHER, LESS COMMON CITRUS FRUITS . . .
AT LEAST IN THE U.S.

ALONGSIDE THE ORANGES, lemons, limes, grapefruit, and tangerines that grace produce selections in a brightly hued range of orange to yellow to green, the citrus family includes less prominent, although equally flavorful and brilliantly tinted, relatives.

❯ **KUMQUATS** are a small citrus fruit, looking rather like orange fingerlings, that grow on a small shrubby tree with dark green, attractive shiny leaves. They originated in China and were unknown in the West until they were brought to England as a landscaping ornamental, not an edible, in 1846. From there they spread across Europe and to the Americas as a garden shrub to enjoy for its looks rather than its fruit. Kumquats are pretty, and like all citrus, their blossoms are quite fragrant. Their fruit also tastes wonderful, raw or cooked, like powerful, tart little oranges.

❯ **BITTER ORANGE** refers to a species of orange that was once popular, but has declined in importance. There are several varieties, all of which grow on small evergreen trees. Some are probably native to southwestern China and northwestern India, but the variety still used most comes from Vietnam. That one, *amara,* is the orange used in marmalade, the grafting stock for the orange flavoring in triple sec and curaçao, and the orange blossoms used in orange-flower water. Another bitter orange variety, bergamot, is named for the ancient city of Pergamon, now in Turkey, where it was cultivated. Small, rough, and slightly pear-shaped, it was the main orange of the ancient Mediterranean. Still popular in Mediterranean countries, bergamots are candied, made into sweet preserves, and used in perfumery and in earlier times were infused in tea. A third variety became so popular in Spain they are known now as Seville oranges. Most are exported to Britain to be used in marmalade. Bitter oranges of the Seville variety were imported to St. Augustine, Florida, by the Spanish and are still grown in that state.

❯ **KAFFIR LIME** is another Southeast Asian citrus that is pear-shaped, wrinkled, and green. The fruit is used in cooking, but more so are its floral yet tart leaves, which unfurl double like twins. They are a common flavoring in Thai and other Southeast Asian dishes.

❯ **BUDDHA'S HAND** is a variety of citron that is shaped like a hand with long, curled fingers resembling Buddha's gesture of serenity, although some see the fruit as an octopus with splayed tentacles. It is thought to be the first citrus fruit known in Europe, brought from India by the Greeks and Romans. Seedless and mostly juiceless but very fragrant, it is valued as an offering in Buddhist temples and to perfume rooms and clothing. It is now grown in southern California, where the large Asian population of farmers has added it to that state's huge basket of citrus fruits.

❯ **WHITE SAPOTE,** from central Mexico, is round, usually green, and bitter. It is enjoyed as an eating and culinary delicacy throughout Central America and can be found in Latin American food sections and stores across the United States.

LOUISIANA SEAFOOD IN BAYOU CHILE BROTH WITH SKILLET CORN BREAD BISCOTTI

INGREDIENTS:

Skillet Corn Bread (page 166), at room temperature

16 jumbo whole shrimp (about 12 ounces)

4 cups water

½ cup white wine

1 tablespoon distilled white vinegar

½ teaspoon kosher or fine sea salt

18 fresh cilantro sprigs

2 tablespoons extra virgin olive oil

1 large white onion, halved and thinly sliced

2 cloves garlic, slivered

1 fresh red chile, preferably cayenne, stemmed and slivered

2 or more dashes of Tabasco or other hot sauce

1 pound catfish fillets, cut crosswise into 3-inch-wide pieces

8 oysters in the shell, scrubbed

DOWN ON THE BAYOU OF LOUISIANA, where French is still spoken and French-named Baton Rouge overlooks the mighty Mississippi River, rivers and inlets replete with catfish meet Gulf waters. Shrimp and oysters arrive at the table within a few hours of harvesting. Within easy boating distance, fresh cayenne peppers flourish on the tiny Avery Island off the coast of New Orleans. Its small acreage is totally dedicated to the production of what has become a worldwide recognized brand of hot sauce: Tabasco. For the cook, the confluence provides a treasure trove of local ingredients for a dish with zydeco rhythm. To accompany it, rather than crackers, crunchy corn bread biscotti pick up all the seafood juices.

1. First make the corn bread and set it aside.

2. Preheat the oven to 425°F.

3. Cut the corn bread into pieces ¾ to 1 inch wide by 4 inches long. Arrange the fingers without touching on a baking sheet, place in the oven, and toast until golden on the bottom, about 10 minutes. Turn them over and continue toasting until golden all around, about 5 minutes more. Set aside.

4. Peel the shrimp, leaving their tails intact and reserving the shells. Devein the shrimp if necessary and set aside.

5. Combine the shrimp shells, water, wine, vinegar, salt, and 6 of the cilantro sprigs in a saucepan and bring to a boil over high heat. Reduce the heat and simmer until the shells are bright pink and the liquid is aromatic, about 10 minutes. Strain the broth into a bowl and discard the solids. Use right away or set aside at room temperature for up to 1 hour.

6. In a large pot or sauté pan wide enough to hold the catfish pieces in 1 layer, heat the oil over medium heat. Add the onion and garlic and sauté until they begin to turn golden, about 10 minutes. Add the shrimp broth, chile, hot sauce, and catfish and bring to a boil over medium-high heat. Reduce the heat to maintain a simmer and cook until the catfish pieces begin to curl up, 3 minutes. Add the shrimp

and oysters and cook just until the shrimp are firm and light pink and the oysters are slightly open, 3 minutes.

7. To serve, ladle the seafood and vegetables into individual wide bowls or deep plates. Moisten with the broth and garnish each bowl with 3 of the corn bread biscotti and a few of the remaining 12 cilantro sprigs. Serve right away, with the remaining biscotti on the side.

AVERY ISLAND AND ITS REMARKABLE PRODUCT

AVERY ISLAND, in the Gulf of Mexico off the coast of New Orleans, is one of nature's most curious and enchanting places. It is one of five salt-domed islands that arose out of a salt plain created when a vast expanse of ocean evaporated. What was left over eons became covered by layer upon layer of alluvial sediment that eventually pushed up as part of the islands' landscape.

Among other wildlife wonders, it became a rookery for the showy snowy egret and other migratory water birds. Under the aegis of its owner, E. A. McIlhenny, it became a wildlife preserve, particularly a bird sanctuary. It also became home to one of the world's most famous and widely distributed bottle sauces: Tabasco. The island lends itself to the farming of acres of cayenne peppers that thrive in its humid, sandy soil. McIlhenny brewed his peppers into a sauce that now appears in big I-use-it-on-everything bottles; medium-size bottles that grace many a table, restaurant to home; and the tiny vial on airplane meal plates. It is one of the most recognized hot sauces in the world.

SHRIMP IN LEMONGRASS COCONUT BROTH

SERVES 4

INGREDIENTS:

⅓ cup unsweetened coconut flakes, for garnish

Kosher or fine sea salt

8 ounces haricots verts, left whole, or young regular green beans, cut in half crosswise

1½ tablespoons peanut or canola oil

2 large cloves garlic, finely chopped

2 tablespoons finely chopped shallot

2 tablespoons coarsely grated peeled fresh ginger

1 to 2 tablespoons chopped small fresh red chile

½ cup coarsely chopped fresh cilantro leaves

1 stalk lemongrass, tender white and light green parts, cut into 2-inch pieces

2½ cups canned unsweetened coconut milk

1½ tablespoons fish sauce, preferably Thai

1½ pounds jumbo (21 to 25) shrimp, shelled, tails left intact, deveined if necessary

4 scallions, trimmed and cut into 2-inch-long slivers, for garnish

1 lime, quartered, for garnish

THE FRENCH DISCOVERED COCONUTS in two of the regions where they explored: the far Pacific and the Caribbean. They encountered lemongrass, ginger, and fish sauce in their incursions into Southeast Asia. In each of these places, they adapted local ingredients to their cooking and the locals integrated French style into their own cuisine. In a nod to such compositions, here is a dish of toothsome shrimp delicately simmered in a broth imbued with lemongrass and coconut milk, served with American-via-France haricots verts for a crisp contrasting green.

1. Toast the coconut flakes in an ungreased skillet over medium-high heat, or in a 350°F oven, or in a microwave oven on high until crisp and golden, about 4 minutes for any method. Set aside.

2. Bring a pot of salted water to boil, add the green beans, and blanch for 2 minutes. Drain, rinse under cold water to stop the cooking, and set aside.

3. Heat the oil in a large, heavy pot over medium-high heat. Add the garlic and shallot and cook until beginning to wilt, 2 minutes. Add the ginger, chile, cilantro, and green beans and stir to mix. Add the lemongrass, coconut milk, and fish sauce, stir again, and bring to a boil, still over medium-high heat. Add the shrimp, reduce the heat to maintain a simmer, and cook just until the shrimp are pink and firm, 3 minutes.

4. Remove and discard the lemongrass pieces. Garnish with the scallion slivers, toasted coconut, and lime wedges and serve.

THE FRENCH IN AMERICA AND AMERICAN FOOD

The first French inroads into the North American continent were scattered and hesitant. The French were too involved in conflicts and machinations in Europe to take much heed of the new land and their rivals who were settling it. But by 1750 there were eighty thousand French in America. Five years later a group of French Acadians, expelled from Nova Scotia by the British, settled near New Orleans and became the population now called Cajuns, who still speak a melodious, rhythmic French patois.

The French proved a great ally to the newly born United States, an alliance that continued throughout the Revolutionary War and beyond. In 1803 Jefferson, a great admirer of France and all things French, purchased the Louisiana Territory from Napoleon, and the largest French territory in the New World became part of the nascent American nation.

The effect the French had on American culture has been enormous and undeniable. The French influenced how our cities look, their layout, avenues, and monuments. They shaped American architecture, especially in the South, bringing such forms as the gallery, post-on-sill construction. Benjamin Henry Latrobe de Boneval, of Huguenot descent, was America's first professional architect, and Etienne Sulpice Hallet was the one to envision a central dome to crown the United States Capitol. French philosophers influenced the writers of the United States Constitution and the acts of our first presidents.

Americans have been captivated by centuries of towering development in French culinary arts from such early chefs as Escoffier and Brillat-Savarin, encyclopedias such as *Larousse Gastronomique,* and later on to Jacques Pépin and Julia Child. In our major cities, French restaurants were long considered irreproachable, and until the flourishing of the American wine industry French wines were the most admired and desired.

SPEAKING OF THE FRENCH . . .

THE IMPACT OF THE FRENCH on the American culinary complex and certainly on the food vocabulary remains considerable. From the French come, among a very small sampling, béarnaise, beurre blanc, and vinaigrette in the sauce category; au gratin and sauté in the cooking methods; crème brûlée and tarte tatin on dessert menus in restaurants and homes both. French bread is spread with Camembert and Brie for a predinner taste treat. Mayonnaise blends tuna and other salads and becomes aioli for seafood from crab to halibut and catfish or just about any vegetable.

SHRIMP ON GRITS WITH DRY VERMOUTH, TOMATO, AND CAPERS

SERVES 4

INGREDIENTS:

Grits (recipe follows),
for serving

6 tablespoons (¾ stick)
butter

3 medium-size tomatoes,
cored, halved, seeded, and
cut into ½-inch chunks

2 large cloves garlic, minced
or pressed

2 teaspoons chopped fresh
thyme

½ teaspoon kosher or
fine sea salt

½ cup dry vermouth

2 tablespoons Dijon mustard

1½ pounds jumbo (21 to 25)
shrimp, with shells and
tails intact, deveined if
necessary

2 teaspoons large capers,
preferably salt-packed,
rinsed

¼ cup chopped fresh flat-leaf
parsley, for garnish

VERMOUTH IS AN AROMATIZED WINE, meaning that unlike a fortified wine in which spirits are introduced to boost the alcohol level, vermouth is infused with additives meant only to confer flavor, including herbs, spices, sugar, roots, flowers, water, and, yes, some alcohol. There are several types of vermouth, but the most popular, well known for its use in martinis, is the dry white developed in France by Joseph Noilly in the nineteenth century. It delivers an especially herbaceous and richly round character to what is a fairly traditional Mediterranean shrimp concoction, but the other twist is a truly American one. A mound of grits makes a striking bed on which to place the colorful shrimp and sauce. And yes, the shrimp are served unpeeled.

1. Make the grits and set aside.

2. Melt 3 tablespoons of the butter in a large sauté pan over medium-high heat. Add the tomatoes, garlic, thyme, and salt and cook until the tomatoes begin to soften and release their juices, 2 minutes. Stir in the vermouth and mustard and cook until bubbling, about 2 minutes. Add the shrimp and capers and cook just until the shrimp are pink and firm, 3 minutes.

3. To serve, spoon the grits onto 4 individual plates. Cut the remaining 3 tablespoons butter into small pieces and divide them over the top of the grits. Top with the shrimp and sauce. Sprinkle the parsley over all and serve right away.

GRITS

OFTEN CALLED *HOMINY GRITS,* which expresses their corn origin, grits play a role in southern cooking as polenta does in Italian cooking and yellow cornmeal does in Mexican. Hominy grits are white, made from white cornmeal, and are more coarsely ground than either polenta or yellow cornmeal. In the American South,

GRITS ARE THE foundation on which to build, the side on which to fill up, or a comfort food merely to stir alone with a pat of butter. A helping of them, in one guise or another, often appears on the table morning as well as night. Like polenta, grits can serve equally as a sauce absorber under scaloppine, stew, or sassy shrimp. For such a bed, 15 minutes of cooking time renders them creamy and soft all through, not al dente.

SERVES 4

3 cups water

1 teaspoon kosher or fine sea salt

¾ cup quick-cooking grits

½ cup milk

Bring the water and salt to a boil in a medium-size pot over high heat. Slowly stir in the grits and then the milk. Reduce the heat to very low, as you would with rice, cover the pot, and cook until creamy soft, 15 minutes. Serve right away or set aside in a warm place for up to 30 minutes.

SAUTEED CLAMS
WITH MACADAMIA NUT AND
GINGER PERSILLADE

SERVES 3 OR 4

INGREDIENTS:

¼ cup peanut or canola oil

1 piece (1 inch) fresh ginger, peeled and cut into ⅛-inch-thick rounds

2 cloves garlic, 1 smashed and peeled, 1 minced or pressed

4 pounds littleneck or cherrystone clams, rinsed

1 teaspoon finely grated peeled fresh ginger

⅓ cup coarsely chopped fresh flat-leaf parsley

⅓ cup roasted macadamia nuts, chopped not too fine

2 teaspoons finely chopped lemon zest

1 lemon, cut into wedges, for serving

1 baguette, warmed, for serving

PERSILLADE IS THE FRENCH NAME FOR A MIXTURE of chopped parsley and garlic. It is used in French cooking as a final fillip for various dishes, such as grilled sardines, sautéed beef, and an estimable potato assemblage called *pommes persillade*. In American cooking, persillade appears early on in the 1918 edition of Fannie Farmer's *Boston Cooking-School Cook Book,* as an embellishment for potatoes. It was the flourish that made New Orleans chef Austin Leslie's signature dish, Fried Chicken Persillade, illustrious. Many have toyed with the mix, adding tarragon, lemon zest, bread crumbs, olive oil, even anchovy (and the mixture invites yet more possibilities). Here, with the addition of ginger and macadamia nuts, the persillade imparts a perfect finish for sautéed clams.

1. Heat the oil in a pot large enough to hold the clams in 1 crowded layer over medium-high heat. Add the ginger rounds and smashed garlic and sauté until sizzling, 30 seconds. Remove and discard the ginger and garlic, leaving the oil in the pot.

2. Add the clams to the pot and sauté, stirring and turning frequently, until they open, 8 to 10 minutes. Turn off the heat and transfer the clams to a platter or individual bowls.

3. Without turning the heat on again, add the minced garlic and grated ginger to the pot and sauté until barely beginning to turn golden, 45 to 60 seconds. Add the parsley, macadamia nuts, and lemon zest, stir to mix, and sprinkle over the clams right away. Serve with the lemon wedges and warm baguette slices on the side.

FANNIE FARMER:
THE DOYENNE OF CLASSIC AMERICAN COOKING

FANNIE FARMER WAS born March 23, 1857, and grew up in Massachusetts. First employed as a "mother's helper," part nanny, part maid, part errand girl, and part cook, Fannie's work brought her into the kitchen, and it was there she found her love.

Seeing her interest, her parents sent her to study at the Boston Cooking School, which primarily trained professional cooks, many of them women who had suffered terrible reversals—widowhood, abandonment, or divorce. In time she became the assistant director of the school and then director. The school had published a book for chefs called *The Boston Cooking-School Cook Book*, but when Fannie saw that housewives needing help were also buying the book, she revised it, gearing it for the home cook. In it she added startling precedents, such as exact measurements, so that results would be dependable. Her updated, revised edition, published in 1896, appealed to the rising number of urban middle-class women who considered homemaking

their career. Fannie, who never married, was dubbed "the mother of level measurement."

In 1902, Fannie left the Boston Cooking School and opened Miss Farmer's Cooking School, again aimed not at chefs-to-be but at ordinary housewives. Over the years she collected the recipes of home cooks around the country, lectured on domestic topics, became very interested in healthful diets, aided doctors in outlining regimens for patients who had many different diseases, and wrote several more cookbooks. Though she died in 1915, her school continued on until 1944, and her *Fannie Farmer Cookbook*, updated in 1979 and again in 1996 by the deft hand of Marion Cunningham, is still in print.

BLAZING MUSSELS WITH SAFFRON, ONION, AND AIOLI

SERVES 4

INGREDIENTS:

Aioli (recipe follows), for serving

4 pounds mussels

3 tablespoons extra virgin olive oil

1 small yellow, white, or sweet onion, thinly sliced

1½ cups white wine

1 teaspoon saffron threads

1 baguette, warmed, for serving

MUSSELS PROLIFERATE UP AND DOWN BOTH AMERICAN COASTS. They also abound on the coasts of France, where they are extolled. Saffron was once a major crop from the spring crocuses of the Provençal hills of France, providing both landscape and dishes with a blazing stroke of almost incandescent yellow. So the dish, mussels, saffron, and all, would hardly be complete without the most famous sauce of France, mayonnaise, and especially the version from southern France, mayonnaise with garlic added, called *aioli*.

1. Make the aioli.

2. Right before cooking, debeard the mussels, if necessary, and scrub the shells under cold running water.

3. Heat the oil in a large, heavy pot over medium-high heat. Add the onion and cook, stirring frequently, until well wilted and just beginning to turn golden, about 5 minutes. Add the wine, bring to a boil, and cook until reduced to 1 cup, 2 to 3 minutes. Stir in the saffron, add the mussels, cover the pot, and cook until the mussels open and become firm, 5 to 7 minutes.

4. Dollop half of the aioli across the mussels and serve right away with the remaining aioli and bread on the side.

AIOLI

AIOLI IS A lusty garlic mayonnaise, dear to its native France, where it is slathered on vegetables, eggs, seafood, meats, and snails if the season is right. In an Italian rendition, it thickens brothy bowls of steamed clams. In Spain, white gazpacho is basically aioli in broth thickened and flavored with pulverized almonds. In America, there's barely a bistro that doesn't offer it to accompany a range of dishes from french fries to plainly cooked vegetables, to simple fish preparations. Aioli makes a glorious sauce dolloped on a homey pot of steamed mussels brightly colored with saffron. And, with a food processor, it's ready in minutes.

MAKES 1 CUP

- 1 slice (1 inch thick) baguette, crust removed, soaked in 1 tablespoon water to soften for 5 minutes
- 3 cloves garlic, coarsely chopped
- 1 large egg, at room temperature
- ¼ cup extra virgin olive oil
- ¼ cup peanut or canola oil
- 1 tablespoon fresh lemon juice
- ¼ teaspoon kosher or fine sea salt
- 1 to 2 tablespoons warm water

Squeeze the bread dry and place it in a food processor. Add the garlic and process to mix into a puree. Add the egg and pulse to mix. With the processor running, add the olive oil and then the peanut oil, both in a slow stream, until you have an emulsion. Add the lemon juice and salt and pulse to mix. Mix in 1 to 2 tablespoons warm water to thin the mixture to a mayonnaise consistency. Use right away or cover and refrigerate for up to 3 days.

BICOASTAL BIVALVES AND THEIR CELEBRATION

BESIDES THE FOURTH OF JULY and baseball's All-Star Game, probably the most traditional of summer festivities in America is the clam bake. Its date for any particular year is not specified, except that it falls between the season's bookends of Memorial Day and Labor Day. The clam bake conjures up images of East Coasters heading for the beaches to dig up clams to steam in a freshly dug fire pit. When the clams have steamed and opened, the revelers dip the tasty meat in melted butter and pop it into their mouths. No plates. No utensils. No formality. The main clams eaten are the East Coast soft-shell clams, also called *steamers, long necks, piss clams,* and *Ipswich clams.* They live in tidal mud flats, most famously along the New England coastline, but are also found from the Carolinas to Canada and even across the Atlantic to Wales.

The East Coast is not the only place for clam bake festivity. In 1879, it seems some venturesome entrepreneurs hoping to embed East Coast oysters in western waters and sell them inadvertently also brought some clams and plunked them down in San Francisco Bay. From there soon the clams crept their way down to Monterey and, by 1960, up the rocky coast as far as Alaska.

The oldest annual recorded clam bake, still going on, dates from 1888 and was originally held as a Quaker school Sunday outing on Horeseneck Beach in Massachusetts. Today the biggest East Coast clam bake takes place in Yarmouth, Maine, and is mirrored on the West Coast in Pismo Beach, California, once called "the clam capital of the world." One difference, contrary to iconographic timing, the Pismo Beach festival is not a summer happening. It takes place in October.

BALSAMIC-GLAZED SEA SCALLOPS ON CAULIFLOWER HORSERADISH PUREE

SERVES 4

INGREDIENTS:

Cauliflower Horseradish
   Puree (recipe follows),
   for serving

1½ pounds sea scallops

Kosher or fine sea salt

3 tablespoons butter

½ cup well-aged balsamic
   vinegar (see facing page)

1 tablespoon fresh tangerine
   juice

SCALLOPS CARRY WITH THEM AN AURA of desire and romance. One of the most recognizable and beloved paintings of the Italian Renaissance depicts Aphrodite, goddess of love, whose name means "born from the foam," rising from the sea on a scallop shell.

Scallops are bivalve mollusks that sit between two beautifully concave to convex ridged "scalloped" shells. The edible white meat that holds the shells together is called the *nut*, a perfect appellation, for it is sweet and chewy and rich as a nut in flavor. Many are the ways that scallops can be served: wrapped in bacon, sauced in cream, skewered, or topped with cheese. Here the fragrant syrup of balsamic vinegar coats the tender seaborne delicacy with a delectable bronze red patina.

1. Make the cauliflower puree and set it aside in a warm place.

2. Pat the scallops dry and sprinkle them with salt.

3. In a sauté pan large enough to hold the scallops in an uncrowded layer, melt the butter over medium heat until foaming. Add the scallops and sauté them until golden on both sides, 3 to 4 minutes total. Transfer the scallops to a plate and set them aside in a warm place.

4. Increase the heat to medium-high, add the vinegar and tangerine juice to the pan, and reduce until thick and sticky, 4 to 5 minutes.

5. To serve, divide the cauliflower puree among 4 individual plates. Nestle the scallops in the puree and spoon the balsamic glaze over them. Serve right away.

CAULIFLOWER HORSERADISH PUREE

CAULIFLOWER IS A MEMBER OF THE BRASSICA FAMILY, a Greek word meaning "clustered like a bunch of grapes." Cauliflower puree, a lacing of cream, and a pinch of horseradish provides a loving cushion for scallops.

MAKES ABOUT 2 CUPS

1 small head cauliflower (about 1¼ pounds)

⅔ cup heavy whipping cream

1 tablespoon horseradish, preferably freshly grated, or bottled

Kosher or fine sea salt

1. Bring a pot of water to a boil. Core the cauliflower and cut it into 1-inch florets. Place the florets in the water and boil until they're mashable, about 10 minutes. Drain and let cool until no longer steaming hot, 1 to 2 minutes.

2. Transfer the cauliflower to a food processor and puree. Add the cream and horseradish and continue pureeing until smooth and fluffy. Season with salt to taste. Use right away or set aside at room temperature for up to 1 hour or refrigerate for up to 2 days and reheat in the microwave just before serving.

BALSAMIC VINEGAR:
WHEN AGE IS DESIRABLE AND A CERTAIN TERROIR IS ESSENTIAL

LIKE FINE WINES, true balsamic vinegar comes with an appellation that states its region of origin. Except, in the case of balsamics, there is only one true region and one appellation: aceto balsamico di Modena, or, in English, balsamic vinegar of Modena. Typically, true balsamic vinegar is made from the must of trebbiano grapes—the mash before it is filtered or fermented. Red or white, the must is boiled over an open fire in copper kettles until 50 percent of the content is lost. The nascent vinegar is then aged in wood barrels for 3 to 5 years for the youngest and up to 150 years for the oldest, with 10 to 50 being typical. With each passing year, the vinegar gains finesse in two ways: It becomes concentrated by evaporation during the summer, and then, in winter, as it rests, it absorbs the flavors of the wood barrel where it is housed for the moment.

The little-known "secret" of this process is that as it decreases in volume, the developing vinegar is moved from one barrel into another of smaller size. For the finest balsamics, each descending-size barrel is made of a different wood and each imbues the aging vinegar with its own particular flavor and aroma. The progression begins with oak and goes on to cherry, mulberry, acacia, juniper, and ash. A more complex and subtle brew evolves with each move.

To understand how serious a matter balsamic vinegar is in its region of origin, consider that there is a board of balsamic vinegar makers that blind-tastes each rendition before giving its maker a stamp of approval and the right to label its bottles aceto balsamico di Modena. Once the certification is earned, a range of excellence is affixed to the batch that spans from "terrific" to "gold quality." Some of the cheaper vinegars have added brown sugar or caramel for color. These cheaper balsamics can serve well as a staple. Like fine wines, the price of the better ones can spike to the heavens, but they are well worth it. They can serve as an unparalleled savory and sweet culinary accent—on simple salads of greens and tender herbs, just a few drops to glisten the leaves (with no further doo-das) or on a bowl of prime-time strawberries, halved and sprinkled with cracked pepper. For the truly adventuresome palate, a fine, thick, almost syrupy balsamic makes a perfect sauce for olive oil ice cream.

CHESAPEAKE BAY
SOFT-SHELL CRABS WITH
WARM RADICCHIO SALAD

INGREDIENTS:

8 soft-shell crabs, cleaned

All-purpose flour, for dusting the crabs

Kosher or fine sea salt

Peanut or canola oil, for frying

2 small or 1 medium-size head radicchio (about 10 ounces total), very coarsely chopped

½ cup chopped fresh flat-leaf parsley leaves

¼ teaspoon kosher or fine sea salt

¼ teaspoon freshly ground black pepper

2 tablespoons extra virgin olive oil

2 strips bacon, sliced crosswise into ¼-inch-wide pieces

2 tablespoons balsamic vinegar

2 teaspoons finely chopped scallions, light green parts only

2 lemons, cut into 8 wedges, for serving

THE SOFT-SHELL DEVELOPMENTAL STAGE is one all crabs go through. To grow, the crab must molt, shedding a smaller shell in trade for the one next size up. In the brief interim, the crabs are tender and edible all through, incipient new shell included. Of all the many types of crab, it is only the blue crab that, when shell-less, is considered elite for the table. To honor that crop, here the crabs are simply sautéed and decked out with a warm radicchio salad.

1. Lightly dust the crabs on both sides with flour and sprinkle lightly with salt. Pour oil to a depth of ¼ inch into a heavy sauté pan and heat over medium-high heat until sizzling. Add as many crabs as will fit without crowding and cook, turning 2 or 3 times, until golden brown on both sides, 5 to 6 minutes altogether. Transfer to a platter and set aside in a warm place. Continue with another batch until all the crabs are cooked.

2. Combine the radicchio, parsley, salt, and pepper in a medium-size bowl and toss to mix.

3. Heat the 2 tablespoons oilve oil in a large, nonreactive sauté pan over medium heat until sizzling. Add the bacon and sauté, stirring frequently, until golden crisp, 5 to 6 minutes. Lift out the bacon with a slotted spoon, leaving the oil in the pan, and transfer to a paper towel. Increase the heat to medium-high and carefully add the vinegar to the pan. Right away, remove from the heat, add the radicchio, and toss to coat thoroughly with the balsamic oil.

4. Arrange the radicchio around the crabs, top with the scallions, and garnish with the lemon wedges. Serve right away, while the radicchio is still warm.

WHY WASHINGTON, DC?

WASHINGTON, DC, along the Potomac River leading into Chesapeake Bay, was chosen by George Washington as the site for the nation's capital and approved by the United States Congress in the Residence Act of 1790. Archaeology shows that people had lived on the site where the short Anacostia River joins the Potomac, in the middle of the city as far back as 2000 BCE. At the time Captain John Smith explored the Anacostia in 1608, Powhatans, the same tribe that troubled the Jamestown settlers hundreds of miles south along the James River, lived on the Virginia side of the Potomac, and the Piscataway people lived on the Maryland side. Another village of the Nacostine tribe was located near present-day Georgetown.

The reason for the early settlements was a simple one. The giant Chesapeake Bay and the legion of rivers flowing into it teemed with food. There were fish galore, including an abundance of meaty shad. Hosts of oysters and other shellfish lay in the riverbeds and bay shores, and the waters abounded with many varieties of crab, from tiny to huge. They could be scooped up by the armful. Survival was not arduous. It was even rather easy, and the land beyond proved rich for crops. Native tribes grew corn, beans, and squash and another inveigling crop: tobacco.

To each side of what was to become Washington, DC, lay Virginia Colony and Maryland Colony, the two largest regions of early American settlement. In 1783, after the conclusion of the Revolutionary War, the newly appointed government of the now christened United States sought to find a seat for the nation's capital. The government was then meeting in New York City and Philadelphia, but many of the leaders—Washington, Jefferson, and Hamilton—had their homes and extensive estates in the South, particularly in Virginia. A deal was struck: A neutral spot between the two burgeoning areas with their different economies would be best.

The final site was fixed just below the Potomac River's Great Falls, the farthest point upstream to which oceangoing boats could navigate. Included were the ports of Georgetown, Alexandria, and those on the Maryland side. However, in a political move to keep Virginia proslavery, Alexandria was later returned to the auspices of the state of Virginia.

Washington appointed a French architect, Pierre Charles L'Enfant, to plan the new city. He designed a grid centered on the new capitol building with broad avenues radiating out, each named for a state. No building was to be higher than the capitol, a rule that still holds. The intersections of the grid and diagonals were to feature plazas and circles, which would in time honor notable Americans. One narrower avenue, Pennsylvania, would connect the capitol to the presidential palace. In September 1791, the entire district was named the Territory of Columbia and the city within the City of Washington, hence, ultimately, Washington, District of Columbia.

The cornerstone of the capitol was laid on October 13, 1792. L'Enfant's successor, Andrew Ellicott, changed the shape of a number of streets and resolved upon a different naming scheme. He rushed to make his plan the first one published, and as a result his plan became the lasting one. North/south streets were numbered, east/west ones called by the alphabet.

Under edict from Washington and subsequent presidents, the city, then just an upstart, was designed to look as stately, powerful, and awe-inspiring as its European rivals, and so all the architects who followed Ellicott have perpetuated the building of massive, neoclassical federal buildings in imposing white marble. Beyond the federal structures, the monuments, and the famed mall connecting them, today the town is full of restaurants, many still serving the wonderful seafood from the Chesapeake Bay, especially the famous blue crabs.

LOBSTER TACOS WITH AVOCADO LIME CREAM AND SINGED SCALLIONS

INGREDIENTS:

2 ripe but firm avocados, preferably Hass, pitted, peeled, and cut into chunks

½ cup half and half

¼ cup fresh lime juice

1 jalapeño chile, stemmed

Kosher or fine sea salt

4 live lobsters
(1¼ to 1½ pounds each)

2 small bunches scallions, white and light green parts only

12 corn tortillas

12 tender fresh cilantro sprig tops

THERE ARE MANY TYPES OF LOBSTER with many names: hummer, langoustine, astakos, spiny. But the truly fine, rich and meaty American ones (*Homarus americanus*), which so prolilferated on America's New England coast that in the early days of the nation prisoners were served them, are also known for the regions that cull them: Maine lobster, Massachusetts lobster, Canadian lobster, and just plain North Atlantic lobster. As an edible they are all deemed elegant.

Tacos might seem not so elegant and certainly not up to the majesty of lobster. But topped with an avocado cream, smartened with singed scallion ribbon and cilantro sprigs and wrapped in a tortilla, lobster reaffirms its sophisticated reputation in a whole new and beguiling form.

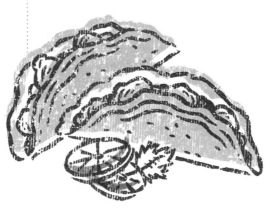

1. Combine the avocados, half and half, lime juice, jalapeño, and ¼ teaspoon salt in a food processor and puree until smooth. Set aside at room temperature for up to several hours.

2. To cook the lobsters, bring 2 large pots of salted water to a rolling boil over high heat. Drop 2 lobsters, head first, into each pot and bring to a boil again. Cover and cook until the shells are bright red and the small legs pull off easily, 10 to 11 minutes. Drain and cool enough to handle.

3. Cut the scallions lengthwise into halves or quarters (depending on thickness) and then crosswise into 3-inch lengths. Heat a heavy skillet over high heat until a drop of water sizzles when dropped in. Add the scallions and stir until they are just slightly wilted and charred in spots, about 1 minute. Set aside.

4. Preheat the oven to 300°F.

5. Meanwhile, extract the lobster meat: Pull off the large front claws from each lobster and crack the shells open with a kitchen mallet or hammer. Remove the small side legs and set them aside for another purpose (see Tip). Break the lobster bodies at the joint between the tail and upper body. With a knife, split the shells along the center of the underside. Remove the meat from the claws, bodies, and tails and cut it into ¾-inch chunks.

6. Warm the tortillas in the oven.

7. To serve, divide the lobster meat among the tortillas. Top with singed scallions, avocado cream, and cilantro sprigs. Fold over the tortillas to enclose the filling. Serve right away, with the remaining sauce on the side.

➲TIP: WHAT ABOUT THE REST OF THE LOBSTER? An Esoteric Side and a Best-Ever Seafood Broth

When cleaning a whole lobster, don't relegate the "remains" to a debris pile in your eagerness for the tender white meat. Here's how to make the most of lobster's extravagant offerings:

From the upper body, spoon out the green part, which is the liver, the marrowlike white part, and the pink-to-orange colored coral, which is the roe, and place them in separate tiny bowls. Offer them alongside the dish as a special treat.

Use the shells and small legs (swimmerets) to make an excellent fish stock. Place them on a baking sheet and roast them in a 400°F oven until slightly golden brown, about 25 minutes. In a medium-size saucepan, heat 1 tablespoon extra virgin olive oil over medium-high heat. Add 1 leek, ½ rib celery, and 1 small carrot, all coarsely chopped, and sauté until the vegetables are wilted, about 5 minutes. Add the lobster shells and swimmerets, along with 1 tablespoon tomato paste, ½ cup white wine, and enough water to come three quarters of the way up the sides of the ingredients. Bring to a boil, reduce the heat to maintain a gentle simmer, and cook until reduced to about 1½ cups, about 30 minutes. Strain through a fine-mesh sieve and use right away, cool and refrigerate for up to 3 days, or freeze for longer.

VEGETABLES: THE VITAL VICTUAL

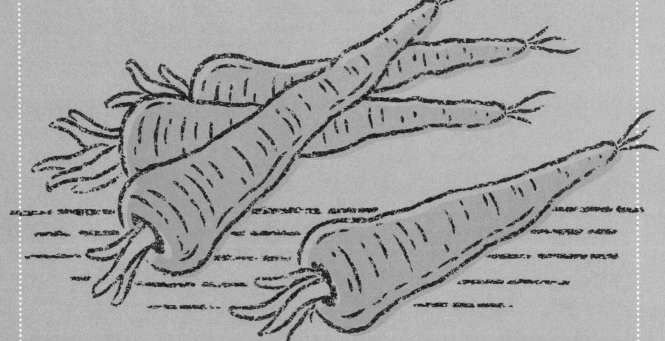

othing compares to the exhilarating tastes of leaves, stems, bulbs, roots, flowers, seeds, tubers, pods, stalks, and sprouts. Some are soft and mellow; some are fibrous and chewy. As they ripen through the yearly seasonal cycle, they present an ever-spinning merry-go-round of taste and texture and color.

As main dishes, vegetables are less weighty while still filling. Simply steamed, roasted, or sautéed, they need only a dollop of butter or oil, a sprinkling of herbs and spices, or a dash of lemon and wine to become the perfect sides.

Following is an array of full vegetable meals. After them comes a promenade of vegetable sides.

Enjoy.

VEGETABLE ENTREES

Whole delectable meals made of vegetables alone are time-honored staples. Sometimes they involve grains, sometimes not. Mixed or stacked, novel and adventurous, or solidly traditional, here are a few of each sort—fun, fabulous, filling, and copious.

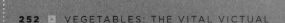

WHITE WINE-SIMMERED VEGETABLE TACOS WITH SASSY SALSA

UPON OCCASION GUESTS ARRIVE FOR DINNER and then announce they are vegetarian. Or perhaps you already knew about their preferences but are pressed for vegetarian ideas. Vegetable tacos are the answer and a happy answer at that. The dish was originally created for our *Good and Plenty: America's New Home Cooking,* when a flock of unexpected visitors who consumed no meat popped up, eager to eat. The dish was a resounding success. It also appeared in our book *The Well-Filled Tortilla,* and now again here, varied with a fun and bold new salsa.

1. Combine the potatoes, tomatoes, zucchini, onion, jalapeño, corn, oregano, salt, and wine in a large pot and bring to a boil over medium-high heat. Reduce the heat and simmer, stirring from time to time, until the potatoes are done, 15 to 20 minutes. Remove from the heat and stir in the cilantro.

2. While the vegetables simmer, make the salsa and warm the tortillas.

3. Spoon some of the vegetables into a warm tortilla, top with a dollop of salsa and another of sour cream, fold, and savor.

SASSY SALSA

IF THE FILLING is the heart of the taco, salsa is the soul. A taco is hardly a taco without one. Here a tomato, onion, and lime juice salsa is tweaked with mint, not the usual leafy cilantro. All together, they add super sass to a purely vegetarian taco—or anywhere else you might use it to accompany simply prepared fish or poultry dishes.

MAKES 1½ CUPS

4 plum or 2 medium-size tomatoes, finely diced

2 tablespoons minced red onion

2 tablespoons fresh lime juice

2 teaspoons finely shredded fresh mint leaves

1½ teaspoons finely chopped jalapeño or serrano chile

2 teaspoons extra virgin olive oil

¾ teaspoon kosher or fine sea salt

Combine the tomatoes, onion, lime juice, mint, chile, oil, and salt in a medium-size bowl and stir to mix. Use right away, set aside at room temperature for up to several hours, or refrigerate overnight.

TAMIL AND CURRY

TAMIL IS SPOKEN by one of the major population groups of India. In Tamil, the word for gravy or spiced sauce is *kari*. The sauce always includes a robust mingling of spices, never a single one. The word *kari* had arrived in English, along with the idea of the gravy and many of the spices in the sauce, by the time of King Richard II in the late 1300s. It went through a number of spellings, including *carrie* and *kaaree*, to the present *curry*. Dishes in curry sauce spread everywhere Indians settled, such as Indonesia and Africa, and also to where those who had been to India returned. Almost all Indian-style dishes that involved a gravy heady with a mix of spices became known as *curries*. Following the éclat the sauce garnered, premixed blends of the spices, simply called *curry* or *curry powder*, followed.

Despite being grouped under a single term, curry powders encompass the arc of spices utilized in Indian cooking. They include turmeric, coriander, mustard, fenugreek, cumin, black pepper, and sometimes anise, clove, cinnamon, and/or chile powder. Curries of other lands where Indian influence spread also often integrate favored local spices—fish paste in Myanmar, lemongrass in Thailand, nutmeg in Java. There is an herb called curry leaf, *kari*, in Tamil. It comes from a pungent tree native to India and Sri Lanka and is also often used in curry gravies much as a bay leaf might be used in Western cooking.

CARROT AND GREEN SPLIT PEA CURRY WITH TAMARIND DATE RELISH

SERVES 4

INGREDIENTS:

- Tamarind Date Relish (recipe follows), for serving
- 1 cup dried split green peas
- 2 tablespoons peanut or canola oil
- 1 medium-size yellow or white onion, coarsely chopped
- 1 tablespoon curry powder
- 1½ teaspoons ground cumin
- ¼ teaspoon cayenne pepper
- ½ teaspoon freshly ground black pepper
- 7 small to medium-size carrots, sliced ½ inch thick on a diagonal
- 6 medium-size Yukon gold or red-skinned potatoes, peeled and cut into ½-inch chunks
- 2 cups water
- 2 teaspoons kosher or fine sea salt
- Steamed Basmati Rice (page 257), for serving
- ¼ cup fresh cilantro leaves, for garnish
- ½ small onion, thinly sliced and sprinkled with salt, for serving
- 1 cup plain Greek yogurt, stirred smooth, for serving

THE MAJORITY OF MEALS PREPARED AROUND THE WORLD consist only of vegetables. Meat, fish, and poultry are rarities, and so the culinary custom in many places is to concoct a meal of a mélange of vegetables. Among the most appealing and popular are Indian curries, now a staple in a varied number of American eateries.

Any vegetable can be the basis, and sweet carrots are one of the best. Here a carrots-for-dinner curry combined with split peas beckons lively Indian seasonings and accompaniments, basmati rice, an intriguing chutney of date and tamarind, tingly salt-wilted onions, and cooling yogurt.

1. Make the relish and set it aside.

2. Place the split peas in a medium-size pot, add water to cover by 1½ inches, and bring to a boil over high heat. Reduce the heat to maintain a brisk simmer and cook uncovered until the peas are soft, 15 to 20 minutes. Drain and set aside.

3. Heat the oil in a large, heavy pot over medium-high heat. Stir in the chopped onion, curry powder, cumin, cayenne, and black pepper and sauté until the onion is translucent and the spices are a little toasty, 3 minutes.

4. Add the carrots, potatoes, water, and salt and bring to a boil. Reduce the

heat to maintain a brisk simmer, partially cover the pot, and cook until the carrots are just beginning to soften, 15 minutes.

5. While the curry simmers, cook the rice and set it aside.

6. Stir the peas into the curry and continue simmering until the vegetables are tender, 5 minutes.

7. Spoon the curry over the rice and sprinkle the cilantro over the top. Put the relish, salted onion, and yogurt in separate bowls and serve on the side.

TAMARIND

THE TAMARIND TREE, or tamar-i-hind, the "date of India" as the Arabs wrote of it, is one of the most common trees of the Indian subcontinent and is an impressive beauty. It can grow taller than sixty-five feet with a canopy spanning an equal footage and remains lushly green year-round except in dry climates. Aside from its shade and aesthetic appeal, its deep red-brown hardwood is useful for its durability in making furniture or flooring. Its pulp, leaves, and bark are reputed to have medicinal applications. But it's from its culinary munificence that the tree achieves its renown.

The fruit, though not a legume, looks like one, with dangling, rusty-brown pods that resemble runner beans or dates.

Unlike legumes, the seeds are not the good part and are discarded. The desired part of the pod is the pulp, which is tangy, indeed a tad sour, but still excites with a trace of sweetness. It is that teeter-totter balance that is the tamarind's draw. It soothes spices and quenches thirst. Indians find it perfect to add a little contrariness to vindaloo, tikka, and curry.

Sometime in the sixteenth century, tamarind was introduced to the Caribbean Islands and Mexico. In those regions it found its way into sauces, for example Jamaican Pickapeppa, but more often was pressed into a refreshing drink, *agua de tamarindo.* But it didn't stay confined to tropical realms. Tamarind is a covert ingredient in English Worcestershire sauce.

TAMARIND DATE RELISH

INDIAN CURRY DISHES always include a medley of spices and a selection of compelling condiments and relishes on the side. These offset the typical Indian spiciness with tart, sweet, or cool tastes. One might find on the table abetting a curry a small dish of *achar,* a potpourri of pickles; yogurt; and a vegetable, herb, or fruit chutney or relish, sometimes sweet, sometimes tangy. Here tamarind in paste form, compacted from the pulp of the tamarind pod, accents the curry's taste spectrum with emphasis on the tart, which contrasts with the poignant sweetness of dried dates. Lacking tamarind, substitute the same amount of ever-so-finely chopped soft, sun-dried apricots plus a splash of lemon. The relish's sweet-tart jammy texture is also a good condiment for pork, chicken, or game dishes.

MAKES ABOUT 2 CUPS

¼ cup tamarind paste

1 cup warm water

1 small yellow or white onion, cut in half lengthwise and thinly sliced

8 ounces pitted dates, cut lengthwise in half

1 piece (½ inch) fresh ginger, peeled and thinly sliced

2 small dried red chiles

¼ cup packed dark brown sugar

½ cup distilled white vinegar

1. Soak the tamarind in ½ cup of the warm water for 10 minutes to soften.

2. Put the tamarind, soaking water, remaining ½ cup warm water, onion, dates, ginger, chiles, brown sugar, and vinegar in a medium-size saucepan and bring to a boil over medium-high heat. Reduce the heat to maintain a gentle simmer. Partially cover the pot and simmer until thick and syrupy, 20 to 30 minutes. Remove from the heat and let the mixture cool.

3. Remove and discard the chiles. Serve the relish right away or store in the refrigerator for up to several weeks.

STEAMED BASMATI RICE

BASMATI RICE IS a direct descendant of the early Himalayan rice and is the main rice cooked in India. Its name means "fragrant" in Hindi and refers to its nutlike flavor and aroma. It is a long-grain rice preferred for thousands of years in the curries of India and Pakistan. Simply steamed, basmati rice serves as the platform for many of the region's vegetable, meat, and seafood offerings. Today basmati rice is also grown in the United States under the names Texmati and Kasmati. The nourishing glory of rice is matched by generosity of volume: A mere cup, when cooked, will provide a bountiful base for four servings.

SERVES 4

1 cup basmati rice
2 cups water

1. Rinse the rice and place it in a medium-size heavy saucepan. Add the water and bring to a boil over medium-high heat.

2. Reduce the heat, adjusting it to maintain the barest simmer. Cover the pot and cook for 22 minutes without lifting the lid. Remove from the heat and set aside to rest and steam dry for at least 15 minutes or up to 1 hour before serving. If the rice needs reheating, sprinkle a little water over the top, cover, and reheat over low heat on the stove or in the microwave.

CAULIFLOWER COUSCOUS
WITH THREE CONDIMENTS

IN AN ORIGINAL NORTH AFRICA-INFLUENCED VEGETABLE consortium, cauliflower heads the table, with, as always in the North African Maghreb—the coastal countries of Africa's northwest corner—chickpeas bubbling alongside. Maghreb-inspired condiments augment the stew with ardor in a peppery harissa paste, a sweet, lemon-flavored apricot relish, and a cooling dilled yogurt served with couscous. The lemon apricot relish and harissa can be made ahead.

1. Make the Lemon Apricot Relish and harissa.

2. Melt the butter in the oil in a large pot over medium-high heat. Add the onion, garlic, cinnamon stick, salt, cumin, caraway seeds, ginger, turmeric, saffron, and water. Stir to mix and bring just to a boil.

3. Add the cauliflower, carrots, tomatoes, zucchini, and chickpeas and cook until the cauliflower and carrots are tender, about 25 minutes. Remove from the heat and let rest for 5 minutes for the juices to settle and the flavors to blend.

4. While the vegetables stew, make the couscous and dilled yogurt.

5. To serve, ladle the stew over the couscous and garnish with the cilantro. Serve with the Lemon Apricot Relish, Harissa, and Dilled Yogurt on the side.

LEMON APRICOT RELISH

MOROCCO IS FAMOUS for its apricots. Virtually tons of them are grown every year. Some come to the market fresh, some are canned, but the majority are sundried to intense and ambrosial concentration. When the dried apricots are joined with lemons in a sweet, fruity relish to accompany couscous stew, magic happens.

MAKES 1½ CUPS

4 medium-size lemons, quartered, seeded, and thinly sliced

½ cup dried apricots, finely chopped

1 teaspoon ground coriander

½ teaspoon dry mustard

1 bay leaf

4 whole cloves

1 piece (1 inch) cinnamon stick

¼ cup honey

2 tablespoons water

1. Combine the lemons, apricots, coriander, mustard, bay leaf, cloves, cinnamon, honey, and water in a medium-size saucepan or microwave-safe bowl and stir to mix. Cover and cook over medium heat on the stove or microwave on high until the lemons are soft, 8 to 10 minutes either way.

2. Remove the cover, stir, and continue cooking until most of the liquid evaporates, about 6 minutes.

3. Let cool, then remove the bay leaf, cloves, and cinnamon stick. Serve at room temperature or chilled. It will keep in an airtight jar in the refrigerator for up to 1 month or more.

HARISSA

THICK AND FORCEFULLY hot, harissa is spooned in small dabs onto the side of the plate to be blended in slowly as one eats. Harissa is at its best shortly after it is made, before it mellows with standing.

MAKES ¼ CUP

½ cup small dried red chiles, such as japones or cayenne, stemmed and broken up but not seeded

1 clove garlic, smashed and peeled

1 teaspoon caraway seeds

½ teaspoon ground cumin

¼ teaspoon ground coriander

¼ to ½ teaspoon kosher or fine sea salt

1 to 2 tablespoons extra virgin olive oil

1. Place the chiles in a small saucepan, add hot water barely to cover, and bring to a boil over high heat. Immediately remove from the heat and set aside to soften for 15 minutes or so.

2. When the chiles are soft, place them in a food processor with 1 tablespoon of their cooking liquid and the garlic, caraway seeds, cumin, coriander, ¼ teaspoon of the salt, and 1 tablespoon of the oil. Process, adding more oil as necessary to make a soft paste. Taste and season with more salt if needed. Use right away or refrigerate for up to 5 days.

RAMBLING COUSCOUS

COUSCOUS IS POSSIBLY ONE OF THE OLDEST PASTAS KNOWN, dating at least to the tenth century. Scholars aren't sure whether the little beadlike pasta originated in West or North Africa, where in both areas it was made with millet and sorghum as well as wheat. It soon spread via nomads, invaders, sailors, and traders across to Egypt, on around the Mediterranean bend to Israel and Jordan, and across that warm sea to Sicily, Madeira, Turkey, and Greece.

In most of the homelands, meat and poultry were and are rare, expensive, and reserved for special events, but all produce a splendid abundance of vegetables. It is common, therefore, that a hotchpotch of garden bounty serves as a marvelous stew spooned over couscous. Eventually couscous made its way to France, England, and South and North America via the coming of the North African people, who found it so basic they simply called it "food."

RAISIN COUSCOUS

RICE WAS A latecomer to North Africa, but wheat dough made into a kind of pasta dates back at least to the Romans, if not the Berbers. The nomads of North Africa created a way to make a pasta noodle small and plump enough to soak up every drop of simmering stew. Couscous cooks in moments, just right for a weary, wandering people.

SERVES 4

4 cups water

3 tablespoons butter

½ teaspoon kosher or fine sea salt

⅓ cup raisins

2 cups couscous

1. Combine the water, butter, and salt in a large pot and bring to a boil over high heat. Stir in the raisins, add the couscous, and stir to mix. Remove from the heat and set aside for 5 minutes, until the grains are beginning to soften. Mix with a fork and your fingers to plump the grains. Cover and set aside in a warm place for 5 minutes longer.

2. Serve right away or set aside and reheat briefly. Fluff the grains just before serving.

DILLED YOGURT

ALTHOUGH YOGURT CIRCLES the Mediterranean, it is not usually a condiment to the forthright dishes of North Africa. However, a cooling spoon or two of it alongside a couscous offers a welcome and ready way to temper their typical fieriness.

MAKES 1 CUP

1 clove garlic

1 teaspoon kosher or fine sea salt

1 cup plain Greek yogurt

2 teaspoons chopped fresh dill

Combine the garlic and salt on a cutting surface and chop them together until minced. Transfer to a small bowl, add the yogurt and dill, and whisk to smooth. Use right away or refrigerate for up to overnight.

CAULIFLOWER AND NETTLE GRATIN

THERE'S A VENTURESOME NEW VEGETABLE, though indeed it is quite ancient, showing up in produce markets: nettles. There are more than forty species of them. The one mainly used in cooking, is the stinging nettle. Never fear. Though you must take care to handle them with tongs or rubber gloves before cooking, through a culinary alchemy the sting of stinging nettles goes away when they are cooked, and abracadabra, they add a deep vegetable green and herb flavor to the food they are in.

With creamy white cauliflower, cheese, and nutmeg, stinging nettles bake into an anything-but-ordinary gratin, and out comes a fine, filling meal. The same amount of spinach may be substituted for the nettles.

1. Place the cauliflower florets, lemon juice, and enough water to cover in a large bowl. Set aside for at least 30 minutes and up to 1 hour to crisp.

2. Preheat the oven to 350°F.

3. Bring a large pot of water to a boil over high heat. Drain the florets and add them to the pot. Cover the pot and blanch the florets, still over high heat, until they begin to soften, 3 to 5 minutes. Pour them into a colander, shake dry, and transfer them to an 11-by-7-by-1½-inch baking dish to cool.

4. Meanwhile, bring another pot of water to boil over high heat. Using tongs so you don't get stung, plunge the nettles into the pot and blanch for 2 minutes. Drain and coarsely chop.

5. Add the nettles, cheese, salt, pepper, nutmeg, and 4 tablespoons of the melted butter to the dish with the cauliflower and toss to coat. Place in the oven and cook until the cheese is beginning to melt, about 10 minutes.

6. Sprinkle the bread crumbs over the top and drizzle the remaining 2 tablespoons butter over all. Continue baking until the cheese is completely melted and the crumbs are beginning to turn golden, about 15 minutes. Serve right away.

SERVES 4 TO 6

INGREDIENTS:

2 large heads cauliflower (about 4 pounds), cored and cut into 1-inch florets

½ cup fresh lemon juice

4 ounces young nettle tops and leaves

2 cups grated sharp white cheddar cheese, such as Vermont or Canadian white cheddar

½ teaspoon kosher or fine sea salt

¼ teaspoon freshly ground black pepper

Pinch of grated nutmeg, preferably freshly grated

6 tablespoons (¾ stick) butter, melted

2 cups bread crumbs, preferably homemade (page 41)

DANDELION GREENS
IN EGG CUSTARD "PIE" WITH A
POTATO CRUST

INGREDIENTS:

Vegetable oil, for greasing the baking dish

1 large or 2 small bunches dandelion greens, tough stem bottoms trimmed, leaves cut crosswise at ½-inch intervals (about 6 packed cups)

1½ cups plain Greek yogurt

½ cup crumbled feta cheese

8 tablespoons (1 stick) butter, melted

1¼ teaspoons kosher or fine sea salt

¾ teaspoon freshly ground black pepper

2 large eggs

1 cup half-and-half

2 medium-size russet potatoes, unpeeled, sliced ⅛ to ¼ inch thick

1 cup bread crumbs, preferably homemade (page 41)

IN THE LAWNS AND GARDENS ACROSS THE UNITED STATES dandelions are considered an annoying weed, but in truth their leaves provide a wonderful, mildly bitter, edible green collected, simmered, and savored in many parts of the world. African Americans knew them from their home continent and embraced them along with kale, mustard, turnip, and collards in a "mess of greens" and quichelike pies, topped as likely with potato as with pastry.

1. Preheat the oven to 375°F. Lightly grease a 1½- to 2-inch-deep 2-quart baking dish. Bring a large pot of water to a boil over high heat.

2. Add the dandelion greens to the boiling water, press them down so they are submerged, and blanch just until bright green and limp, about 1½ minutes. Drain in a colander, rinse under cold water to stop the cooking, and set aside in the colander.

3. Whisk together the yogurt, feta, butter, salt, and pepper in a medium-size bowl. Whisk in the eggs and half-and-half. Squeeze the dandelion greens to remove any remaining liquid without wringing them dry and stir them into the bowl. Set aside.

4. To assemble the pie, cover the bottom of the baking dish with an overlapping layer of potato slices. Pour in the yogurt and egg mixture and cover with another layer of potato slices. Cover and bake until the potatoes are tender, 1 to 1¼ hours.

5. Remove the cover and sprinkle the bread crumbs over the top. Continue baking until the custard is set and the bread crumbs are golden, about 20 minutes longer. Serve right away.

EGGPLANT, POTATO, AND WALNUT CASSEROLE WITH WHITE SAUCE ICING

SERVES 4 TO 6

INGREDIENTS:

- White Sauce Icing (recipe follows)
- ½ to ¾ cup extra virgin olive oil
- 1 medium-size onion, finely chopped
- 3 cloves garlic, chopped
- 2 large tomatoes, finely chopped
- 1 tablespoon tomato paste
- 2 tablespoons brandy
- ½ cup dry white wine
- 2 teaspoons chopped fresh oregano leaves or ¾ teaspoon dried
- ¼ teaspoon ground allspice
- ¼ teaspoon ground cinnamon
- 1 teaspoon kosher or fine sea salt
- ½ teaspoon freshly ground black pepper
- 1½ cups finely chopped walnuts
- 2 medium-size eggplants, ends trimmed, sliced lengthwise ¼ inch thick
- 2 large russet potatoes, peeled and cut into ¼-inch-thick rounds

EGGPLANTS COMING FROM THE EAST and tomatoes from the west met in Greece and fell in love. The combination is an affair that, perhaps, made the classic Greek dish moussaka almost synonymous with Greek cuisine. Although the meaty version of the dish is the most well known, here the meat is traded for walnuts to make a richer vegetarian version. Topped with a white sauce icing, the result is a lush, warming vegetable casserole. When preparing the dish, keep in mind that eggplant eagerly absorbs oil and can slurp up huge amounts: Best to use a delicate hand when adding oil to the pan for sautéing the eggplant, just enough to grease the pan generously, but not so much as to float the slices.

1. Make the white sauce icing and set it aside.

2. Heat 2 tablespoons of the olive oil in a medium-size sauté pan over medium-high heat. Add the onion and garlic and sauté until well wilted, about 5 minutes.

3. Add the tomatoes, tomato paste, brandy, wine, oregano, allspice, cinnamon, salt, and pepper and bring to a boil. Cook briskly until most of the liquid is absorbed and you can see the bottom of the pan when you stir, about 8 minutes. Stir in the walnuts, which should make the sauce quite thick.

Remove from the heat and set aside.

4. Pour enough of the remaining oil into a large skillet to cover the bottom lightly and heat over medium heat. Add as many eggplant slices as will fit in a single layer and sauté, turning once, until wilted, 2 to 3 minutes. Transfer the slices to paper towels to drain and continue with another batch, judiciously adding a little more oil to the pan for each batch, until all the slices are wilted.

5. In the same pan, fry the potato slices in batches in the same way, judiciously oiling the pan as you go and setting the slices on paper towels to drain.

6. Preheat the oven to 350°F.

7. Arrange half of the potato slices in an overlapping layer on the bottom of an 11-by-7-by-1½-inch baking dish. Arrange half of the eggplant slices over the potatoes. Spread the tomato-walnut sauce on the top of the eggplant. Arrange the second half of the eggplant slices over the sauce and top with the second half of the potato slices.

8. Pour the white sauce evenly over the top and bake until the dish is bubbling and the top is lightly golden, 1 hour. Remove from the oven and let rest for 10 to 15 minutes, then serve warm.

A SHORT SOUL FOOD GLOSSARY

WHEN AFRICANS WERE brought to America they needed to adapt to unfamiliar food. Because they didn't have words for their newfound ingredients or dishes, they made up names. The lively nomenclature still exists as part of rich American English.

The slaves loved greens. They recognized dandelions but didn't know some found in their new environment. So any and all of them became a *mess of greens.*

The water used to boil the greens, very nutritious but shunned by the less adventuresome plantation owners, became *pot likker.* Real alcoholic "likker" was mostly forbidden.

Milk, eggs, onion, and flour were added to scraps of catfish and fried up. It is said crumbs were tossed to the dogs to keep them quiet while the food was transferred to the table, and so bready fritters became known as *hush puppies.*

From the Angolan word for okra—*kingombo*—came *gumbo,* one of the signature stews of the American South that includes the vegetable. Native Americans taught the slaves how to season and thicken with sassafras, which was called *filé.* The combined dish was called *filé gumbo.*

The Congo word for peanut, *nguba,* became the shared term *goober* and *goober pea.*

With only the poorer parts of meat available from a hog, good use was made of every inch. The intestines, well cleaned and fried crisp, became a favored snack called *chitterlings* by the English speakers, abbreviated to *chitlins* and *gut strut.*

Corn bread batter was heaped on a spade or hoe to cook over an open fire for a quick snack. It became *hoecakes.* Baked in a round skillet or other batter pan, the bread was called *corn pone,* a term for the shape of the pan.

Gritty ground corn with a little milk and sugar added to make a puddinglike treat became *po' folks dessert in a glass.* When eaten plain, it took on the simple shortcut and apt name *grits.*

In the 1960s, with the acknowledgment of African American's vital role in American life, many cultural items were said to have "soul." And so the cuisine became *soul food.*

WHITE SAUCE ICING

A CLASSIC OF EUROPEAN and early American home kitchens, white sauce can be used to blanket vegetables, nap an old-fashioned open-face sandwich like chipped beef or chicken à la king, enfold cheese to sauce scallops Mornay, bind scalloped potatoes, or spread as a smooth and tasty icing over an eggplant casserole. Its basic ingredients are few, and it swirls together quickly either in a pan or in a microwave oven. With the microwave, a bit of time is shaved off, and, best of all, there's no pan to scrub. The sauce can be made up to several days in advance and then reheated on the stove or in a microwave, thinned with a little milk as desired.

MAKES ABOUT 2 CUPS

3 tablespoons butter

3 tablespoons all-purpose flour

1½ cups milk

⅛ teaspoon kosher or sea salt

⅛ teaspoon grated nutmeg, preferably freshly grated

½ cup grated Parmesan cheese (optional)

CASEROLE CHRONICLES

IN AN ARTICLE PUBLISHED ON APRIL 30, 1911, under the heading "A Message to Women," *The New York Times* touts the advantages of casserole cooking. Dishes made in earthenware casserole pots are palatable, says the article, and, more important, they are economical. In a casserole dish the cook can use leftover foods, a mix of vegetables, tough meats, chickens that aren't young, and otherwise wasted leftover gravy. The popularity of casserole cookery, the article claims, is shown in the increasing number of casserole dishes, of all sizes and shapes from individual to huge, oval to round, displayed in shops.

Casserole cooking saves the cook work since the dish is put on the table in the same vessel it is cooked in. And, placed in a silver plate holder, the casserole can break free of its homey origins. It becomes smart enough to set before a gathering.

The article's 1911 predictions were right. Casserole cooking grew so popular in America that by the 1950s casserole dishes were the most common sort of cookware sold, outranking skillets and teakettles. During this time some of America's classic casserole dishes were forged.

Those classics, still fondly remembered and served, run the gamut from tuna and noodles to baked macaroni and cheese, scalloped potatoes, and tamale pie. There were also numerous "company" casseroles created to be classier and fit for parties—pork chops with rice or potatoes or green beans, veal cutlets layered with mushrooms in cream sauce, baked spaghetti, chicken Divan, and the like. Many employed canned soup. By the early 1970s, the glory of casseroles had begun to fade in America. They came to be considered parochial and decidedly pedestrian. Still, a cooking method and the dish that produces such integration of element and flavor cannot be eschewed forever. Casseroles are, after all, quintessential home fare.

Today's new casseroles take their cue from the ancient, the international, and all that has become American cooking now—paella, rabbit and rice, curry and hot pot, eggplant and walnut, and beyond. Way beyond.

Melt the butter in a medium-size saucepan over medium-high heat on the stove or in a medium-size microwave-safe bowl in the microwave until foaming. Add the flour, whisk until the mixture is smooth, and cook until it begins to turn golden, 2 minutes either way. Whisk in the milk and salt and cook until thickened and creamy, about 5 minutes either way. Whisk in the nutmeg and cheese and remove from the heat. Use right away or cool and refrigerate, covered, for up to 5 days. Gently reheat and whisk before using.

SPIRITED VEGETABLE SIDES

Vegetable sides are the entrée's right hand and as such hold many roles. They round out the meal with essential elements. They provide vitamins and minerals. They mediate the entrée with a contrast, and at the same time gild it with texture, color, and flavor.

With the world of vegetables so vast, and what to do with them unlimited, vegetable sides readily offer themselves as one of the most inventive elements of cuisine. It's rightfully long been held that a replete meal must have a vegetable escort. The point is to make it healthful, taste filled, and fun. There follows a fanciful lineup. All are so versatile they can go with any main dish—meat, game, poultry, and fish—so we don't specify. The choice is up to you.

ARTICHOKE NESTS
WITH GARLIC CLOVE "EGGS"

"SUN BLESSED OR FROST KISSED," as growers and purveyors like to explain, globe artichokes make themselves available twice a year. They appear once in the spring "sun blessed," when their leaves are a plump and perfect mossy green, and again in the fall, "frost kissed," with their outer leaves browned from the chill but the inner ones still sweet as a summer day. Either time, the bottoms of their leaves and their disk-shaped hearts offer a singular taste that lures many a nibbler: vegetable, pulpy, and almost as if green tea had saturated a loamy potato. Garlic has long been a companion of artichokes, often offered in a butter dip. Halved lengthwise and their thorny centers scooped out, artichokes form a scrumptious nest for whole garlic. The garlic should be fresh and supple; if the cloves are dry, they won't turn into succulent "eggs" in their artichoke nest. For a fancy first course, drape the nests with an anchovy fillet or two and serve with a warm baguette and a bowl of homemade garlicky mayonnaise (page 243) for dipping.

INGREDIENTS:

- ¾ cup extra virgin olive oil
- ¼ cup fresh lemon juice
- 2 cups water
- 1 teaspoon sugar
- 2 medium-size to large artichokes, tough outer leaves pulled off, stems trimmed, and thorny tops cut off
- 12 whole cloves fresh garlic, peeled
- 1½ teaspoons chopped fresh dill
- 1 teaspoon kosher or fine sea salt

1. Combine the oil, lemon juice, water, and sugar in a pot large enough to hold the artichoke halves in one packed layer.

2. Cut the artichokes in half lengthwise. With a grapefruit spoon or paring knife, remove the thorny centers. Place the artichokes in the pot and turn to coat all around with the liquid. Turn so the cut side is above the water and place 3 garlic cloves in each half. Sprinkle dill and salt over the tops and bring to a boil over high heat. Reduce the heat to maintain a brisk simmer and cover the pot. Cook until the outer leaves of the artichokes are tender and the garlic is soft but still holding its shape, 20 to 25 minutes, depending on the size of the artichokes.

3. With a slotted spoon, transfer the artichoke nests with their eggs to a platter. Increase the heat to high and reduce the liquid until thickened, about 5 minutes. Spoon over the artichokes and serve warm, at room temperature, or chilled.

ASPARAGUS WITH POACHED EGGS

SERVES 4

INGREDIENTS:

1½ pounds large asparagus

2 large eggs

Good-quality extra virgin olive oil

Condiment salt (page 286), for serving

COOKS HAVE THOUGHT UP DOZENS OF WAYS to treat asparagus spears: beurre blanc sauce, brown butter, mayonnaise, tartar sauce, numerous versions of vinaigrette, extras such as shallot, chives, or capers, to name a few. For all sizes of spears, pencil thin to thick as a thumb, a simple preparation calls for the spears to be cooked quickly to preserve their emerald color. Poached egg is added to adorn the simplicity, along with a splash of extra-special olive oil and a finishing sprinkle of one of the newly available sea salts.

1. Bring a large pot of water to a boil. Trim the bottoms of the asparagus spears up to where the white meets the green. If the spears are quite thick, almost as wide as a thumb, peel them with a vegetable peeler. If they are smaller, leave them unpeeled. Slide the asparagus spears into the water and cook, uncovered, until tender but still crisp and bright green, 2 to 6 minutes, depending on the size of the spears. Drain and rinse under cool water to stop the cooking. Pat dry with cloth or paper towels and arrange the spears on a platter.

2. Pour water to a depth of 1½ inches into a medium-size sauté pan and bring to a soft simmer over medium-high heat. Gently crack the eggs into the water and poach, adjusting the heat as necessary so the water never boils. When the eggs are almost firm, spoon water over the top continuously until the whites are completely firm and the yolks are still runny, 3 to 4 minutes. With a slotted spoon, one by one lift the eggs out of the water, gently shake off excess water, set them on the asparagus, and break open the yolks.

3. Drizzle with olive oil, sprinkle salt across the top, and serve.

MULTI-HUED BEETS
IN WARM GREEN GODDESS DRESSING

NOTHING CAN MATCH BEETS for natural vegetable sweetness, and the sweetness becomes even more concentrated when they are roasted. Once roasted, they take to embellishments and dressings with open embrace, especially a dashing Green Goddess dressing, which ornaments them with aplomb.

1. Preheat the oven to 400°F.

2. Rinse the beets and place them, still wet, in a baking dish large enough to hold them in an uncrowded layer. Add the oil, turn to coat, and cover the dish. Place in the oven and cook until fork-tender, about 1 hour, plus a little more if the beets are large. Remove, let cool enough to handle, and, while still warm, slip off the skins. Set aside.

3. While the beets roast, make the dressing.

4. To serve, cut the beets lengthwise into halves if small or ½-inch-wide wedges if large. Drizzle the sauce across the top and serve warm.

WARM GREEN GODDESS DRESSING

IN 1923 in the kitchen of the Palace Hotel, one of the hotels that survived the great San Francisco earthquake and fire to live on, chef Philip Roemer decided to honor a hit play that had come to town and its cast members who were residing in the hotel and dining in his restaurant. The play was called *The Green Goddess,* and he created a salad dressing with the same name. His original was a cold mayonnaise dressing replete with licoricey tarragon and chervil and made tangy with sour cream. However, for a dinner side dish, especially on roasted beets, a creamy, warm rendition blankets the vegetables with a more snug pleasure. The dressing well adorns fish, shellfish, or many another vegetable, particularly asparagus.

MAKES ¾ CUP

¼ cup heavy whipping cream

½ teaspoon dry mustard

1 small clove garlic, minced or pressed

½ cup mayonnaise

¼ cup chopped fresh flat-leaf parsley

2 tablespoons finely chopped scallion, light green parts only

1 tablespoon white wine vinegar

½ teaspoon chopped fresh tarragon

1 anchovy fillet, minced, or ¼ teaspoon Worcestershire sauce

Whisk together the cream, mustard, and garlic in a small saucepan and bring to a boil over medium heat. Add the mayonnaise, parsley, scallion, vinegar, tarragon, and anchovy and continue whisking until the mixture is just coming to a boil again. Use right away or set aside and reheat on the stove or in a microwave just before serving. (This does not store well.)

LA FAMILLE: VITTLES AND JAZZ

IN 1958, BENJAMIN JAMES AND WILLETTE GAINE MURRAY (the sister of Benjamin's wife, Viola), both from South Carolina, opened one of the most famous southern cuisine restaurants serving the foods of African ancestry. They were helped by Viola, and Willette's husband, Oswald Craine. The restaurant was called La Famille and was located in New York at 2017 Fifth Avenue near 125th Street in Harlem. Among the dishes offered were corn bread, fried chicken, black-eyed peas, and string beans. The bustling café quickly became a jazz club as well and attracted an international crowd. It spread to three dining rooms, and more than three hundred people would gather on Sunday nights when the jazz bands performed.

Both owners had come from southern poverty. When she moved north, Willette Murray had to march on picket lines in the 1930s to win her first job on 125th Street, washing glasses at a dime-store lunch counter. She later worked as a dining room host and assistant banquet manager at Harlem's renowned Hotel Theresa, which sits at the intersection of Adam Clayton Powell Jr. Boulevard and Martin Luther King Jr. Boulevard. The hotel was a vibrant center of African American life in the mid-twentieth century. Other hotels had long refused black guests, and so black businessmen, performers, and athletes all gathered at the Theresa. Guests included Josephine Baker, Louis Armstrong, Dorothy Dandridge, Duke Ellington, Lena Horne, Muhammad Ali, Dinah Washington, Ray Charles, Little Richard, and Jimi Hendrix. When he was turned away from other hotels for the opening of the United Nations in 1960, Fidel Castro booked a room there.

Willette and her family took advantage of the confluence and began to serve the foods they all loved. The hotel closed in 1967, though it has been declared a landmark by the city of New York. The restaurant was sold in 1989 and continued to serve up jazz with the foods of African origin. But it eventually fell victim to the disappearance of old Harlem. Willette died in 1995 and sadly La Famille had closed by then.

BROCCOLI WITH FENNEL, CREAM, AND GREEN PEPPERCORNS

THOMAS JEFFERSON BROUGHT BROCCOLI TO AMERICA from Europe, where it had grown wild before being widely cultivated, and planted it at Monticello. In 1775, John Randolph, a fellow Virginian, described it saying "the stems will eat like asparagus and the heads like cauliflower." Along with familiar carrots and peas, it has became one of the most desired vegetables in America. Here it is served creamed with two unexpected cohorts, fennel bulb and green peppercorns, giving the broccoli a little contrasting snap.

1. Place the broccoli florets in a large sauté pan and add enough water to barely cover. Bring to a boil over high heat, drain immediately, and return the florets to the pan.

2. Add the cream, fennel, garlic, and salt and bring to a boil over medium-high heat. Cook briskly, stirring once or twice, until the cream is bubbling up and almost gone, about 5 minutes. Stir in the lemon juice and peppercorns and serve.

SERVES 4

INGREDIENTS:

4 cups broccoli florets

1 cup heavy whipping cream

⅓ cup coarsely chopped fennel bulb

1 small clove garlic, minced

½ teaspoon kosher or fine sea salt

1 tablespoon fresh lemon juice

1 teaspoon green peppercorns, cracked with a mallet

FENNEL IN ALL ITS SPLENDOR

FENNEL IN ALL ITS PARTS serves the household. In the garden, it attracts the anise swallowtail butterfly as a place to deposit her eggs. Its stately, tall stems topped with brilliant yellow flowers attract the eye of the flower arranger.

It also delights the cook. The bulbs are used fresh, thinly sliced, and doused in lemon or cooked and often dressed with a cream sauce. The fronds make a fragrant bed for fish or, chopped, an intriguing change from parsley as a garnish. The flowers, left to dry, provide a most exotic and fragrant spice: fennel pollen. Once gone to seed, fennel becomes a spice used in many cuisines, especially Italian, where it provides the "sweet" in sweet Italian sausage. With such capabilities, it's not surprising that slices of the bulb infused in cream can enhance an everyday vegetable like broccoli and pull out its charms.

OLIVE OIL TERMINOLOGY AND USES

OLIVE OIL IS PRODUCED IN NUMEROUS COUNTRIES, among them Greece, Italy, Spain, Turkey, Morocco, South Africa, Australia, and the United States.

In the wide world of olive oils, the sensory delights vary in almost countless ways. Each oil has a set of particular sensations: a first nose, then a bouquet as it opens; a first taste, then plural tastes as it makes itself known to different spots on the tongue. As with wines, these nuances are determined by the oil's terroir, that is, place of origin, including the soil, climate, and geography of the region and the way the olives and their processing is handled, artfully or indifferently, by the people who turn the harvest into oleaginous liquid for consumption.

The method of production is of prime importance, and the oil's label must state how the oil was extracted, as well as the acidity of the outcome and whether it was filtered. (If the oil has not been filtered, it may be cloudy; some prefer it that way.) These have become international rules established by the International Olive Oil Council (IOOC), of which the United States is not yet a member. The United States has its own classifications, based on such terms as Grade A Fancy and Grade B Choice, with different acidity allowances from the international system. California is urging the United States to join and conform to with the international standards.

Following is a list of the different grades, from the highest quality (those generally used as a dressing, finish, or dip for bread) to those of slightly diminished caliber but still excellently flavorful (more generally used as a cooking medium or ingredient) and finally to those altered to extract strong flavor and to those used for lamps, soap, and fuel.

EXTRA VIRGIN OLIVE OIL: All olive oils labeled this way have been expressed under heavy pressure without heat or water, often from pristine, unbruised olives, meaning just on the edge of being ripe and within thirty-six hours after picking. Other times the oil is made from olives that have just reached their ripeness and either have dropped or can be shaken from the tree. There are two methods of first pressing for extra virgin and virgin oils: the traditional way in which the olives are made into a paste using stone presses and a modern way in which metal centrifuges are used. The stone-ground method has a slight flavor advantage over modern centrifuging in that the stones impart no heat to the paste; centrifuging produces some heat. The term *cold pressed* is without meaning and is only a marketing tactic now. It comes from the fact that hot water was sometimes used in the first pressing to extract more oil, resulting in a slightly inferior product.

Each extra virgin olive oil has a distinctive "personality" of first and secondary flavors derived from its origins that range from a little bitter to a little peppery. Terms for some of the flavor nuances are *grassy, alfalfa, artichoke, fruity,* and *loamy.* To receive the classification of extra virgin in IOOC standards, the oil must have less than 0.8 percent acidity.

VIRGIN OLIVE OIL: This is olive oil that has been pressed in the same way as extra virgin oil, but the oil comes from riper olives, olives stored longer, or less superior olives, or else mechanical centrifuges have involved more heat than desired for extra virgin. As a result, the oil has a higher acidity level, albeit still quite low, between 1 and 2 percent. The result is essentially low-grade extra virgin oil and an oil with a somewhat less distinct personality than extra virgin oils that also turn rancid more quickly. It offers a less expensive alternative for general table and kitchen use.

PURE OLIVE OIL: The result of a second round of pressing or chemical processing of the mash left over from the first pressing, pure olive oil is lighter in color and blander in taste than extra virgin or virgin olive oil. Its acidity level is between 2 and 3 percent. It is useful as a general all-purpose olive oil. *Pure* refers to the fact that no nonolive oil is added. Some have been treated chemically to lower the smoke point, making them a good medium for frying. Some have been blended with virgin or extra virgin oil for flavor.

REFINED OLIVE OIL: These oils are made by chemically treating pure olive oil to remove any strong taste. The acidity level is higher than 3.3 percent. The flavor and odor can often be less than pleasing. Again, the smoke point is increased to allow for higher-heat frying.

LIGHT OR EXTRA LIGHT OLIVE OIL: This olive oil is made from a mixture of refined oil and the low-quality, chemically processed pure oils. It has exactly the same number of calories as other olives oils while being essentially devoid of flavor.

OLIVE POMACE OIL: Here the oil is collected from the olive mash left after all the other pressings and is often then treated with solvents such as for refined oils, but more so. It must be designated *pomace* to distinguish it. To be sold, it is usually blended with a bit of virgin oil to provide a taste element to an otherwise not-so-tasty oil. Most olive oil aficionados categorically state that pomace oil is not worth culinary use and may not even be healthy to consume. However, it has long enjoyed a nonculinary use as a cosmetic application. Armenian, Greek, and Turkish women of old would rub some into the scalp to achieve a smooth scalp and shiny hair.

BLENDED OILS: There are many blended oils on the market. They contain various amounts of extra virgin, virgin, pure, and olive oil. By IOOC rules, the quality of the oil, amounts, and region of origin should be specified. However, considerable corruption exists in the olive oil exportation market, and buyers should exercise caution.

LAMPANTE: These oils are not suitable as food. They are directed toward olive oil's long-standing use in oil-burning lamps and are mostly used in the industrial market.

THE IDEAL ENVIRONMENT for storing olive oil is 57°F and in a dark area, so not near the stove. It should also be tightly closed and stored in the original container, or in carafes made of tinted glass or porcelain, not clear glass. Never store olive oil in plastic or reactive metal as it can absorb particulates from those materials. Olive oil can can be refrigerated and in low temperatures will turn cloudy, but will clarify again when warmed.

BRUSSELS SPROUTS
WITH PANCETTA AND TANGERINE

INGREDIENTS:

12 ounces Brussels sprouts, bottoms trimmed off, tough outer leaves removed, sliced into ¼-inch-thick rounds

2 tablespoons butter

3 ounces thinly sliced pancetta, coarsely chopped

2 tablespoons fresh tangerine juice

¼ cup chopped tangerine peel

BRUSSELS SPROUTS ARE SO DARLING, their tight ball form so intriguing, who can resist them? Here is a recipe that takes advantage of their nutritional goodness while taming their hard-to-fork round shape. Combined with a citrus companion, tangerine, and seasoned with pancetta, they make a fine accompaniment to salmon, pork roast or chops, and winter holiday turkey or goose.

1. Bring a large pot of water to a boil over high heat. Add the Brussels sprouts and blanch for 1½ minutes. The water will not return to a boil. Drain in a colander, rinse under cool water to stop the cooking, and set aside in the colander.

2. Heat a large, heavy sauté pan over medium-high heat. Add the butter and pancetta and cook until the pancetta is slightly crisp, about 5 minutes. Add the Brussels sprouts, tangerine juice, and chopped tangerine peel and sauté until the Brussels sprouts are barely wilted, about 2 minutes. Serve right away.

WHAT IS A TANGERINE?

THE FIRST TANGERINES ARRIVED IN EUROPE in 1841 from Tangier, Morocco. At first they were called *tangerine oranges* and later just *tangerines.* Curious vegetables, fruits, and other items arriving in northern Europe at this time were often being called by what was thought to be their country of origin. The little citrus delicacy now streaming in from Tangier became the tangerine.

Tangerines bear a loose skin, making them easy to peel and devour, thus a fine fast treat. The fruit also divides easily into discrete segments, rendering them agreeably sharable. At the same time, their vibrant citrus flavor, their juiciness, and their unique tang distinguishes them as a little more brazen than oranges and a rather right mix with vegetables. For this reason, they are popular in salads and make for a provocative counterpoint to a pungent brassica like Brussels sprouts.

Although they started out the same, after much cultivation tangerines are now actually quite different from mandarin oranges. Clementines are yet another close cousin. Their peak season is from November to March, which is why, in the days when good children received a sweet and bad ones a lump of coal, the treat good children found in Christmas stockings was often a brilliant red-orange delectable tangerine.

CARAMELIZED CARROT COINS
AND WALNUTS IN MAPLE SYRUP

CARROTS BELONG TO THE PARSLEY FAMILY and are cousins of celery, parsnips, fennel, dill, and coriander. They arrived in America on ships before the *Mayflower* and prospered in fields and gardens. A glaze of America's tawny maple syrup bronzes and caramelizes them while walnuts add rich nuggets of munch.

1. Place the carrots in a medium-size pan, add water to cover by 1 inch, and bring to a boil over medium-high heat. Cook until easy to pierce with a fork, about 7 minutes, then drain.

2. Melt the butter in a medium-size skillet over medium heat. Add the carrots, walnuts, maple syrup, and salt. Bring to a boil and simmer briskly, stirring frequently, until the syrup is almost completely reduced and turning brown on the bottom of the pan, about 10 minutes. Serve.

INGREDIENTS:

7 medium-size carrots, cut into ¼-inch-thick rounds (4 cups)

1 tablespoon butter

⅔ cup walnut halves or large pieces

⅓ cup maple syrup

⅛ teaspoon kosher or fine sea salt

SAUTEED CAULIFLOWER
WITH CELERY AND CARAWAY

INGREDIENTS:

6 tablespoons (¾ stick) butter

2 small or 1 large cauliflower, cored and cut into 1-inch florets (about 4 cups)

3 ribs celery, sliced crosswise ¼ inch thick (about 1 cup)

½ cup white wine

½ cup water

1 teaspoon caraway seeds

1½ teaspoons kosher or fine sea salt

1 teaspoon freshly ground white pepper

1 tablespoon finely chopped celery leaves

HOW TO PICK A CAULIFLOWER? The buds of the florets should be fine, compact, and regular, looking like tiny beads. The green leaves around the stem should not be limp. The head should be heavy for its size; it is not a lightweight sort of vegetable. Cauliflower is best fresh but will keep for up to one week or so in the refrigerator. It is a vegetable that simply cries out for butter, lots of it, browned and foamy. Add to that white wine, celery, both rib and leaf, and aromatic caraway, and you have a dish for a president.

1. Melt the butter in a medium-size sauté pan over medium-high heat until foaming gently. Add the cauliflower and celery and stir until well coated with butter and lightly browned all around, about 5 minutes.

2. Stir in the wine, water, caraway, salt, and pepper. Cover the pan and simmer over medium heat until the cauliflower is soft throughout and all the liquid is absorbed, about 15 minutes. Sprinkle with the celery leaves and serve right away, while warm.

BRAISED CELERY À LA VICTOR

CELERY, though long enjoying some status as a side vegetable in continental cuisine, doesn't hold a strong place in the panoply of American vegetable sides. Or it didn't until one day in the early 1900s Victor Hirtzler, chef de cuisine of San Francisco's renowned Hotel St. Francis, did everyone's table a great favor with his braised celery under a tarragon-accented vinaigrette. Here the vinaigrette is swapped for a topping of lemon juice without the oil, letting the broth and butter serve that purpose, and a caper garnish is added for glamour.

SERVES 4

INGREDIENTS:

2 bunches celery

1 cup low-sodium chicken broth or water

2 tablespoons butter

1 tablespoon fresh lemon juice

2 teaspoons capers, preferably salt-packed, rinsed

1 teaspoon chopped fresh tarragon or ½ teaspoon dried

1 tablespoon chopped fresh flat-leaf parsley

Kosher or fine sea salt

1. Trim the tops off the celery and remove the tough outer ribs, leaving the rest of the ribs connected in their bunches. Cut the bunches lengthwise into 4 sections and rinse them. Place in a sauté pan large enough to hold the quarters lying down. Add the broth and butter and bring to a boil over medium-high heat. Reduce the heat to maintain a brisk simmer, cover, and cook until fork-tender, about 15 minutes.

2. With a slotted spoon, transfer the celery to a platter. Combine the lemon juice, capers, tarragon, and parsley in a small bowl. Whisk in 1 tablespoon of the cooking liquid, along with salt to taste. Pour over the celery and serve warm, at room temperature, or chilled.

EGGPLANT AND WHOLE SHALLOTS
STEWED IN RED WINE

INGREDIENTS:

2 medium-size eggplants

1 cup extra virgin olive oil

12 medium-size shallots, peeled

6 to 8 cloves garlic, slivered

4 medium-size tomatoes, coarsely chopped

¾ cup red wine

1 bay leaf

1 teaspoon kosher or fine sea salt

½ teaspoon freshly ground black pepper

¼ cup shredded fresh basil leaves

6 whole fresh basil leaves, for garnish

DESPITE THE RESTRAINED USE OF EGGPLANT in classic American cooking, it is one of the most important food crops in the world. Although it has a number of names in different parts of the world, the name *eggplant* developed in the English-speaking world because the cultivars that first arrived in Europe were yellow or white and resembled goose eggs. Today the most common eggplants are quite large and ovoid with a dark purple skin; those of the Asian variety are long and narrow, colored white to yellow to green, to reddish, bright pink, black, and even striped. Eggplant entered American culinary parlance by its popularity in multiple cuisines, namely Japanese, Spanish, French, Italian, Greek, Thai, Indian. An eggplant recipe first appeared in a Spanish cookbook in 1520. Taking direction from there, wine-simmered eggplant softens to a fleecelike texture in this deeply flavored vegetable side.

1. Trim off the ends of the eggplants and discard them. Cut the eggplants into ½-inch cubes.

2. Heat the oil in a large, heavy sauté pan over medium heat. Add the eggplant cubes, shallots, and garlic and sauté, stirring frequently, until the eggplant wilts, 10 to 12 minutes.

3. Stir in the tomatoes, wine, bay leaf, salt, and pepper. Simmer uncovered without stirring again until the oil rises to the top and the eggplant is very soft and beginning to stick to the bottom of the pan, 45 to 50 minutes.

4. Remove the pan from the heat and set aside to cool for 10 to 15 minutes. Stir in the shredded basil and serve warm or at room temperature. Garnish with the whole basil leaves just before serving.

SWEET AND SOUR LEEKS
WITH LEMON AND HONEY

WHILE THE "SWEET AND SOUR" DESCRIPTION might at first conjure a Chinese combination of ingredients and flavors, the sweet and sour leeks here lean more to a European style of interweaving those two flavors. The dish, which includes a surprise boost from a bouquet of fresh herbs, exploits the range of tastes and colors the onion family provides: softly oniony in white to light green shreds from the leeks; slightly sharp and crunchy white to purple specks with the shallot; aromatic, full-up green with the specks of chive. It's a condiment-like side preparation that will add personality to simply prepared pork, chicken, and fish.

1. Combine the shallot, garlic, mustard, honey, chile flakes, vinegar, 2 tablespoons lemon juice, and olive oil in a food processor and process just until blended. Stir in the parsley, chives, chopped thyme, tarragon, and salt. Use right away or set aside at room temperature for up to 4 hours.

2. To prepare the leeks, halve them lengthwise, cut them crosswise into 3- to 4-inch lengths, and cut each length into ¼-inch-wide shreds. (There should be about 4 cups.) Submerge the shreds in plenty of water, changing it 2 or 3 times if necessary, to wash away all of the grit, then lift out the shreds and transfer them to a colander to drain. Set aside.

3. Pour water to a depth of 3 inches into a large pot. Add the juice of ½ lemon and the thyme sprigs and bring to a boil over medium-high heat. Add as many leeks as will fit and still stay submerged and cook until barely wilted and still bright, 2 to 3 minutes. With a wire strainer, transfer to a colander and continue with another batch if necessary. Pat the wilted leeks dry and transfer them to a serving bowl.

4. Add the sweet-sour sauce mixture to the leeks and turn gently to mix. Serve warm, at room temperature, or chilled.

SERVES 4 TO 6

INGREDIENTS:

1 small shallot, coarsely chopped

½ small clove garlic, coarsely chopped

½ teaspoon Dijon mustard

½ tablespoon honey

⅛ teaspoon red chile flakes

2 tablespoons white wine vinegar

2 tablespoons fresh lemon juice

¼ cup extra virgin olive oil

2 teaspoons chopped fresh parsley

2 teaspoons chopped fresh chives

½ teaspoon chopped fresh thyme

½ teaspoon chopped fresh tarragon or a small pinch of dried

¼ teaspoon kosher or fine sea salt

2 large or 4 medium-size leeks, white and light green parts only

Juice of ½ lemon

2 fresh thyme sprigs

PORTOBELLO MUSHROOMS WITH PUNCHY CELERY CHOP

SERVES 4

INGREDIENTS:

4 very large or 8 small portobello mushrooms (about 1 pound), stems snapped off, caps wiped

Extra virgin olive oil, for brushing the mushroom caps

Kosher or fine sea salt

2 tablespoons butter

1 cup coarse bread crumbs, preferably homemade (page 41)

½ cup chopped fresh flat-leaf parsley

1 tablespoon chopped celery leaves from the inner, tender ribs

1 large clove garlic, minced or pressed

1 teaspoon cracked green peppercorns

PORTOBELLO MUSHROOMS HAVE BECOME SUCH A FAVORITE of chefs and home cooks alike that the mushroom offerings in farmers' markets and supermarkets now routinely include them and recipes are not shy in calling for them. Portobellos are in actuality mature cremini, or brown, mushrooms. They range in size from about 2 inches to a hefty 4 to 5 inches in diameter. The large, dense, meaty ones, something like mushroom giants, can serve as a starter plate. Sautéed and embellished with bread crumbs, they make a bold side dish for any entrée or pasta dish.

1. Preheat the broiler or preheat the oven to 500°F.

2. Brush the mushroom caps with a light film of oil and lightly sprinkle them with salt. Place the caps, top side down, under the broiler and cook until sweating, 3 or 4 minutes. Turn over the caps so they are top side up and continue broiling until soft but still holding their shape, 3 to 5 minutes more.

3. While the mushrooms broil, melt the butter in a sauté pan over medium-high heat. Add the bread crumbs, stir to mix, and sauté until the crumbs are golden but still soft, 2 to 3 minutes. Add the parsley, celery leaves, garlic, and cracked peppercorns. Stir to mix, season with salt, and remove from the heat.

4. Transfer the mushrooms to a platter, underside up. Heap the bread crumb mixture into the centers and serve.

CELERY CITY

SOME TIME AROUND 1600, the Potawatomi Indians moved from the East Coast over to what is now southern Michigan. They called the river where they settled Ki, and the spot where the river churned Kikalamezo, meaning "boiling" water because it gurgled with hundreds of bubbling springs. The Potawatomi ceded the land to the United States and moved away in 1827. By 1833 a population of new settlers moving west had formed a town. They established a college and, making the Potawatomi word more English, called the place Kalamazoo.

The land was fertile, the location desirable, and in the next five years Kalamazoo saw more land sales than anywhere else at any time in American history. The town was thriving, and in 1856 it attracted a Scotsman named George Taylor, who began experimenting with celery seed he had brought from England. At first some of his neighbors refused to eat his crop, calling it poisonous, but he convinced the Burdick House, the most fashionable hotel and food establishment in town, to put the vegetable, which he would provide free of charge, on the menu. Celery caught on.

Soon celery fields covered the entire north side of town and beyond. By 1871 the amount of celery shipped from Kalamazoo by rail was second only to shipments from Detroit. By 1910, more than six pages of the *Kalamazoo City Directory* were devoted to celery growers. Celery packers sprang up. Other states started sending celery to Kalamazoo for packaging, and every corner in town boasted people peddling bunches of celery. It was being grown and shipped year-round. Travelers passing through town by rail and automobile were overrun by celery hawkers. As late as 1939, more than a thousand mucky acres—celery from wild to tame likes a wet, boggy milieu—were planted with celery, and Kalamazoo took on another name, "Celery City." Pascal celery, the most common variety grown and used in the U.S., is sometimes called *Kalamazoo celery*.

In its salad days, Kalamazoo's baseball team was named "The Celery Pickers." The dance team was "The Celery Cloggers." Patent medicines were compounded from celery. It was touted to be "ever soothing" and an aphrodisiac. Recipes were developed for celery soup, braised celery, steamed celery. It became known for one of its primary uses, along with onions and carrots, as a base flavoring for sauces. The vegetable was also lauded for what would now be called its ecological value. It grows in what is otherwise considered wasteland, bogs, banks, and drainage fields. By 2000 most of the celery growing had died out. Only one farm remained. The beds had given way to flower growing. Still, the old celery flats were declared a historic area and the name Celery City lingers on.

MAPLE-GLAZED LITTLE ONIONS

INGREDIENTS:

16 little boiling onions, peeled

2 tablespoons maple syrup, preferably grade B (facing page)

2 teaspoons apple cider vinegar

1 tablespoon butter, melted

THE USES OF AMERICA'S OWN NATIVE SWEETENER ARE LEGION. We mostly know it as a syrup that we pour on pancakes and waffles, drizzle on ice cream, add to sweet potatoes, baked apples, and pies to infuse them with maple syrup's unique and sweet sapidity. It makes a sugary crust on ham, gives a zing to salad dressing, and imparts a brilliant glaze to vegetables. But the syrup has other culinary uses, too, some quite savory; for example, as a contrast to the bite of little onions. Little boiling onions, larger than pearl onions and so much easier to peel, are still small enough to serve whole without slicing or chopping. With a touch of cider vinegar, butter, and maple syrup, the dish is a northwoods triumph.

1. Preheat the oven to 375°F.

2. Place the onions in a baking dish large enough to hold them in one layer. Pour the maple syrup, cider vinegar, and butter over them and turn to coat all around. Cover the dish and bake, shaking the dish 2 or 3 times to rotate the onions, until glazed and easily pierced with a fork, about 25 minutes. Serve warm or at room temperature.

MAPLE SYRUP:
AMERICA'S OWN SUGAR

NO ONE KNOWS EXACTLY WHEN or how the sweetness of maple sap was chanced upon, but long before Europeans landed on the coasts, the Algonquin and other people of the Northeast became aware of the glorious fluid.

Native to North America, the rock maple—also known as the *hard maple* and *sugar maple*—stands in large and grand old forests. To produce sugar, the trunk must be at least 12 inches in diameter, and it takes 30 years for it to grow to that size. The Native Americans gashed the bark of the maple in a V shape and caught the dripping sap in hollowed-out logs, birch bark bowls, or clay vessels. They dropped hot rocks into the sap to boil off the water content and later cooked the now dark, rich fluid to concentration over a campfire. Often they reduced the sap to a crystal stage, like brown sugar, making it easier to carry with them in deerskin pouches.

The first white man to make maple sugar was reportedly a French missionary in 1690, who, along with other settlers, had been taught how by the northern tribes. Soon many Europeans came to tap the sweet. They bored holes in the trees with augers, spiked in wooden or metal spouts, and hung wooden buckets from the spouts, which, once filled, they slung on shoulder yokes to carry to fires where the syrup was boiled in iron kettles. At first they reduced the sap to crystals. With white sugar scarce and expensive, maple sugar was the only source of sugar to sprinkle on food for many pioneers for many decades.

By the twentieth century, sap collectors began using plastic tubing to act as faucets to collect the sap. Large networks of tubes could be arranged to gather the sap from many trees and guide it to storage tanks without intermediary contraptions. Nowadays vacuum pumps draw the sap and state-of-the-art stainless steel boiling systems evaporate the water and concentrate the sugar. As of old, sapping is done in the spring season and those collecting it stay in sugar camps throughout the process.

Today, across the Northeast to Minnesota and through much of eastern Canada, maple syrup is considered a pantry staple to use on much more than pancakes. In those places, the late-season, darker brown, denser, more intensely flavored grade B maple syrup is preferred over early-season, lighter-colored, milder-tasting grade A, especially for marinades, and glazing everything from bacon to little onions. A specialty of the region is a traditional "natural" snow cone, called *sugar on snow.* In spring, when the late-season maple sap is being boiled down to turn it to syrup and snow still lies on the ground, ladles of the boiling syrup are poured over bowls of fresh snow. The syrup immediately becomes as hard as a crackly caramel, a perfect candy topping for the icy snow underneath. In some places, the same treat is made with shaved ice.

There's nothing quite like American maple syrup. The flavor of it defies description. Yet, while all have the distinctive "maple" taste, the syrups from different areas, like wine, emit hints of soil and climate from their regions. Nothing is added to the syrup; it is simply and only maple syrup.

FRENCH-FRIED
ONION RINGS

SERVES 4 TO 6

INGREDIENTS:

2 large yellow, white or
   sweet onions, sliced into
   ¼-inch-thick rings,
   rings separated

1 cup milk

1 cup all-purpose flour

Peanut or canola oil, for
   deep-frying

Kosher or fine sea salt

LITTLE IS KNOWN ABOUT HOW THE FRITTER MET THE ONION and came out French. A fritter is a piece of fruit, meat, fish, or vegetable that is coated in batter or dusted with flour and deep-fried. It can also be a fried dollop of plain dough. Somewhere along the line, and probably in many places over time, onions found themselves fritterized.

The first recipe for battered onion rings in America appeared in a Crisco ad in 1933 in the *New York Times Magazine.* It called for the onion to be sliced and the slices punched free into ever-diminishing circles. Meanwhile, the term *French* became the popular descriptive for deep-frying, whether the object of the hot oil treatment was battered or not. Along this meandering path, the onion ring became a fritter and then became "French" fried. The tasty savory quickly soared to an all-American favorite, a heap of them appearing with hamburgers, steaks, chops, and sandwiches. The rings can be wide or thin, twice fried or once, beer or water or soda battered, but one thing about them is for sure: A sprinkling of salt overall, postfrying, is an absolute requisite of their lure.

1. Place the onion rings in a large bowl, pour the milk over them, and toss to coat. Set aside. Spread the flour on a large plate. Set aside.

2. Pour oil to a depth of 1½ inches into a large, deep pot and heat over medium-high heat until a sprinkle of water dropped in instantly sizzles. A few at a time, lift out of the milk as many onion rings as will fit in the pot without crowding. Shake them to get rid of any excess milk and put them on the plate with the flour. Turn to coat the onion rings thoroughly and gently place them in the oil. Fry, using tongs to separate and turn the rings, until golden and crispy, 2 to 3 minutes altogether. Transfer to paper towels to drain and sprinkle with salt. Continue with another round until all the rings are fried. Serve right away.

SWEET AMERICAN ONIONS

ALTHOUGH ALL MANNER OF ONIONS ARE A STAPLE OF THE AMERICAN LARDER, in relatively recent times we have reveled in modern varieties of sweet onions. Most likely sweet onions began as a packet of tart Bermuda onion seeds brought to Texas in 1898 and planted near the town of Cotulla. By 1907, more than a thousand trainloads of onions had been shipped from Texas to other parts of America, a number that doubled in the following year. Thousands have been shipped ever since. Onions are still one of the main vegetables grown in Texas.

Onion growers, however, were looking for new varieties, more disease resistant and also better adapted to the south Texas climate. Texas A&M University and the U.S. Department of Agriculture worked together to begin an onion-propagating program in 1933. They examined the onion's chemical compounds and from that developed the first fully sweet American onion, the Texas Grano. By 1940, it was noted that the Texas Grano changed again, ripening ten days earlier than usual and with larger bulbs than the grandparent, the Bermuda onion. It was named 502 for the field in which it was first produced.

By 1952, the 502 had parented the Excel onion and then the hybrid called the Granex. In the same year, to outmaneuver the wily weeds of Texas, some Granex onions were transplanted to Toombs County, Georgia, near a town named Vidalia, where earlier Bermuda onions had already been introduced. The farmer who planted them, Moses Coleman, discovered the new onions were sweet. Lacking enough seed, he had to struggle to increase his crop. Yet all the while he managed to sell the crop for more money than other onion growers were able to sell their harvest of regular onions. Soon neighboring onion farmers followed his lead.

These Georgia onions became known as Vidalia onions and have become America's most popular sweet onion. Now there are about 225 Georgia growers, cultivating around fourteen thousand acres of Vidalia onions. Only those farmers living in thirteen particular Georgia counties, where the soil and climate are most conducive to the vegetable's sweetness, are allowed to grow the onion. Vidalia onions are harvested from late April to mid-June and are available until December.

But Vidalias are by no means the only sweet onion now produced in America. In addition, there are:

WALLA WALLA ONIONS, named for the Washington city, are not an offspring of the Texas strains. Their forefather was brought from the island of Corsica in the late 1880s. As with Georgia and its Vidalias, the area Walla Wallas can be grown in is strictly specified. They are available from June through August.

MAUI ONIONS, from the island of Maui in Hawaii, are grown in volcanic soil that contributes to their sweetness. They, like Vidalias, are a hybrid of Texas Grano and Granex onions. They are shaped like a flattened globe and are available from April to June.

SPRINGSWEETS AND 1015S. SpringSweets are the first sweet onion to reach the market, in late March. The 1015s are named for the recommended planting date, October 15th. The prime time for 1015s is April through June. They can be the size of softballs and are highly recommended for onion rings (facing page).

IMPERIAL SWEETS, grown in the Imperial Valley of California, are available from late April through early June.

NUMEX, developed by agriculturalists in New Mexico, are planted in the fall and come to market in mid-June.

CULINARY SALTS:
CRYSTALLINE TREASURES FOR THE KITCHEN AND TABLE

MOST CULINARY SALTS ARE PRODUCED FROM THE EVAPORATION OF SALTY WATERS, which leaves behind salt crystals. Salts can be found virtually everywhere on the globe. Their crystals are formed within environments that contain other minerals, so that what results are salt compounds, such as calcium salts, magnesium salts, and salts with various other chloride compounds, as well as clay particles and other particulates. Depending on the kind and amount of these minerals, the salt may have a bitterness, a murky color, or a pleasing hue.

How salt winds up on the table, more or less "pure," and in what size crystals depends on the processing between the source and the intended destination. Whatever the method, the mineral content and/or the crystal size and shape are altered during the process, which affects the color and texture. Here's a brief glossary of the wide range of culinary salts available today and their uses in the kitchen and on the table.

KITCHEN SALTS
These are the salts kept on the kitchen counter or by the stove to season dishes as they cook. Other than the highly processed and granulated salt that used to be all that was available, there are two other types:

KOSHER SALT is processed from either sea salt or mined salt to a granular stage and then pressed to form small, pyramid-shaped flaky crystals with a texture somewhere between granulated and fine sea salt. Because of their shape, the crystals adhere to raw meat yet dissolve slowly enough

so that the meat is cleansed as dictated by Jewish law by drawing out blood without desiccating it; thus it is "koshered." Kosher salt has become a salt of choice for chefs and home cooks who appreciate its clean taste and its ability to season without clouding sauces and brines.

FINE SEA SALT is achieved by evaporating seawater until its salt content is rendered to a crystalline stage. The crystals are then crushed to achieve small, uniform particles of a size between granulated and kosher salt. They dissolve somewhat rapidly, giving the impression of being quite salty at first taste.

Measure for measure, by volume, kosher salt, with its slightly larger crystals, will fill a teaspoon more quickly than fine sea salt. But the difference is not significant enough to make a point of it in recipes that call for a mere teaspoon or so.

CONDIMENT SALTS
When salt is set on the table as a condiment, there's a bit more drama surrounding it. Condiment salts show personality. Some are crunchier, some softer; some are drier, some moist; some seem quite "salty" and others mild. Some need grinding, while others are easily sprinkled over food. As a group, they have captured the hearts of cooks and diners who want to add a few grains as a finishing touch to the dish just before it's eaten. In general, condiment salts are used in larger crystals than are kitchen salts. As they differ somewhat in flavor, the option of which to use is the chef's choice.

VARIETAL SEA SALTS make up most of what are now called *Condiment Salts.* From Brittany to Portugal and Sicily, around the world to Japan, Australia, Hawaii, the coast of northern California, and the coast of Maine, to name but a few of many places, sea salts are harvested from offshore saline pools where ocean water has evaporated, either naturally or deliberately by human intervention, leaving salt crystals. There is a mind-boggling number of choices available, but three standouts are the incandescent white, soft-crystal ones from Maldon off the British coast; the peachy-coral-colored flaky crystals from the Murray River in New South Wales, Australia; and the deep-rose-colored ones from the Red Sea.

SEL GRIS, OR GRAY SALT, is so called for the way it is colored by particulates in the clay bottoms of the saline pools off the Brittany coast in the northwest of France. Another prized gray sea salt comes from the Emilia-Romagna region of Italy. Gray salt is the star of the kitchen-to-table scenario. It straddles the line between simple kitchen salt and jazzier condiment salt. It dissolves readily enough in soups, stews, braises, and other liquid mediums and also enhances as a finishing salt.

FLEUR DE SEL, perhaps the most prized of condiment salts, comes from the surface of salt evaporation ponds or shallow salt basins off the coast of Brittany in northwestern France, the exact same place as sel gris. But fleur de sel's journey to the table is more complicated and refined. *Fleur* is flower; *sel* is salt, and, interestingly, in the recent craze over condiment salts, it's the Breton name that has become commonly used to describe this special salt. There it "blooms," like the cream that rises to the surface of milk, atop sel gris. On calm warm days, the gray salt, hand-raked to the edge of the beds, forms multifaceted white crystals that are harvested before they sink and become gray again.

ROCK SALTS

are mined from underground salt deposits formed when the oceans receded millennia ago. For culinary purposes, most rock salts are finely granulated, and additives such as iodine and anticaking compounds are mixed in to make ordinary table salt. Coarse rock salt was highly prized for pickling or as a bed for high-heat baking, but these uses have fallen by the wayside. Recently, however, some rock salts have become regarded as a condiment, most notably the pretty pink bead-size crystals from the Himalayas and the glitzy Bolivian rock salt, which looks like a large pink quartz crystal.

While there is a certain academic appeal in taste-testing the differences among condiment salts, the bottom line is that salt is pretty much salt when it comes to NaCl, its chemical compound. The relevant variations are in the texture, size of crystals, and moisture content and eye appeal from color more than in taste.

MOSAIC OF BELL PEPPERS STUFFED WITH EGGPLANT, OLIVES, AND CAPERS

SERVES 4

INGREDIENTS:

¼ cup extra virgin olive oil

1 large eggplant, cut into ¼-inch dice

½ cup white wine

½ teaspoon kosher or fine sea salt

16 kalamata olives, pitted and chopped

2 tablespoons capers, preferably salt-packed, rinsed

2 tablespoons tomato paste

1 large clove garlic, minced or pressed

1 teaspoon chopped lemon zest

1 teaspoon chopped fresh oregano or ½ teaspoon dried

4 medium-size bell peppers, preferably a mix of colors

1 cup water

BELL PEPPERS BELONG TO A RAGTAG FAMILY OF VEGETABLES so diverse its assembled members look like a white elephant sale. On his first voyage to America, Columbus found the peppers, and although he hadn't found the Eastern spice islands he was seeking, he was gratified to have found something spicy enough to claim as a pepper. He took a ton of them back to Spain. There it was clear they fit in as a perfect companion to eggplant, olives, and capers, and the robust herbs of the Mediterranean climate. Soon they were joined by the tomato. The shape of bell peppers, like a box, allowed them not just to be added to the great vegetable mixes of the Mediterranean, but to hold them as well. And that is the presentation here. The flavors of all unite dynamically. From green peppers, expect a rather immature and grassy flavor added to the mix, from red peppers a sweet spicy one, and from yellow and purple a mild indulgence.

1. Heat the oil in a large skillet over medium-high heat. Add the eggplant, stir to coat with the oil, and reduce the heat to medium. Stir in the wine and salt and cook, stirring frequently, until the eggplant is well wilted and juicy, 10 minutes. Mix in the olives, capers, tomato paste, garlic, zest, and oregano and cook, stirring frequently, until the eggplant is very soft, 5 minutes. Remove from the heat and set aside to cool while preparing the peppers.

2. Slice the tops off the peppers to make ¼-inch-thick caps. Remove the cores and seeds and fill the peppers with the eggplant mixture. Arrange them upright in one tightly packed layer in a wide pot, top with the caps,

and pour the water around (not over) the peppers. Bring to a boil over high heat, reduce the heat to maintain a simmer, cover, and cook until the peppers are soft but not collapsing, 25 to 30 minutes. Serve warm, at room temperature, or chilled.

THE CUNNING CAPER FAMILY

CAPPARALES, THE ORDER of flowering plants to which edible capers belong, consists of four families, 111 genera, and thousands of species. In short, the caper family bush—most are shrubs, not trees—is enormous.

The name of the order derives from *kapparis*, first used to mean any tart bud. The bud of the caper that is sprinkled on salmon, over carpaccio, tossed into salads, and fried for a crunchy flavor explosion comes from the dominant branch of the order, which startlingly includes such flowers as stock, the crucifixion thorns, scurvy grass, the prolific nasturtium, the tufted rose of Jericho, marsh cress, cuckoo flowers, and sea kale. The best capers to buy are those that are packed in salt. These are available in bulk and in vacuum-sealed pouches in gourmet markets. You can store the salted capers for a year or more; once rinsed, you can cover them with fresh water and keep them for several months in the refrigerator. The more commonly found jarred capers are bottled in a vinegar brine and are more astringent than the salt-packed ones. You can enhance them by soaking them in several changes of fresh water to dilute the vinegar infusion.

A MOUND OF
MASHED POTATOES

SERVES 4 OR MORE

INGREDIENTS:

2 pounds russet or other mashing potatoes, peeled and cut into 1-inch chunks

3 to 4 cloves garlic, coarsely chopped

Kosher or fine sea salt, for salting the cooking water and seasoning the potatoes

4 tablespoons (½ stick) butter

¾ cup half-and-half

Freshly ground white pepper

MASHED POTATOES ARE ICONIC IN AMERICAN COOKING. Hardly a soul doesn't revere and welcome a bowlful of them set piping hot on the table. The mash might be smooth and fluffy or chunky with the potatoes barely pulverized—or any gradation in between. Each seems to satisfy. In today's markets you can select from Yukon golds, Kennebecs, German Butterballs, Yellow Finns; all make fine mashed potatoes. Still, russet potatoes reign for turning out the fluffiest, most lofty hummock. In a new American cuisine approach, garlic is cooked with the potatoes as they boil, giving them a prebutter jump on flavor. Half-and-half is then whisked in as they are mashed, turning them creamy and light. A few twists of freshly ground white pepper over the top just before serving completes the reach to a peak. They've been known to make babies clap with delight, grown men to get teary with joy, and all of us to dig in.

1. Place the potatoes and garlic in a large pot, add water to cover by 2 inches, and salt generously. Bring to a boil over high heat and cook briskly until the chunks easily separate into smaller pieces with a fork but are not collapsing, 12 minutes or so, depending on the type of potato. Drain in a colander, shake gently, and return to the pot. Add the butter and, without stirring, partially cover and set aside in a warm place to dry a bit, 5 to 6 minutes.

2. Return the pot to the burner over medium-low heat and coarsely mash the potatoes with a potato masher or sturdy wire whisk. Add half of the half-and-half and continue mashing until the potatoes are almost smooth. Add the remaining half-and-half and mash vigorously until as smooth and fluffy as you like. Season to taste with salt.

3. Coarsely grind some white pepper over the top and serve hot.

⊕ Cook potatoes in plenty of well-salted water and never crowd them in the pot.

⊕ Cook them briskly and quickly in roiling, not merely simmering, water.

⊕ Once cooked and drained, potatoes need some resting time back in their cooking pot, 5 to 6 minutes, with or without the butter dollop on top. This prevents them from being soggy when mashed.

⊕ A food processor is not a good tool for mashing potatoes. Instead, use a potato masher or sturdy wire whisk and some elbow grease and whisk with vigor. This method keeps the potatoes from becoming gluey, and it works whether you want your mashed potatoes chunky or ethereal. For very fine, smooth, and airy mashed potatoes, use an old-fashioned potato ricer, still available in hardware stores of yesteryear and up-to-date kitchenware stores. A food mill also works as does a handheld electric mixer.

ONE POTATO, TWO POTATO, THREE . . . THE POTATO PEELER

IT MAY BE HARD TO IMAGINE that the potato peeler was a matter of serious invention, but it was, and several types now exist. No one knows if the early Incas peeled any of the more than three hundred varieties of potatoes they ate, but European and American potato eaters found the peel and the little potato "eyes" unappealing and quickly developed ways to rid the tuber of its skin.

The first sort of home peeler invented looked much like a knife, with a blade extending from a wooden or plastic handle. The blade was thicker along the back edge than a knife's, the better to rest a thumb on for heft when scraping. This sort of peeler is called a *Yorkshire* or *Lancaster peeler,* announcing an English claim to the design, but in 1885 Vincent van Gogh (who was Dutch) painted a French village woman using such a peeler and then a group of people eating the potatoes, so quite likely other countries had such peelers.

The second sort of peeler looks like the safety razors men use to shave or the yoke that harnesses two oxen and is aptly called the *Y-peeler* or *yoke peeler.* It's also known as the *Rex peeler* and *speed peeler.* The gizmo is shaped like a Y with the metal peeling blade resting between the two arms of the Y. It is a quick peeler with a barrier bar to keep the peeler from digging too deeply into the potato flesh.

The third sort of peeler comes from Down Under. It was designed around 1947 by a company called Dalsonware in Melbourne, Australia. They call it the Dalson Classic Aussie Peeler. It consists of a longish handle, the lower part to grip, the upper part holding at top and bottom a partially swiveling blade. The same sort of peeler can be found in almost every American kitchen's utility drawer, most often with a metal handle, sometimes with a rubber grip.

The first commercial potato peeler was invented by the Hobart Company in 1928. Its introduction led to the development of the potato chip because huge amounts of potatoes could be peeled quickly, making it feasible to turn out crisp slices by the bagful. In large potato-processing factories, a recent innovation uses three laser beams to zap the skin off a potato in one second. It is not yet known what this device will lead to.

A HAYSTACK OF SHOESTRING FRIES

SERVES 4 TO 6

INGREDIENTS:

3 large russet or Kennebec potatoes

Peanut or canola oil, for deep-frying

Kosher or fine sea salt

FISH AND CHIPS, STEAK FRITES, a crunchy salad topping, a plateful for a snack—there's almost nowhere you can't take shoestring potatoes. These come out particularly crisp and delicious due to rinsing away much of the starch before frying. It's important to fry them in small batches and take care to adjust the heat between rounds so that the oil stays hot enough to sizzle the potatoes but not so hot as to boil up and over the pot.

1. Fill a large bowl with cold water.

2. Peel the potatoes and cut them into shoestrings ¼ inch wide using the julienne blade of a food processor or a chef's knife. Place them in the cold water as you go. Change the water 3 or 4 times until it runs clear.

3. Drain the potatoes in a large colander and shake as dry as possible. Spread on kitchen towels, making 2 or 3 layers as necessary so that the shoestrings are not crowded. Top the last layer with a clean kitchen towel, loosely roll up the layers like a jelly roll, and set aside for at least 30 minutes and up to 2 hours.

4. To cook the potatoes, line a baking sheet with paper towels. Pour oil to a depth of 2 inches into a large pot and heat over high heat until a shoestring dropped in sizzles and rises to the top right away.

5. Fry the potatoes one handful at a time until golden, about 5 minutes. With a wire strainer, remove the potatoes, shake gently to remove excess oil, and transfer to the paper-towel-lined baking sheet. Sprinkle lightly with salt and continue with another batch until all the potatoes are fried.

THE FRENCH FRY FRACAS, OR WHO PUT THE FRENCH IN THE FRY?

THERE ARE A NUMBER OF THEORIES about why we call fried potatoes french fries. Some of the theories agree with one another; others contradict. Here are a few:

The term *French-fried potatoes* dates from Thomas Jefferson's time when he noted that while living in France he had just supped on pommes de terre frites à cru, en petites tranches, or "potatoes, cut into thin strands and fried as is [meaning without previous cooking]." The dish was cooked by his French chef, Honoré Julien.

A Belgian explanation claims that the term *french fries* was coined by British and American soldiers arriving in Belgium during World War I, where they first sampled the fries. They thought them to be French because French was what the Belgians spoke. Yet the term french fry was in use in America far earlier than World War I. Still, the story makes for a nice patriotic reinforcement for the Belgians' claim that fried potatoes are their own. Despite the glory the fry gives them, the French also think the fried potatoes are of Belgian origin.

In contradiction, recipes for fried potatoes begin to appear in French cookbooks as early as the mid-1700s, soon after the potato docked in Marseilles, Calais, or Bretagne, and was finally determined to be not only edible but delectable. One of the first is Menon's *Les Soupers de la Cour.*

Professor Paul Ilegems, curator of the Friet museum in Antwerp, believes, however, that Saint Teresa of Ávila first fried the potatoes that French way.

The English call the potatoes *chips*. In England the term *french fry* is used primarily in American-style fast-food restaurants.

While we enjoy ketchup on our french fries, in the British Isles chips are served with salt and vinegar, gravy, mayonnaise, pepper sauce, curry sauce, and "mushy" peas (an Indian interpretation from when Britain ruled India).

In Quebec, there's a variation called *poutine,* namely fries with gravy and cheese.

In Vietnam, a former French colony, the fries are served with butter and sugar.

In America, they are ubiquitous as a side with burgers and steaks and, when served alone, considered a major comfort.

HERBED MUSCLE FRIES

INGREDIENTS:

2 to 2½ pounds potatoes, such as russet, Yukon gold, or other nonwaxy types, peeled or not and cut into ½-inch-thick wedges

⅓ cup extra virgin olive oil

⅓ cup water

1 teaspoon finely chopped fresh rosemary, thyme, or oregano

1 teaspoon kosher or fine sea salt

½ teaspoon freshly ground black pepper

¼ cup fresh lemon juice

IN AN UNUSUAL TWIST ON "FRIED" POTATOES, oil and water combined provide the cooking medium and the oven provides the heat for a thick, semicrisp, hardy potato wedge. Each wedge has more muscle to it than a thin fried potato yet has the soft center of a baked potato. The final fillip, a sprinkling of fresh lemon juice, contrary to what you might think, adds seasoning without diminishing the crispness. And with so little oil! To peel or not to peel the potatoes is a matter of personal choice, and if the potatoes are very small, such as tiny fingerlings, leave them whole with their skin on.

1. Preheat the oven to 425°F.

2. Spread the potatoes on a rimmed baking sheet large enough to hold them in one uncrowded layer. Add the oil, water, herb, salt, and pepper and toss to coat. Bake, turning twice, until the potatoes are lightly golden and beginning to crisp, about 45 minutes.

3. Add the lemon juice, turn to coat, and continue baking until the potatoes are golden and very crisp, 10 to 15 minutes more. Serve hot.

LUTHER BURBANK AND THE RUSSET BURBANK POTATO

THE RUSSET BURBANK POTATO IS A LARGE BROWN-SKINNED, WHITE-FLESHED POTATO that is by far the most common potato cooked in America and also the most widely grown from state to state. Americans do just about everything one can do with russets: bake them, mash them, fry them, scallop them.

Strange, considering the russet is a baby as potatoes go, only about 125 years old. It did not spring up self-spawned; rather it was developed by one of America's most famous horticulturists, Luther Burbank.

Luther Burbank was born in Lancaster, Massachusetts, in 1849, the thirteenth of eighteen children. He was raised on a farm and attended only elementary school. When he was twenty-one, his father died and he used the small inheritance he received to buy a seventeen-acre piece of a land near his family farm. With a natural instinct for botany, he began developing a bigger, better potato, and rather quickly he had produced a wonderfully large, firm, tasty tuber, of a color no potato was before: russet. Suppliers and other farmers wanted it. It was named the Burbank potato, and in 1875, a year after he developed it, Burbank sold both his farm and the rights to his potato.

California, everyone said, was a Garden of Eden, proliferating in fruit and vegetables. Burbank left the East Coast and with his sale money bought a four-acre plot in Santa Rosa, California. Before his death in 1926, he proceeded to originate eight hundred strains of plant varieties. His hybrids ranged from fruits and flowers to grains, grasses, and vegetables. They included the Santa Rosa plum, the Elberta and the freestone peach, the Flaming Gold nectarine, the Shasta daisy and fire poppy, ten kinds of cherries, ten kinds of strawberries, eleven quinces, four grapes, four pears, two figs, and one almond. Along with the potato he evolved twenty-six kinds of vegetables. All told, his accomplishments ring out like verses in "The Twelve Days of Christmas," times one hundred.

Scientists despaired of his process; Burbank was not one for keeping detailed notes. He wanted only results. In 1893 he published a descriptive catalog of some of his best varieties, titled *New Creations in Fruits and Flowers*. He also published an essay on child rearing called "The Training of the Human Plant." The advice in this case was thankfully abstract. Though Burbank married twice, he had no children of his own. He lived simply and shared a best-friend relationship with guru Paramahansa Yogananda. He wrote several more books on his methods and results, including an eight-volume set called *How Plants Are Trained to Work for Man* and a treatise called *Partner of Nature*.

HASSELBACK BAKED POTATOES

SERVES 4

INGREDIENTS:

Olive oil, for greasing baking dish

4 Yukon gold, Yellow Finn, or russet potatoes (7 to 9 ounces each), peeled

6 tablespoons (¾ stick) butter, melted

Kosher or fine sea salt, for sprinkling on the potatoes

½ cup fine bread crumbs, preferably homemade from a baguette or similar loaf (page 41)

¼ cup finely grated Parmesan or other hard cheese

½ teaspoon hot or sweet Hungarian paprika

THE TEMPLATE FOR CLASSIC BAKED POTATOES and their toppings rotated on plates seemingly for eons. The potato was baked whole, pierced or not, oiled or not, foiled or not, plopped on a plate, split and squeezed and filled with butter, sour cream and chives, or perhaps all three. Or it was sliced, stacked with layers of butter, milk, and flour, and spooned out, now scalloped. Or, once baked, the center was scooped out from within the skin casing, then mashed and buttered, maybe cheesed, returned to the skin and the oven once more. Now along has come the baked potato Hasselback style by way of Swedish ingenuity. The raw potato is peeled, sliced across like a carapace, and baked. The done potato is topped with cheese and crumbs and rebaked to a gumptious crustiness. Why Hasselback? The potato manner is eponymously named for the original chef and owner of Scandic Hasselbacken Restaurant in Stockholm.

1. Preheat the oven to 425°F. Lightly grease a baking dish large enough to hold the potatoes without crowding.

2. Cut a thin slice off one long side of each potato so that it stays steady as you slice. Place a potato, squared-off side down, on a cutting board. Arrange 2 chopsticks or similar small sticks the long way, abutting but not under the potato. The chopsticks will work as a stop for the knife as you slice before it cuts all the way through the potato. Cut the potato crosswise from top to bottom, stopping when the knife meets the chopsticks, at ¼-inch intervals to make thin slices as far as the knife can go without slicing all the way through. Gently separate the slices, taking care not to break the potato apart. Set it in the baking dish and brush the top with some of the melted butter, letting some drip down through the crevices of the fanned-out slices. Lightly sprinkle salt over the top. Repeat with the remaining potatoes.

3. Cover the baking dish loosely and bake the potatoes until a fork easily pierces at the center, 50 to 60 minutes.

4. While the potatoes bake, combine the bread crumbs, Parmesan, paprika, and remaining butter in a small bowl. Stir gently to mix and set aside.

5. When the potatoes are cooked, remove them from the oven. Pat the bread crumb mixture across the top of the potatoes, pressing a little into the crevices between the slices as you go. Return the potatoes to the oven and continue baking, uncovered, until the topping is very golden and a bit sizzling, about 5 minutes. Serve right away.

ROUND TRIP ROOTS

THERE IS A CHRONOLOGY to how potatoes arrived on the American Plate. To start, they come from Chili and Peru, specifically dating from around 8000 BCE. In the 1500s, Pedro de Cieza de Leon, a Spanish conquistador, likened them to chestnuts. Gonzalo Jimenez de Quesada, another Spanish explorer, took them to Spain in lieu of gold, where the Spanish thought they were truffles. The potato was then carried to Italy, England, Belgium, and Germany, and in 1588 the Irish first tried them when they were found in the holds of the shipwrecked Spanish Armada. It took two more centuries before the French were encouraged to cultivate them by Antoine-Augustin Parmentier, who declared that potatoes were not poisonous. Louis XVI let him have a hundred "useless" acres outside Paris for potatoes, which Parmentier guarded zealously to prevent theft.

As they were not considered a people food, they were not widely grown in North America until the eighteenth century, when Scotch-Irish settlers brought the potato with them and carried them west as they pioneered farther and farther inland. By 1836, the potato had reached Idaho, and then, from 1845 on, the Irish, pushed out of Ireland by the potato famine, planted still more of them in their new land. In short, potatoes came from us and then returned to us again. We took to them cooked in every way. They became our mainstay, our comfort food, our fry, our chip, and our great love.

ON POTATOES FROM AMERICA'S FIRST COOKBOOK

AS THE POTATO meandered along its indirect path from South to North America, some thoughts about the spud were written in the first cookbook penned by an American, Amelia Simmons, published in 1796. Simmons was a domestic worker in colonial America. Her *American Cookery* is chock full of colonial recipes, advice on "the art of dressing viands, fish, poultry and vegetables," and includes a glossary of cooking terms of the times. Most are no longer in use, but their sound and meanings remain charming and useful. On the potato she wrote:

"A roast Potato is brought on with roast beef, a steake, a chop, or fricassee; good boiled with a boiled dish; make an excellent stuffing for a turkey, water or wild fowl; make a good pie, and a good starch for many uses.

"I may be pardoned by observing, that the Irish have preserved a genuine mealy rich Potato, for a century, which takes rank of any known in any other kingdom.

"All Potatoes should be dug before the raining seasons in the fall, well drying in the sun, kept from frost and dampness during the winter, in the spring removed from the cellar to a dry loft, and spread thin, and stirred and dried, or they will grow and thereby be injured for cookery."

POTATO AND CELERY ROOT LATKES WITH PEAR COMPOTE

MAKES ABOUT 20 LATKES

INGREDIENTS:

Pear Compote (recipe
   follows), for serving

3 large russet potatoes,
   peeled and coarsely
   grated (5 to 6 cups)

1 medium-size celery root,
   peeled and coarsely
   grated (about 2 cups)

1 small onion, finely chopped

3 large eggs

1 teaspoon kosher or fine
   sea salt

½ teaspoon freshly ground
   black pepper

½ cup all-purpose flour, plus
   more as necessary

Peanut or canola oil, for
   frying

AS POTATOES CIRCUMNAVIGATED THE WORLD, in almost every cuisine they met, potato cakes were made from them. In preparation the potatoes were boiled, mashed, or grated, and sometimes roasted. Other times they were minced or grated raw. Among the best known of this last method are the Jewish potato pancakes called *latkes* that are traditionally served during Hanukkah. Several theories have taken root about why cakes of this latter-day vegetable rose to claim a place at such an old celebration. One thought is that the cakes are fried and the oil signifies what was needed to light the everlasting light in the ancient temple, which, scant as it was, lasted for eight nights. Another theory is that rich and filling latkes were what Judith used to put Holofernes to sleep, enabling her to relieve him of his head to end the Assyrian siege on the Hebrews.

Of course, potatoes could not have been the vegetable of Judith's latkes, but celery root could have been included. Celery root grows wild all around the Mediterranean and to this day, cultivated and tamed, is gathered and used for both food and seasoning. And although latkes are customarily topped with applesauce, small pears were a venerated fruit of bygone times and befit the latkes perfectly.

1. Make the compote.

2. Place the grated potatoes in a colander and press down on them to extract as much excess liquid as possible. Combine the potatoes, celery root, onion, eggs, salt, and pepper in a large bowl and stir to mix. Starting with

½ cup, add enough flour to make a mixture just dry enough to pat into cakes, adding more flour as necessary.

3. Pour oil to a depth of ¼ inch into a large, heavy sauté pan and set it over medium-high heat until hot enough to immediately sizzle a drop of water. Pat the latke batter into 4- to 5-inch-wide patties, ¼ inch or so thick. Fry the patties, in batches without crowding in the pan, until golden on the bottom, 2 to 3 minutes. Turn them over and fry on the second side until golden and crispy but still soft in the center, about 4 minutes more. Transfer to paper towels to drain and continue with another round until all the latkes are cooked.

4. Serve right away, while still hot and crisp, with the pear compote on the side.

PEAR COMPOTE

PEARS ORIGINATED NEAR the Caucasus Mountains and became so enormously popular in Europe from the Middle Ages on that there were at one time more than a thousand varieties. No native pears grew in America, but in 1629 the Massachusetts Bay Company ordered pear seeds from England. Pears that are raised from seed rather than root stock tend to stray in variety; they don't stay true to the original kind. American pears became even more varied than their European progenitors.

Pear growers in the United States yearly produce over a million tons of fruit, more than half of them Bartletts, but Anjou and Comice are also popular. A compote of pear is sweet and lush enough to put on pancakes or ice cream as well as potato cakes, or to serve in a bowl to spoon up like applesauce.

MAKES 2 CUPS

3 ripe but firm pears, such as Bartlett, Anjou, or Comice, peeled, cored, and cut into 1-inch chunks

2 tablespoons fresh lemon juice

2 tablespoons dark brown sugar

¼ teaspoon freshly ground white pepper

1. Combine the pears, lemon juice, brown sugar, and pepper in a medium-size saucepan and bring to a gentle boil over medium-low heat, stirring from time to time. Cover and cook until the pears are easily mashable, 13 to 15 minutes, depending on the ripeness of the pears.

2. Remove from the heat, cool slightly, and mash with a potato masher or puree in a food processor until as smooth or chunky as you like. Cool to room temperature and serve. The sauce can be stored in the refrigerator for up to 3 days.

SPAGHETTI SQUASH WITH BACON, PINE NUTS, AND BALSAMIC VINEGAR

SERVES 4

INGREDIENTS:

1 spaghetti squash (3 pounds), halved lengthwise and seeds removed

4 thin slices bacon

2 tablespoons balsamic vinegar

1 teaspoon fresh lemon juice

¼ cup extra virgin olive oil

2 tablespoons chopped fresh flat-leaf parsley leaves

¼ teaspoon kosher or fine sea salt

⅛ teaspoon freshly ground black pepper

⅓ cup pine nuts, toasted

LOOKING LIKE A LARGE, PALE YELLOW FOOTBALL with rounded ends, spaghetti squash has a unique texture. When cooked, the pulp comes out in strands as thick and long as spaghetti noodles. Cut in half, the squash can be oven-baked in less than half an hour or microwaved in a rapid fifteen minutes. The long threads of vegetable goodness can then be forked out, topped, garnished, herbed, buttered, or tossed with cheese, nuts, or other vegetables in simple, exorbitant, conservative, or outrageous splendor. Here bacon, pine nuts, and a touch of lemon juice and vinegar produce an ambrosial warm salad.

1. If oven-baking, preheat the oven to 375°F.

2. Place the squash, cut sides down, on a baking sheet or microwave-safe dish. Cover and cook until collapsing and soft all the way through, about 45 minutes in the oven, 15 minutes in the microwave. Place the bacon alongside the squash on the baking sheet for the last 20 to 25 minutes, or place the slices between 2 paper towels and microwave until crisp, 3 to 4 minutes. Remove and let cool enough to handle.

3. Scoop the squash out of its shell and place the strands on a platter. In a small bowl, stir together the vinegar, lemon juice, olive oil, parsley, salt, and pepper. Pour over the squash. Sprinkle the pine nuts and crumble the bacon over the top and toss gently to mix. Serve right away or at room temperature.

KNOW YOUR SQUASH

SQUASHES, WHETHER THE THIN-SKINNED SUMMER VARIETY or the thick- to hard-skinned winter variety, are all members of the same genus, *Cucurbita.* All have edible flowers and seeds, though the flowers of the summer squash and the roasted seeds of the winter ones are preferred. Here's a rundown of the family.

SUMMER SQUASH

Mostly variants of the botanical branch *Cucurbita pepo*, summer squash are picked before they mature fully. They have tender skin, crisp texture, and flavors that are fresh, mild, and light. When purchasing summer squash, look for rigid, not flaccid, ones with glossy skins and that feel compact. If you are using them for a quick sauté or steaming, small to medium-size ones have the best flavor and texture. For longer cooking and for stuffing, the larger, seedier ones are the choice. Included among the summer squashes are:

❯ **YELLOW SQUASH:** *Crookneck* and *Straightneck.* Round bulbous body extended into a curved or straight narrow neck, bright yellow.

❯ **PATTYPAN:** Disk shaped with a scalloped edge, pale green, white, or gold.

❯ **SCALLOPINI:** Round with a scalloped edge like pattypan, dark green.

❯ **ZUCCHINI:** Long and cylindrical, from light to dark green to golden. Sometimes called *summer squash.*

WINTER SQUASH

Winter squashes are generally harvested when fully mature. They have hard, thick shells that range from dark green to pale yellow, golden, and deep orange-red, sometimes striped or mottled, and large, developed seeds. Depending on the variety, the flesh is soft and buttery or even stringy. Their flavors are deep and honeyed to fruity and nutty. Because of the thick protective shell, winter squash keep for many months and in fact improve with storage because their sugars continue to develop off the vine. When purchasing winter squash whole, look for deep skin color and a solid feel. When the squash is already cut, look for moist, good-colored flesh with no dryness or softening around the edges. Common varieties include:

❯ **ACORN:** Oval, with a ridged shell, dark green skin, soft and sweet pulp.

❯ **BANANA:** Long and pale yellow, mild and creamy taste.

❯ **BUTTERNUT:** Roundish, orange to tan skin, dark, sweet flavor, tops for soups and purees.

❯ **DANISH:** Like acorn but more golden skin, yellower flesh, milder taste.

❯ **DELICATA:** Shaped like a fat cucumber, yellow with green-tinted orange stripes similar in flavor to Sweet Dumpling (see below).

❯ **HUBBARD:** Large, bluish-gray skin, orange flesh, mild and slightly stringy.

❯ **KABOCHA:** A Japanese variety introduced to America a few decades ago with a taste and texture like a cross between butternut and acorn.

❯ **PUMPKIN:** From six inches in diameter to more than a hundred pounds in weight, bright orange to pale to white-skinned, dense buttery flesh; the large ones are the squash carved into Halloween lanterns all across America.

❯ **SPAGHETTI:** Large football shape with rounded ends, pale yellow skin, almost white inner flesh that separates into long strands.

❯ **SWEET DUMPLING:** Small and roundish like a tiny pumpkin, yellow with green-tinted orange stripes, very deep flavor.

❯ **TURBAN***:* Round with a turban-shaped hat of green and white, striped yellow and white below.

TURNIPS, RUTABAGAS, AND PARSNIPS:
A ROOT VEGETABLE BONANZA

SERVES 4 TO 6

INGREDIENTS:

Kosher or fine sea salt

12 ounces turnips

12 ounces rutabagas

8 ounces parsnips

½ cup sour cream

2 tablespoons chopped fresh
flat-leaf parsley

⅛ teaspoon grated nutmeg,
preferably freshly grated

WHEN THE POTATO BECAME EMBRACED by the Europeans and later North Americans, it usurped the former place of turnips, rutabagas, and parsnips as the beloved root vegetable side dish. That was unfortunate, because with the snubbing a bouquet of exquisite tastes went missing. Turnips have a radishlike top note. Rutabagas are a flavor cross between turnips and cabbage and have a brassica essence. Parsnips, sometimes thought of as a white carrot, are dulcet in a more honeyed way than their orange carrot cousins. As a trio, together they bring earthy warmth to the table from fall through winter and bestow a rust, sienna, ocher rainbow swirl around poultry or meat roasts and chops.

1. Bring a large pot of salted water to boil over high heat.

2. Peel the vegetables, trim away their root and top ends, and cut them into ¼-inch-thick half-rounds or quarter-rounds, depending on their diameter, so that they are approximately the same size.

3. Add the vegetables and cook briskly over high heat until tender but still holding their shape, about 5 minutes. Drain in a colander and set aside.

4. Whisk together the sour cream, parsley, and nutmeg in a small bowl.

5. Transfer the cooked vegetables to a serving bowl. Add the sour cream mixture and toss gently to mix. Serve right away.

BLACK-EYED PEAS
WITH SUNDRIED TOMATOES AND
CORN BREAD CRUMBLE

ORIGINALLY A NATIVE OF AFRICA, BLACK-EYED PEAS first traveled with the slave trade to the West Indies and from there to America. George Washington Carver promoted planting them both for nutrition and reviving the soil. Black-eyed peas and corn bread became a typical southern lunch food during the Civil War, when Sherman stripped the countryside of crops. He didn't take the peas and corn that he considered animal fodder, so both transmuted into "good luck" food to the decimated South. The "good luck" tradition continues, with black-eyed peas serving as a token New Year's food in the South.

1. First make the corn bread and cut it into wedges. Cut enough wedges into small chunks to make 2 cups. Set the chunks and the remaining wedges aside.

2. Place the olive oil and pancetta in a medium-size pot over medium-high heat. Cook, stirring from time to time, until the pancetta begins to turn golden around the edges, about 3 minutes. Add the onion, thyme, and tomatoes and stir to mix. Add the black-eyed peas, water, and salt, stir to mix, and bring to a boil. Reduce the heat to maintain a brisk simmer and cook uncovered until the liquid is almost gone, about 15 minutes.

3. While the peas cook, melt the butter in a medium-size sauté pan over medium-high heat. Add the corn bread chunks and cook, tossing gently, until golden and toasty, about 3 minutes. Transfer to paper towels and set aside until the peas finish cooking.

4. When the peas are done, spoon them into a serving dish. Top with the toasted corn bread crumble, sprinkle the parsley over all, and serve with the remaining corn bread wedges on the side if desired.

SERVES 4

INGREDIENTS:

- 2 cups coarsely cut-up Skillet Corn Bread (page 166)
- 1½ tablespoons extra virgin olive oil
- 4 thin slices pancetta, coarsely chopped
- ½ cup finely chopped white onion
- 1 teaspoon chopped fresh thyme or ½ teaspoon dried
- ⅔ cup sundried tomatoes, coarsely chopped
- 4 cups cooked black-eyed peas
- 3 cups water
- 1 teaspoon kosher or fine sea salt
- 2½ tablespoons butter
- ¼ cup chopped fresh flat-leaf or curly parsley, for garnish

THE BEAN'S TANGLED VINE

THE COMMON BEAN was domesticated close to seven thousand years ago in two areas of the New World, Meso America and the Andes. About three thousand years ago, it, along with corn and squash, had become a main food of peoples living many miles apart, from the natives of the northeastern woodlands of North America to those at the tip of Chile.

Around 1500 CE, explorers to the Americas began to restock the food stores of their ships with American beans, which when dry would last the length of the voyage. They soon became a staple in many European countries, providing food through the barren winter, spreading as far north as Scandinavia, east through Armenia, and beyond to far Asia.

Beans inspire a tangle of names based on size, shape, color, and utter whimsy. Some American ones are calypso, Pennsylvania Dutch lazy wife beans, rattlesnake beans, red valentine beans, rice beans, soldier beans, stink beans, tongue of fire beans, Jacob's cattle beans, and zebra beans.

MINNEAPOLIS BROWN BEAN CAKES WITH CHEESE MELT

SO MANY SWEDES IMMIGRATED TO MINNESOTA and to its major city, Minneapolis, in the 1800s that at one point one-fourth of the region's population was Swedish. They brought their drollness, their acumen, their subtle humor, and their food, including a famous bean dish called *bruna bönor*. It is made from a soft brown bean—developed for their northern soil—that is baked in a casserole, touched with molasses, and given a perking twist with white vinegar.

A bean cake done with true Swedish brown beans or similar ones offers an intriguing vegetable patty to accompany a meal. What is that

INGREDIENTS:

3 cups cooked Swedish brown or white beans

¼ cup water

2 tablespoons molasses

2 teaspoons distilled white vinegar

⅛ teaspoon ground allspice

½ to ¾ teaspoon kosher or fine sea salt

4 to 5 tablespoons all-purpose flour

4 to 6 tablespoons (½ to ¾ stick) butter

1 cup grated Havarti or other mild soft cheese

1 tablespoon chopped fresh dill

A TRIO OF BEAN CAKES

NEW WORLD BEANS TRAVELED TO EVERY LAND and, with every group returning to the Americas, reappeared in new guises. Who can count the many versions of bean soups, bean casseroles, bean side dishes, bean salads? Some are named for cities; some maintain ethnic influences; some are named for the sort of bean or how many types of beans are used in the composition. Altogether the numerous dishes reveal that beans are a satisfying, sought-after food that flourishes to full flavor under almost any flaunt and fancy. Among the ways to enjoy the humble bean is in a bean cake. Depending on the bean and the cuisine, the cake can take on many enhancements. Three are on these pages—one with northern European origins, one with South American origins, and one with Mediterranean/Middle Eastern origins.

mysterious dark tinge of sweetness? Following the Swedish penchant, the cakes are browned in butter and more butter. Cheese as a topping follows the copious use of cheese in Swedish cooking. The pungent wild rue used so freely in Sweden is a hard-to-find herb in the States and is replaced with dill, another favorite herb in Scandinavia. Real Swedish brown beans can be found in specialty food stores, but in the meantime the cakes can be made from common white beans found in every grocery store.

THE POWER OF MINNEAPOLIS

MINNEAPOLIS SITS AT THE BASE OF THE MISSISSIPPI RIVER'S only gorge and waterfall. The early settlers in the area realized they could harness power from the cascading water for industry, and given that the city lay conveniently near the immense wheat fields of the Great Plains, grain milling was the obvious choice. By 1880 flour mills were booming, and in 1928 twenty-seven of them merged to become General Mills. In 1869, another early miller, Charles Pillsbury, established the Pillsbury Flour Mills Company in the city. Ever expanding, General Mills bought Pillsbury in 2001.

As all this was unfolding, pushed by population pressure and agricultural hardship, around 1840 a tidal wave of Swedish and Norwegian immigrants started arriving in Minnesota. Immigration agents had promised them inexpensive acreage to farm in a climate like their own, but nearby Minneapolis needed laborers. By 1910 Swedes were the largest ethnic group in Minneapolis.

Time wrought many changes, and by the time the millennium turned, many of the mills had moved to distant cities. The Swedes and other Scandinavians stayed. To this day they have left their mark on the politics, arts, religions, and definitely the humor of Minnesota. Also

the food. Nowhere else in the country can a shopper so readily buy Swedish meatballs, potato sausage, lutfisk, lingonberry jam, rue for flavoring, aquavit to tipple, and brown beans for signature baked brown beans, often turned into slightly sweet and scrumptious bean cakes.

1. Place the beans, water, molasses, vinegar, allspice, and salt in a food processor and process into a crumbly puree. Starting with 4 tablespoons, add enough flour to make a sticky, doughlike mixture.

2. Melt 3 tablespoons of the butter in a heavy skillet over medium-high heat. Taking about ¼ cup of the bean mixture in your hand, form it into a ball, then press it into a patty about 3 inches in diameter and ¼ to ½ inch thick. Place as many patties in the skillet as will fit in a single, uncrowded layer and fry until crispy on the outside while still soft on the inside, 3 to 4 minutes per side.

3. Place about 1 tablespoon of the cheese on each patty, cover with a lid, and continue frying until the cheese is melted, about 1 minute more. Transfer the patties to a platter and keep warm, and continue with another batch until all the bean cakes are cooked.

4. Sprinkle dill over all and serve warm.

ALBUQUERQUE BLACK BEAN CAKES WITH CHIPOTLE CHILE CREAM

BLACK BEANS ARE A VARIETY OF KIDNEY BEANS also known as *turtle beans, frijoles negros, Spanish black beans, Tampico beans, Venezuelan beans,* and *caviar criollo.* They have been cultivated for more than seven thousand years and are the main bean of most South and Central American as well as Caribbean cuisines. The beans are not curved and indented like most of their cousins; rather they are shaped more like oval beads or black-eyed peas. Their sleek ebony skin covers a white interior, and when cooked they assume a creamy texture and a sweeter hint to their taste than most beans. Not only do they make for a great side vegetable on their own; they also serve as a fine burrito layer, a legumy mix with rice, and an earthy chew in stews, and they mash into one of the tastiest of bean cakes. The take here is Central American, the type of bean cake, nutty and magnanimous, that might show up in an El Salvadoran, Guatemalan, or Nicaraguan restaurant, any of which can be found in a lively American city such as Albuquerque with its mix of people and cuisines of all those countries.

MAKES ABOUT 12 PATTIES

INGREDIENTS:

Chipotle Chile Cream
(recipe follows),
for serving

3 cups cooked black beans

1 small yellow or white onion,
finely chopped

1 jalapeño chile, finely
chopped

½ teaspoon kosher or
fine sea salt

¼ teaspoon ground cumin

Peanut or canola oil,
for frying

Fresh cilantro sprigs,
for garnish

1. Make the Chipotle Chile Cream.

2. Mash the beans to a textured puree using a food processor or potato masher. Transfer to a bowl and stir in the onion, jalapeño, salt, and cumin. In ¼-cup amounts, form the mixture into patties about 3 inches in diameter and ¼ to ½ inch thick.

3. Lightly coat a heavy skillet with oil and heat over medium-high heat. Put in as many patties as will fit in a single, uncrowded layer and fry until golden and toasty on both sides, about 1 minute per side. Transfer to a platter and keep warm, and continue with another batch, adding more oil to the pan as needed, until all the patties are cooked.

4. Place a small dollop of the chipotle chile cream atop each bean cake, garnish each with a few sprigs of cilantro, and serve warm, with the remaining chipotle chile cream on the side.

THE VILLA OF DUQUE DE ALBUQUERQUE

ALBUQUERQUE WAS FIRST SETTLED IN THE LATE 1600S by Spanish missionaries on a site that had been abandoned by Pueblo people. The place was lovely with the nearby Sandia Mountains glowing a bright reddish pink at sunset. Albuquerque thrived in part because the Rio Grande flows through it, and in the 1800s settlers from eastern states and other European countries began to arrive, many following one of the main wagon train routes across the land, the Sante Fe Trail. Then in 1880, the Atchison, Topeka, and Santa Fe Railway rolled into town. The surrounding land had already come under the control of the United States as the New Mexico Territory. Routes for cattle drives nearby had already brought ranchers, herders, and outlaws. The University of New Mexico, boasting Pueblo revival architecture, was located in the center of what was then still a sleepy little hamlet. By 1900 Albuquerque had eight thousand inhabitants with all the up-to-date urban amenities, including an electric tram. When, in 1912, the Territory of New Mexico was granted statehood, Santa Fe, though now far smaller than Albuquerque, was named as capital.

Albuquerque remains New Mexico's largest city. The city's population and food reflect every layer of its settlement, but at the base and dominating lies a fusion of the cooking of the earliest peoples to arrive, the Pueblo and the Spanish. Albuquerque is an epicenter of Southwest cuisine. You can still get a great burger there from an old Route 66 café, but mostly you find tortillerias rolling out corn and flour tortillas and burrito and Navajo taco quick-stop joints where the tortillas are filled with black beans and roasted meats. More elegant restaurants offer sophisticated tamales and rellenos placed on black bean cakes and topped with smoky salsas.

CHIPOTLE CHILE CREAM

CHIPOTLES CAN BE found dried, usually packaged in cellophane, or moist, canned in a thick blend of tomatoes, vinegar, and spices called *adobo* sauce. For this recipe the canned ones in adobo sauce are best, due to their suppleness and agreeable coating. One small can provides enough chile heat for many recipes, so once the can is opened, transfer them to a glass or plastic container and store them in the refrigerator.

MAKES 1 CUP

1 cup crème fraîche or ½ cup heavy whipping cream mixed with ½ cup sour cream

2 teaspoons minced chipotle chiles in adobo sauce

1 teaspoon fresh lime juice

¾ teaspoon kosher or fine sea salt

Combine the crème fraîche, chipotle chiles, lime juice, and salt in a bowl and whisk to mix and smooth. Use right away or store in the refrigerator for up to 2 days.

GLENDALE CHICKPEA CAKES WITH TOMATO AND SESAME SEED TOPPING

CHICKPEAS ARE A CLOSE RELATIVE OF BEANS and, like beans, a member of the legume family, a near enough cousin to also be called garbanzo "bean." Chickpeas are one of the oldest legumes grown and were a staple food of southern Eurasia and their early wandering people who came down from above the Caspian Sea, including the ancient Armenians.

Chickpeas have remained an honored food of Armenians, the first of whom arrived in America in 1618. Armenian cooks simmer them in stews and soups, toast them to nibble, and press them into crunchy, nutlike, delectable patties or balls. By far the largest numbers of Armenian immigrants made their way west to California, especially to the town of Glendale on the edge of Los Angeles. They took chickpeas with them. This cake is reminiscent of their glorious culinary heritage.

INGREDIENTS:

Tomato and Sesame Seed Topping (recipe follows), for serving

2¼ cups cooked chickpeas

2 cloves garlic, chopped

⅓ cup water

3 tablespoons tahini (sesame paste), stirred smooth (page 55)

¾ teaspoon kosher or fine sea salt

½ cup all-purpose flour, plus extra for kneading and shaping the cakes

Extra virgin olive oil, for frying

1. Make the topping.

2. Place the chickpeas and garlic in a food processor and process until crumbly. Add the water, tahini, and salt and process until well blended and somewhat pureed but not yet smooth. Add the flour and process until you have a sticky doughlike mixture that collects around the processor blade.

3. Transfer the mixture to a floured board and with floured hands knead in enough extra flour to make a soft, cohesive ball. This will take up to ¾ cup extra flour.

4. Divide the dough into 12 portions. With floured hands, roll each portion into a ball, then press it into a cake about 3 inches in diameter and ¼ inch thick. The cakes may be prepared to this point, covered with plastic wrap, and set aside at room temperature for up to a few hours.

5. Lightly coat a heavy skillet and heat over medium-high heat until hot enough to sizzle a tiny pinch of the dough. Add as many patties as will fit in a single uncrowded layer and fry until golden, 2 minutes per side. Transfer the cakes to a platter and continue with another round until all are fried.

6. To serve, garnish each cake with a dollop of the topping and serve warm.

TOMATO AND SESAME SEED TOPPING

AS AN OLD and thriving culture, Armenians have had the advantage of incorporating new foods into traditional favorites. They have long employed sesame and mint in their dishes, and as hot peppers and tomatoes became available, they were woven into an innovative topping of old and new, which can go on any bean cake.

MAKES ABOUT ⅔ CUP

2 teaspoons sesame seeds

1 medium-large tomato, finely chopped (about ⅔ cup)

1 teaspoon finely shredded fresh mint leaves

½ teaspoon hot or sweet Hungarian paprika, or to taste

¼ teaspoon salt

1. Lightly toast the sesame seeds in an ungreased skillet or microwave oven until beginning to pop, 2 to 3 minutes either way.

2. Combine the toasted seeds, tomato, mint, paprika, and salt in a small bowl and toss gently to mix. Use right away or set aside at room temperature for up to several hours, but don't refrigerate.

GLENDALE, FROM RANCHO TO SUBURB

IN 1784 A CORPORAL IN THE SPANISH ARMY OF BAJA, California, received a land grant on the edge of the Sierra Madre mountains near Mission Los Angeles. His grandson, Teodoro Verdugo, built a home there called Verdugo Adobe, which today is the oldest building in Glendale, the town that grew around it.

As early as 1880, the location and booming economy of Glendale attracted immigrant populations, so that by 1906 it was named the fastest-growing city in America. Soon freeways crossed the original ranch, and both businesses and people continued to arrive. From 1915 on, multitudes of Armenians migrated there, and today Glendale is the city with the largest Armenian population in the United States. People of Armenian heritage make up 40 percent of the population, and they have changed the city, giving it a lively ethnic strain. Glendale houses a rarity in most cities, a plethora of Armenian restaurants serving *sarma, shish kebabs,* and *basturma.* Stores sell the freshest figs, quince, and eggplant. Dishes are flavored with sumac, Aleppo pepper, pomegranate, and sesame paste, as in the fresh and tasty Armenian-style chickpea cakes.

THANK YOU GEORGE WASHINGTON CARVER

FOR DECADES AFTER the Civil War, the growing of cotton depleted the soil in much of the South and made it extremely difficult to grow food crops. One man, George Washington Carver (1864 to 1943), an African American botanist, inventor, and educator who spent forty-seven years at Tuskegee University, changed the culture. Carver, who was born into slavery in Diamond, Missouri, taught poor farm workers and planters to rotate the food crops they grew in order to replenish the nitrogen in the soil and mitigate the build-up of pests that attack only one crop. He especially promoted the planting of peanuts—for which he offered one hundred and five recipes—as well as soy beans and yams.

Meanwhile, in his laboratory, he worked to advance the cultivation of new and diverse crops such as cowpeas, pecans, and broccoli. In time, he invented and developed virtually hundreds of plant products. They included peanut butter and more than three hundred other foods that were derived from peanuts. A hundred more came from sweet potatoes.

Carver's research was lauded by Presidents Theodore Roosevelt and Franklin Roosevelt, who designated his boyhood home in Diamond a national monument. Carver is still celebrated today for having changed the way Americans grow and prepare food.

GRAINS TO MAKE A MEAL

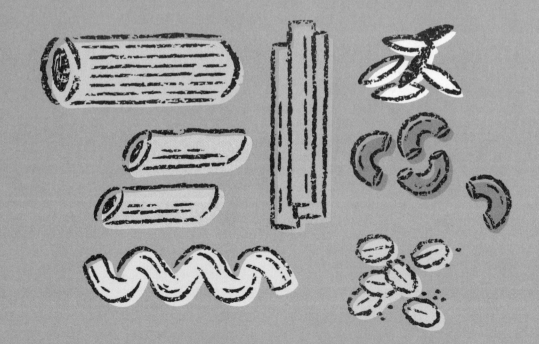

atural grasses grew on all the continents of the globe except the Americas and Australia. As people learned to harvest and then plant them, they became the most important staple of the human diet: grain.

Among the tall grassy stalks that flourished across the steppes of Europe and Asia and the plains of Africa were millet, barley, wheat, and rice. North America had no such grain grasses. They were brought here. Today North America is one of the major producers and exporters of cereal grains, growing enough to feed the world.

America had the perfect soils and conditions to produce grains. In the center there were vast expanses of plowable earth, much of it alluvial, with open lands that went on for hundreds of miles. The temperate climate cycled from a germinating cold winter

THE STATE OF PASTA IN THE STATES

- Ravioli are a specialty of the Italian American community in Providence, Rhode Island.

- The word "macaroni" comes from a Sicilian word for the force needed in the dough-making process.

- In eighteenth century England, when many young aristocratic men returned from foreign travels with airs, they were called "macaronis" for their affectations. It's in this vein that Yankee Doodle, upon sticking a feather in his hat, was called "macaroni."

- Thomas Jefferson brought macaroni to America after visiting Naples.

- Pasta is shredded, cut, and twisted into more than six hundred shapes.

- Semolina, the flour from which pasta is made, is the coarsely milled endosperm of durum wheat, which is then milled into flour.

- The first American pasta factory was opened in Brooklyn, New York, in 1848 by a Frenchman named Antoine Zerega. He installed one horse in his basement to drive the equipment and dried the strands on his roof.

- Most Americans eat pasta at least forty times a year, close to once a week, amounting to fourteen pounds a year.

- To be called a noodle, pasta must have egg in it.

- Most of America's durum wheat is grown in North Dakota. There the Wheat Commission prints T-shirts reading "Mouth Droolin', Athlete Fuelin', People Pleasin' Pasta."

- It takes 16,548 kernels of wheat to make one pound of pasta.

- Pasta with meatballs may have its roots in Sicily, but the combination became a dinnertime favorite in America.

to maturing hot summer, perfect for wheat. Outer lowlands and wetlands offered ideal acreage for rice. Northern temperatures and thinner soils favored barley and oats, even millet. Wild rice, an aquatic grass whose seeds are eaten, is the only native grain on the continent.

The first wheat was planted here in 1777 as a hobby crop. Now wheat is grown in forty-two of the fifty states. Rice was first grown in 1694 and by 1700 was a major crop. Wheat and rice became foundations integral to the American diet as it evolved. Bread, rolls, and crackers took a place at every meal. Rice came to sit as a pillow under meat and vegetable or as a companion to the dish. Both in many forms—boxed, toasted, and baked—became the focus of our breakfast menu. When new ethnic groups arrived with more expansive ideas, grains marched onto our plates as the cardinal ingredient of big and bold dinner dishes. We discovered pasta. We took to risotto. We found bulgur pilaf.

Starting with noodles topped with tomato sauce or inundated with rich cheddar cheese, we have gone on to devise pasta dishes tossed with robust and tender vegetables, seafood, sausages, oils, and cream. We simmer rice with tidbits of all sorts. We add the harvest of our gardens and leas to wheaty pilaf. Our own wild rice bewitchingly fills casseroles. Each is a bounteous meal.

PASTA
WITH GRAPE TOMATOES, CORN, AND POACHED EGGS

WHEN FARMERS MOVED ONTO THE GREAT PLAINS, they created a cornucopia. Wheat could grow in fields so vast that the edges couldn't be seen. By August of any year, all vistas were obscured by forests of corn over six feet high. Gardens of vegetables thrived. From that abundance comes a Great Plains homage to pasta. The noodles are from winter wheat. Scattered over them are kernels of the plains' most famed crop, corn. Small tomatoes add a red and juicy adornment. To top it all comes a poached egg, a farm-honored food that adds a special and unusual country note to pasta.

1. Bring a large pot of salted water to a boil. Add the pasta and cook until al dente, 2 to 4 minutes for fresh pasta, according to the package directions for dried. Drain the pasta briefly, return it to the pot still moist, and set it aside in a warm place (see Tip, page 318).

2. Line a plate with paper towels. To poach the eggs, fill a sauté pan with water to a depth of 1½ inches and bring it to a boil over high heat. Reduce the heat to low and, when the water is just simmering, gently crack each egg into the water. Gently cook the eggs until the whites are just set, about 5 minutes. With a slotted spoon, lift out each egg and set it on the prepared plate. Set aside at room temperature while preparing the sauce.

3. To make the sauce, heat the oil in a large sauté pan over medium-high heat. Add the tomatoes, corn, garlic, and ¼ teaspoon salt and stir to mix. Cook until the tomatoes are barely wilted, about 3 minutes. Remove from the heat and stir in the Parmesan cheese and basil.

4. To serve, divide the pasta among 4 individual wide bowls. Spoon the sauce over the pasta. Gently set an egg over the top of each dish and serve right away.

PASTA AND HOMEMADE MEATBALLS
WITH TWO-PEPPER TOMATO SAUCE

SERVES 3 OR 4

INGREDIENTS:

Kosher or fine sea salt

8 ounces dried pasta, such as spaghetti or bucatini

12 ounces ground pork

¾ cup bread crumbs, preferably homemade (page 41)

1 large egg

2 teaspoons fresh lemon juice

½ teaspoon hot Hungarian paprika

½ teaspoon chopped fresh sage or ¼ teaspoon crumbled dried

¼ cup extra virgin olive oil

1 medium-size yellow or white onion, chopped

¾ cup chopped pasilla chile or chopped green bell pepper mixed with a pinch of chopped jalapeño

⅔ cup white wine

1¾ cups (one 14.5-ounce can) canned diced tomatoes, with juices

1 tablespoon tomato paste

¼ cup chopped fresh flat-leaf parsley, for serving

½ medium-size red or green bell pepper, seeded and slivered, for serving

½ cup grated Parmesan, Romano, or aged Asiago cheese, for serving

THE INVENTION OF THE FLOUR NOODLE IS VERY OLD, and it has been dried for later rehydrating equally as long. Pasta as a version of noodle came to Italy via the Arabs of Sicily and from Sicily to America. Nowadays there are many different pasta dishes on the American plate, with toppings from tomato to basil, meat to vegetable, cream to olive oil, but meatballs still reign as the most popular. Red tomato sauce with meatballs served over pasta is a fill-'em-up plateful loved by a population that loves a full plate. Here a venturesome version boasts a few new touches: mild-to-a-bit-nippy pasilla pepper along with bell pepper in the sauce; in the meatballs, a dash of lemon; and slivers of raw bell pepper for a fresh topper. Of the 600 different shapes of pasta, for this dish good old spaghetti or similar bucatini is the prime choice.

1. Bring a large pot of salted water to a boil. Add the spaghetti and cook until al dente. Drain the spaghetti briefly, return it to the pot still moist, and set it aside in a warm place (see Tip, page 318).

2. Combine the pork, bread crumbs, egg, lemon juice, paprika, sage, and ³⁄₄ teaspoon salt in a medium-size bowl and mix with your hands to blend well. Form into balls about 1 inch in diameter, setting the balls on a plate as you go. You should wind up with 18 to 20 meatballs. Set aside at room temperature for up to 30 minutes while preparing the sauce or cover and refrigerate for up to 2 days.

3. To make the sauce, heat 3 tablespoons of the olive oil in a large skillet over medium-high heat. Add the onion, pasilla chile, and 4 meatballs, mashing them to mix in with the vegetables. Reduce the heat to low and cook until the meat is slightly browned and the vegetables are wilted, about 15 minutes, stirring occasionally. Increase the heat to high, add the wine, and cook until the wine is mostly evaporated but the mixture is still moist, 3 minutes. Stir in the tomatoes with their juices and the tomato paste and bring to a boil. Reduce the heat to maintain a simmer, cover, and cook until the sauce is reduced and thickened, 40 minutes.

4. While the sauce simmers, heat the remaining 1 tablespoon olive oil in a separate large sauté pan over medium heat. Add the remaining meatballs and cook, turning often, until browned all around and firm, about 10 minutes. Stir the meatballs and any pan juices into the sauce and continue simmering, uncovered, until the sauce is richly colored and the meatballs are cooked through, 15 minutes.

THE STORY OF WHEAT, THE PASTE OF PASTA

WHEAT, ALONG WITH BARLEY AND MILLET, was one of the first domesticated grains. Two types were the first to be changed from wild to domestic, meaning they could no longer seed themselves but needed purposeful planting. One was emmer wheat, the most widespread during ancient times. The other was einkorn wheat, which was widely cultivated up to the Iron Age and sustained populations in much of Europe. Though never as widespread as emmer, nor is its yield as great, it is more resistant to cold, heat, drought, and disease. Modern wheat, shorter and husk free, followed. It is now the most widely cultivated in the world.

There are several versions of modern wheat grown and some ancient varieties are still planted. Today in America six sorts are cultivated, depending on soil, climate, and use for food, much of it on the Great Plains.

HARD RED SPRING WHEAT is hard, brown, high in protein and gluten. It is used for bread and hard baked goods. Planted in spring and harvested by fall, it is common to the deeper soils and wetter part of the prairie.

HARD RED WINTER WHEAT is hard and brownish and fairly high in protein. It is planted in the fall, stays dormant over winter, and appears with spring's warming for early harvesting. It is used for bread and hard baked goods. Most unbleached, all-purpose flour is milled from it. It also is mixed with softer flours, so-called "enriched," to increase their nutrition.

SOFT RED WINTER WHEAT is used for cakes, crusts, muffins, and biscuits and is often packaged as cake flour or pastry flour. Sometimes baking powder and salt are added and it is sold as "self-rising."

HARD WHITE WHEAT is hard, pale, and opaque. It is grown in drier zones and is used for bread and beer.

SOFT WHITE WHEAT, light of color and low in protein, is grown in wetter zones. It is used for piecrusts and pastry, and much pastry flour is made from it.

DURUM WHEAT, an ancient variety, is still the second-most widely cultivated wheat today. It is hard and translucent; it is the wheat ground to make semolina, the flour used to make pasta.

5. To serve, place the spaghetti on a large platter or individual plates. Spoon the sauce and meatballs over the top, garnish with the parsley, bell pepper slivers, and cheese and serve right away.

IF IT WEREN'T FOR THEM!
INVENTORS WHO HELPED BRING PASTA TO THE TABLE

CYRUS McCORMICK OF ROCKBRIDGE COUNTY, VIRGINIA, perfected the idea of a mechanical reaper to harvest wheat in 1831. His company, first called the McCormick Harvesting Machine Company, became International Harvester. With his machine a farmer who could reap only two acres a day with scythes and sickles could now harvest eight. William Seward, later President Lincoln's Secretary of State, said that due to McCormick's machine "the line of civilization moves westward thirty miles each year."

FROM 1607 ON, grist mills sprang up all over America. George Washington had one at Mount Vernon.

OLIVER EVANS of Newport, Delaware, invented the gravity-fed automated grist mill in the 1780s and patented it in 1790 when the U.S. Patent Office first opened.

JOHN DEERE, a blacksmith who lived in Grand Detour, Illinois, noticed that the cast-iron plow was not working well on prairie soil and, remembering how he used to polish the needles for his tailor father to help push them through leather, invented the polished-steel plow in 1837. Deere moved to Moline, Illinois, where he founded Deere and Company, the world's largest provider of agricultural equipment.

JOSEPH DART of Buffalo, New York, devised the grain elevator in 1843. At first steam powered, it lifted grain from rivers and lakes to storage bins to await milling. Buffalo became the largest grain port in the world.

FRANKLIN HIRAM KING of Whitewater, Wisconsin, invented the cylindrical silo for storing grain in 1889. To this day it is an iconic edifice across American farmlands.

➲ TIP: THE VERSATILITY OF PASTA AND A HANDY TRICK. A dish of pasta offers numerous advantages to a time-pressed cook: Foremost, it easily enfolds almost any vegetable, from tomatoes, onions, garlic, squash, mushrooms, peppers, corn, and olives to all manner of greens—sturdy choys, mustard greens, and chard as well as the more delicate spinach leaves and pea shoots. Sauces with ground meat, sausage, seafood, eggs, nuts, and cheese can round out its protein profile. In other words, it's a wide open game, to be determined by what's on hand or what is desired.

Fresh commercial pasta is widely available and makes for a very quick meal. Some cooks like to make their own pasta now and again, but most home cooks turn to the array of dried pastas on the market shelves, many of which are of very good quality. For extra ease, dried pasta can be prepared and kept warm at the back of the stove for a brief while. Here's how:

Bring a large pot of salted water to a boil over high heat. Add the pasta and cook until al dente, using the package instructions as a guideline. Then—and here's a key point—very quickly drain the pasta in a colander and return it right away to the pot while it's still quite wet. Cover and set aside in a warm place, such as the back of the stove. This way the pasta will stay moist and warm and not become gluey for up to 20 minutes.

CABIN FEVER PASTA
WITH JERKY

ON A BLUSTERY DAY WHEN YOU PREFER TO STAY INSIDE and have nothing for dinner except what you can scramble up from the cupboard and refrigerator, why not use America's long-lasting meat as the key note for a delectable pasta dish? Small pieces of jerky plump up perfectly. In fact all the ingredients of a beef jerky sauce can come from backpack or pantry: garlic, onions, canned tomato, chile pepper, and red wine. If your garden or market doesn't have fresh sage, America's most plentiful native herb, to fry for a garnish, you can substitute a teaspoon of dried sage added to the sauce while it is cooking. The composition is named for those who love to take themselves into the wild, far away from the stores, but it makes an unusual meal for those who prefer to hide out in their cozy home. For the outdoor or indoor adventurer, buffalo and elk jerky make gumptious jerky choices.

1. Bring a large pot of salted water to a boil. Add the spaghetti and cook until al dente. Drain the spaghetti briefly, return it to the pot still warm, and set it aside in a warm place (see Tip, facing page).

COME GET YOUR JERKY IN AUSTIN, NEVADA

SINCE THERE ARE MILES and miles to cover in Nevada between towns, a supply of jerky in the car helps tide travelers over. In Austin, Nevada, as the snow melts and visitors begin to arrive, not only can you find commercial jerky in the town's one remaining grocery, its hardware store, and two gas stations, but there is also a munching supply in its four bars. Individual purveyors show up with pickup trucks to peddle their own homemade jerky made with meat obtained from their hunting and their herding. Each has a private recipe of spices and a secret method of drying. The cattle of Austin feed on brambly sage and pungent grasses, as do the abundant herds of deer and antelope, so without extra seasonings, each and every one is sassy and savory.

SERVES 4

INGREDIENTS:

Kosher or fine sea salt

12 ounces spaghetti or other dried pasta

¼ cup extra virgin olive oil

16 large fresh sage leaves or 1 teaspoon dried

1 medium-size white or yellow onion, halved and thinly sliced

3 large cloves garlic, coarsely chopped

1 teaspoon red chile flakes

2 ounces good-quality beef, buffalo, or elk jerky

10 canned plum tomatoes, coarsely chopped, with juices (from two 1-pound 12-ounce cans; reserve extras for another use)

1 cup red wine

½ cup freshly grated Parmesan cheese, for serving

THE JOURNEY OF JERKY

THE FIRST INHABITANTS OF THE AMERICAS were hunters or simple agriculturalists. None had herds of domestic animals to provide meat, and in fact there were no sorts of indigenous animals suitable for domestication. Deer, elk, and buffalo are too recalcitrant to stay fenced in and follow orders, and llamas were needed more for pack-animal purposes than for meat. Even when the native peoples wanted meat, they usually had to hunt for it. If they were too far from home to bring the meat back fresh, they dried it in strips over campfires.

The Spanish in Peru learned the native word *charqui,* the term for dried meat, and brought the term north. From them the pioneers heading west picked up the technique of drying the meat they hunted or raised and also picked up the term. Only they mispronounced it, calling it *jerky.* Such dried meat became an American staple for trappers, explorers, anyone snowbound in a cabin or far from a store, and also for mountaineers, trailblazers, and long-distance travelers. Indeed, even today as you travel rural roads, there are peddlers and food stands everywhere selling beef, venison, and elk jerky. You can also buy jerky in convenience stores. All make a terrific pasta as you camp or cabin it, in or out of town.

2. Heat the oil in a medium-size sauté pan over medium-high heat. Add the sage leaves if using fresh and fry, turning once, until beginning to crisp, 30 to 45 seconds. Transfer the leaves to a paper towel to drain, leaving the oil in the pan.

3. Add the onion, garlic, red chile flakes, and jerky to the pan. Sauté over medium heat until the onion wilts, 3 to 5 minutes. Increase the heat to medium-high, add the tomatoes and their juices, the red wine, and the sage if using dried, and bring to a boil. Cook, stirring from time to time, until the mixture is thickened and saucy, 10 to 12 minutes. Season with salt to taste.

4. Top the pasta with the ragout, garnish with the fried sage leaves, and serve with the Parmesan cheese on the side.

IMPERIAL LINGUINE WITH ROASTED SALMON, WRINKLED OLIVES, AND SALMON CAVIAR CREAM

PASTA IMPERIAL WAS SO NAMED TO DENOTE ITS PLACE on a noble's dinner table. Its sauce includes caviar, a delicacy that a laborer or miner can't easily afford. But as classy as the dish is, it jumps class boundaries with the new, not-too-costly caviars available from American waters. Salmon caviar studs the treat here, made its most luxurious with yet another deluxe ingredient, heavy cream. Fresh linguine turns the dish yet more lavish, but dried linguine also works fine.

1. Preheat the broiler or oven to 500°F. Lightly grease a baking sheet with oil. Bring a large pot of salted water to a boil over high heat.

2. Place the olives in a small bowl, cover with warm water, and set aside for 30 minutes to soak out some of the saltiness.

3. Add the linguine to the boiling water and cook until al dente, 2 to 3 minutes for fresh linguine or according to the package instructions for dried. Drain the pasta briefly, return it to the pot still moist, and set it aside in a warm place (see Tip, page 318).

4. Combine the lemon juice and extra virgin olive oil in a small saucepan and bring to a boil over high heat. Reduce the heat to medium and whisk in the cream. Cook until the mixture is bubbling up and thickened, 3 to 5 minutes. Set aside in a warm place until ready to serve.

NATIVE CAVIARS

SINCE THE MID-1970s, the price of Russian caviars has increased to almost unaffordable as the beluga and sevruga sturgeons were overfished beyond sustainability. In response, American entrepreneurs began to scout their home waters, both fresh and saline, for replacements. They found sturgeon caviar in the Missouri, Mississippi, Sacramento, and Columbia Rivers. They hit upon golden whitefish caviar from inland waters on both sides of the country, Lake Michigan and Flathead Lake in Montana, of all places. In the oceans' waters they discovered the roe of flying fish, tiny, crunchy orange-to-red beadlets that the Japanese had long celebrated, as well as herring roe found on lengths of kelp where the fish deposit their eggs.

Among all the newbies, salmon roe stands out as an exemplar of caviar perfection. The eggs have a zingy taste of the sea but are not too salty; they're a translucent bright red-orange color and are just the right size to provide a pleasing pop as they are bitten. Most gourmet grocery stores carry these delectable local caviars at the fish counter during the winter holidays, and the price is right.

5. Sprinkle both sides of the salmon fillets with salt, set them on the baking sheet, and place in the oven. Cook without turning until firm on the outside and still rosy in the center, 6 to 7 minutes. Remove and set aside for 5 minutes for the juices to settle.

6. Divide the pasta among 4 individual plates and dot the top of each with olives. Place a salmon fillet in the middle of each pasta bed. Spoon the sauce on top, sprinkle the caviar over all, and serve right away.

DECONSTRUCTED LASAGNE WITH CREAMED SPINACH, CHANTERELLES, AND PINE NUTS

ALTHOUGH FIRST USED TO DESCRIBE A METHOD of critical thinking as applied to interpreting text, *deconstructing* now simply means dividing something into its components in order to understand its whole. Deconstructed lasagne follows the theme. It's a facile assembly, no architectonic building required. The elements are cooked separately, gently tossed together, and served on a platter. It's a family dish of the highest order.

1. Preheat the oven to 400°F. Lightly grease a baking sheet.

2. Spread the chanterelles in a single layer on the baking sheet and sprinkle lightly with salt. Place in the oven and roast until they are beginning to dry out and turn golden, about 15 minutes. Spread the pine nuts on the baking sheet, keeping them separate from the chanterelles, and toast until golden, about 5 minutes. Remove the baking sheet from the oven and set aside.

3. Make the creamed spinach.

4. Bring a large pot of salted water to a boil. Break the lasagne sheets into approximately 4-by-1-inch pieces, add to the water, and cook until al dente, about 7 minutes. Drain the noodles and return them to the pot. Add the chanterelles and toss to mix. Gently stir in the creamed spinach, tomato, and mozzarella and season with salt. Transfer to a large platter or serving bowl, sprinkle the pine nuts over the top, and serve right away.

SERVES 4

INGREDIENTS:

Oil, for greasing the baking sheet

8 ounces chanterelle mushrooms, wiped clean, stem ends trimmed and cut lengthwise into ½-inch-thick slices

Kosher or fine sea salt

¼ cup pine nuts

Creamed Spinach with Chèvre (recipe follows)

12 ounces lasagne noodles

1 large ripe red tomato, cored and cut into ½-inch dice

4 ounces fresh mozzarella cheese, cut into ½-inch pieces

THE AMERICAN PINE NUT AND THE TRIBES OF THE WEST

PINE NUTS ARE THE EDIBLE SEEDS of pine trees. Among all the types of pine trees that glorify the globe, about twenty-eight produce seeds large enough to eat.

North America is blessed with some of the most fruitful and tasty of those species that bear nuts large enough to be a food crop, in particular the single-leaf piñon, the Mexican piñon, and the Colorado piñon. These constituted a major source of food for many Native American tribes, among them the Paiutes and Washoe of the Great Basin, the Hopi of the Southwest, and the Shoshone of the Rocky Mountains.

Pine nuts are not generated by pine trees on a yearly or even predictable basis. An area of pine forest will produce nut-bearing cones about once every seven years. The nuts contain the highest amount of protein of any nut or seed. Before the coming of white settlers, and even up until World War II, the mountains and valleys these native people occupied were lush with fertile pine trees and produced virtually millions of tons of pine nuts. Huge numbers of trees have been taken down for fuel, for construction, to clear land for ranches, farms, and cities. Today, instead of harvesting and selling our own pine nuts, we import about eight million pounds of them a year from Italy and China, usually shelled. In their shells, the pine nuts keep for a long time. Unfortunately, once shelled and transported, they lose much of their flavor. Many of the tribes who once lived on the nuts continue to have exclusive rights to harvest them. Often at roadside stands, farmers' markets, and local grocery stores around the West, and choosy markets in the East, rich, still full-flavored American native pine nuts are available.

CREAMED SPINACH WITH CHEVRE

CREAMED SPINACH IS a standard side dish in classic steak houses and seafood restaurants. It is often deemed velvety enough with just the spinach and cream. Other times a little tarragon, nutmeg, or a touch of dill is added. To unite a scattered lasagne, creamed spinach gussied up with goat cheese is a smart choice. It also makes a tempting filling for ravioli or blanket for broiled whole mushrooms. Soft goat cheeses vary widely on the mild-to-tangy taste spectrum. For creamed spinach, choose one that is at the tangy end.

MAKES 2 CUPS

1 pound fresh baby spinach, leaves and tender stems only

1 tablespoon butter

1 large clove garlic, minced or pressed

1 cup heavy whipping cream

½ cup soft goat cheese, at room temperature

Kosher or fine sea salt

Freshly ground black or white pepper

1. Rinse and drain the spinach and place it, still wet, in a large pot over medium-high heat or in a microwave-safe bowl on high and cook, stirring once or twice, until thoroughly wilted but still bright green, about 5 minutes either way. Drain and, when cool enough to handle, squeeze out as much water as you can and finely chop the spinach.

2. Melt the butter in a large sauté pan over medium heat. Add the garlic and sauté until softened, about 2 minutes. Add the cream and goat cheese and whisk until smooth and beginning to boil and thicken, about 2 minutes. Stir in the spinach and season with salt and pepper. Serve right away or set aside and reheat briefly before using.

SHRIMP RAVIOLI IN WONTON WRAPPERS
WITH SHRIMP CURLS AND
GINGER CHIVE OIL

THE SECOND PASTA DISH, after spaghetti with red sauce, that met with wild approval in America was ravioli. Rather than a simple noodle, ravioli are made by stuffing rounds or squares of pasta dough with a filling, something like a pillow. To make ravioli from scratch Italian style is an endeavor, but there's a shortcut that relies on prepared fresh wonton wrappers. Wonton wrappers have the same ingredients as Italian egg pasta and a similar taste and soft texture when cooked. They are available in the refrigerated produce section of many supermarkets, usually in packages of forty-eight, alongside the miso and tofu. Unused wrappers keep in the refrigerator for up to one month.

The pasta squares can be stuffed with anything. Use the time saved with the wonton wrapper shortcut to prepare an extraordinary filling. Here, cued by Asian pasta, shrimp is sauced in a light oil emulsion of lime and ginger, which takes the ravioli in a truly special direction.

1. Bring a small pot of water to a boil. Add the chives, then strain them out right away. Spread the chives on a paper towel and squeeze to wring out the water. Transfer to a food processor, add the ginger and oil, and process until emulsified, about 1 minute. Season with salt to taste and set aside.

2. Pull off the shells and tails from the

SERVES 4

INGREDIENTS:

1 cup (2 to 3 bunches) coarsely chopped fresh chives

1 teaspoon peeled fresh ginger, pressed in a garlic press, peel reserved

½ cup peanut or extra virgin olive oil

Kosher or fine sea salt

1 pound extra large shrimp (26 to 30)

2 teaspoons fresh lime juice

2 tablespoons chopped fresh cilantro leaves

1 teaspoon minced or pressed garlic

⅛ teaspoon Asian sesame oil

32 wonton wrappers

shrimp and devein them. Set the shells and tails aside. Cut 8 of the shrimp in half lengthwise and set aside in the refrigerator. Coarsely chop the remaining shrimp in the food processor. Add the lime juice, cilantro, garlic, and sesame oil and process until finely chopped almost to a paste. Season with salt.

3. Place about 2 teaspoons of the chopped shrimp mixture in the center of each of 16 wonton squares. Top each with another square and seal around the edges with water. The ravioli may be cooked right away or covered with a barely damp towel and set aside in the refrigerator for up to 2 hours.

4. To cook the ravioli, fill a deep, wide pot three-quarters full of water and bring to a boil over high heat. Add the reserved shrimp shells and tails, along with the reserved ginger peel. Cook briskly until the shrimp shells and tails are quite pink and the water smells aromatic, 5 minutes. With a wire strainer, lift out and discard the shell and tails and ginger peel. Bring the broth to a boil again, add the shrimp halves, and cook until they curl and turn pink, 2 to 3 minutes. Remove them with the wire strainer and set aside in a warm place.

5. With the broth boiling, slide as many ravioli as will fit without crowding into the pot and cook until they are soft and opaque all the way through, 3 to 4 minutes. Lift them out with the wire strainer and transfer them to a large plate. Continue with another batch, topping off the broth with more water if necessary, until all the ravioli are cooked.

6. To serve, divide the ravioli and some of the broth from their resting plate among 4 large, high-lipped serving plates. Set 4 of the cooked shrimp spirals around each serving of the ravioli and drizzle with a generous amount of ginger chive oil over all. Serve right away.

PEANUT OIL

WHEN AFRICANS WERE BROUGHT TO THE AMERICAS, along with them came one of their main foods, the groundnut, or peanut.

Peanuts contain a veritable vat of oil that is nutritious, containing 40 to 50 percent fat, 20 to 50 percent protein, 10 to 20 percent carbohydrate, and 6 to 8 percent valuable fatty acids. In addition, peanut oil has a high smoke point—the temperature at which it begins to smoke—far higher than olive oil, and so it rapidly became widely selected as a frying medium. The people of South Carolina were using significant amounts of peanut oil for cooking by 1800. The culminating value of the oil, of course, is the fact that it emits the flavor and aroma of peanuts so that when used to fry or as a taste-enhancing drizzle, a trace of pulsy peanut comes with it.

BULGUR, SWEET POTATO, AND KALAMATA OLIVE PILAF

TWO FOODS, ONE FROM AFAR AND ONE FROM CLOSER TO HOME, began to appear on our plates in new ways in the last decades of the twentieth century. The first, bulgur, is a wheat product resulting from wheat kernels that have been saturated with steam until plump, dried, and then crushed into fine, medium-size, or coarse granules. As a grain base for pilafs, with lamb, poultry, or vegetables, it had been the staple across much of the Old World for millennia—and still is. The second, sweet potatoes from the New World, have long been boiled, baked, roasted, or pureed for pie. They also turn out great french fries, potato chips, and mashes. Put together with onion, herb, and olive, the result is a pilaf at once nutty and mellow, softly sweet with a salty kick. Diners will savor the first helping and request seconds right away. It's a comfort food and filling meal that begs for repeats.

1. Heat the olive oil in a medium-size pot over medium-high heat. Add the onion, sweet potato, and bulgur and sauté until the onion and bulgur are golden brown and translucent, 6 to 8 minutes.

2. Add the broth, wine, olives, oregano, salt, and pepper and stir to mix. Bring to a boil, reduce the heat to low, cover, and simmer until the bulgur is soft all the way through, 15 to 20 minutes. Remove from the heat and set aside with the lid on to steam and fluff up for 5 to 10 minutes.

3. Transfer the pilaf to a bowl, sprinkle the parsley over the top, and serve.

SERVES 6 TO 8

INGREDIENTS:

- 2 tablespoons extra virgin olive oil
- 1 medium-size yellow or white onion, finely chopped (about ¾ cup)
- 1 large sweet potato (about 12 ounces), peeled and cut into ¼-inch pieces
- ¾ cup medium-grind bulgur
- 1 cup low-sodium chicken broth or water
- ⅓ cup white wine
- ⅓ cup pitted kalamata olives, chopped
- 1 tablespoon fresh oregano leaves, chopped
- ½ teaspoon kosher or fine sea salt
- ¼ teaspoon freshly ground black pepper
- 2 tablespoons chopped fresh parsley, for garnish

GERMANS IN AMERICA

People who claim all or some German descent are one of the most sizable groups to immigrate to North American shores, and today they make up an enormous proportion of the American population. But what is little known are the twists and turns that compelled so many German speakers to leave their homes for the unknown frontier of the New World.

The first German immigrants came early. Several settlers of Jamestown in 1607 were Germans, and Peter Minuet, the governor of Dutch New Netherlands in 1626 and later the Swedish colony in Delaware, was from Germany. Then in 1683, thirteen families of German Mennonites seeking religious freedom arrived and founded Germantown just north of where Philadelphia now sits. They were followed throughout the 1700s by waves of other small German-speaking religious groups: the Swiss Mennonites, Baptist Dunkers, Schwenkfelders, Amish, Waldensians, and many belonging to the major religious sects, Lutherans and the Reformed Church. The majority found homes in Pennsylvania. Most came as "redemptioners"; that is, they agreed to work for up to seven years in exchange for free boat passage. They worked their years mostly building the Conestoga wagons that carried pioneers west and, once free, found land to farm. They were joined by Roman Catholic Germans who had been expelled from Austria and settled Ebenezer, Georgia, and the Moravians, who started a new city, Bethlehem, Pennsylvania.

By the 1820s, the Pennsylvania "Dutch," as the Germans were called, had introduced the custom of a decorated tree at Christmas, Santa Claus, the Easter bunny, and Easter eggs. Germans had entered the world of trade, John Jacob Astor being the most prominent.

FREEDOM TO GROW

IN THE DECADE OF THE 1850s, more than one million German immigrants streamed into America, 215,000 in 1854 alone. One of them was Adolphus Busch from the Rhineland, who settled in St. Louis and, taking advantage of the Great Plains' overflowing grains, started a company called

Anheuser-Busch Brewing Company. Another was Margarethe Schurz, who opened America's first kindergarten. By 1860 there were 1.3 million German immigrants in America running two hundred German-language newspapers and Germans had become a powerful political bloc.

DIRT AND DETERMINATION

THEN, IN 1872, a large number of German Mennonite farming families who had escaped religious persecution earlier in the century by settling on the broad steppes of Ukraine had their right to live there revoked by the tsarist rulers. Still seeking religious freedom, they decided to move to America. With them they brought the hard winter wheat they had grown on the steppes and, as the Kansas and Nebraska territories had soil much like what they knew, headed for America's newly opened, as yet unfarmed Great Plains.

More than a hundred thousand arrived the first year. They built communal houses, negotiated for plots, and established villages. In due time they spread out across Kansas, Nebraska, the Dakotas, and Minnesota. They bought livestock and introduced the practice of constructing half-buried sod houses before they built permanent house-barn, dual-purpose homes. They wasted no time in planting gardens, orchards, and flowerbeds with seeds, bulbs, and cuttings

they carried with them. They realized they had at hand the perfect environment to grow the grains they knew—wheat, barley, rye—and discovered they could add an American crop they had never known before, corn. There is little doubt that the German Mennonites were hugely instrumental in turning the Great Plains into the breadbasket of America.

All told some fifty-eight million people of German descent reside in America. With them and their forefathers also came their foods: the frankfurter or hot dog of baseball fame, some say the hamburger from the German ships sailing out of Hamburg with cargoes of immigrants; pickled cabbage and cucumbers; breaded chops; soups; delicatessen fare; pretzels; pumpernickel; Bavarian breads, buns, and rolls; all kinds of kuchen (cakes); and noodles before they were called pasta. And for drinking, fruity, full-bodied white wines in Rhineland style and many brews of beer.

RISOTTO WITH WOODLAND MUSHROOMS AND CHICKPEAS

INGREDIENTS:

4½ cups water

¾ cup dried mushrooms, such as morels, shiitake caps, or chanterelles

6 tablespoons (¾ stick) butter

6 ounces fresh button mushrooms, stems trimmed, sliced ¼ inch thick

1 teaspoon kosher or fine sea salt

2 teaspoons fresh lemon juice

⅓ cup finely chopped yellow or white onion

1¼ cups Arborio or other risotto rice

½ cup white wine

¾ cup cooked chickpeas

½ cup freshly grated Parmesan cheese

THE RISOTTOS OF NORTHERN ITALY ARE TEXTURAL, creamy rice dishes quite unlike any other. They can be straightforward, with only meat broth and Parmesan cheese supplying richness to the rice. Or they can enfold an unusual combination of foods in a one-dish meal. The boon of risottos for home cooking is that with the medium of toothsome rice, the ingredients can be specially thought out or spontaneously put together with components from a pantry expedition. The Texas rice industry has recognized the flavor absorption advantage of risotto rice and now produces domestic Arborio and other risotto rices. Here an American take offers fresh and dried mushrooms, which lend a woodsy nose and make the dish suave. Chickpeas add substance and round out the protein value. The water used to soak the dried mushrooms so they plump up acts like a light vegetable broth, so there's no need for a meat stock. The dish is vegetarian.

1. Combine the water and dried mushrooms in a small saucepan. Set aside to rehydrate for 20 minutes or so. Lift the mushrooms out of the water, coarsely chop them, and set them aside.

2. Heat the soaking water over high heat until almost boiling. Set it aside and keep warm.

3. Melt 2 tablespoons of the butter in a large sauté pan over medium-high heat. Add the fresh mushrooms, salt, and lemon juice and sauté until barely cooked, about 5 minutes. Transfer the mushrooms to a bowl and set aside in a warm place.

4. Add the remaining butter to the sauté pan over medium-high heat. Add the onion and sauté until wilted, 2 to 3 minutes. Add the rice and rehydrated dried mushrooms and sauté until the rice becomes translucent, 2 to 3 minutes.

5. Add the wine and stir gently and continuously with a wooden spoon until absorbed, 2 to 3 minutes. Add ½ cup of the warm mushroom-soaking liquid and continue stirring until it is absorbed, 2 minutes.

6. Add 2 cups more of the soaking liquid ½ cup at a time, stirring until each addition is completely absorbed and making sure the rice doesn't stick to the bottom of the pan.

7. Add the remaining 2 cups soaking liquid and the chickpeas and cook, stirring from time to time until the rice is just al dente and the liquid is mostly absorbed but the mixture is still very moist and creamy, 10 to 15 minutes, depending on the dimensions of the pan.

8. Remove from the heat and stir in the Parmesan cheese. Top with the sautéed fresh mushrooms and serve right away.

⊙ TIPS: A PERFECT RISOTTO is creamy and still somewhat moist with al dente grains that invite you to chew them. To achieve this, risotto requires risotto rice, which is plump and short to medium grain. Risotto rice has been developed to cook up soft on the outside yet remain firm in the center. Regular long-grain, short-grain, or brown rices are not the same and cannot make a proper risotto. Familiar varieties of risotto rice are Arborio, Carnaroli, and Vialone Nano.

Parmesan cheese is the spiritual essence of moist risottos, so it is essential to use the good sort, preferably Parmigiano Reggiano, a fine aged Asiago or grana, or one of the new American Parmesans. All fit the bill.

Risotto is best served in individual wide, shallow bowls.

RISOTTO WITH ELK SUMMER SAUSAGE AND EDAMAME

SERVES 4

INGREDIENTS:

4½ cups low-sodium chicken broth

4 tablespoons (½ stick) butter

⅓ cup thinly sliced scallion, white and light green parts only

1 cup Arborio or other risotto rice

½ cup white wine

Large pinch of saffron threads

5 ounces elk or other summer sausage, cut into ½-inch cubes (about 1 cup)

¾ cup shelled edamame, defrosted if frozen

⅓ cup freshly grated Parmesan cheese

THE WORD *FUSION* **DOESN'T BEGIN TO DESCRIBE** how melded American cooking has become. Of all the out-there ideas explored, developed, and kept or rejected on the fascinating journey to seek out the best and most delicious of what American integrated cuisine can be, a risotto of game and Japanese edamame (fresh soybeans) comes close to number one. Fresh or frozen lima beans or fresh fava beans can substitute. Diversions with the dish continue. Rather than onion, the risotto features scallions, and it employs saffron, usually found in the more basic risotto Milanese. Another element shows up to preserve the risotto tradition: a healthy amount of Parmesan cheese.

1. Heat the broth in a small saucepan over high heat until almost boiling. Set aside and keep warm.

2. Melt the butter in a large saucepan or sauté pan over medium-high heat. Add the scallion and sauté until wilted, 1 to 2 minutes.

Add the rice and sauté until translucent, about 2 minutes.

3. Add the wine and stir gently and continuously with a wooden spoon until absorbed, 2 to 3 minutes. Add ½ cup of the broth and continue stirring until it is absorbed, 2 minutes.

4. Add 2 cups more of the broth ½ cup at a time, stirring until each addition is completely absorbed and making sure the rice doesn't stick to the bottom of the pan.

5. Stir the saffron into the remaining 2 cups broth and add it to the rice along with the sausage. Continue stirring until the rice is al dente and most of the liquid is absorbed but the mixture

is still moist and creamy, 10 to 15 minutes, depending on the dimensions of the pan.

6. Stir in the edamame and cheese and serve right away.

THE SUMMER IN SUMMER SAUSAGE

SUMMER SAUSAGE REFERS to any sausage that can be kept without refrigeration. It evolved as a way to preserve meat for later use either as a cold cut or in cooked dishes. Hunters made summer sausage to keep game meat—elk, venison, and moose—although beef and pork are more common fodder nowadays. Once the meat is seasoned, always including salt (an important component in the curing process) and stuffed into a sausage casing, the preserving can be managed in two ways: by drying or by smoking. As with other sausages, an essential part of the formula and savor is the seasoning mix. In the basic version, mustard seed, black pepper, garlic, and sugar are used.

A celebrated Mennonite variation employs beef as the meat. In other summer sausage variations, such as Italian fresh salami or French cervelat, the meat might be pork animated with hot pepper or herbs.

Despite its name—and who knows how it got the appellation?—summer sausage is usually made in the fall, at the end of hunting season.

RISOTTO WITH SHRIMP, SCALLOPS, AND SUNDRIED TOMATOES

INGREDIENTS:

- 4½ cups low-sodium chicken broth
- 2 tablespoons butter
- ¾ cup sundried tomatoes in oil, drained, oil reserved, coarsely chopped
- ¼ cup finely chopped yellow or white onion
- ½ cup coarsely chopped celery leaves with some rib
- 1¼ cups Arborio or other risotto rice
- ½ cup white wine
- 8 ounces large sea scallops, cut into ½-inch cubes
- 12 extra large fresh shrimp peeled, deveined (if necessary), tails left on
- ⅓ cup grated Parmesan cheese
- 2 tablespoons chopped flat-leaf parsley or cilantro, for garnish

FROM THEIR NORTHERN ITALY ORIGIN came three renditions of risotto. One is vegetable risotto, containing legumes or fresh garden accents; the second offers bits of savory meats, such as bacon or sausage; and the third features glorious shellfish, such as clams, mussels, and shrimp. Wine accentuates them. Combining cheese with shellfish is not a thought that might come immediately to mind in American cooking, but it turns out it's a cultivated pairing around the northern Mediterranean from Greece to Spain, including Italy and Sicily. It takes advantage of both the waters and the shores they lap against.

1. Heat the broth in a small saucepan over high heat until almost boiling. Set aside and keep warm.

2. Melt the butter in 2 tablespoons of the reserved sundried tomato oil in a wide saucepan or deep sauté pan over medium-high heat. Add the onion and celery and sauté until transparent, about 2 minutes. Add the rice and sauté until it becomes translucent, about 2 minutes.

3. Add the wine and stir gently and continuously with a wooden spoon until absorbed, 2 to 3 minutes. Add ½ cup of the broth and continue stirring until it is absorbed. Add 2 cups more of the broth ½ cup at a time, stirring until each addition is completely absorbed and making sure the rice doesn't stick to the bottom of the pan.

4. Add the remaining 2 cups broth and the tomatoes and continue stirring until the rice is al dente and most of the liquid is absorbed but the mixture

is still moist and creamy, 10 to 15 minutes, depending on the dimensions of the pan.

5. Add the scallops and shrimp, stir gently to mix them in, and continue cooking until the scallops are barely firm and the shrimp is barely pink, 4 to 5 minutes.

6. Remove from the heat and stir in the cheese. Sprinkle the parsley over the top and serve right away.

HOW RICE GOT TO THE UNITED STATES

IN 1685 A DUTCH SHIP WITH AN ENGLISH CAPTAIN sailed from the island of Madagascar lying to the east of South Africa, around Africa's horn, up and across the Atlantic Ocean, where it encountered a terrible storm. Battered and limping, it inched its way into the port of Charleston, South Carolina, then called Charles Towne, where helpful colonists set about repairing the boat. To repay the helpers, the captain made a gift to a local planter of a small amount of "Golden Seede Rice" taken from the fields of Africa. It proved to be far more than the modest gift the captain intended. Instead it turned into a comestible that was an economic boon of incalculable measure to North America. The precious golden seeds of rice, named for their color, became the forerunner of America's most famous rice, Carolina Golden.

The low-lying marshlands washed by the tidal rivers of the Carolinas and Georgia had been of little use before. The land was flat and fertile, but twice-a-day tides pushed so much fresh river water up that nothing would grow there. But rice could, and from the first field of rice the colonists planted came the next and next, until rice fields virtually blanketed the Carolinas and surrounding states.

Rice became a crop that, almost more than any other, established the demand for slaves. Rice farming is extremely hand-labor-intensive. Even with an ox-drawn plow, a small rice plantation of a few hundred acres required as many as three hundred laborers to prepare the soil, plant, harvest, and thresh the grain. On the sweat of this labor, Carolina Gold grew so splendidly it became the standard of high-quality rice throughout the world.

Then came the Civil War, which effectively ended the plantation era. Atlantic coast hurricanes were also intermittently devastating the rice crop. Although returning soldiers parceled out plantation lands into smaller rice fields, the high labor costs put the rice business into a depression. That is, until 1884, the year that the machine age entered every aspect of American agricultural life. In the same year an Iowa wheat farmer pointed out that the broad prairie land of western Louisiana and eastern Texas had soils that, like Iowa's, could hold up heavy equipment, and America's rice industry moved to Arkansas, Louisiana, Mississippi, Missouri, and Texas. Rice growers took to mechanization and dry field cultivation.

Even farther west, the Gold Rush in California brought an influx of forty thousand Chinese workers whose staple food was rice. To feed them, rice production nearby became essential. Again with mechanization, the farmers in the delta region of the Sacramento River found rice would grow on the alluvial riverbanks where no other crop had succeeded. By 1920 California had turned into one of America's main rice-producing states. Recently, southern Florida has joined in. Nowadays, rice remains a major American crop; rather than being exported, 90 percent of it is consumed within America.

WILD RICE AND PECANS:
TWO ALL-AMERICAN FOODS

WILD RICE

ACROSS THE NORTHERN GREAT PLAINS, where many forest-rimmed lakes and rivers embroider the land, there prosper large expanses of America's only indigenous grain-producing grass, wild rice.

Wild rice is any of four species of grass plants that grow submerged in shallow ponds and slow-flowing streams. Often only the flowering head of the grass rises above the water.

By far the most widely known and harvested is *Zizania palustris* from North American waters. As Americans eschewed it for cultivated wheat, corn, and rye, it became a scarce and rarely eaten commodity.

Late in the twentieth century, as the grain's great nutritional value was determined to be a storehouse of protein and minerals, wild rice increased in popularity. To meet the interest, commercial cultivation began, that is, insofar as wild rice can be cultivated. Dry field planting failed, so cultivated wild rice is grown in artificial or dyked lakes alongside natural bodies of water. Still the term *cultivated* cannot really apply. Wild rice is essentially unchanged from its wild form. Its seeds cannot be planted directly but must be germinated in water, although a hardier variety with a more shatterproof, easier sprouting kernel has been developed. As a crop it is merely "encouraged" and harvested as before. A better term for its cultivation is probably *farm grown*. There are companies that still harvest "wild" wild rice by canoe and it is worth seeking them out for their excellent product.

Wild rice has an incomparable taste and texture. Its flavor is far more seedlike than conventional rice's, and its grains, even when cooked, retain a nutty toothsomeness that still smacks of the wild, as if, for serving, it would better suit a bark plate than a china one.

PECANS

SETTLERS FIRST STEPPING ONTO AMERICAN SOIL came upon a broad, sheltering, previously unknown hardwood tree. It produced nuts in such abundance that tribal people not only gathered them in quantity to feast on but also made a fermented drink from the nut meat, called *powcohicora,* which Europeans truncated into *hickory*. The nut itself they called *paccan,* a generic term meaning any nut so hard it had to be cracked with a stone, which Europeans changed to *pecan*.

The hickory tree grew from the Atlantic coast all the way to the Mississippi and into the river valleys of Mexico. It was particularly copious across the South, and Native Americans there long cultivated the tree.

The demand for the nut so increased that a call came out to develop hickories with bigger, better nuts. In 1822, a South Carolina farmer named Abner Landrum chanced on a way to graft domestic plants from superior wild selections, but his innovation was lost until 1876, when a former slave from Louisiana, known simply as Antoine, rediscovered Landrum's propagation technique and cloned 126 trees.

The hickory is a gorgeous, prepossessing tree that grows to more than a hundred feet tall and can live to be a thousand years old. Today the tree is most widely raised in Georgia, Louisiana, Mississippi, Florida, New Mexico, and Texas, where it is the state tree. Next to peanuts, pecans are the second most popular nut in America. They are most often associated with pecan pie, pecan pralines, and as a crumble on sweet potato soufflé. They also have found contemporary uses, in salads, meat crusts (page 152, Pecan-Crusted Elk Medallions with Apple Jalapeño Jam), and stuffings; toasted for a snack; in cookies; or, as here, in a singular and satisfying dinner pie.

WILD RICE AND PECAN CUSTARD IN A CRUST: A SAVORY AMERICAN PIE

THERE IS SOMETHING GRATIFYING about an eggy quiche-style pie for dinner. Like a potpie or dessert pie, the meal comes in a crunchy, flaky pleasing crust. Sometimes the custard filling stands alone, and sometimes it contains surprise elements. The diversion here is a different, sweetly mollifying all-American quiche. America's native grain, wild rice, and native nut, the pecan, commingle with rustic warmth and woodsy appeal. Two of the preparations can be done in advance: making the pastry dough and cooking the wild rice. With those set aside in the refrigerator, the cook is free until it's time to finish the recipe and bake a beautiful pie up to two days later.

1. Make and chill the pastry dough. Bring it to room temperature when ready to use.

2. Combine the wild rice with 1 cup of water in a small, heavy pot and bring to a boil over high heat. Reduce the heat to low, cover the pot, and cook until the grains break open and puff out, 30 to 50 minutes, depending on the age and quality of the rice. Remove from the heat, drain off any remaining water, and set aside at room temperature for up to several hours or store in the refrigerator overnight.

3. When ready to make the pie, preheat the oven to 375°F.

4. Roll out the pastry dough and line a 9-inch pie or tart pan with it. Set aside in the refrigerator.

5. Toast the pecans in a microwave oven or ungreased skillet over medium-high heat until lightly golden, about 3 minutes either way. Melt the butter in a small pan over medium heat until foaming. Add the onion and cook until it begins to wilt, about 2 minutes.

SERVES 6

INGREDIENTS:

Pastry Dough (recipe follows)

½ cup wild rice

2 tablespoons chopped pecans

2 tablespoons butter

2 tablespoons chopped yellow or white onion

4 large eggs

2 cups half-and-half

Pinch of kosher or fine sea salt

6. Lightly beat the eggs in a large bowl. Add the half-and-half and whisk until well blended. Stir in the onion, pecans, wild rice, and salt. Pour the mixture into the crust and bake until the top is rising up and golden brown, 40 to 45 minutes.

7. Serve the pie warm or at room temperature.

PASTRY DOUGH

WHEN WHEAT FLOUR and shortening are bound with a little water, the result is magical. From that simple formula, cooks and cuisines have developed a world of pastries for an astounding number of dishes, piquant to sweet, baked to fried. It's quite a wonder. Here's an easy rendition of that miracle, made easier and more rapid using a food processor. The dough is useful for wherever you'd like a pastry in the dish. If the dough is to be used for a sweet pie, one tablespoon sugar can be added.

MAKES ONE 9-INCH CRUST

1½ cups unbleached all-purpose flour

Pinch of kosher or fine sea salt

8 tablespoons (1 stick) cold butter, cut into ½-inch-thick pieces

3 tablespoons cold water, plus more as needed

1. Combine the flour and salt in a food processor (see Tips) and pulse once or twice to mix. Add the butter to the processor bowl and pulse until the mixture is crumbly but not coming together in a ball. Add the 2 tablespoons water and pulse again until a pinch of the mixture just comes together when pressed. If the mixture is too dry, add a bit more water, 1 teaspoon at a time.

2. Gather all the dough together, wrap it in plastic wrap, and press to form a smooth ball. Chill in the refrigerator for 1 hour or up to 2 days. Bring to room temperature before rolling it out.

⊙TIPS: EASY, NO-TROUBLE PASTRY DOUGH.

⊕ To get a small amount of truly cold water for making pastry, drop a few ice cubes into a cup of water and let sit for a few minutes while you begin the recipe.

⊕ When making pastry dough in a food processor, don't be tempted to run the machine until the mixture comes together on its own. By then it will be overworked and won't bake up light and flaky. Rather, gather it up while it is still not quite cohering but comes together when a small piece is pinched.

⊕ Don't skip the chilling: Chilling dough in the refrigerator allows time for the dough to relax and become firm enough to roll out smoothly without breaking apart.

⊕ You can also make pastry dough by hand using fork or pastry cutter.

QUINOA BURGERS
WITH TOFU, CHARD, SHIITAKES, AND DICED TOMATO SALSA

OFTEN IN CREATING DISHES TO SUIT EVERYONE—not too spicy, fitting for vegetarians—necessity turns into serendipity. One such is the most satisfying quinoa veggie burger. Quinoa originated in the Andes of South America and has been an essential food for more than six thousand years. There it is called the mother of all grains. It is light and fluffy, grassy in taste, and so appealing it has lately taken America by storm. Combined with tofu, the nutrition pedigree of a quinoa burger becomes double blue ribbon. A forthright tomato salsa brings all together in a new American burger that tells a scrumptious taste tale of both the Old and New Worlds.

1. Rinse and drain the quinoa and place it in a medium-size pot with 1 cup water. Bring to a boil, cover, and simmer until the water is absorbed, 10 to 15 minutes, depending on the size of the pot.

2. In a medium-size bowl, using your hands, knead together the mushrooms, tofu, bread crumbs, quinoa, chard, shallot, chives, ginger, zest, eggs, salt, and pepper to taste, until the mixture coheres. Divide it into 6 portions and pat each into a ¾-inch-thick burger. Set aside in the refrigerator to chill for 15 to 30 minutes.

3. Make the salsa.

4. Melt the butter in a large skillet over medium-high heat until foaming. Place as many burgers as will fit in the skillet without touching and fry, turning once, until golden on both sides, 7 to 8 minutes per side. Transfer to a platter and repeat until all the burgers are cooked.

5. Garnish each burger with a dollop of the salsa and serve alongside a basket with the toasted buns, if using.

MAKES SIX 3½-INCH PATTIES

INGREDIENTS:

½ cup quinoa

⅔ cup finely chopped shiitake mushroom caps

½ of a 14-ounce carton firm tofu, mashed with a fork

1½ cups fine bread crumbs, preferably homemade (page 41)

1 cup thinly shredded chard, blanched for 1 minute

1 tablespoon minced shallot

1 tablespoon finely chopped fresh chives

1 teaspoon minced peeled fresh ginger

1 teaspoon minced lemon zest

2 large eggs, lightly beaten

1 teaspoon kosher or fine sea salt

Freshly ground black pepper

Diced Tomato Salsa (recipe follows), for serving

3 tablespoons butter

Toasted buns for serving (optional)

DICED TOMATO SALSA

A RELATIVE OF THE MANY Mexican and Latin American salsas, this one is similar to an Old World vinaigrette but with more substance. It can be used to crown and add pizzazz to plain grilled fish or chicken breasts or simply cooked vegetables, such as potatoes, summer squash, and cauliflower, or to dress a salad of sturdy leaves like escarole or chicories. The salsa is best used the day it is made; after that, its brightness fades.

MAKES ½ CUP

1 medium-size ripe tomato, peeled, seeded, and cut into ¼-inch dice

1 tablespoon minced red or white onion

1 tablespoon chopped fresh cilantro leaves

1 teaspoon finely chopped fresh green or red chile

1 teaspoon chopped fresh mint leaves

1 tablespoon fresh lime juice

1 tablespoon extra virgin olive oil

½ teaspoon kosher or fine sea salt

Mix together all the ingredients in a small bowl. Use right away or set aside at room temperature for up to several hours.

QUINOA:
A NEW WORLD GRAIN OF GOODNESS

QUINOA is a life-sustaining plant native to the Andes Mountains in what is now Peru and Bolivia. Rather than a true cereal grain like rice, wheat, and corn, quinoa is not the kernel of a grass but instead a seed gathered from a member of the goosefoot, or *Chenopodium,* genus, which includes beets and rhubarb. Though it fed the Aztec and Inca civilizations that peopled those high-altitude places, somewhere along the way, through time, it got shuffled aside for grain imports from the Old World, wheat and rice, and the New World's other great grain, corn, and remained in the shadows until recently. So new is quinoa to modern American cooking that a mention of it in writing requires help with its pronunciation (keen-wah). It has indeed been rediscovered, thanks to contemporary chefs and many fairly recent cookbooks devoted to grains. It is now grown in the Colorado Rockies.

OTHER GRAINS OF THE PLAINS

BARLEY

Barley, along with einkorn and emmer wheats, was the first grain tamed from wild grasses. Half the United States production is used as animal feed. A large part of the rest is used for malting and is a key ingredient in beer and whiskey production. It's also a main ingredient in soups and stews. In some places and during hard times it has been used as a coffee substitute. It comes hulled, with hulls still on, dehulled with bran and germ, and pearl.

BUCKWHEAT

Buckwheat is not a grain, but rather like quinoa is a flowering plant with a grainlike seed. Buckwheat, sometimes also *beechwheat,* comes from the resemblance of its triangular seeds to the large nuts of the beech tree and its wheatlike use. There are two main genera plus a weedlike cousin. One is native to Eurasia; the other is indigenous to America, where it has been grown since colonial days. In Europe it has long been used in its raw, untoasted kernel form, as a porridge called *kasha.* It has undergone a resurgence in America, especially in breakfast cereal, due to its full-bodied taste and its nutrition. It is gluten-free and rich in protein.

CORN, OR MAIZE

Corn is the most widely grown crop in the Americas. Sweet (or green) corn is eaten straight off the cob at countless summer picnics and backyard barbecues; as kernels in muffins, pancakes, spoon breads, and chowder (Crowded Chowder with Cod, Shrimp, and Corn, page 69); creamed for a classic American side dish, and more. There are other corns besides sweet corn, each with a different advantage.

Dent corn, also called field corn, has kernels with both hard and soft starch that become dented in the middle with maturity. It is used to make hominy grits and for animal feed.

Flint corn has hard horned or rounded short and flat kernels. Much is grown in South America and Europe. It is used for polenta. Flint corn has two additional varieties, one called waxy, for its appearance; it is used to make a starch thickener for cooking. The second is popcorn, which is grown on small ears and has pointed kernels with a hard exterior.

Two other types are Indian corn, with multicolored kernels, used for autumn holiday table decorations, and flour corn, also known as soft corn or squaw corn. Sometimes blue in color, it is mostly grown for baked goods, blue corn tortillas, and beer.

MILLET

Millets are a small-seeded cereal crop of which there are many varieties. It is usually cooked into a porridge or a couscous-like dish in African cuisine. In America, it is mostly used for animal, particularly bird, feed.

OATS

During the time wheat and barley were being domesticated, oats probably grew alongside them as a weed in Asia Minor. Though the popularity of oats was slow to spread, the fact that they grew more successfully than wheat in cold and rough climates made them a mainstay of the harsh-weather areas of Europe. In those places, oat porridge became sustenance food. Elsewhere, oats were mostly thought of as animal food.

Oats come to the table in six ways: oat groats, or whole oats, needing long cooking; oat bran, much used in baking; steel-cut, or Irish, oats, groats that are chopped into tiny pebbles; rolled or old-fashioned oats, groats flattened by large rollers, the sort in the familiar round box; instant oats, which are chopped groats precooked, dried, and smashed; and oat flour, which has no gluten. And, the most popular form in America, in little Os (called Cheerios), a breakfast cereal introduced in 1941, still today America's best-selling cereal.

RYE

Rye is a member of the wheat and barley family. It originally grew wild in eastern Turkey and was used early, probably in mixes with other grains. It is grown on every continent, in the United States largely in the Great Plains, and, as well as being used for bread and crackers, it is distilled into whiskey.

SWEETS IN PROFUSION

n America, with its abundance of food and its love of full plates, dessert, as might be expected, has become big, not just big in flavor, but big in offering a composite of edible pleasures. It's not just a slice of pie, but pie with ice cream on top; not just a slice of cake but cake with icing and a sauce; not simple fruit, but fruit spiced and gilded. Desserts have also changed with the mix of peoples and cultures and the flavors, fruits, and innovations they have added to the menu. Every land across the globe has its own sweets, and now in America we savor them all and mix and match them in bold fashion.

Starting from scratch as all great desserts should, the three steps that led to America's phenomenal copiousness and variety of desserts are: One, place something sweet in a bowl. The nation was discovered in a hunt for a sugar source, and soon sugar was planted right on the land. Honey bees were brought to Jamestown in 1622 and had swarmed all the way to California by 1851, well in advance of settlers. The northern woods had native maple syrup. Pecans were here and so were berries. More nuts and fruit were brought along with butter and flour and spices. And from America's southern neighbor, Mexico, two previously unheard of delights were swirled in: chocolate and vanilla.

Two, stir in a new way of eating. Hardworking immigrants had no time for afternoon tea break with tiers of sweetmeats. Instead, a large dinner evolved to cap the long workday, and the day's sweet treat became linked to it as the pinnacle.

Three, sprinkle in people and culinary delicacies from all around the world. Mix all together, bake, and serve.

Out of the oven came incomparable confectionery innovations: the all-American pie and the sweet that could be tucked away in a lunch pail or purse, the cookie. There also sprang up regional variations like Boston cream pie, which isn't pie at all, Florida's Key lime pie, and southwestern sopapillas.

Following is a string of new confections created with all of America's wonderful ingredients in mind. We start with a Bittersweet Chocolate and Espresso Butterscotch Pie and move on to one filled with lime curd and crusted with Hawaii's macadamia nuts. A traditional apple crisp replaces ice cream with yogurt cream. A Tequila Sunset Cake melds a popular drink into a dulcet batter, while another cake features Middle Eastern sesame in both batter and icing. Indoor S'Mores require no fire, and an Italian-style tiramisu is soaked with New Orleans's own Southern Comfort, and far more.

BUY ME CRACKER JACK

IN 1893, a man named Frederick "Fritz" Rueckheim coated popcorn and peanuts with caramelized molasses and later sugar. At first it stuck together too much, but by 1896 Fritz's brother Louis had figured out how to keep the coated morsels from adhering. Louis gave the treat to a salesman, who in the vernacular of the time declared it "crackerjack!" "So it is," said Fritz, and he trademarked the name.

Twelve years later (1908), Jack Norworth penned a tune called "Take Me Out to the Ball Game" during a thirty-minute subway ride. With music by Albert Von Tilzer, the song became the standard to be sung during the seventh-inning stretch at virtually every baseball game nationwide still today and included the line "Buy me some peanuts and Cracker Jack. I don't care if I never get back."

In 1912 the Cracker Jack Company added a prize in every box, and between the song and the prize, a caramel icon was indelibly fixed in the American psyche. In 1918, the images of Sailor Jack and his dog, Bingo, were placed on the wax-coated package, where they remain today.

Cracker Jack became enshrined in popular culture. Shirley Temple sang of Cracker Jack bands as a twist on "The Good Ship Lollipop." In *Breakfast at Tiffany's*, Holly Golightly's wedding ring comes from a Cracker Jack box. Alfalfa of the Little Rascals eats six boxes to find a ring to give to Darla.

How American is caramel-coated Cracker Jack? July 4 may be Independence Day, but July 5 is Cracker Jack Day.

BITTERSWEET CHOCOLATE AND ESPRESSO BUTTERSCOTCH PIE IN SHORTBREAD CRUST

EARLY ON, Americans took to two energizing indulgences that arrived like ingestible comets from two directions. Chocolate, an American native avidly relished by the Aztecs and the Maya, shot north but also went east to Europe, only to U-turn back to American shores. Coffee flew from the Arab world, and when it touched down on American soil, it became a national drink. Separately along the way, sugar had been added to enhance both. Every now and then the two collided: chocolate nibbled with coffee, coffee sipped with chocolate, and sometimes the two were blended. Here they sit layered in two ardently rich strata, one darkly earnest, the other stealthily thrilling. And underneath? A simple-and-easy crust made of the delicate crumbles of shortbread cookie.

1. Make and bake the shortbread crust and set it aside at room temperature.

2. Make the espresso butterscotch and set it aside to cool.

3. When ready to make the pie, preheat the oven to 375°F.

4. Place the cream in a small, heavy saucepan over medium-low heat until beginning to steam (do not let it boil). Add the chocolate and whisk gently until the chocolate melts and the mixture is smooth and glossy, 2 to 3 minutes. Whisk in the egg, remove the pan from the heat, and set it aside to cool and thicken slightly, 5 minutes or so.

MAKES ONE 9-INCH PIE

INGREDIENTS:

**Shortbread Crust
(recipe follows)**

Espresso Butterscotch (page 347)

1 cup heavy whipping cream

10 ounces bittersweet chocolate, broken into 1-inch chunks

1 large egg, lightly beaten

5. Pour the cooled chocolate mixture into the crust and bake until firm but still soft to the touch and a knife inserted in the center comes out a little moist, 13 to 15 minutes. Set it aside to cool until no longer piping hot.

6. Pour the espresso butterscotch over the chocolate and spread it evenly across the top. The butterscotch will still be somewhat runny but will thicken with refrigeration. Loosely cover the pie and refrigerate for at least 2 hours and up to 3 days.

7. Just before serving, remove the pie from the refrigerator and serve cool.

⊙**TIPS:** A SHORT AND SWEET DREAM OF A DOUGH. Broadly speaking, the term *short* in baking parlance means a dough made flaky or crumbly with fat. A shortening can be solid vegetable oil (think Crisco); lard, usually pork; or butter, salted or sweet. For a sweet shortbread that comes out meltingly tender with a pleasing sandy crunch and is perfectly balanced, the formula lies with its very basic ingredients—flour, butter, and sugar. The true glory of shortbread is its versatility. As with most good things, one might want to expand upon the pleasure:

⊕ Before cooking, mix finely ground walnuts, pecans, hazelnuts, pistachios, or macadamias into the dough.

⊕ Do as the Scots do and make cookies: Press the dough into a square or round pan, keeping it about ½ inch thick. Score the dough halfway through, so it can easily be divided into parts after baking. Serve the shortbread cookies as is or embellish them with a drizzle or two of plain melted chocolate or with a bowl of warm butterscotch sauce for dipping.

⊕ Crumble the cooked shortbread on top of ice cream.

⊕ Top rounds of the cooked dough with juicy summer fruit, such as sliced strawberries or peaches, and top the fruit with lightly whipped cream, as in strawberry or other fruit shortcakes.

SHORTBREAD CRUST

SHORTBREAD IS ONE of the simplest of all confections. It is the humble compound of the basic sweet biscuit, the modest sugar cookie, and the plain shortcake. It consists of only flour, butter, and sugar. There isn't even water in the dough. Since the mixture is pliable, not only can it take any shape as a cookie, it also makes an amazingly elegant pastry crust, uncomplicated yet adaptable enough to take on any filling. To top it all, it is fast and easy to make.

MAKES ONE 9-INCH CRUST

¾ cup unbleached all-purpose flour, plus extra for pressing the dough into the pie pan

¼ cup confectioners' sugar

8 tablespoons (1 stick) butter, cold and cut up

1. Preheat the oven to 375°F.

2. Combine the flour, confectioners' sugar, and butter in a small bowl or food processor and blend until the mixture is pebbly but holds together when gathered up. With floured fingers, press the dough across the bottom and up the sides of a 9-inch pie pan or removable-bottom tart pan. Place in the oven and bake until just golden brown and crisp, 18 to 20 minutes. Remove and set aside to cool.

ESPRESSO BUTTERSCOTCH

BUTTERSCOTCH IS THE mellifluous combination of butter and brown sugar fused together by heating. When cooled, the two ingredients result in a tempting candy. When the simmering mixture reaches the consistency of heavy syrup, if cream is stirred in it remains saucy rather than hardening into candy. Add a second tempting taste, coffee, and the alluring result is this espresso butterscotch. Besides pie filling, it makes a stunning ice cream topping, icing for cake, or

THE CONSTITUTIONAL CAFE

COFFEE DRINKING AND coffee houses were so entrenched in America by the time of the Revolutionary War that the Continental Congress declared the beverage the national drink. Who knows what Constitutional amendments were hammered out as the delegates hammered back coffee in small coffee chat-and-chew establishments?

dipping sauce for breadsticks to finish a meal in a sweet, simple, and uncomplicated way.

MAKES 1 CUP

1 cup packed dark brown sugar

1 vanilla bean, split lengthwise, or 1 teaspoon pure vanilla extract

¼ cup brewed espresso coffee

4 tablespoons (½ stick) butter, cut into pieces

¾ cup heavy whipping cream

¼ teaspoon kosher or fine sea salt

1. Place the sugar and vanilla in a heavy pot over medium heat. Cook, stirring occasionally, until the sugar is very soft and fragrant and beginning to melt, about 5 minutes. Add the coffee and butter and stir until the mixture is well blended, about 2 minutes.

2. Add the cream and salt and bring to a simmer. Stirring all the while, simmer until the sauce is the consistency of thick honey, about 15 minutes. Remove from the heat and take out the vanilla pod if used. Serve hot or cold, depending on how it's to be used.

PINK GRAPEFRUIT PIE WITH LEMON GRAHAM CRACKER CRUST AND DOUBLE CREAM

INGREDIENTS:

Lemon Graham Cracker Crust (recipe follows)

⅔ cup strained fresh pink grapefruit juice

¼ cup strained fresh orange juice

1 tablespoon fresh lemon juice

Grated zest of 1 large grapefruit

1 can (14 ounces) sweetened condensed milk, preferably organic

4 large egg yolks

¾ cup heavy whipping cream

¼ cup confectioners' sugar

¼ cup sour cream

IN 1823 grapefruit was brought to Florida, and twenty years later the first grapefruit were shipped to New York and Philadelphia and the American passion for the fruit began. Grapefruit became a traditional breakfast starter, but, unlike its cousins, orange, lemon, and lime, it has rarely appeared in sweets. It's too bad, for grapefruit can turn into a tingly, sweet-tart pie as scrumptious as lemon meringue or Key lime, but different. Underpinned with a crunchy graham cracker crust, it is truly a surprise crowd pleaser, and its pretty rose and yellow juicy main ingredient is available year-round.

1. Make and bake the crust and set it aside at room temperature. Keep the oven on.

2. Whisk together the grapefruit juice, orange juice, lemon juice, zest, sweetened condensed milk, and egg yolks in a medium-size bowl until thoroughly blended. Pour into the prepared crust and bake until just firm to the touch, about 12 minutes. Remove from the oven and set aside at room temperature to cool and set.

3. When ready to serve, whip the cream to stiff peaks in a medium-size bowl. Whip in the sugar and sour cream until just mixed. Dollop some of the cream mixture on each piece of pie.

LEMON GRAHAM CRACKER CRUST

IT WASN'T LONG AFTER nutritious graham wheat flour was developed in 1829 by diet-conscious Sylvester Graham that the graham cracker appeared. The crackers became a household staple especially for families with children. Cooks found another advantage to the crackers. Crumbled fine with a little butter added, graham crackers make a toasty, cookielike piecrust.

MAKES ONE 9-INCH CRUST

13 full-size graham cracker sheets (4 perforated crackers per sheet), preferably organic

1 tablespoon grated lemon zest

¼ cup sugar

6 tablespoons (¾ stick) butter, melted

2 tablespoons water, or more if needed

1. Preheat the oven to 350°F.

2. Pulverize the crackers in a food processor. Add the lemon zest, sugar, butter, and 2 tablespoons water to the processor and process until the mixture holds together. Add a little more water if necessary.

3. Place the crumb mixture in a 9-inch pie pan or removable-bottom tart pan and press it evenly over the bottom and up the sides of the pan. Place the pan in the oven and bake for 12 to 15 minutes, depending on how crisp you want the crust. Remove from the oven and let cool until firm.

A CONDENSED HISTORY OF CONDENSED MILK

AMERICAN ENTREPRENEUR AND INVENTOR Gail Borden was born in Norwich, New York, in 1801. As a young man he drifted through a wide variety of jobs, but underneath there was always one love, inventing. He began experimenting with ways of preserving medicines and developing sustainable foods for the army, which led him to think about the process of condensing. In 1852, during a transatlantic trip, he found that the cows on board became too seasick to be milked. He also knew that fresh milk, which was then transported in unsanitary barrels, spoiled quickly. Seeing that the children on board were suffering from lack of dairy, he worked on devising a machine that condensed milk, a goal he realized in 1853. The machine he invented evaporated 87 percent of milk's water content. Packed in an airtight container, the milk stayed good for three days.

Borden was granted a patent for his condensed milk in 1856 and formed Borden Incorporated. His first canned product appeared in 1864 under the still-used name Eagle Brand Sweetened Condensed Milk. "Sweetened" had been added to the product name because added sugar inhibits bacteria. Because soldiers needed milk that didn't spoil, the Civil War proved Borden's greatest boon, and his company became enormously successful. When it was discovered that condensing removed nutrients, vitamin D was added.

Condensed and evaporated milk (canned, partially dehydrated milk with no sugar added) soon found uses in the home kitchen. It could be employed for baking, making ice cream and candy, and for its richness in cream pies, and so entered mainstream American cuisine in all those facets. The Borden Company no longer exists, but many of its products are now produced by other companies, including its original—condensed milk.

LIME CURD COCONUT MERINGUE PIE WITH MACADAMIA NUT CRUST

MAKES ONE 9-INCH PIE

INGREDIENTS:

Macadamia Nut Crust
(recipe follows)

4 large eggs, separated,
at room temperature

1 large egg

1¼ cups sugar

3 tablespoons cornstarch

5 tablespoons butter, cut up

½ cup fresh lime juice

1½ tablespoons unsweetened
coconut flakes

IN THE NURSERY RHYME *CURD* REFERS TO A DAIRY PRODUCT, like Little Miss Muffet's curds and whey. In baking, curds are soft, spreadable pastes thickened with egg and butter. A curd is the kind of custard, often lemon flavored, used to slather on scones or fill tarts. A lemon curd is nice, but a lime curd is bold. Here astringent lime juice is mixed colada style with coconut and simmered into a curd. It is then poured into a scrumptious crust of crushed macadamia nuts.

1. Make and bake the crust and set it aside at room temperature. Keep the oven on.

2. Whisk together the 4 egg yolks, the whole egg, 1 cup of the sugar, and the cornstarch in a medium-size saucepan over medium heat. Add the butter and lime juice and cook, stirring frequently with a wooden spoon, until the mixture is barely simmering and just thick enough to coat the spoon, about 5 minutes. Set the pan aside off the heat.

3. Beat the 4 egg whites in a large bowl until soft peaks form. Slowly add the remaining ¼ cup sugar, continuing to beat, until the mixture is smooth and glossy and stiff peaks form.

4. Spread the lime curd evenly over the baked crust. Spread the beaten egg whites evenly over the top and, using the flat side of a knife or your fingers, lift the meringue into multiple peaks. Sprinkle the coconut over all and bake until the egg whites form into a meringue with golden peaks, about 15 minutes. Remove and set aside in a cool place for 1 to 2 hours and up to 4 hours before serving. Refrigerate any leftover pie.

MACADAMIA NUT CRUST

SMOOTHLY BUTTERY and marvelously crunchy, macadamia nuts are delightful for munching. But when ground, their unctuous oil makes a nutty shortening, perfect for binding together a toothsome piecrust or cookie dough.

MAKES ONE 9-INCH CRUST

2 cups toasted, salted macadamia nuts

¾ cup all-purpose flour, plus extra for pressing the dough into the pie pan

2 tablespoons sugar

3 tablespoons butter, cut up

2 tablespoons cold water

1. Finely chop the macadamia nuts in a food processor. Add the flour and sugar and pulse briefly to mix. Add the butter and pulse until the mixture is crumbly. Add the water and pulse briefly again, just until the water is incorporated. Gather the dough into a ball, wrap it in plastic wrap, and press into a smooth disk. Refrigerate for at least 30 minutes and up to 2 days or freeze for up to 1 week. Bring to room temperature before using.

2. When ready to bake, preheat the oven to 350°F.

3. With floured fingers, press the dough into a 9-inch pie pan or removable-bottom tart pan. Prick the bottom all over with a fork and bake until golden brown, about 25 minutes. Set aside at room temperature to cool and firm.

TIP: MACADAMIA NUT COOKIES. The dough for the Macadamia Nut Crust can be turned into macadamia nut cookies: Make a batch of dough and set it aside. Keep some extra macadamia nuts for studding the cookies.

With floured fingers, press the dough into whatever size cookies you'd like and place them 1 inch apart on an ungreased baking sheet. Top each cookie with a whole nut and bake at 350°F until golden and cooked through, about 25 minutes. Cool to room temperature and serve. Or store at room temperature, not tightly sealed, for up to 3 days.

FREE-FORM PLUM TART WITH PINE NUTS

MAKES ONE 9-INCH TART

INGREDIENTS:

Pastry Dough (page 338)

2 tablespoons butter, melted, plus extra for greasing the baking sheet

⅓ cup coarsely ground pine nuts

2½ tablespoons sugar

¼ teaspoon ground coriander

All-purpose flour, for rolling out the dough

8 small to medium-size red plums, halved, pitted, and each half quartered

A FREE-FORM TART REQUIRES NO PIE PAN OR TART RING; rather, you make the dough, roll it out, apply a fresh fruit layer across the top, and roll up the dough edges to rim the fruit. Sometimes the shape formed is more or less round; sometimes it's rather . . . well, free-form. The shape of the dough matters not, for what's important is the sweet fruit filling, which often leaks just enough around the free-form edges to become quite caramelized, adding extra snap to the flaky crust. The fruit filling is undeniably seductive.

1. Make the dough, adding 1 tablespoon of the sugar when you combine the flour and salt in Step 1.

2. When ready to make the tart, preheat the oven to 400°F. Lightly butter a large baking sheet.

3. Combine the pine nuts, 1 tablespoon of the sugar, and the coriander in a small bowl. Set aside.

4. Lightly flour a flat surface and roll out the dough into a 12- to 13-inch circle, rectangle, or other shape, adding a little more flour as you go to keep it from sticking to the surface. Transfer the dough to the baking sheet.

5. Sprinkle the pine nut mixture over the dough, leaving a 2-inch border around the edges. Arrange the plums over the top. Fold the edges of the dough up and over the fruit to encircle it with a 2- to 3-inch border, leaving the center exposed. Brush the melted butter over the fruit and the dough border and sprinkle the remaining 1½ tablespoons sugar over all.

6. Place the tart in the oven and bake until the crust is quite golden and the plum juices are bubbly, 40 to 45 minutes. Remove and cool slightly before serving.

➤TIPS: FRUIT TARTS APLENTY. Plums are not the only fruit that can be baked to bubbling in a sculpted crust. Using 4 to 5 cups of readied fruit, try:

⊕ Sweet or sour cherries, pitted and sugared to taste

⊕ Apricot halves, pitted and arranged cut sides down

⊕ Peaches or nectarines, peeled, pitted, and sliced ½ inch thick

⊕ Blueberries, alone or in combination with raspberries, glazed with red currant jelly thinned with a little port wine

⊕ Apples, peeled, cored, and sliced ¼ to ½ inch thick

⊕ Fresh figs, halved lengthwise and arranged cut sides down, glazed after baking with apricot jam thinned with a little orange liqueur

⊕ Rhubarb, cut into ½-inch pieces, alone or combined with stemmed and halved strawberries, tossed with sugar

A PLUM VERSUS A SUGARPLUM?

WHEN THE EARLY COLONISTS ARRIVED ON THE SHORES of North America, to their surprise they found wild plums growing along the coasts. The fruit wasn't quite like the Old World plum, but rather a New World variety. With cultivation and hybridization, plums have changed over time. Many of today's common varieties were developed by America's famous botanist, Luther Burbank.

None, though, is a sugarplum. In fact, a sugarplum is not a plum at all. It is a sort of candy developed around 1600. Traditionally it was composed of a tiny sugar-coated seed, usually a coriander and later an anise seed. Argument arose over how many times the seed needed to be dipped and thus coated in multiple layers of sugar—10, some confectioners claimed; others, 12. The resulting candy was much the size and shape of a plum—hence the name—often dyed colors, with a taste that started off sweet and ended with a salvo of spice from the buried seed. Sometimes a wire was embedded like a stick or stalk in the candy, forming a sort of early lollipop. As the candy evolved, eventually little bits of fruit were employed as the center of the "plum."

The candies snowballed into enormous popularity. They became the treat to put in a Christmas stocking. Strange how a candy so idolized and renowned faded from confectioners' counters. But visions of them still dance in our heads. No fairy is more famous than the Nutcracker's Sugarplum Fairy, and sugarplums very much linger in our terms of endearment.

APPLE CARDAMOM CRISP WITH BREAD CRUMB TOPPING AND YOGURT CREAM

INGREDIENTS:

Yogurt Cream (recipe follows), for serving

2 cups bread crumbs, preferably homemade (page 41), lightly toasted

½ cup packed dark brown sugar

½ cup all-purpose flour

6 tablespoons (¾ stick) butter, at room temperature, cut up

2 pounds apples, such as Fuji, Gala, or Gravenstein, peeled, quartered, cored, and thinly sliced (about 6 cups)

1 tablespoon sugar

2 teaspoons fresh lemon juice

⅛ teaspoon cardamom seeds, crushed

THE APPLE CRISP, to parody the famous saying, is as American as apple pie. Indeed, crisps in general are an American dessert invention, and the very first ones were apple. Orchards of apples bloom in glorious profusion across the country every spring, and their fruit is plentiful. Rather than a crust, a crisp has only a crunchy topping, and the crisp here is a modern take on the American tradition. Two things update it: It features bread crumbs as the crunch rather than the more customary nut, usually walnut, and, it employs sweetened yogurt rather than whipped cream for the sauce.

1. Make the yogurt cream.

2. Preheat the oven to 375°F.

3. Combine the bread crumbs, brown sugar, flour, and butter in a bowl and use your fingers to mix them into a coarse meal. Set the topping aside.

4. In a 13-by-9-by-2-inch or other 2-quart-capacity baking dish, toss together the apples, sugar, lemon juice, and cardamom seeds and spread the fruit mixture across the bottom of the pan. Using your fingers or a spatula, spread the bread crumb topping mixture over all. Bake until the top is golden and crispy and the apples are soft but not yet collapsing, about 40 minutes. Serve the crisp warm or at room temperature, topped with the yogurt cream.

YOGURT CREAM

YOGURT IS A MAGICAL FOOD, healthful, easy to digest, and hospitable to flavorings both savory and sweet. It's also receptive to variations in texture, from thin enough to make a refreshing iced drink to thick enough to spread like soft cheese. It all depends on how much water you add or how much whey you drain off the yogurt base. Taking thick yogurt a step more ambrosial, a sweetened yogurt cream can replace whipped cream, crème fraîche, or sour cream dolloped on poached fruit and pies.

MAKES ABOUT 1 CUP

2 cups plain Greek yogurt

2 teaspoons confectioners' sugar

1. Place a colander in a bowl large enough so it can sit above the bottom of the bowl and above the liquid as it drains off. Line the colander with several layers of cheesecloth, enough to make a very fine sieve. Place the yogurt in the colander and set it aside at room temperature until the drained yogurt is thick and creamy as you'd like, 1 to 3 hours, depending on the thickness of the yogurt to begin with.

2. Transfer the yogurt to a bowl and whisk in the confectioners' sugar. Use right away or refrigerate for up to 3 days.

BAKED APPLE BABBLE

IF YOU RAMBLE THROUGH the chronology of American cookbooks, a number of fruit and flour desserts pop up, mostly with apple. Beside savoring, the joy of them is in their names.

APPLE CRISPS. Though absent from Fannie Farmer's 1896 cookbook, two show up in 1924, in *Everybody's Cook Book* by Isabel Ely Lord and aptly in the *Appleton Post-Crescent* newspaper from Appleton, Wisconsin. Crisps are topped with a mix of crumbs or a crumble of flour, butter, and sugar or a single piecrust.

APPLE GRUNTS. Grunts of apple topped with clumps of biscuits show up in early American, Amish, and Pennsylvania Dutch cookery, named, so some say, because upon the first bite the partaker grunts in satisfaction. Others explain that as they were baked in a Dutch oven over an open fire, the desserts "grunted" as they boiled. The same composition shows up under other names, in particular *cobbler, pandowdy,* and *slump.*

BROWN BETTYS. A lot like crisps, brown bettys feature layer after layer of fruit, usually apple, with a sprinkle of crisp makings between each one. A *betty* is a colonial term for a baked pudding, and the brown is because it calls for brown sugar.

BAKED APPLES. Sometimes also called *bird's nest pudding,* these are whole cored apples, their centers filled with sugar, nuts, and spice, sometimes encased in a pastry crust.

APPLE CRUMBLES. The British term for apple crisp, crumbles first appeared in England and America during World War II. There was little butter and flour during the war years, so a lesser way to make a crunchy addition to the baked fruit had to be created, and bread crumbs alone worked.

APPLE PIES. The root of the word *pie* comes from Greek *pita* and traveled through time and rhyme to English nursery chants. Fruit-filled ones are an American innovation, and apple-filled ones ranging from one to four inches in height are the country's all-time front runner.

SOURDOUGH CRUMB CAKE WITH GREEN TEA AND CANDIED GINGER SYRUP

MAKES ONE 8-INCH CAKE

INGREDIENTS:

Butter and all-purpose flour, for preparing the cake pan

2 tablespoons all-purpose flour

½ teaspoon baking powder

½ teaspoon ground ginger

⅛ teaspoon kosher or fine sea salt

6 large eggs, at room temperature

¾ cup sugar

1 cup fresh bread crumbs, preferably homemade from a sourdough baguette (page 41)

Green Tea and Candied Ginger Syrup (recipe follows)

CONTEMPORARY AND UNUSUAL, Sourdough Crumb Cake with its syrup combines two inspirations. The first comes from the classic larder and, like bread pudding, uses stale bread. The second involves an innovative way to use one of the new additions to the modern American pantry, green tea. The texture of the cake is like sponge cake. Made without shortening or leavening, it gains its soft yellow color from eggs and its rise from the air that's whipped into them. A soaking of a green tea and candied ginger syrup makes it a lively offering.

1. Preheat the oven to 325°F. Lightly butter and flour an 8-inch cake pan.

2. Using a fork, mix together the 2 tablespoons flour, baking powder, ginger, and salt in a small bowl. Set aside.

3. Combine the eggs and sugar in a large mixing bowl and beat until creamy, light-colored, aerated, and thick enough for the beater to make deep rivulets, about 15 minutes.

4. Fold in the flour mixture and bread crumbs.

5. Pour the batter into the pan and bake until springy and no longer moist in the center, 35 to 40 minutes. Remove and set aside to cool.

6. While the cake bakes, make the syrup.

7. Remove the cake from the pan and set it on a rimmed platter. Pour some of the syrup over the top, let it soak in for 1 to 2 minutes, and then pour on a little more at 2-minute intervals. Pour the last of the syrup down the sides of the cake. Set aside for at least 30 minutes so the cake can soak up the syrup before serving.

GREEN TEA AND CANDIED GINGER SYRUP

GREEN TEA WAS the most popular sort of tea imbibed most everywhere up until the 1900s. It was the tea dumped into Boston Bay, inciting the American Revolution. Green tea tastes light and fresh, like a spring day, with scents of newly grown grass, warm sun, and clean air. A syrup of it imbued with ginger transforms a cake into a venturesome dessert.

MAKES 1 CUP

**2 good-quality green tea bags or
 1 tablespoon loose green tea leaves**

1 cup boiling water

¾ cup sugar

**¼ cup finely chopped candied
 (crystallized) ginger**

1. Steep the tea in the boiling water for 3 minutes, not longer or the tea will become too bitter. Remove the tea bags or strain out the leaves and pour the tea into a small saucepan. Add the sugar and bring to a boil over medium-high heat. Cook until the mixture is syrupy and thickly drips off a spoon, about 10 minutes.

2. Stir in the candied ginger, remove from the heat, and set aside until cooled but still a little warm. Use right away or store in the refrigerator for up to 1 week and reheat before using.

TEQUILA SUNSET CAKE WITH TROPICAL FRUIT FILLING

MAKES ONE 9-INCH CAKE

INGREDIENTS:

Butter and all-purpose flour, for preparing the cake pan

8 tablespoons (1 stick) butter, at room temperature

¾ cup sugar

3 large eggs

1 cup plain Greek yogurt

2 teaspoons grated lemon zest

1¾ cups all-purpose flour

1 teaspoon baking powder

½ teaspoon baking soda

¼ teaspoon kosher or fine sea salt

1 cup unsweetened coconut flakes, lightly toasted (see Tip, page 197)

1 cup canned mandarin orange segments or ½-inch cubes fresh pineapple or a mixture

Tequila Lime Syrup (recipe follows)

WHAT BETTER WAY IS THERE TO GREET THE EVENING than watching the sunset with a tequila cocktail in hand? Here's one, a cake soaked in a tequila and lime syrup that evokes the same feeling of tranquillity. It emerges from the oven with a texture much like that of a pound cake, and like a pound cake, it is ready to sponge up any punctuating syrup. A filling of coconut and fruit in the center adds levels of flavor like the gradations of sunset's colors. For simplicity, though, the cake can be served unfilled.

1. Preheat the oven to 350°F. Butter and flour a 9-inch cake pan.

2. Cream together the 8 tablespoons butter and sugar in a large bowl. Beat in the eggs one at a time, then the yogurt and zest. Sift the flour, baking powder, baking soda, and salt into the bowl and beat to mix well.

3. Pour half the batter into the prepared cake pan. Sprinkle the coconut flakes across the top and dot with the fruit. Pour the remaining batter over the fruit. Bake until the edges of the cake are pulling away from the pan and

a knife inserted in the center comes out clean, about 40 minutes. Set aside to cool.

4. While the cake bakes, make and cool the tequila lime syrup.

5. When it is cool enough to handle, remove the cake from its pan and place it on a large rimmed plate. Pour some of the syrup over the top, let it soak in for 1 to 2 minutes, then at 2-minute intervals, slowly pour on the remaining syrup. Set aside at room temperature so the cake can soak up the syrup for 2 hours before serving.

TEQUILA LIME SYRUP

THE PHRASE TEQUILA SUNSET has come to conjure thoughts of island indolence where you can watch the tropical sun disappear into the water, yet the tequila sunset cocktail was actually invented at the Biltmore Hotel in downtown Phoenix, Arizona. Originally made of tequila, crème de cassis, lime juice, and club soda, it is now contrived more popularly with tequila, orange juice, and grenadine syrup. The juice and sweet red syrup, having more solids, sink to the bottom of the glass to form a tri-part stack of colors the hotel bartender thought reminiscent of a sunset. Like the original, a fruit juice concoction readily reduces to a syrup for a soaking liquid reminiscent of the cocktail and bows to the descending sun.

MAKES 1 CUP

1 cup sugar

½ cup tequila

¼ cup fresh lime juice

¼ cup water

1 tablespoon cranberry or pomegranate juice

Combine the sugar, tequila, lime juice, water, and cranberry juice in a small saucepan and bring to a boil over high heat. Reduce the heat to maintain a boil without overflowing and cook until thickened enough to loosely coat a spoon, 10 to 12 minutes. Remove from the heat and cool until the bubbling stops. Use right away or store in the refrigerator for up to several weeks. To use as a syrup again, gently reheat on the stovetop or in a microwave. Or, to make into a refreshing drink, mix a tablespoon or so into a glass of cold seltzer.

TEQUILA:
AND HOW IT CAME TO BE

TEQUILA, the beverage par excellence of Mexico, is made from the heart, or core, of the blue agave cactus after the spiky leaves are removed. Legend has it that long before the Spanish arrived tequila was created when a bolt of lightning struck an agave field. The bolt penetrated the heart of the plant, and the heat of the lightning not only cooked the heart but caused it to ferment. The nearby villagers noticed a fragrant juice pouring out and, in awe, decided to taste the juice. A few sips later they deemed it nectar, a miraculous gift from the gods, and have been making it ever since.

In 1873 the initial distilleries to export tequila to the United States were owned by Don Cenobio Sauza, followed by Don José María Guadalupe de Cuervo, whose family received the first license to make tequila from the king of Spain in 1795. Prohibition and World War II almost halted exportation. In the 1940s, with the invention of the margarita—there are four stories of how this drink originated—the popularity of tequila in the states began to soar. Today, exports of tequila to the United States are enormous. Most people know only mass-produced kinds, which are generally mixed, or the slightly better "gold." With even stricter guidelines for premium versions, as with bourbons and scotches, handcrafted boutique tequilas of 100 percent blue agave, such as Patron Añejo and El Tesorio Paradiso, are now being produced.

SESAME CAKE WITH SESAME ICING

MAKES ONE 9-INCH CAKE

INGREDIENTS:

1 tablespoon white sesame
seeds

Butter and all-purpose flour,
for preparing the cake pan

⅓ cup all-purpose flour

1½ cups fine bread crumbs,
preferable homemade
(page 41)

½ cup sugar

1 teaspoon baking soda

1 teaspoon ground cinnamon

¼ teaspoon ground cloves

⅛ teaspoon freshly grated
nutmeg, preferably freshly
grated

¼ teaspoon kosher or
fine sea salt

½ cup tahini (page 55),
at room temperature

1 cup fresh orange juice

2 tablespoons grated orange
zest

½ cup water

¼ teaspoon orange blossom
water, triple sec, or other
orange liqueur

Sesame Icing
(recipe follows)

WHEN ALI BABA UTTERED THE MAGIC PHRASE "OPEN SESAME!" in *A Thousand and One Nights* to gain entrance to a cave full of treasure, he used the word *sesame* not because it was strange but because it was so common it was easily overlooked. From Indonesia to India to Egypt and the Mediterranean, the seeds played such a prevalent culinary role that people didn't even use the full name. They just called it *sa*.

The plant's rosy or white flowers produce seeds that, when pressed, burst with an earthy oil, which is still widely used for its burnished flavor. The cake here is low rising, warm and crumbly and, when iced with a sweet frosting of more sesame, it's easy to see why the little seed kept the ancients enthralled.

1. Spread the sesame seeds out in a dry skillet and toast over medium-high heat until beginning to pop and turn golden, about 4 minutes. Set aside.

2. Preheat the oven to 350°F. Lightly butter and flour a 9-inch cake pan.

3. Sift the ⅓ cup flour into a large bowl. Add the bread crumbs, sugar, baking soda, cinnamon, cloves, nutmeg, and salt and stir with a fork to mix.

4. Combine the tahini, orange juice, zest, water, and orange blossom water in a food processor and process until well blended. Add the tahini mixture to the bowl with the dry ingredients and beat to blend thoroughly.

5. Pour the batter into the pan and bake until the edges are pulling away from the pan and a knife inserted in the center comes out clean, 30 minutes. Remove the cake from the oven and set aside to cool.

6. While the cake cools, make the icing.

7. Remove the cake from the pan and place it on a platter. Drizzle the icing over the top, sprinkle the toasted sesame seeds over the icing, and serve.

SESAME ICING

AN ICING THAT contains the same flavoring as the cake intensifies the whole experience. Bronzed with sugar and reduced to a glaze, sesame icing makes sesame cake both opulent and exotic. The sprinkling of toasty seeds over the icing triples the inscrutable aura.

MAKES ¾ CUP

¼ cup tahini, at room temperature (page 55)

½ cup confectioners' sugar

½ teaspoon pure vanilla extract

1½ tablespoons boiling water

Combine the tahini, sugar, vanilla, and boiling water in a food processor or small bowl and process or beat until smooth. Use right away or store in the refrigerator for up to 3 months. Heat gently if too firm to pour before using.

BEFORE SUGAR THERE WAS HONEY:
BUT NOT EVERYWHERE!

THE ANCESTORS OF MOST OF THE CAKES AND TREATS of today were sweetened with honey, not sugar. Surprising as it may seem, honeybees did not live everywhere. Honeybees lived only in Europe west of the Ural Mountains. Their honey was a favorite of the early Indo-Europeans, who carried honeybees and honey around the world.

The uses of honey were legion. Honey was drizzled on grain puddings and breads. Long before beer and wine, it was discovered that honey could be turned into an intoxicating beverage called *mead,* which could be fermented in only a few days. Mead was dispensed like water from a spring. Once beer and wine were developed, the taste for honey did not die. Honey was stirred into both.

Honey was added to cakes. It was used to coat cheese, make honey vinegar, polish metal, and as an undercoat for murals, and its attendant beeswax was used to make candles. It was also considered a strengthener. Soldiers trained on diets of nothing but honey, and when they were given leave, it was called a "honeymoon."

The flavor of their honey reflected the particular flower the bees were nectaring on. So, in cooking, honey adds flavor in a way that other sugars do not. Along with sweetness, it bequeaths the savor of the flowers, herbs, and even trees. Since the color of honey comes from plant pigments, honey also colors food. Honey still plays a major role as sweetener and colorant not just in desserts, but in stews, sauces, and salad dressings as well.

ANOTHER KIND OF HONEY

AS WELL AS by its sapor, honey is judged by its thickness, and there is a long-standing joke told about that. In the time of the sultans, a woman lived to be one hundred years old. The sultan was so impressed that he offered her as a gift her choice of a strapping young man or a barrel of honey. She chose the young man. "What would I do with the honey?" she asked. "I haven't got any teeth to chew it."

FLOURLESS CHOCOLATE CAKE WITH FERNET BRANCA CREAM AND RASPBERRIES

MAKES ONE 8-INCH CAKE

INGREDIENTS:

Butter and sugar, for preparing the cake pan

10 ounces good-quality dark chocolate, bittersweet or semisweet or a mixture, broken into large chunks

8 tablespoons (1 stick) butter

2 tablespoons water

5 large eggs, at room temperature, separated

½ cup granulated sugar

2 teaspoons Fernet Branca (facing page)

1 cup heavy whipping cream

2 tablespoons confectioners' sugar

2 cups fresh raspberries, for garnish

AMERICANS ARE AVID FOR CHOCOLATE, as is clear from the amount of it produced and consumed here every year. No restaurant can escape having a selection of chocolate desserts on the menu, and among the most readily ordered is any cake that features a molten chocolate fudgelike center. That exact sort of cake can be turned out at home with very few ingredients—in fact with no flour at all. The recipe is straightforward and uncomplicated, yet the result is anything but. The cake would be enough, but it becomes an over-the-top sensation when capped with an herb-liqueur-laced whipped cream and whole raspberries. If it's not raspberry season, frozen raspberries with a sprinkle of sugar make a fine stand-in. Ouzo or triple sec can substitute for Fernet Branca.

1. Preheat the oven to 325°F. Butter and sugar an 8-inch cake pan.

2. Melt the chocolate, 8 tablespoons butter, and water together in a microwave-safe bowl in a microwave oven on medium-high or a small saucepan over low heat until the chocolate chunks are soft all the way through but still hold their shape, about 2 minutes either way. Whisk the mixture until it is smooth and glossy. Set aside.

3. Combine the egg yolks and ½ cup granulated sugar in a large mixing bowl and beat until creamy, pale colored, and the consistency of a runny pudding, 3 minutes. Add the chocolate mixture and 1 teaspoon of the Fernet and continue beating until well blended.

4. Beat the egg whites until soft peaks form. Gently stir them into the chocolate mixture, a third at a time. Pour the batter into the pan and bake until a knife inserted in the center comes out mostly clean and the cake is pulling away from the sides of the pan, about 33 minutes. Remove from the oven and let cool to room temperature. Remove the cake from its pan and place on a serving plate.

5. Beat the cream and confectioners' sugar together until soft peaks form. Add the remaining 1 teaspoon Fernet and blend it in. Set aside until ready to serve.

6. Slice the cake into portions. Top each portion with a generous dollop of the whipped cream, garnish with the raspberries, and serve.

FERNET BRANCA:
AN OLD-FASHIONED MEDICINE, A NEW-FASHIONED MIXER

FERNET BRANCA, PRONOUNCED "FERNETTE," is a bitter digestive liqueur that has recently become the darling of cocktail mixologists. Its origin is unclear, but most likely it was created in Milan, Italy, in the mid-1800s by an herbalist named Bernardino Branca. To this day his family keeps the formula a closely guarded secret.

Whatever its origin, Fernet Branca as a substance has an intriguing profile: It is claimed that it can cure a hangover, soothe the stomach, subdue anxiety, and banish what all else one might want to go away. It was brought to the United States in the suitcases of Italian immigrants. Fernet Branca was not on the list of proscribed alcoholic drinks during Prohibition, even though it was 80 proof, because it had been imported under the aegis of medicine. Its curative powers were not called into question, because it did indeed offer pain relief due to the inclusion of opiates. The Branca family was able to establish a legal distillery in New York City a year before the prohibition of alcohol was repealed.

As for its taste, Fernet Branca is spicy, bitter, herbaceous, and pucker making. It is far less sweet and licoricy than Jägermeister or Underberg, two other popular bitter digestives. In a small swallow, Fernet reveals its complex makeup as it meets the tongue and passes to the throat. Just right for a mixologist's playful blending of spirits or a cook's playful blending of flavors in dessert cream to top a dense chocolate cake.

SOUTHERN COMFORT TIRAMISU

MAKES A 8½ x 5½" CAKE

INGREDIENTS:

Sheet Sponge Cake
   (recipe follows)

2 large egg yolks

¼ cup plus 2 teaspoons
   superfine sugar

¼ cup Southern Comfort

1 cup (about 8 ounces)
   mascarpone cheese,
   at room temperature

¼ cup heavy whipping cream

½ cup brewed espresso or
   other strong coffee

1 tablespoon cocoa powder,
   for sifting over the top

TIRAMISU, A LATECOMER TO ITALIAN "CLASSIC" CUISINE, emanated from Treviso sometime in the mid- to late 1980s. Traditionally it's an enticing layered montage of thin sponge cake and a zabaglione-like cream, each moistened with a syrup of espresso and rum. Taking away the rum and adding instead an infusion of Southern Comfort and cream gives it a dynamic American edge. Tiramisu is traditionally made with ladyfingers; here they are exchanged for a homemade sponge cake. To excel, the tiramisu requires superfine, or bakers', sugar.

1. Make and bake the sheet sponge cake and set it aside.

2. Pour water to a depth of 1 inch into a large pot. Place a steamer trivet in the pot; it should sit above the water. Bring the water to a simmer over medium heat.

3. Whisk together the egg yolks, ¼ cup sugar, and 2 tablespoons of the Southern Comfort in a medium-size heatproof bowl. Set the bowl over the simmering water. Adjust the heat to maintain a simmer and whisk the mixture until it is thick and well heated, about 3 minutes. Remove the bowl from the pan and beat the mixture until it is doubled in volume. Add the mascarpone and cream and beat until the mixture is smooth. Set aside.

4. Whisk together the espresso, the remaining 2 teaspoons sugar, and the remaining 2 tablespoons Southern Comfort in a small bowl.

5. To assemble the tiramisu, cut the sheet cake into 4 equal rectangles. Place 1 layer on a platter and drizzle one fourth of the espresso mixture over it. Spread one fourth of the Southern Comfort mixture across the top and cover with a second rectangle of cake. Continue layering in the same way, ending up with the remainder of the Southern Comfort mixture. Sift the cocoa powder over the top.

6. Refrigerate for at least 6 hours, overnight if possible, before seving.

SHEET SPONGE CAKE

A GENOISE IS a type of sponge cake named for the city of Genoa. A classic génoise formula uses no leavening—air generated by mixing the batter gives it its spring. As well as offering a porous layer for tiramisu or other soaked and filled cakes, it can be turned into a jelly roll. It also provides the structural and spongy layers in buttercream-filled cakes, can be baked in madeleine cookie molds, or be shaped into ladyfingers. In short, a génoise is a dessert maker's ideal building block.

MAKES 1 LARGE CAKE

Butter and all-purpose flour, for preparing the baking sheet

4 large eggs, at room temperature

½ cup superfine sugar

½ teaspoon pure vanilla extract

3 tablespoons butter, melted and still warm

1 cup cake (pastry) flour

1. Preheat the oven to 350°F. Lightly butter and flour a rimmed 11-by-17-by-1-inch baking sheet.

2. Combine the eggs and sugar in a large, warm bowl and beat with an electric mixer until tripled in bulk and the consistency of soft whipped cream.

3. Beat in the vanilla and then slowly beat in the melted butter. Sift the flour into the bowl and fold it in with a spatula just until mixed in.

4. Pour the batter onto the prepared baking sheet and with a rubber spatula gently coax it to the edges of the pan, taking care not to deflate it. Place the baking sheet in the oven and bake until the cake pulls away from the edges of the pan and springs back when pressed with a finger, 15 to 20 minutes. Remove and set aside to cool.

SOUTHERN COMFORT:
A SWEET SOPORIFIC IN THE GLASS AND IN A CAKE

THE TALE OF SOUTHERN COMFORT is somewhat of a Horatio Alger story, if not exactly rags to riches. As it is told:

By the late nineteenth century, New Orleans was abuzz with commerce, much of it entering the city via riverboat and much of it whiskey. The whiskeys flowing into the delta hub were not by any means all of comparable caliber. One arriving keg could be mellifluous, another searing. Enter M. W. Heron, who owned a bar on Bourbon Street. In 1874, looking to guarantee a quality drink for his customers, he concocted a peachy, bourbon-based beverage laced with citrus, vanilla, and cinnamon. (The exact recipe is a secret, generations old, and closely held to this day.) The drink was dubbed Southern Comfort, and at first it was served somewhat home style, directly out of the barrel, jigger by jigger. The "doctored" bourbon at Mr. Heron's bar became a runaway hit.

In 1889, Heron, clearly an enterprising character, opened another bar, this time in Memphis, Tennessee. There demand for Southern Comfort warranted bottling it for take-home at what now seems a ridiculously low price of $2.50 per bottle.

In 1904, Heron took his brew to the World's Fair in St. Louis, Missouri, where it was awarded a gold medal. He opened a third bar there and created the St. Louis cocktail, a glass of Southern Comfort served with a twist of lemon and signage saying "Limit 2 to a customer. (No gentleman would ask for more.)"

HAZELNUT AND FIG SPICE CAKE WITH CANDIED CARROT RIBBONS

MAKES ONE 9-INCH CAKE

INGREDIENTS:

Butter and all-purpose flour, for preparing the cake pan

1 cup hazelnuts (filberts)

1 cup milk

1 tablespoon distilled white vinegar

2 cups all-purpose flour

1 teaspoon baking soda

1 teaspoon baking powder

¼ teaspoon ground cinnamon

¼ teaspoon ground cloves

¼ teaspoon ground allspice

1½ cups sugar

1 cup hazelnut oil

2 large eggs

1 teaspoon pure vanilla extract

1 cup finely chopped dried Calimyrna figs

Hazelnut Caramel (recipe follows)

Candied Carrot Ribbons (page 368), for garnish

1 cup sour cream, for serving

FRUITED SPICE CAKES BEGAN TO APPEAR in the Middle Ages, when, along with dried fruit, ingredients as diverse as cooked beets and carrots were added. The cakes were served most often during Christmastime. Such cakes were frosted with marzipan and decorated with holly leaves. The version here takes luscious hazelnut caramel for a frosting and candied carrots for a garnish. In a pinch, peanut or olive oil can substitute for hazelnut oil. Unlike almonds, walnuts, or pine nuts, all of which can be quickly toasted in an oven or microwave to coax out their nutty essence, hazelnuts require a deep toasting on the stove top in a heavy skillet until they seem charred almost beyond salvation.

1. Preheat the oven to 350°F. Lightly butter and flour a 9-inch cake pan.

2. Heat a heavy skillet over high heat. When it begins to smoke, add the hazelnuts and cook, stirring frequently, until toasted and charred all around, about 10 minutes. Transfer the nuts to a kitchen towel, cover with another towel, and set aside just until cool enough to handle. With your hands, rub the nuts around between the towels to loosen the skins. With your fingers, remove as much more of the skins as will slip away. Finely chop them and set aside.

3. Combine the milk and vinegar in a small bowl and set aside.

4. Sift together the flour, baking soda, baking powder, cinnamon, cloves, and allspice and set aside.

5. Place the sugar and hazelnut oil in a large bowl and beat until well blended. Beat in the eggs. Beat in the flour mixture, alternating with the milk, adding each a third at a time. Mix in the vanilla, hazelnuts, and figs. Pour the batter into the pan and bake until a knife inserted in the center comes out clean, about 55 minutes. Remove from the oven and set aside to cool.

6. While the cake bakes and cools, make the hazelnut caramel and candied carrot ribbons.

7. When ready to serve, remove the cake from the pan and transfer to a plate. Drizzle the caramel across the top of the cake. Strew the carrot ribbons over all and serve with sour cream on the side.

HAZELNUT CARAMEL

HAZELNUTS, also called *filberts,* spread across Europe after the last Ice Age. The name *hazelnut* comes from an early word for "helmet" or "headdress," and filbert from their August harvest time, which is near St. Filbert's Day. They are smooth and round and hold a plump kernel that smacks a bit of warm, dark wood. There are more than a hundred varieties, most grown around the Black Sea, but the Willamette Valley in the state of Oregon produces a sizable crop.

It's hard to quantify the popularity of caramel and the avidness of its fans. The soft, thickly sweet concoction of brown sugar and sometimes cream or butter comes as a candy, syrup, or filling for ice cream or cake. The flavor of both hazelnuts and caramel is memorable, but a marriage of the two is indelible.

MAKES 1 CUP

1 cup sugar

1½ teaspoons light corn syrup

½ cup water

⅓ cup heavy whipping cream

⅓ cup toasted, skinned, and finely chopped hazelnuts (Step 2, facing page)

1 teaspoon hazelnut, olive, or peanut oil

1. Combine the sugar, corn syrup, and water in a small, heavy saucepan or cast-iron skillet and bring to a boil over medium heat. Cook until the mixture is golden and thickly coats a wooden spoon, 12 to 15 minutes. Remove from the heat and whisk in the cream and then the hazelnuts. When the mixture is no longer boiling, whisk in the oil.

2. Use right away or cool and refrigerate for up to several weeks. Reheat in the microwave or on the stove top before using.

FRUIT HASH

THROUGH THE AGES, dried figs and nuts have often been principal ingredients in fruit mélanges. There are many such hodgepodges of fruits and other tidbits. Among them are:

- A confetti, originally a sweetmeat of Italian cooking, consisted of candied nuts, dried fruits, and candy dragées thrown to a crowd at festivals. The mixture might include figs and raisins; almonds, hazelnuts, and walnuts; and candies or candied fruit, sometimes spiced with cinnamon or clove. In poor times the tossed candies were plaster imitations. Later these were replaced by tatters and shreds of paper.

- A macédoine, or macedonia, is a medley of cooked or fresh fruits, sometimes with nuts and spices. The patchwork of goodies is named for Macedonia, home of a veritable patchwork of peoples. In America, the mosaic is tossed with a sweet cream or yogurt dressing and often includes miniature marshmallows.

- Fruit salads are jumbles of fresh fruit; they include watermelon and other melons, along with a mix of berries and stone fruit, in summer; apples, pears, grapes, oranges, and grapefruit in the colder months. Mostly they are not sauced or dressed but just left in the synthesis of the different sweet, flavorful juices.

- A tutti-frutti is a mixture of fruits in brandy. The confederacy needs to sit for a week or so to become preserved in the liquor. A tutti-frutti can be replenished with new fruit and a dash more brandy as it's consumed. The name, however, has also come to refer to the scattering of candied fruits in ice cream, chocolate, taffy, or other candies.

CANDIED CARROT RIBBONS

CARROTS ARE the sturdy culinary workers whose dulcet earthiness can carry a dish from ordinary to extraordinary. Here carrots' natural sugariness is accentuated by candying.

MAKES 3 CUPS

3 medium-size carrots, peeled

2 cups sugar

1 cup water

1. Shave the carrots lengthwise with a vegetable peeler to make long thin ribbons.

2. Combine 1½ cups of the sugar and the water in a medium-size saucepan and bring to a boil over high heat. Add the carrot ribbons and cook for 1 minute. Drain and shake out the excess moisture from the ribbons. Spread them out on paper towels, separating them so they're not in clumps. Set aside until completely cool and no longer moist.

3. Sprinkle the remaining ½ cup sugar over the carrot ribbons and, using your fingers, toss gently to mix and coat the ribbons. Spread them out on dry paper towels and set aside for at least 1 hour and up to 4 hours.

TWO-TIERED CHEESECAKE WITH PINE NUT CRUST AND GREEN GRAPE CHAMPAGNE TOPPING

AMERICA HAS UMPTEEN VERSIONS OF SEDUCTIVE, moist cheesecakes, and yet every now and again comes a new take. The cheesecake here begins with a delicate pine nut crust. Over that lies the gentle but ripened lushness of cream cheese and soft chèvre. Crowning that is a sugared tart layer of sweetened sour cream flavored with vanilla. Over all flows a river of grapes simmered in champagne. From nadir to apex, it's divine.

INGREDIENTS:

Pine Nut Crust
(recipe follows)

1½ pounds cream cheese,
at room temperature

3 tablespoons soft chèvre
cheese, at room
temperature

1 cup plus 1 tablespoon sugar

4 large eggs

1½ teaspoons pure vanilla
extract

2 cups sour cream

⅛ teaspoon kosher or
fine sea salt

Green Grape Champagne
Topping (page 370)

1. Make the crust, press it into a prepared springform cake pan, and set it aside.

2. Preheat the oven to 325°F.

3. Combine the cream cheese, chèvre, and 1 cup sugar in a food processor and process until smooth. Add the eggs and 1 teaspoon of the vanilla and process until well blended. (Do not overbeat or the filling will get too airy.)

4. Pour the cream cheese mixture into the crust and bake until a knife inserted in the center comes out almost clean and the cake is still a bit jiggly, about 50 minutes. Remove from the oven and set aside.

5. While the cake sits, increase the oven temperature to 450°F.

6. Whisk together the sour cream, the remaining 1 tablespoon sugar, remaining ½ teaspoon vanilla, and the salt in a small bowl. Spread the mixture evenly across the top of the cake, return the pan to the oven, and bake until the sour cream topping has firmed up, about 8 minutes. Remove the cake from the oven, release the pan's spring lever, and set aside to cool.

7. When completely cool, remove the pan ring, leaving the cake on the pan bottom, and place in the refrigerator to chill until set all the way through, at least 4 hours and up to overnight.

8. While the cake chills, make the green grape topping and chill it.

9. When ready to serve, pour some of the grape topping over the top of the cake. Cut the cake into portions and spoon the rest of the topping over each.

PINE NUT CRUST

CHEESECAKES often feature a sprinkling of nuts on top, as delectable a place for them as in a nut crust on the bottom. Pine nuts impart a sublime touch of resin and enough oil that they require no butter to press nicely into a delectable crust.

MAKES ONE 9-INCH CRUST

**Butter and all-purpose flour,
    for preparing the cake pan**

2 cups pine nuts

5 tablespoons sugar

¼ cup all-purpose flour

**2½ tablespoons triple sec or other
    orange-flavored liqueur**

1. Lightly butter and flour a 9-inch springform cake pan.

2. Place the pine nuts, sugar, flour, and triple sec in a food processor and process until finely ground and well mixed. Press the pine nut mixture across the bottom of the pan and 2 inches up the side to form a crust. Use right away or set aside in the refrigerator for up to several hours before using.

GREEN GRAPE CHAMPAGNE TOPPING

CHEESECAKE PURISTS would have no extra flavors in their cheesecake. For nonpurists, toppings on cheesecakes have become quotidian. A topping of grapes cooked in champagne is anything but.

MAKES ABOUT 1½ CUPS

2 cups seedless green grapes, halved

1¼ cups sugar

¾ cup brut champagne

1. Place the grapes, sugar, and champagne in a medium-size saucepan and bring to a boil over medium-high heat. Reduce the heat to maintain a brisk simmer and cook until the grapes have wilted and released their juices, about 5 minutes. With a slotted spoon, transfer the grapes to a bowl. Continue cooking the syrup at a brisk simmer until it is thick and heavy when dripped off a spoon, about 20 minutes, depending on the juiciness of the grapes. As the syrup cooks, pour the liquid released by the grapes in the bowl back into the saucepan 3 or 4 times.

2. Stir the grapes back into the saucepan, remove the pan from the heat, and allow to cool. Chill the topping in the refrigerator until set. It will keep in the refrigerator for up to 3 weeks.

THE BIG "CHEESECAKE"

FROM ITS EARLIEST DAYS, the largest city by population in the United States has always had a *new* in its name: New Angoulême, New Amsterdam, New Orange, New York.

It started as a Native American village. The Dutch built a citadel for protection on the lower tip of what was called by the natives Manna-hata Island. Huguenots came, then Sephardic Jews, then the English, and then everybody came. Originally the city consisted of a number of scattered hubs, but in 1898 all of them were consolidated into a single city of five distinct boroughs—the Bronx, Brooklyn, Queens, Staten Island, and Manhattan.

FOOD, GLORIOUS FOOD

NO AMERICAN CITY has seen or housed more diverse populations. As a result, New York City developed into a great fulcrum for food. Every ethnic group that arrived added a culinary variant to what was available to eat. Irish taverns with pub foods mark the city like polka dots. Greenwich Village became Italian, with every sort of cheese and pasta and sauce sold in small mom-and-pop groceries and served in small restaurants. A huge meatpacking district grew up on the far west side around 14th Street, and a major fish market moved in down on Fulton Street. From the inflow of Chinese in the late 1800s came a vibrant Chinatown offering dumplings and stir-fries. Russian tea houses opened in the 1920s and Russian restaurants in the 1990s. Greeks opened diners all across town in the 1940s. A stream of Puerto Ricans came bringing stews, beans, and plantains. The Japanese added delicate tempuras, noodle dishes, and, later, sushis. The immigrants of the last decades have once again changed country of origin, many being from Southeast Asia, India, Pakistan, and the Middle East.

At the center of the city's culinary sampling, a particular core stands out. Beginning in the late 1800s, Germans and European Jews joined the city swell and brought with them three towering and singularly New York culinary specialties for which the city is still famous: unmatched delicatessens with corned beef, pastrami, smoked fish, rye breads, and salads; the bagel, which in time has turned into an all-American breakfast food, though some claim the best are still found only in New York; and the New York–style cheesecake.

A SWEET BROADWAY STAR

NEW YORK CHEESECAKE achieved fame, and probably fortune, when it appeared in Lindy's and Junior's, both popular and notorious restaurants for the crowds of Broadway stars, gamblers, and writers like Damon Runyon they attracted. The cheese came from upstate, including dairies that had developed creamy cheeses like French Neufchatel, and the Empire Cheese Company of New York, which manufactured a brand called Philadelphia Cream Cheese. With that, plus eggs, cream, and sugar, came a cheesecake that was simple and unadorned and caught the heart of the city. Despite the antiquity of cakes made with cheese, New Yorkers contend there really was no cheesecake until New York cheesecake. Today New York remains a global hub. It houses the biggest theater life, centered near flashy Times Square. World-famous sports teams play in renowned arenas. The country's major radio and television networks air from there, and the main newspaper, *The New York Times*, culls the most prestige of any in the country. Still, nowhere can you eat like you can eat in New York.

For unclear reasons, the city bears the nickname The Big Apple. No one really knows why, but considering the texture, the mix of flavors, the tartness, hidden sweetness, and the way the city fills you up like its celebrated dessert, it could equally be called The Big Cheesecake.

WALNUT BUNDT CAKE SOAKED IN COFFEE SYRUP

MAKES ONE 10-INCH CAKE

INGREDIENTS:

8 tablespoons (1 stick) butter, at room temperature, plus extra for preparing the cake pan

¾ cup raw sugar, plus 2 tablespoons for coating the cake pan

2 cups all-purpose flour

1 teaspoon baking powder

1 teaspoon baking soda

¼ teaspoon ground cinnamon

¼ teaspoon ground cloves

1 cup granulated sugar

2 large eggs

1 cup plain Greek yogurt

1 cup walnuts pieces, finely chopped

Coffee Syrup (recipe follows)

ONE WOULD THINK WALNUT CAKE, rather crunchy, nut laden, and syrup soaked, is a bit out of the ordinary. Perhaps, but while not often seen, it is a glorious contribution to the American dessert menu and as easy a cake to create as can be. Variations were brought here by a number of ethnic groups. Here is a version bound to become mainstream, with a terrific pairing of coffee with the walnuts. A top dusting of raw sugar coating the Bundt pan adds a lavish crunch to the exterior. Lacking a Bundt pan, a loaf pan will do.

1. Preheat the oven to 350°F. Lightly butter a 10-inch Bundt pan and sprinkle the 2 tablespoons raw sugar across the bottom and up the sides.

2. Sift together the flour, baking powder, baking soda, cinnamon, and cloves. Set aside.

3. Combine the 8 tablespoons butter, granulated sugar, and ¾ cup raw sugar in a large bowl and beat until well mixed and creamy. Beat in the eggs, 1 at a time. Beat in the dry ingredients, alternating with the yogurt, adding a third of each at a time. Stir in the walnuts. Spoon the batter into the Bundt pan and bake until a knife inserted in the center comes out clean, about 45 minutes. Remove from the oven and let cool for 15 to 20 minutes.

4. While the cake bakes and cools, make the coffee syrup.

5. When the cake and syrup are cool, loosen the cake around the circumference and inner tube, leaving the cake in the pan. Pour one-third of the coffee syrup over the cake and let sit for 10 minutes for the syrup to soak in. Repeat twice more with one-third of the syrup each time. Place a plate large enough to cover the Bundt pan on top of the cake and set aside for 1 to 2 hours.

6. Invert the plate and pan so the cake is right side up and let sit for another 1 to 2 hours so the syrup soaks all through the cake. Remove the cake from the Bundt pan and serve.

COFFEE SYRUP

IN EUROPE, cakes emerged as a late-afternoon treat to be served with a glass of sherry, a cup of tea, or a cup of coffee. In America, where cake and coffee are a favorite pairing, it seems a natural move to merge the two. A rich coffee syrup slathered right on, and soaked *in,* the cake is, at least to Americans, obvious.

MAKES ¾ CUP

½ cup strong brewed coffee

½ cup sugar

½ cup honey

¼ cup water

Combine the coffee, sugar, honey, and water in a small saucepan and bring to a boil over high heat. Adjust the heat to maintain a boil without overflowing and cook until the mixture is reduced and thickened enough to drip slowly off a spoon, 15 minutes. Remove from the heat and set aside until the bubbling stops. Use right away or store in the refrigerator for up to several weeks. Gently reheat on the stove top or in the microwave before using.

THE BUNDT PAN

THE BUNDT PAN, the greatest cake pan design of recent decades, is manufactured in Minnesota, a region settled by later-day Vikings. Nordic Ware, the company manufacturing the pans, gives heed to its Scandinavian origins.

It is appropriate. The word *cake* is of Viking origin, coming from the Old Norse term *kaka.* Through the rough-hewn Viking warriors and their incursions into Britain, the word crept into English as *cake.* From England the term crossed the ocean into North America, where English won out as the official language.

Flash forward to 1950, when at the behest of the Minneapolis Hadassah women's group (not quite Scandinavian, but nonetheless northern) Nordic Ware's Bundt cake pan appeared. The Hadassah women wanted a fluted cake pan like the bund pan they had used in their native Germany so that they could make kugelhopf or bundkuchen—what we might call a coffee cake. The pan proved a phenomenal success.

In Germany the pans had been made of breakable ceramic or very heavy cast iron. David Dalquist, the founder of Nordic Ware, created a sculpted and fluted pan of lighter aluminum that due to its shape provided even heat and uniform cooking all through the batter. The fluting also resulted in a graceful-looking cake that could easily be cut into pieces of the exact same size. Dalquist added the silent *t* to the Hadassah ladies' bund request so he could patent the pan.

The pan sold rather sluggishly until the 1966 Pillsbury Bake-Off contest, when a lollapalooza called Tunnel of Fudge Cake, baked in a Nordic Bundt form, won second place. The recipe entered the annals of innovative American baking delights and made a celebrity out of a diminutive Houston mother of five, Ella Helfrich.

It also changed the fortunes of Dalquist's small company. More than fifty million Bundt pans have subsequently sold. Designs of more intricate flutes, lines, and peaks have come along. Some of the original pans have found their rightful place in the Smithsonian Institution, and November 15 has been declared national Bundt Cake Day.

INDOOR S'MORES WITH DARK CHOCOLATE, MARSHMALLOWS, AND SNICKERDOODLES

INGREDIENTS:

12 Snickerdoodles
(recipe follows)

¾ cup (5 ounces) bittersweet
chocolate chips

12 gourmet marshmallows

FOR THE PAST 80 YEARS, just about every person who went camping has reveled in s'mores, a sandwich of a campfire-toasted marshmallow and a piece of Hershey chocolate bar squeezed between two graham crackers. A bite into one is gooey, chocolaty, crunchy, and nary a lip emerges that doesn't need wiping. The treat was first described in the *Girl Scout Handbook* of 1927. In the twenty-first century, chefs began putting s'mores on menus, even in fancy restaurants. Here a redesigned s'more is not only still a kids' treat but also one for the urbane adult. The size of an individual pie, they feature dark chocolate, fancy marshmallows, and replace the boxed cracker with a homemade snickerdoodle made with equal amounts of cinnamon and nostalgia. You don't have to build a campfire. These s'mores are oven friendly and you'll definitely want "some more."

1. Make the snickerdoodles.

2. Preheat the oven to 375°F.

3. Place 6 of the snickerdoodles on an ungreased cookie sheet large enough to hold them without touching. Place a generous 2 tablespoons of the chocolate chips over each and set 2 marshmallows on top of the chocolate. Cover with another snickerdoodle and place in the oven until the chocolate melts and the marshmallows are oozingly soft, 5 to 6 minutes. Serve right away.

DECONSTRUCTED S'MORES

CHOCOLATE BELLIES UP TO THE BAR

ALTHOUGH IN 1657 the first hot chocolate house was opened in London, and by 1674 chocolate was showing up all over Europe, in the United States its native origin remained unknown for another century. It had to be reintroduced, and that occurred only in 1764, when John Hannon, an Irish chocolate maker, brought a batch of beans from the West Indies to Dorchester, Massachusetts. There he sought the help of an American named Dr. James Baker to refine the cacao beans, and the pair soon built America's first chocolate mill that, by 1780, was making Baker's Chocolate.

Although about 1829 cocoa powder for Dutch chocolate and cocoa butter for bars were popping up in Europe, and in 1881 Daniel Peter and Henri Nestlé added dairy to make milk chocolate. But America was lagging. Then along came Milton Hershey. Hershey, born to a Mennonite family, had signed on as an apprentice to a candy maker in Lancaster, Pennsylvania, at the age of ten. By eighteen he had opened a candy store in Philadelphia, then moved to Denver, Colorado, to learn how to make caramels. He returned to Lancaster to open a caramel company, then at the World's Fair in Chicago in 1893 bought some chocolate-making equipment. The rest, as they say, is history. American chocolate making was under way.

Since the Swiss wouldn't share the secret of how to make milk chocolate, Hershey had to find his own way. He sold his caramel business to devote himself to his milk chocolate innovation. By the early 1900s he began making milk chocolate bars, wafers, and other shapes. He established a company town near where he was born and named it after himself. In 1907 he invented the chocolate "kiss."

Hershey bars and Kisses are exported to more than ninety nations. Today the company also makes Almond Joy, Mounds, Reese's Peanut Butter Cups, Kit Kat Wafers, Twizzlers, and more.

While Hershey was busy putting his chocolate equipment to great use, in 1911 candy store owners Frank and Ethel Mars turned their daughter-in-law's favorite milk shake into a solid bar they called the Milky Way. They went on to create the Mars Bar, Snickers, Dove chocolate, Twix, and Three Musketeers. The Mars company is still family owned and exports to as many countries as Hershey's. Mars also produces M&M's, possibly America's most famous chocolate candy.

EVEN MARSHMALLOWS HAVE A STORY

THE MARSHMALLOW WAS ONCE a much more "green" candy, made from a kind of mallow that grows in salt marshes; hence the name *marshmallow*. That mallow grows in abundance up and down the eastern United States near the shore and saltwater inlets, and folks began to use the sweet sap from the plant to make a confection that was well liked and sought after. In time, the sap was discarded and gelatin was adopted, but the name stayed the same.

By the 1880s confectioners found they could make marshmallows in molds made of modified cornstarch, just like jelly beans, candy corn, and today's gummy bears. The next advancement came in 1948, when a marshmallow manufacturer found he could push the gooey ingredients through a long tube and simply snip the mixture into even round measures as it emerged, creating today's popular flat-ended marshmallow.

With the cornstarch molds, candy makers then realized they could make marshmallows into other three-dimensional shapes. The most famous version is Peeps—chicks, as well as bunnies and other holiday figures. But nothing beats a campfire-toasted marshmallow on its own or as the centerpiece of freshly made s'mores.

SNICKERDOODLES

THE MASHUP OF *SNICKER*—a derisive laugh—and *doodle,* which implies a somewhat offhand activity, is not an obvious coupling for a cookie name. Maybe the name was intended just to bring a sense of mirth to the cookies—a nineteenth-century New England creation. Certainly making them is easy fun. One caution, though: Snickerdoodles need to be taken out of the oven just before you think they are done, when they are quite soft. Otherwise they become too hard as they cool.

MAKES TWELVE 5½-INCH COOKIES

1 cup all-purpose flour, plus extra for shaping the dough

½ teaspoon baking soda

Pinch of kosher or fine sea salt

8 tablespoons (1 stick) butter, at room temperature

¾ cup granulated sugar

1 large egg

½ teaspoon pure vanilla extract

1½ teaspoons raw sugar

¼ teaspoon ground cinnamon

1. Combine 1 cup flour, the baking soda, and the salt in a small bowl and stir with a fork to mix. Set aside.

2. Beat the butter and granulated sugar together in a medium-size bowl until thoroughly blended and becoming creamy, 2 minutes. Beat in the egg and vanilla. Add the dry ingredients and continue beating just until the dough gathers together. Form into a ball, wrap it in plastic wrap, and refrigerate for 30 minutes to firm slightly. (The dough may be refrigerated for up to 2 days. Bring to room temperature before proceeding.)

3. When ready to bake, preheat the oven to 375°F.

4. With floured hands, divide the dough into 12 portions and roll each into a ball. Press each ball into a 4½-inch flat round. Place the rounds on ungreased cookie sheets as you go, leaving 2 inches or so between them to allow room for expansion during cooking (they will sprawl another inch).

5. Mix together the raw sugar and cinnamon and lightly sprinkle each cookie with the mixture. Bake until lightly golden around the edges and on the bottom but still quite soft in the centers, 8 to 10 minutes. Remove from the oven and set aside to cool on the cookie sheets for 5 minutes. With a metal spatula, transfer the cookies to a plate without stacking them.

6. Use right away or keep loosely covered at room temperature for up to 3 days.

AMERICAN COOKIE AND BERRY TRIFLE WITH MUSCAT SABAYON

A CLASSIC ENGLISH TRIFLE IS A LAYERED WHIMSY of pound cake, jam, and custard. It is also generously laced with sherry or a liqueur, which is soaked up by the cake, leading to its alternate sobriquet, *tipsy pudding.* With a few alterations, the trifle can be turned into an ad hoc American treat boasting an abundance of summer's fresh berries. A 3-minute sabayon featuring muscat wine replaces sherried custard, and crisp sugar cookies replace the pound cake. Berries—red, blue, and purple—plus whipped cream make up the other layers, until the whole concoction comes out rather like a vertical berry shortcake, made more intriguing with the tang of wine.

1. Place 2½ cups of the berries and the lemon zest in a food processor and puree. Set the puree aside.

2. Toast the almonds in a microwave or dry skillet over medium-high heat until golden, about 5 minutes either way. When cool enough to handle, finely chop them.

3. Whip the cream together with the confectioners' sugar until soft peaks form. Set aside.

4. Prepare a large bowl of ice water. To make the sabayon, fill a medium-size saucepan with water to a depth of 2 inches and bring it to a boil. Whisk together the egg yolks, granulated sugar, wine, and salt in a medium-size stainless-steel bowl. Place the bowl over the boiling water, being careful that the bottom of the bowl doesn't touch the water, and cook, continuing to whisk, until the egg yolk mixture is thick enough to coat a spoon, 2½ to 3 minutes. Set the bowl in the ice water

MAKES A 2-QUART TRIFLE

INGREDIENTS:

5 cups mixed berries, such as strawberries (quartered), blueberries, raspberries, blackberries

1 teaspoon grated or finely chopped lemon zest

6 tablespoons coarsely chopped whole blanched almonds

2 cups heavy whipping cream

¼ cup confectioners' sugar

8 large egg yolks

½ cup granulated sugar

¾ cup red or white muscat or other dessert wine

Small pinch of kosher or fine sea salt

2 cups broken-up Snickerdoodles (see facing page) or good-quality sugar cookies

bath, whisk briefly until cool, then fold in half of the whipped cream. Set aside.

5. To assemble the trifle, spread one-third of the sabayon on the bottom of a 2-quart glass bowl. Arrange one-third of the cookies over the sabayon. Spread one-third of the pureed berries over the cookies and one-third of the whipped cream over the berries, then one-third of the whole berries over the whipped cream. Sprinkle one-third of the almonds over all. Starting with the sabayon, repeat the layers two more times, ending with the almonds.

6. Cover and refrigerate for at least 3 hours, up to overnight. Serve chilled, spooning into separate bowls.

THE ALL-AMERICAN COOKIE AND THE GIRL SCOUTS

CHOCOLATE CHIP TO OATMEAL, peanut butter with its distinctive fork-tine stamp to macadamia chunk, gingersnap to cinnamony snickerdoodle, lace to simple sugar, the cookie is a uniquely American specialty. We are, in fact, famous for cookies. Some are considered triumphant only when baked at home—the commercial versions being mere imitations. Others, like Fig Newtons and Oreos were commercial innovations from the start. Bakeries display legions of cookies, lined up in separate trays like soldiers.

All, however, bear certain commonalities that announce them as a cookie. They are by and large flat, melting and spreading out in the oven's heat. Most of all, whether as small as a silver dollar or as large as saucers, they are sized for the individual. Indeed, what we love most about cookies is that they are a "to each his own" treat.

Of the lot, the sugar cookie, a certain plain Jane, is the "mother of all cookies." No hidden gems, melted drops, crunchy inserts—just flour, butter, and sugar, the basics any cook might have in the pantry.

DOING THEIR DUTY

THE GIRL SCOUTS, needing money to fund their many activities and charities, early on realized the uniqueness and all-embracing appeal and locked on to the All-American cookie as their special gold mine. Hence, once a year they knock on the door, stand in front of your supermarket, or tempt you outside the gym. They are selling their Girl Scout cookies—the biggest brand of cookie sold across all fifty states.

In 1917, five years after the Girl Scouts were established, the first Girl Scout cookies were made in home kitchens by Scout members and their mothers. The first recipe, for—guess what?—a plain sugar cookie, appeared in the Scout magazine and it was estimated that six to seven dozen could be made for between 25 and 35 cents and sold for the same price per dozen.

The demand was great and home ovens couldn't produce enough, so by 1935 the Scouts began to buy commercial cookies to sell. In 1948 they hired bakers across the country and in a few years offered three varieties: sandwich, shortbread, and chocolate mint. In 1956, they added a vanilla-cream-filled cookie. By 1966, a peanut butter cookie had joined the troop.

In 1978, the Scouts settled on just four national bakers to keep the cookies consistent, and the package designs were changed to reflect the new composition of Girl Scout members, girls of every shape, size, and color. In the 1990s low-fat and sugar-free cookies were added. Today, to maintain ties to the past, three types of cookies are mandatory: shortbread, peanut butter, and thin mint. After that, any region can offer special selections but the overall bestseller is the thin mint.

PEACHES IN CHAMOMILE CHERRY WINE SYRUP
WITH TOASTED WHOLE PISTACHIOS

SOFT COLORS, SOOTHING AROMAS, AND GENTLE FLAVORS mingle into an uncomplicated summer dessert of poached fruit in a fragrant syrup, unadorned, save for a sprinkling of toasted pistachios. Stepping beyond the usual, the syrup is made from cherry wine infused with the perfume of chamomile. Freestone peaches are the preferred choice. For the wine, in place of cherry, strawberry or blackberry will do, as would white zinfandel, often called *blush*. All together, they turn into an irresistible bouquet of tastes and smells to finish a meal.

1. Combine the wine, water, chamomile flowers, lemon juice, and sugar in a heavy saucepan large enough to hold the peach halves in 1 layer. Stir to mix and bring to a boil over high heat. Add the peaches, skin sides up, and reduce the heat to maintain a brisk simmer. Cook until the peaches are just tender, 8 minutes. Gently, so as not to bruise them, transfer the peaches to a large

INGREDIENTS:

- 1 bottle (750 ml) cherry wine, other fruit wine, or white zinfandel
- 1½ cups water
- 2 tablespoons chamomile tea flowers
- 2 tablespoons fresh lemon juice
- 1 cup sugar
- 4 ripe but firm peaches, preferably freestone, washed and gently dried with a towel to defuzz, halved and pitted
- ¾ cup shelled salted pistachio nuts
- ½ cup heavy whipping cream, sour cream, or plain Greek yogurt, for garnish

dish using a slotted spoon. Set aside until cool enough to handle. When cool, with your fingers, lift off the skins and return the peaches to the dish.

2. While the peaches cool, bring the liquid remaining in the saucepan to a boil over high heat. Reduce the heat to maintain a brisk simmer and cook until the liquid is reduced to a thick syrup that coats a spoon, about 20 minutes. Remove from the heat and let cool until no longer hot, about 15 minutes.

3. Pour the syrup over the peaches and chill for at least 3 hours and up to overnight, before serving.

4. When ready to serve, toast the pistachios in a microwave or dry skillet over medium heat until beginning to brown, about 4 minutes either way. Lightly whip the heavy cream until thickened.

5. Arrange the peach halves, half of them facing up, half of them facing down, in a high-rimmed serving dish. Pour the syrup over them, sprinkle the pistachios all around, and garnish each peach half with a dollop of whipped cream, sour cream, or yogurt.

WHEN SOUR CREAM AND YOGURT WERE CALLED *CLABBERED MILK*

CLABBERED MILK is a cultured milk product, soured or curdled so as to become thick, much like yogurt or buttermilk or the French crème frâiche. It was also often called *soured milk* in old recipes. The term was used a century ago mostly in the American South and Midwest. In England, it was called *clabbered cream.*

The dairy maids in early creameries who made the thickened milk were called *clabber girls,* and when Herman Hulman, a German immigrant, first developed baking powder in Terre Haute, Indiana, it was used to make the milk thicken faster, so the powder came to be branded Clabber Girl. It was discovered that baking powder could also make cakes rise. That is its main use today, and though the reason for her being on the label is unknown by most people, Hulman's Clabber Girl still smiles at us from our grocery baking shelves.

THE ENGLISH AND THEIR INFLUENCE IN AMERICA

No people coming to America have been a greater determinant of American culture than the English. America adopted their language, many of their laws, their customs, and, at first, their cooking. And the country was under British rule until gaining independence at the end of the American Revolution.

The first enduring English settlement in America was the Jamestown Colony in Virginia in 1607. It was followed by a group of Protestant separatists who chartered a ship called the *Mayflower* and founded a colony that they named Plymouth. Virginia was named for Queen Elizabeth, the Virgin Queen; English Catholics settled in Maryland and Quakers in Pennsylvania. Most of the American founding fathers were of English ancestry. They wrote the Declaration of Independence and the Constitution and set a standard of English etiquette and custom for the country. By 1790, half the entire population of the country were of English descent. Believing that language was the major organizing principle, the leaders pushed for English to prevail as the singular national language. Countless cities, counties, and even states take their names from English place names: New Hampshire, New Jersey, Boston, Rochester, Bristol, Lancaster, Birmingham, Raleigh, and far more.

Though their cuisine has never been considered stellar, indeed the opposite, for a long while their culinary bill of fare also dominated American food. The idea of a roast—called a *joint* in England—or a bird as centerpiece of a meal comes from the English. The hearty American breakfast, with bacon or sausage and eggs, toast and jam, follows English custom. Our pea soup is their pease porridge. Our traditional cheeses, such as cheddar, mimic their traditional cheeses. And of course, let's not forget tea.

CUSTARD AND CUSTOM

ENGLISH SWEETS have shaped those in America as well. Their muffins peddled by the muffin man, their scones, their famous butterscotch, taffy, and toffee candies, many of our holiday sweets, especially Christmas ones, emanate from England. All found a place on the American platter.

And then there is pudding. To the English, the word means dessert in general, the final course of the dinner, but the word morphed in America to mean the soft custards and their kin that also stem from English tradition.

Today almost 9 percent of Americans, more than 25 million, are of English descent. The states with the most are no longer in New England, but rather California, Florida, Texas, Utah, Idaho, and Wyoming, though many still inhabit New York and Massachusetts as of old. England is still considered our closest ally. Our concern for their royals, their politics, their arts, and music remain strong. And, of course, we still speak English, albeit with our own accent.

ROASTED PEARS WITH RUM CARAMEL SAUCE AND CHOCOLATE SAUCE

SERVES 4

INGREDIENTS:

Rum Caramel Sauce
(recipe follows),
for serving

Chocolate Sauce
(page 383), for serving

4 ripe but firm pears,
such as Anjou, Bartlett,
or Comice

2 tablespoons butter, melted

2 tablespoons dark brown
sugar

2 tablespoons dark rum

TAWNY OCHER, BROWN GOLD, LIME GREEN, RUSTY RED—one sort of pear or another is always present at the market. Pears are preferred fruit for poaching or roasting for dessert. Roasting rather than poaching them means no poaching liquid needs to be made. In the oven they soften as they turn a golden, candied brown. For topping, why stop at one? Two sauces, chocolate and caramel, convert them into a black and tan fruit sundae.

1. Preheat the oven to 400°F.

2. Make the sauces.

3. Peel the pears with a vegetable peeler, leaving the stems intact. Trim the bottom of each so that it is flat enough to stand upright. Use a paper towel to hold the pear steady so it doesn't wiggle around in your hand and, with a paring knife, core each from the bottom, still leaving the stems on. Stand the cored pears in a nonreactive baking pan large enough to hold them snugly side by side.

4. Whisk together the butter, brown sugar, and rum in a small bowl. Pour the mixture over the pears, place them in the oven, and roast, basting 2 or 3 times, until they can barely be pierced with a fork (they'll cook more as they cool), about 30 minutes. Remove the pan from the oven and set aside in a warm place until ready to serve.

5. To serve, gently warm the sauces, if necessary. Stand one pear on each of 4 individual serving plates. Spoon some of the rum caramel sauce over the top, letting it run down the pear and pool on the bottom of the plate. Drizzle

some chocolate sauce over and around each pear to create a fanciful pattern and serve right away.

RUM CARAMEL SAUCE

THE BEAUTIES OF CARAMEL are many. It is so satin, so tantalizing, so sweet, so tasty, and also so accepting. It graciously combines with added flavor elements like vanilla, ginger, anise, cinnamon, brandy, and bourbon. Here the flavor of the caramel is mirrored in dark, full-bodied rum. Sugar-based like the sauce itself, it's almost like reuniting twins.

MAKES ABOUT 1½ CUPS

2 cups packed dark brown sugar

1 cup heavy whipping cream

¼ cup dark rum

1. Combine the brown sugar, cream, and rum in a heavy saucepan and whisk to mix. Bring to a boil over medium-high heat. Reduce the heat to maintain a brisk simmer, and cook, whisking occasionally, until thick enough to drizzle from a spoon in threads, about 10 minutes.

2. Remove the pan from the heat and set aside in a warm place until ready to serve. Or cool and refrigerate until ready to use, up to 1 month or so. Reheat gently before using.

CHOCOLATE SAUCE

CHOCOLATE SAUCE can be spooned over vanilla ice cream or drizzled over a fudge brownie or frozen bananas, making them simply fantastic. Chocolate bars and chips have become darker and more chocolaty, and a whole lot bolder, containing a high percentage of often organic cocoa. With them and three more ingredients, homemade chocolate sauce reaches new heights.

MAKES ABOUT ¾ CUP

4 ounces bittersweet chocolate, coarsely chopped, or chocolate chips

½ cup heavy whipping cream

1 tablespoon butter, cut up

2 tablespoons water

1. Combine the chocolate, cream, butter, and water in a small, heavy saucepan. Set the pan over medium heat and cook, stirring from time to time at the start and then constantly at the end, until smooth, shiny, thickened, but not boiling, about 4 minutes.

2. Remove from the heat, whisk to smooth, and set aside in a warm place until ready to serve. Or cool and refrigerate for up to 1 month. Reheat gently before using.

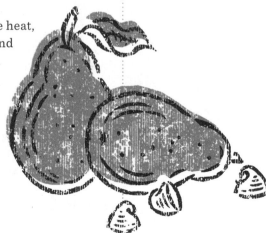

FIGS POACHED IN ZINFANDEL
WITH ZINFANDEL CLOVE GRANITA

INGREDIENTS:

Zinfandel Clove Granita
(recipe follows), for
serving

1 cup granulated sugar

1 cup water

2 cups zinfandel wine

12 ripe but firm fresh figs,
such as Black Mission,
Brown Turkey, or Kadota

1 cup heavy whipping cream

2 tablespoons confectioners'
sugar

12 fresh mint leaves,
for garnish

A FIG IS NOT A SINGLE FRUIT but almost fifteen hundred tiny fruits clustered in one green, yellow, brown, or purple black skin. Bite into one and there's no escaping its exotic sweetness. Poaching a fig in lusty, big-fruited red zinfandel and serving it with a slushy ice, now with a twist of clove, supplies yet more pleasure. You will want to stay a fig prisoner forever.

1. Make the granita and store in the freezer for up to several days.

2. To cook the figs, combine the sugar, water, and wine in a large, heavy saucepan and stir to mix. Bring to a boil over medium-high heat, stirring to dissolve the sugar. Add the figs, and adjust the heat to maintain a simmer. Cook until the figs are a little wrinkled and slightly soft but maintain their shape, 10 minutes. Remove the pan from the heat and let the figs cool in the liquid. When cool, refrigerate the figs and their poaching liquid together until chilled, at least 2 hours and up to 2 days.

3. Whip the cream together with the confectioners' sugar until soft peaks form.

4. To serve, place 3 poached figs on each of 4 individual serving plates. Spoon some of the poaching liquid over and around them. Set a scoop of the granita to one side and garnish with the mint leaves. Top with a dollop of the cream.

ZINFANDEL CLOVE GRANITA

A GRANITA is a semifrozen dessert rather like a sorbet but coarser. It originated in Sicily, and true to its homeland cuisine, its main characteristic is an intense flavor. An adventurous rendition of it comes from spicy zinfandel, a mainly California wine with an almost cult following of those who gravitate toward big, heavy, spicy reds. Cloves add pungency. When the granita base is cooked, they soften enough to be almost chewable, so leaving them in adds a surprise. If you're a lucky one who gets a whole clove, savor it. It will also freshen the breath.

MAKES 1½ CUPS

1 bottle (750 ml) zinfandel wine

2 cups sugar

1 tablespoon fresh lemon juice

6 whole cloves

1. Combine the wine, sugar, lemon juice, and cloves in a medium-size saucepan and bring to a boil over medium-high heat. Reduce the heat to maintain a brisk simmer and cook until the mixture begins to thicken, 15 minutes. Remove the saucepan from the heat and set it aside until completely cool.

2. When cool, transfer the mixture to a glass or stainless-steel bowl and place it in the freezer until ice crystals form around the edges and across the top but the center is still somewhat slushy, 1 to 2 hours. Whisk to break up the crystals and return the bowl to the freezer until the mixture is half frozen, about 2 hours.

3. Whisk one more time to break up the crystals and make an evenly granulated mixture. Return to the freezer until frozen all the way through, at least 2 to 3 hours and up to several days.

4. When ready to serve, remove the granita from the freezer and set aside at room temperature until just soft enough to break up the ice with a fork. With the fork, mix again, breaking up the ice, until scoopable. Use right away.

THE FRUIT ROUTE FROM EAST TO WEST

THE SPICE ROUTE that caravans took over mountain and valley from the far, Far East to Western markets is famous. But the fruits of Asia and Europe also took similar long treks to reach the Western Hemisphere.

❯ Christopher Columbus introduced citrus fruits to the island of Haiti in 1493, transporting the seeds of sweet orange, sour orange, citron, lemon, lime, and pomelo trees. By 1563, the Spanish brought the citrus to St. Augustine, Florida.

❯ The Massachusetts Bay Company that supported the Plymouth colony sent seeds of pear trees to New England. In 1629 Captain John Smith reported that trees from the peach seeds he brought to Virginia were sprouting. Then, too, William Blackstone began planting apple trees in Boston.

❯ Other colonists brought seeds of cherry, plum, quince, and pomegranate, along with hazelnut. In 1707, Spanish mission records reported that apricot, mulberry, orange, peach, fig, quince, apple, and pear trees were flourishing near their settlements.

❯ In 1733, General James Oglethorpe imported five hundred white mulberry trees. Meanwhile Henry Laurens, a landowner in South Carolina, ushered in olives, limes, ever-bearing strawberry, red raspberry, apples, plums and white grapes. Black pear trees were planted in Massachusetts, as were Black Mission figs in Texas and California.

❯ The first American fruit tree nursery was opened in 1737 by Robert Prince in Flushing, New York, and one of his most enthusiastic customers was Thomas Jefferson whose favorite fruit was the peach.

❯ Banana trees were among the last to arrive. Introduced by the Spanish explorers, they were a green, hard plantain later bred into the big plump bananas we know today.

OLIVE OIL CARDAMOM ICE CREAM WITH AMERICAN HAROSET

MAKES 3½ CUPS

INGREDIENTS:

American Haroset
(recipe follows) for
serving

2 large eggs

1½ cups whole milk

½ cup sugar

¼ teaspoon cardamom seeds

½ teaspoon pure vanilla
extract

1½ cups heavy whipping
cream

½ cup extra virgin olive oil

THE GOOD NEWS IS THAT, even without an ice cream machine, a home cook can turn out to-die-for ice cream. It takes attention, but intermittently. The joy of ice cream is that it can go beyond the prosaic to something provocatively different. Olive oil ice cream steps beyond vanilla and outclasses *dulce de leche*. Many an ancillary flavor can be added, such as fruit, chips, nuts, or spices. Cardamom, long dubbed the spice of paradise, introduces extraordinary savor to an opulent ice cream, while an American take on haroset, a Sephardic compote, crowns the lush pairing.

1. Make the haroset.

2. Lightly beat the eggs in a medium-size bowl. Set aside.

3. Whisk the milk, sugar, and cardamom seeds together in a medium-size saucepan and set over medium heat until just beginning to simmer.

4. Whisking briskly, slowly stream the hot milk mixture into the eggs. Pour the combined mixture back into the saucepan and cook over medium-low heat, stirring frequently, until the custard thickens enough to lightly coat a spoon, 15 to 20 minutes, depending on the size of the saucepan. Remove the pan from the heat, stir in the vanilla, and let the custard cool until it is no longer hot to the touch, 8 to 10 minutes.

5. Strain the custard through a fine-mesh sieve into a 1-quart container. In a separate bowl, whisk the cream and oil together until thoroughly blended. Whisk this mixture into the strained custard. Cover with plastic wrap and

refrigerate until chilled, at least 1 hour and up to overnight.

6. To turn the custard cream into ice cream, remove it from the refrigerator, whisk it smooth, and place it in the freezer. Leave until frozen.

7. To serve, scoop out portions of ice cream into bowls. Top with spoonfuls of the haroset.

AMERICAN HAROSET

AT THE JEWISH PASSOVER SEDER, there are a number of symbolic foods requisite to the service and the meal. Bitter herbs, usually horseradish, represent the bitterness of slavery. A fresh green, usually salt-dipped parsley, depicts the renewal of life and the return of spring. To symbolize the mortar the Jewish slaves had to use when they built the palaces of Egypt, there is haroset. Among northern European Jews, haroset is a mixture of nuts, apples, cinnamon, and wine. Among southern European and Near Eastern Jews, haroset is made up of dates, almonds, lemon, and spices, and there are many variations in between. Here haroset, with the inclusion of dried cranberries, gets the American treatment and takes leave of the seder table. As an assortment of fruits, nuts, spice, and sweet wine, it makes an ideal topping for ice cream.

MAKES ABOUT 1 CUP

2 tablespoons shelled salted pistachios

2 tablespoons slivered almonds

¼ cup diced dried apricots (6 to 7 halves)

¼ cup dried cranberries

2 tablespoons chopped lemon rind

⅛ teaspoon ground cloves

⅛ teaspoon ground cinnamon

½ cup Marsala wine

¼ cup water, plus more if necessary

3 tablespoons honey

1. Place the pistachios on a cutting board, cover with a cloth or paper towel, and roll them around to loosen the skins. Discard the skins and coarsely chop the nuts. Place them and the almonds in a skillet or a microwave over medium-high heat and toast until golden, 4 minutes either way.

2. Place the dried apricots and cranberries, the lemon rind, cloves, cinnamon, wine, ¼ cup water, honey, and toasted nuts in a small saucepan over medium-high heat. When the liquid begins to boil, reduce the heat to maintain a quiet simmer and cook until the fruits are soft and the mixture is sticky but still moist, 15 minutes. If necessary, add a bit more water to prevent the fruits from sticking to the bottom of the pan.

3. Cool and use right away or store in the refrigerator indefinitely. It will keep for months, but you'll have eaten it in no time.

CONVERSION TABLES

PLEASE NOTE that all conversions are approximate but close enough to be useful when converting from one system to another.

OVEN TEMPERATURES

FAHRENHEIT	GAS MARK	CELSIUS
250	1/2	120
275	1	140
300	2	150
325	3	160
350	4	180
375	5	190
400	6	200
425	7	220
450	8	230
475	9	240
500	10	260

NOTE: Reduce the temperature by 20°C (68°F) for fan-assisted ovens.

APPROXIMATE EQUIVALENTS

1 stick butter = 8 tbs = 4 oz = 1/2 cup = 115 g

1 cup all-purpose presifted flour = 4.7 oz

1 cup granulated sugar = 8 oz = 220 g

1 cup (firmly packed) brown sugar = 6 oz = 220 g to 230 g

1 cup confectioners' sugar = 4.5 oz = 115 g

1 cup honey or syrup = 12 oz

1 cup grated cheese = 4 oz

1 cup dried beans = 6 oz

1 large egg = about 2 oz or about 3 tbs

1 egg yolk = about 1 tbs

1 egg white = about 2 tbs

LIQUID CONVERSIONS

U.S.	IMPERIAL	METRIC
2 tbs	1 fl oz	30 ml
3 tbs	1 1/2 fl oz	45 ml
1/4 cup	2 fl oz	60 ml
1/3 cup	2 1/2 fl oz	75 ml
1/3 cup + 1 tbs	3 fl oz	90 ml
1/3 cup + 2 tbs	3 1/2 fl oz	100 ml
1/2 cup	4 fl oz	125 ml
2/3 cup	5 fl oz	150 ml
3/4 cup	6 fl oz	175 ml
3/4 cup + 2 tbs	7 fl oz	200 ml
1 cup	8 fl oz	250 ml
1 cup + 2 tbs	9 fl oz	275 ml
1 1/4 cups	10 fl oz	300 ml
1 1/3 cups	11 fl oz	325 ml
1 1/2 cups	12 fl oz	350 ml
1 2/3 cups	13 fl oz	375 ml
1 3/4 cups	14 fl oz	400 ml
1 3/4 cups + 2 tbs	15 fl oz	450 ml
2 cups (1 pint)	16 fl oz	500 ml
2 1/2 cups	20 fl oz (1 pint)	600 ml
3 3/4 cups	1 1/2 pints	900 ml
4 cups	1 3/4 pints	1 liter

WEIGHT CONVERSIONS

US/UK	METRIC	US/UK	METRIC
1/2 oz	15 g	7 oz	200 g
1 oz	30 g	8 oz	250 g
1 1/2 oz	45 g	9 oz	275 g
2 oz	60 g	10 oz	300 g
2 1/2 oz	75 g	11 oz	325 g
3 oz	90 g	12 oz	350 g
3 1/2 oz	100 g	13 oz	375 g
4 oz	125 g	14 oz	400 g
5 oz	150 g	15 oz	450 g
6 oz	175 g	1 lb	500 g

INDEx

Caviar(s):
native, 322
salmon, cream, imperial
  linguine with roasted
  salmon, wrinkled olives
  and, 321–22
Celery:
braised, à la Victor, 277
chop, punchy, portobello
  mushrooms with, 280
sautéed cauliflower with, and
  caraway, 276
Celery City, Kalamazoo, Mich.,
  as, 281
Celery root and potato latkes
  with pear compote,
  298–99
Chamomile cherry wine syrup,
  379–80
Champagne green grape topping,
  370
Chanterelles:
creamy chicken soup with egg
  noodles and, 62
deconstructed lasagne with
  creamed spinach, pine nuts
  and, 323–24
Chanteys, or shanties, 184
Chard, 9
quinoa burgers with tofu,
  shiitakes, diced tomato
  salsa and, 339–40
vegetable soup with red bell
  pepper pesto, 52–53
Chardonnay, 90
Napa Valley pot roast with
  leeks and, 89–90
Cheddar cheese:
American rarebit with
  bourbon, pickled shallot,
  and bacon bits, 15
cauliflower and nettle gratin,
  261
-stuffed burgers, 102–3

white, zucchini fritters with,
  and fried parsley topping,
  26–27
Cheese. See also specific cheeses
crisps, lacy, 49–50
herbed quesadillas with
  cantaloupe, orange, and
  onion salsa, 16–17
melt, Minneapolis brown bean
  cakes with cheese, 305–6
-stuffed burgers two ways, 106
Cheesecake:
New York, 371
two-tiered, with pine nut crust
  and green grape champagne
  topping, 369–70
Cherry(ies), 385
sour, sauce, 151
wine chamomile syrup,
  379–80
Chesapeake Bay soft-shell crabs
  with warm radicchio salad,
  246
Chestnut mash, creamy, 123–24
Chevre, creamed spinach with,
  324
Chicago, 104
Chicken(s), 171–97
beer-battered, with
  Cumberland Gap jelly,
  186–87
breasts in coffee, vanilla,
  sundried tomato, and
  currant cream, 178
crispy oven, with potato and
  broccolini salad, 183–84
Dominique, 191
ethnic dishes, 195
garlic-soused, 173
mole, mock, with toasted
  pumpkin seeds and ancho
  chile paste, 180–82
Parmesan and cracker-crusted,
  with lemon cream, 185

potpie under filo crust, 194–95
prairie, 189
roast, stuffed with bulgur,
  yellow squash, and bell
  pepper pilaf, 190–91
roast, with walnut pesto and
  shredded basil, 188–89
with shallots, vinegar, capers,
  and sage, 179
soup, creamy, with
  chanterelles and egg
  noodles, 62
soup, ethnic variations on, 64
soup with toasted tortilla
  strips and goat cheese, 65
spatchcocked, with
  mozzarella and baby beets,
  176–77
tandoori-style beer-can, 193
wings, peanut-crusted, with
  Southeast Asian dipping
  sauce, 38–39
yellow curry, with green
  beans, coconut spice, and
  saffron rice, 196–97
Chicken liver:
chopped, 41
taquitos with ruby grapefruit
  peanut salsa, 18–19
Chickpea(s):
beet, and almond dip with pita
  chips, 9
cakes with tomato and sesame
  seed topping, Glendale,
  309–10
lamb shanks with black olives,
  golden raisins and, 118–19
risotto with woodland
  mushrooms and, 330–31
Chicory, wilted, and green apple,
  135–36
Chile(s):
ancho, paste, 181
chipotle, cream, 308

roast, caraway-crusted, with
balsamic-glazed pears, 208
roast, with honey-rum glaze
on braised red cabbage,
206–7
Durum wheat, 314
Dutch oven(s), 88
pot roast with fennel, butter
lettuce, and pancetta, 87

Edamame:
bruschetta with minced
scallion, lemon zest, and
black sesame seeds, 10–11
risotto with elk summer
sausage and, 332–33
Egg(s), 171–72
custard "pie," dandelion
greens in, with a potato
crust, 262
noodles, creamy chicken soup
with chanterelles and, 62
poached, asparagus with,
268
poached, pasta with grape
tomatoes, corn and, 315
Eggplant, 24
Cornish game hens baked with
green olives and, 198
half-moons with red bell
pepper slices, feta, and
green olive chop, 23–24
mosaic of bell peppers stuffed
with olives, capers and,
288–89
potato, and walnut casserole
with white sauce icing,
263–65
and whole shallots stewed in
red wine, 278

Elk (wapiti), 153, 320
medallions, pecan-crusted,
with apple jalapeño jam,
152–53
summer sausage, risotto with
edamame and, 332–33
English culinary influences,
381
chicken soup, 64
Cumberland sauce, 187
trifle, 377–78
Escoffier, August, 169
Espresso butterscotch and
bittersweet chocolate pie in
shortbread crust, 345–47
Evans, Oliver, 318

Farmer, Fannie, 241
Fennel, 271
broccoli with cream, green
peppercorns and, 271
crisp baby artichokes, lemon
rounds and, 21–22
mustard greens, and feta in
crenellated filo cups, 34–35
Fernet Branca, 363
cream, flourless chocolate
cake with raspberries and,
362–63
Feta, 31
date, and prosciutto roll-ups,
31
eggplant half-moons with red
bell pepper slices, green
olive chop and, 23–24
lentil and romaine soup with
salted lemon rounds and,
56–57
mustard greens, and fennel in
crenellated filo cups, 34–35

Fig(s), 385
and hazelnut spice cake with
candied carrot ribbons,
366–68
poached in zinfandel with
zinfandel clove granita,
384–85
whiskey-soaked, with mint
and currant pesto, 29–30
Filet mignon with tarragon
shallot butter, 80
Filo:
crust, chicken potpie under,
194–95
cups, crenellated, mustard
greens, fennel, and feta in,
34–35
dough, tip for using fresh and
frozen, 33
parcels, savory, 33
pie, leek, potato, and dill,
32–33
sherried mushroom coils,
36
Fish and shellfish, 212–49.
See also Salmon; Tuna
clams, sautéed, with
macadamia nut and ginger
persillade, 240
cod, 71
crabs, soft-shell, Chesapeake
Bay, with warm radicchio
salad, 246
crowded chowder with cod,
shrimp, and corn, 69–70
fishy facts about, 214
halibut, grilled, with grape
leaf salsa, 229
lobster tacos with avocado
lime cream and singed
scallions, 248–49
Louisiana seafood in bayou
chile broth with skillet corn
bread biscotti, 234–35